THE ENGLISH BOOK TRADE

THE UNSPEAKABLE CURLL

"THE DISTRESSED POET." BY HOGARTH
The first state of the plate showing on the wall a picture of Pope beating Curll
[*Frontispiece*

THE
UNSPEAKABLE
CURLL

BEING SOME ACCOUNT OF
EDMUND CURLL, BOOKSELLER
TO WHICH IS ADDED A FULL LIST OF HIS BOOKS

BY

RALPH STRAUS

[1927]

AUGUSTUS M. KELLEY · PUBLISHERS
NEW YORK 1970

First Edition 1927

(London: Chapman & Hall Ltd., 1927)

Reprinted 1970 by

AUGUSTUS M. KELLEY · PUBLISHERS

REPRINTS OF ECONOMIC CLASSICS

New York New York 10001

I S B N 0 678 00649 0

L C N 72 117504

PRINTED IN THE UNITED STATES OF AMERICA

by SENTRY PRESS, NEW YORK, N. Y. 10019

CONTENTS

TO

J. C. SQUIRE,
A VERY OLD FRIEND

LIST OF ILLUSTRATIONS

LIST OF ILLUSTRATIONS

PART I

THE MAN

CHAPTER ONE

A NEW ARRIVAL IN GRUB STREET (1706)

Hence Bards, like Proteus long in vain tied down,
Escape in Monsters, and amaze the Town.
Hence Miscellanies spring, the weekly Boast
Of Curl's chaste Press and Lintot's rubric Post :
Hence hymning Tyburn's Elegiac Lines,
Hence Journals, Medleys, Mer'cries, Magazines ;
Sepulchral Lies, our holy Walls to grace,
And New-Year Odes, and all the Grub-Street Race.

Pope, *The Dunciad.*

I

THIS is the story, so far as I can piece it together, of a rather scandalous, but very remarkable, person. It is a curious and sometimes baffling story, for its hero is not always easy to understand, but it is also a somewhat comical story, and as such I shall endeavour to tell it.

To most people, I suppose, the very name of Edmund Curll will be unknown, and even those whose inclinations have led them to make a study of literature in England during the first half of the eighteenth century and know something of his tempestuous career, may express surprise that any detailed attention should be paid to so contemptible a scoundrel. Almost certainly that is how they will describe him. Why trouble yourself, they may ask, about a miserable wretch for whom no right-minded man has ever been able to find a good word ? Did he not earn a living by publishing obscene books for which he was rightly punished ? Was he not the most rascally of " pirates " ? Surely a vulgarer, more dishonourable money-grubbing bully of a fellow never disgraced the Republic of Letters with his presence ? The man, they will tell you, was an impudent pest, and if amongst the hundreds of books that he published one or two were not without merit, there never lived a rogue who better deserved the appalling reputation that has always been his. And there are scores of authorities whom they may quote. Hardly a great man of his own time, hardly a critic of later days, but has consigned Edmund Curll to the gutter.

There never was a man who was called by so many names. There never was a man who succeeded in irritating almost beyond endurance so many of his betters. And nothing could make him see the " error " of his ways : he just continued to irritate. If, for instance, objection was raised to some book of his of the bawdier kind, it would as likely as not be followed by another even more scandalously improper. If a furious author declared that a book of his, published by Curll, was wholly unauthorized, he would probably find that a " Second Volume " of his work was being advertised as " Corrected by the Author Himself." Occasionally the bookseller went too far, and then there was trouble, sometimes wholly grotesque. All kinds of ludicrous misadventures came his way. He was given an " emetick " on a celebrated occasion by Pope, he was beaten by Westminster schoolboys, he was several times imprisoned, and once he stood in the pillory. Actions were brought against him in the Courts, he was almost annually lampooned, and a word was even coined from his name to describe his regrettable methods of business. Pachydermatously Curll continued to exist.

With a little manipulation—thoroughly in keeping with the period—he could be nicely whitewashed. Nowadays all kinds of odd folk are put through the process, with highly entertaining results. And it would be quite possible to write a full-dress biography of the bookseller which he might have described as " proper for Families " to read. That, however, would be a dull business, and might cause you to take him as a wholly serious figure : a clear mistake. At the same time there is not the smallest doubt in my mind that he was a much bigger man than even his few apologists believed him to be. He was big in the sense that he had ideas and demanded and obtained attention for them. In the face of all kinds of opposition he refused to be ignored. And behind the very tall, shambling figure, loose-lipped and goggle-eyed, that the little world of London came to know so well, there lurked the soul of a fighter. All the while he was thundering out : " I'm as good as you, and probably better." And though some of his escapades might lead you to think so, he was no mere buffoon. Moreover, in spite of the peculiar character of some of his publications, he was a man with a genuine love for good books and by no means without taste in the matter of their production. So far from being the illiterate impostor that some would call him, he could and did wield a clever, if occasionally too flowery pen. In the preparation of some of his books he went to endless trouble, and if at times his methods were questionable, they were certainly no worse than those adopted—by his enemy Pope amongst others—against him.

He was called impudent liar, and accused of forgery, theft, immorality, and even something like murder. To me, innocent of whitewashing intentions, it would seem that in an age that was astonishingly coarse and given to the crudest personalities, almost his greatest crime was his ability and determination to give the public what it wanted.

He was not, of course, a respectable person. I have no doubt that he was what most people would call a thoroughly bad lot. It seems that he drank—at other people's expense—and I gather that he was exceedingly fond of the other sex. More than a bit of a rake, in fact. They did say that the most dreadful folk were often to be found in his shop. . . . But if he was a rogue, he was a comical rogue, and he carried his impudence to lengths which must command admiration. When he is playing his least reputable trick, and bringing it off, you are so far from regretting the fact as to smile with satisfaction. And he could smile at himself. He could even make money by repeating the libel against himself. Indubitably he was the finest showman of his day.

Looking, indeed, at the man and his work, I am inclined to believe that he was one of those men who are fated to live before their time. He was almost the first to realize the enormous value of publicity, and managed to keep himself in the public eye, even when they shut him away in prison. In his advertisements he reached a position which has hardly been passed by your American super-salesman of to-day. I do not deny that they were generally misleading, but for sheer ingenuity they would be hard to beat. As for his title-pages, they were marvels of optimistic inaccuracy. Curll, I feel sure, must have been the inventor of the gentle art of window-dressing. And as I see him, very cunning, very impudent, money-grubbing all the time though he was, he becomes something other than the unconscionable villain that his enemies—and it is to be noted that for the most part these were the bigger men of the time—painted him. I see him as more than a bit of a pioneer : an adventurous, picturesque, comical scamp with an agreeable habit of getting his own way.

Were he living to-day, I can see him enriched and resplendent : distinctly a magnate. The small shop in Bayswater would have become metamorphosed into the world-famed emporium in Regent Street. The " interests " of its proprietor would have been enlarged. His profile would have become familiar to newspaper readers, and the Stock Exchange would be taking note of his movements. We superior ones might always have laughed at him, but he would have had our secret admiration. He would not be in Parliament, unless, perchance, a grateful Government had sent him to the House of Lords, but as a keen politician—he was an ardent Tory the whole of the time that party was in power, and an excellent Whig thereafter—he would be working quietly in the background. Almost certainly he would come to own theatres and cinema-palaces—the theatre seems to have been his favourite relaxation—and we should not be surprised to learn that after his second successful bankruptcy he had secretly purchased at least one of our great " dailies," and was " reflecting public opinion " as newspaper owners fondly imagine they do. He would still be the object of bitter attacks for his " unscrupulous " methods in business, but there would be a touch of romance and melodrama in his " life-story " very much to the public taste, and his death would cause the head-lines to be even more flaring than usual.

Is this too whimsical a fancy ?

Let us look at his story.

II

We should begin, I feel, on a sober note. There must be some suggestion of a background. As it happens, Curll emerges from complete obscurity suddenly, and meetly, in a newspaper advertisement. Let us take a glimpse, then, at the literary world of the time. . . .

Were it not for their advertisements and their love of personal abuse, the newspapers of Queen Anne's day would make dull enough reading. They were single sheets, badly printed, devoid of head-lines, and wretchedly cramped. The politicians had realized the importance of disguised propaganda, but the Special Correspondent able to exploit it had not yet been invented. The advertisements, however, could be delightfully scurrilous, and nobody bothered to call a spade by any other name. There were exceptions, of course, like the official and monotonous *London Gazette* and the still youthful and very cautious *Daily Courant*, but in general there was a lack of dignity, and editors cannot have sat too comfortably in their chairs. So often they were being hurried off to prison at the request of some offended peer. No doubt they thoroughly deserved all they got, but I question whether some of the " great men " were very much better than they. It may have been a " glorious " age, but it was also an age of singular corruption. Never-

theless, it is possible to obtain from these newspapers a
not too inaccurate bird's-eye view of " the Town," and
a close study of them is essential if one is to understand
the metropolitan world at the time of Curll's arrival in
its midst.

Then, as now, the centre of newspaperdom was Fleet
Street, and here, too, were to be found many of the best
book-shops.   It was a Fleet Street, however, very
different from the overcrowded thoroughfare of to-day.
Ned Ward might complain in his *London Spy* of " the
Ratling of Coaches, loud as the Cataracts of Nile," but
I fancy that if we could return to the year 1706, at which
date this story may conveniently be allowed to begin,
our first impression would be one of a strange stillness
and peace.   The houses would seem very small and low,
and the people out of a hurry.   There would be a coun-
trified air over the place.   The coaches might be making
a rumble over the cobbled stones, but it would be difficult
to believe that we were actually in London.   Yet soon
enough well-known landmarks would remove our doubts.
We should see St. Paul's, but lately bereft of its scaffold-
ing, and the Gates of the Temple.   To the West we
should find Temple Bar in position—not for a hundred
and fifty years was it to be removed to Theobald's Park
—and although St. Dunstan's Church might be present-
ing an unfamiliar appearance, we should catch a glimpse
of a St. Clement Danes little different from what it is
to-day.   Then, looking closer, we should see a number
of book-shops each with its own sign over the doorway,
some the ground-floor of houses, but others little better
than huts or stalls propped up against the walls.   Particularly in the neighbourhood of St. Dunstan's we
should find a whole row of them, and an almost equal
number outside the Bar, ranging up to St. Clement
Danes and in the alleys, long since demolished, to North
and South.

And for a moment we might wonder a little.   Where
were the great publishing houses ?   From what lordly
buildings were the great morning " dailies " being rushed

out to the world ? At that time, however, not only were the newspapers and books issued from the same little shops, but the publishing and the selling of them had not yet become two separate trades. (Even to-day a few provincial booksellers continue to issue their own books.) And so it happened that the great ones like " genial " Jacob Tonson were equally satisfied with their humbler brethren to have their wares sold over a counter. Old and new books could be bought at the same shop, even if the new ones might generally be confined to those that bore the proprietor's name on their title-page. Many of these bookseller-publishers, indeed, were continually advertising their willingness to purchase " parcels " of books and even whole libraries, though since Charles II.'s time important collections had often been sold by auction when they came into the market. As for the newspapers, they enjoyed very small circulations, but were supplemented by the regular appearance of broadsides and pamphlets which dealt with matters of ephemeral interest. . . .

With regard to the writers themselves, it was a time of transition. Dryden had been dead a few years, and Pope was not yet ready to step into his shoes. Congreve was going blind, and Wycherley was an old man losing whatever popularity had been his. Nobody realized that Swift was so soon to become unofficial Prime Minister, and although his *Tale of a Tub* had exhibited his powers of satire, twenty years were to pass before *Gulliver* saw the light. Defoe, never in his lifetime allowed to enjoy the position that posterity has given him, was in Edinburgh and showing no sign of a *Robinson Crusoe*. Addison had published his Italian Travels and *The Campaign*, but not *Cato*. He was a member of the Kit-Cat Club, and had recently succeeded John Locke in an official position. Two years were to pass before he was to enter Parliament. His friend Steele had written plays, but his *Tatler* was unborn. Gay had published nothing at all. Of the lesser men Matthew Prior had printed several satirical pieces, but was better known as a politician. Nicholas

Rowe, soon to be very busy with the first illustrated edition of Shakespeare, had been disappointed with a comedy " which pleased nobody but its author," and was about to produce his now-forgotten *Ulysses*. Garth had done little since his *Dispensary* had appeared seven years before, Young was at Oxford, and Arbuthnot had not yet shown his unusual wit. A city physician called Richard Blackmore had been knighted for some curious reason, and every year was producing " everlasting," if very virtuous, poems which laid him open to general ridicule. John Dennis was playing critic, and Lord Halifax—" full-blown Bufo, puffed by every quill "— Mæcenas. Translations from the classics and modern French authors were beginning to be popular, and a single set of verses could still excite the whole town.

Now the conditions under which the work of the great writers was produced are fairly well understood, but frequently there was trouble in the publishing world, and it may be well to say a few words about it. " Writers," observed Goldsmith, speaking of this time, " were sufficiently esteemed by the great, and not rewarded enough by the booksellers to set them above dependance." He might have added that not all writers would have accepted reward, or, indeed, that the booksellers themselves were not always in a position to offer it. As with literature itself, so with the machinery necessary to bring it before the public, it was a time of transition. The older patronage of the great nobles was falling into disuse, which meant that the booksellers were coming to occupy a new and more important position. Yet authorship was still so far from being a " profession " as to be considered the last refuge of a failure. A big reading public had not yet appeared, and this led to " working agreements," sometimes of the most complicated nature, amongst the booksellers. Most important, the question of copyright was in its infancy, and piracy was rampant.

At the accession of Queen Anne no regular Copyright Act had been passed, and a measure of 1709–10, though

NICHOLAS ROWE.
(From the painting in the National Portrait Gallery.)

[To face p. 10.

it safeguarded the publisher to some extent, was not to be very helpful to the author. If you chose to " enter " your proposed publication at Stationers' Hall, you could bring an action against anybody unwise enough to produce a " spurious " edition. Actually this was seldom done—I do not know why—and, as we shall see, hardly a season passed without some indecorous squabble, either between author and bookseller, or between two or more booksellers issuing rival editions of the same book. There were, however, piracies and piracies, and if one is to understand Curll's peculiar position, one must be able to distinguish between the various forms.

Most common of all such piracies was the cheap reprint of a recently issued and popular book. Any number of unscrupulous printers could be found ready and eager to make a little money in this way. Printing was inexpensive, and hawkers were not yet in a position to demand very high wages. There was a man called Henry Hills, living in Blackfriars, who for years issued penny and twopenny reprints of every sermon or poem that had caught the popular taste. There was nothing to stop him, and, indeed, he could argue with some justice that he was acting " for the Benefit of the Poor "—words often to be found on the title-pages of his ill-printed pamphlets. He, undoubtedly, was the worst " offender," but he was only one of many. Occasionally, however, the announcement of a new book in the advertising columns would at once lead to warnings against it. It might be " unauthorized " or " printed from an imperfect copy " or even " an impudent fraud " ; and you would be exhorted to wait for the " genuine " edition that would be ready " early next month." But there was another possibility. The new book, wholly or in part, might be immediately disowned by its alleged author.

Yet while it would be idle to pretend that the first-class booksellers made a practice of issuing new books other than by direct treaty with their authors, it must be understood that a publisher who issued a book without its author's express sanction was not necessarily a low-minded villain. Very often he purchased manuscripts that had been " handed about " for a considerable time, or packets of old letters from those to whom they had been written, and considered himself at full liberty to make what use he chose of property thus legally acquired. To us this might seem wholly inexcusable, but for him there is something to be said. Many years were to pass before the vexed questions of copyright were to be thrashed out, and even to-day one or two anomalies are allowed to remain. Moreover, it is a fact that there were authors at this time, and not only those of the second class, who, so far from objecting to see their work brought in this roundabout way to the printing press, secretly connived at some such transaction. And if this seems strange, it is to be remembered that there is little in common between the man of letters of those days and the hard-working author of to-day. True, there were hack-writers then as now—we shall be hearing something about those whom Curll employed—but the idea that it was derogatory for a gentleman to accept payment for what he might write was still widely held, and even in cases where an author disclaimed all knowledge of a book issued as his, it was not always the publisher who was in the wrong. Questions of expediency would often dictate a policy of tortuous approach and what Pope called " genteel prevarication." A poet might " hand round " copies of verses " meant only for friends," but he was not always angry, one imagines, whatever he might say to the contrary, when one or other of these copies found its way into the hands of an enterprising bookseller.

I do not wish to make too much of the matter, but it does so happen that Curll was far from being a Henry Hills : so far, indeed, that he himself suffered from the man's activities on more than a single occasion. Although he may have done so, there is no positive evidence that he ever *reprinted* a rival's publication,[1] and none that he

---

[1] Though I admit that I am in some doubt as to the procedure adopted with *The Dunciad* in 1728 and some of Pope's later poems.

was guilty of deliberate theft. Even when he assigned to authors work that was not of a certainty theirs, there was generally some very good reason to suppose that they were not wholly ignorant of its composition. This, of course, is not to say that his methods of obtaining " copy " were always above suspicion, nor that his habit of advertising old books under some wonderful new title was other than regrettable ; but in justice to him it must be realized that he was by no means alone in considering that the possession of a manuscript lawfully acquired carried with it a right to print.

III

I have mentioned the old newspaper advertisements. They can be exceedingly diverting. The new books naturally fill columns, but they may be sandwiched in between the oddest and most inappropriate announcements. At one moment you may be reading that a butler is required, who, if he can play the violin and the flute, will not be asked to wear livery ; at the next you will be invited to buy good Bohea tea at 12s. the pound, or warned against some impudent impostor just now disturbing the town with his presence. All kinds of unlikely objects are lost, from "the Side Door of a Chariot painted Coffee Colour " to a baronet's lady. Houses are to be let for rents which would cause a stampede to-day, and apprentices, who have taken a dislike to their masters and "gone away," are urged to return. Of all the varied announcements, however, those that deal with medical matters are by far the most regular, and here it is to be noted that quite a number of the booksellers—though not the most reputable of them—added to their incomes by issuing quack-medical books or selling some " infallible remedy." Sometimes they did both. This is not altogether surprising. The medical profession had not yet fully organized itself, and it was difficult for the ordinary layman always to distinguish between the regular practitioner and the quack. When the Queen's own oculist, the egregious and illiterate Sir William Read, could fill half a column most days in the newspapers advertising his marvellous cures, and fashionable physicians crowded their houses with " magic " apparatus, it was small wonder that quackery flourished.

These quacks, indeed, played a large part in the life of the day.   Take a look, for instance, at the *Courants* and the *Post-Boys* of January, 1705/6.   In that month, I dare say, thirty booksellers were regularly advertising their wares, but there is little enough of purely literary interest.   On the other hand, columns are devoted to quack nostrums and " medical " books.

Thus at the Pestle and Mortar on Snow Hill, there is a " Person who has Great Experience in curing Lunaticks "—surely a useful fellow when you remember the horrors of Bedlam, then open, as an agreeable entertainment, to the " curious Publick."   Your costive children need not be frightened by abominable mixtures, but may enjoy the most admirable " purging Sugar Plumbs." A Mr. John Watts is prepared to supply you with a set of artificial teeth so firm that you can actually eat with their assistance.   True, you must never remove them—one patient is delighted to tell you that his own set has remained in his mouth for five years on end—but our notions of hygiene are not those of our less delicate ancestors.   Then there is a Mr. Thomas Paine, of Cirencester who has unselfishly left his native Gloucestershire in order to save his fellow-creatures in London from the ravages of cancer.   A Mr. John Hill implores you not to be led astray by sham or misleading advertisements, when his own most efficacious " drawing Ointment and Plaister " is there to cure any sickness you may happen to have.   Mr. Honorato Fornello, " Gent, no Physician," as he is good enough to tell you, " could hardly be perswaded to publish his Dissolution Salt "— an early Eno, no doubt—but does so with almost tiresome regularity.   And as with the remedies, so with the books.   They keep pouring from the press.   Only one need be mentioned here.   This was a translation of

Chirurgia Curiosa, the work, we are told, of that famous
High Dutchman, Matthæus Gothofredus Purmanus,
published by " R[ichard] Smith at the Angel and Bible "
in conjunction with two partners.

This Richard Smith is of interest to us. Little is
known about him. According to John Dunton [1] " he
was born with auspicious Starrs, has made several
Auctions with good Success, and increases daily, both
in Fame and Riches." In the previous year he had
published several books, including Captain Martin
Bladen's translation of Cæsar's *Commentaries,* and the
same author's *Solon,* a dramatic piece never acted, and
printed, it would seem, without Bladen's permission.
He remained at the Angel and Bible until October, 1707,
when he removed to a " warehouse " in " the Inner
Walk of Exeter Change in the Strand." And there is no
reason to doubt that he was the " Mr. Smith " to whom
in some unspecified year a certain Edmund Curll—the
name is also spelt Curl—had been apprenticed, and who
now in this month of January, 1705/6, set up for himself
a few doors away beneath his own sign of the Peacock,
in the identical small shop from which more than twenty
years later the *Dunciad* with its furious attack on himself
was to be issued.

IV

Who was this man, and where did he come from ?
The biographers have little to say of his earlier life.
There is even some uncertainty about the date of his
birth. When he died in 1747, the newspapers gave his
age as seventy-two, but in one of his own pamphlets
Curll gives the " Year of my Nativity " as 1683. *The
New and General Biographical Dictionary,* which appeared
in 1798, states that he was born in the West of England,
and Curll himself tells us that he was the son of a tradesman. The *Dictionary* further informs us that " after
passing through several menial capacities," he arrived at
" the degree of a bookseller's man." Afterwards he is

[1] *Life and Errors,* 1705.

supposed to have " kept a stall " and to have taken " a shop in the purlieus of Covent Garden," but no details are given. In 1712 he wrote a short life of Dr. Walter Curll, Lord Bishop of Winchester in the reign of Charles I., but gives no hint that they might be related.

I confess that I have not thought it worth while to embark upon any genealogical excavations. Edmund Curll's story must begin at the time of his arrival at the Peacock, with a wife and a small son, a stock of books, and some very clear notions as to what he proposed to do.

C. Julius Cæsar's

COMMENTARIES

OF HIS

WARS in *Gaul*,

AND

CIVIL WAR with *Pompey*.

To which is Added
Aulus Hirtius, or *Oppius*'s Supplement of
the *Alexandrian*, *African* and *Spanish*
Wars.

With the AUTHOR'S LIFE.

Adorn'd with Sculptures from the Designs of the
Famous *PALLADIO*.

Made *English* from the Original *Latin*
By Captain *MARTIN BLADEN*.

The SECOND EDITION Improv'd,

With Notes explaining the most difficult Places, the Ancient and
Modern Geography exactly compar'd, and *Dionysius Vossius's*
Supplement collected from *Plutarch*, *Appian*, *Dion*, &c. which
makes a Connexion between the Wars in *Gaul* and Civil War
with *Pompey*.

LONDON,

Printed for *R. Smith* without *Temple* Bar; and Sold
by *Cha. Smith* at the *Buck* between the Two *Temple* Gates in *Fleetstreet*, and *E. Curll* at the *Peacock*
near St. *Clement*'s Church in the *Strand*. 1706.

POSSIBLY THE EARLIEST BOOK TO BEAR CURLL'S NAME.

[To face p. 17.

CHAPTER TWO

TRICKS OF THE TRADE, AND A PAMPHLET OR TWO
(1706–1715)

Long live old *Curl*! he ne'er to publish fears
The Speeches, Verses, and Last Wills of Peers.
How oft has he a Publick Spirit shown,
And pleas'd our Ears regardless of his own?
But to give Merit due, though *Curl*'s the Fame,
Are not his Brother-Booksellers the same?
Can Statutes keep the British Press in awe,
When that sells best, that's most against the Law?

James Bramston, *The Man of Taste.*

I

ALL his life Curll had an inquisitive nose. He liked to be "in the know." That meant going about, and keeping his ears widely open. He was not, as we shall see, a shy man, and he could talk very well. I imagine that he did not dislike the sound of his own voice. I can see him, even as a very young man, addressing any audience there happened to be, with a pleased excitement, an unbounded belief in himself, and now and again a hint of agreeable mystery. The names of the great ones must constantly have been on his lips, and at times you would have wanted to laugh at the fellow's conceit. And yet was there not something about the Master of the Peacock which suggested that he would never be content to follow the staid course that his great contemporary was to map out for his industrious apprentice? Yes, you knew soon enough that he was one of those men who push themselves on—somehow or other.

It was a lucky chance, too, I fancy, that had apprenticed him to Richard Smith, for under that auspiciously-starred man, he must have mastered the auctioneer's art. At an auction the chief figure may talk as much as he likes. How good an auctioneer old Richard may have been we do not know—unlike the great Millington, he remains unsung—but with a ready tongue and a flair for wording his announcements in an attractive way, his pupil probably enticed a large public to his afternoon sales, conducted, by the way, not in his shop, but in some neighbouring house of call.

In his Elegy to Edward Millington, Tom Brown gives a picture of the famous auctioneer, which may well have applied to the younger man.

> " How oft has he, with strained Eloquence,
> Affirm'd the Leaves contain'd a world of Sense,
> When all's insipid dull Impertinence.
> Come, Gentlemen, come, bid me what you please ;
> Upon my word, it is a curious Piece,
> Done by a learned Hand, and neatly bound :
> What say you, come, I'll put it up one Pound :
> One Pound, once, twice ? Fifteen : who bids a Crown;
> Then shakes his Head with an affected Frown ;
> Good-lack-a day, 'tis strange ; then strikes a Blow,
> And in a feigned Passion bids it go :
> Then in his Hand another Piece he takes,
> And in its Praise a long Harangue he makes ;
> And tells 'em that 'tis writ in lofty Verse,
> One that is out of Print, and very scarce ;
> Then with high Language, and a stately Look,
> He sets a lofty Price upon the Book :
> Five Pound, Four Pound, three Pound, he cries aloud,
> And holds it up, and shows it to the Crowd,
> With Arm erect, the Bidders to provoke,
> To raise the Price before th' impending Stroke :
> This in the Throng does Emulation breed,
> And makes 'em strive each other to outbid,
> While he descants upon their learned Heats,
> And his facetious Dialect repeats :
> For none like him for certain knew so well,
> By way of *Auction* any Goods to sell."

The Dutch method, you notice, was the only one practised.

Actually the first of Curll's sales to be mentioned in the

newspapers took place on February 28th, 1705/6, at the Temple Coffee-House, but before the year was out numerous other auctions had been held, all widely advertised. It would be tedious to quote from these announcements, but it is a fact that you find in them a freshness and a sparkle that are absent from his rivals' more prosaic accounts. He introduced what to-day we should call the personal touch. So you might be told something about the late owner of the books, or be given alluring details of some particular rarity. And as with his auctions, so with the books in his shop. Unlike his rivals, he would be drawing your attention each week to something different—a parcel of books from Holland or Spain, a collection of modern French authors, a poetical display and the like. Always, too, there would be some particular appeal. You might not be an ardent collector of books, but—only come to the Peacock! The rare folios of last week's announcements might all have been sold, but the equally interesting and valuable quartos from the old Manor House in Essex or the " curious " collection from my Lord So-and-So's library in Kent would prove very much to your liking. And surely, you were expected to believe, no bookseller had ever advertised so profusely before !

Sales at auction, however, were to be but one branch, and that a minor one, of the business that Curll proposed to build up. As early as March this year, he was advertising the first of the many new books in which, to use his own phrase, he " had an interest." Here, of course, there were fresh risks to be faced. If the public were to be given what it wanted—and on that point Curll was never in two minds—manuscripts of the right kind must be procured, preferably with the author's consent, but if necessary without it. And here, I admit, manuscripts *were* constantly " coming his way " in the most mysterious manner all through his chequered career. According to his own accounts, these were often " given " him by various important people, and it is a fact that through all his troubles he retained powerful friends. Politics may have accounted for some of them, but not for all. There must have been something about him—sheer persistence, perhaps, combined with tact— which invited feelings other than those of ridicule or scorn. At the same time the bookseller did not mind to what trouble he was put so long as he obtained what he wanted. He travelled about, he watched, he put two and two together. I can picture him in his early days hearing that a library was likely to come into the market, and lobbying carefully to be " called in " as an expert. And why, indeed, should he not be called in ? A keen new man with nothing (as yet) against him. So I can see him examining a country house library with his short-sighted eyes, wondering as he picks up some rare and perhaps rather naughty work whether the time has not come for a " modernized " edition, and finally asking to be shown any odd " papers " that the family may happen to possess. The papers are duly produced. " Ah, yes," I can hear the bookseller murmuring, half to himself and half to the would-be vendor, " not of great *public* interest, I am afraid, though diverting to—to ourselves. No commercial value, of course. None. And yet, you know, Sir, I could almost bring myself to print if―― " The mutterings become vaguer, and—somehow the bundle of old papers has changed hands. . . . Curll must have been collecting such things all his life.

If, however, he did decide to print, it was necessary to be cautious. Partners, acknowledged or " sleeping," had therefore to be found. They were found in some abundance. Throughout his career they were constantly changing, but there was rarely a time when one or other of his " brothers " was not " in the firm." [1] But although in most cases there was in these early days little danger of any unpleasant prosecution, it might occasionally happen that anonymity or the use of some

---

[1] Of such partners, the first was Egbert Sanger, who had been apprenticed to Lintott, and others who helped Curll at this time were the John Morphew who issued so many of Swift's pamphlets, John Pemberton, at one time more or less officially employed by Parliament, and the faithful and, I suspect, long-suffering James Roberts.

THE
ANTIQUITIES

OF

St *PETER* s,

OR THE

ABBEY CHURCH

OF

WESTMINSTER:

CONTAINING

All the INSCRIPTIONS, EPITAPHS, &c.
upon the TOMBS and GRAVE-STONES;
with the *Lives, Marriages,* and *Iſſue,* of the moſt
Eminent Perſonages therein repoſited; and their
COATS of ARMS truly Emblazon'd.

By J. C. M. D. *Fellow of the Royal Society.*

Adorn'd with Draughts of the TOMBS, curiouſly Engraven.

From hence we may that Antique Pile behold,
Where Royal Heads receive the Sacred Gold;
It gives them Crowns, and does their Aſhes keep,
There made like Gods, like Mortals there they ſleep;
Making the Circle of their Reign complete,
Thoſe Suns of Empire, where they riſe they ſet.   *Waller.*

LONDON:

Printed by *J. N.* and Sold by JOHN MORPHEW
near *Stationers-Hall.* MDCCXI.

" SOME OF HIS MOST VALUABLE PUBLICATIONS ARE WITHOUT HIS NAME."

[*To face p.* 21.

agent's name would be expedient, and it was for this reason (though perhaps the liking for a touch of mystery which is inherent in every good showman may have had something to do with it) that more than half the books for whose appearance Curll was wholly or in part responsible do not bear his name. Here, too, a curious point is to be noted. You might suppose that if a man had decided to issue certain unseemly books in addition to his ordinary publications, he would confine the use of his name to the latter, but this is far from being the case with Curll. Some of his most valuable publications are without his name, and others of the least reputable character bear it. Indeed there come moments when you are tempted to believe that he deliberately meant the presence of his name on a title-page to imply a certain alluring naughtiness in the book. . . .

In the year 1706 he published but four books, none of particular importance, though it may be noted that one was a religious treatise that met with considerable success and another a " 2nd Edition Improv'd " of Bladen's *Cæsar*, which differed not at all from Smith's edition of the previous year. At the beginning of 1707, however, there came the first of his many little " differences " with the trade. Rumours arose that this new and very pushing bookseller had secured a manuscript of more than usual interest, a collection of poems, in fact, by the celebrated Mr. Matthew Prior. How these poems came into his hands we do not know, but with two doubtful exceptions they were genuine. Mr. Tonson at once made known his disapproval.

" Whereas," said he in the *Daily Courant* of January 24th, " it is Reported that there is now Printing a Collection of Poems which the Publishers intend to call Mr. Prior's, This is therefore to inform the World, that all the Genuine Copys of what Mr. Prior has hitherto written, do of right belong, and are now in the hands of Jacob Tonson, who intends very speedily to publish a correct Edition of them."

The " correct Edition " did not appear for nearly two

years, but Curll's publication was issued within the week. Who precisely his partners were in this venture is uncertain. The names of R. Burrough and J. Baker are to be found with his on the title-page, but the earlier advertisements make no mention of them, their place being taken by E[dward] Place, who was Pomfret's publisher, and Egbert Sanger. Later notices include only Baker's name and that of Charles Smith. It is not a matter of any importance—though to-day this thin volume will fetch £50 or more at auction—but it illustrates the difficulties which beset Curll's bibliographer. Here he did not attempt to hide his own connection with a book, though he mixed up his ostensible and hidden partners in a very curious way. Later on he took much more curious steps. . . .

Of his other early books little need be said in this place, though it is to be noticed that in conjunction with a man called Jeffrey Wale, who went bankrupt in the same year, he issued a text of Petronius which was the first to be printed in England. His others included a comedy, two poems by Blackmore, Rowe's version of Boileau's *Lutrin* amongst other translations, and one or two of the " Secret Memoirs "—a foretaste of that library of more or less worthless " Lives " for which he was to become so notorious. Two or three of his little tricks, however, were already causing unfavourable comment, and may be mentioned.

In 1708 public attention was being drawn to a Latin poem called *Callipædia*. New texts had appeared, and translations were promised. Curll announced that a translation by the celebrated Mr. Rowe was in the press and would " speedily be publish'd." Undoubtedly Rowe had been approached about the matter, but that was all that had been done. On the other hand, Curll fully intended to produce such a book, and said so. The " speedily " might be unduly optimistic, but it was the usual word. And if the book did not appear until 1712, four years later, was it Curll's fault ? Even if the translation, when it really was printed, did not happen to be more than a quarter Rowe's work, could the book-seller be blamed ? But the important point was this : by his early insertion of a notice he was able to say with something like truth that he had been first in the field, and complain with every appearance of righteous indignation that certain unscrupulous fellows had illegitimately intruded into a scheme of his own.

Another little device is typical of the man's delightfully cool cheek. In the *Post Boy* for March 14th, 1708, he was advertising the publication of a new edition of the Works of Rochester and Roscommon " with some Memoirs," but the book was not to be found in his shop. A day or so later he was apologizing for the delay, but there were, he said, good enough reasons. Postponement, he explained, had been necessitated " by reason of several Papers sent yesterday, containing a Perfect Copy of my Lord R——'s Mountebank Speech." This speech, it seems, had already been printed " from an imperfect Copy," and naturally the book must not appear until the necessary alterations had been made. And then followed the first of many public appeals for literary assistance. " Those Gentlemen," continued the notice, " that have any Papers by them of the Earl of Rochester's, or Roscommon's, if they please to send 'em as soon as possible, they shall have so many of the Books neatly bound as is proportionable to what they communicate, or any other gratification of the undertaker E. Curll."

What could be fairer ? And is not the practice continued to this day ? Unfortunately Curll could not always wait as long as he might have done. The great thing was to be first in the field. Did a great man die, Curll immediately announced that his " Life " was in the press and would speedily be published. This might or might not be true, but the public would be invited to make the proposed publication as complete as possible. In this way it often happened that a few odd biographical scraps from the newspapers would be mingled with any outside contributions that might have been forthcoming, and some sort of a " Life " be made ready before " the

Family " or the dead man's executors, could publish anything at all.   And if the available material was not enough for a sixpenny or a shilling pamphlet, what could be better, or easier, than to make the " Life " the required length by reprinting anything that the dead man had happened to write ?   True, there would be " Supplements," printed separately, but " bound in " as fresh matter came to hand—incidentally giving birth to a " Second " or a " Third " edition—but there is small wonder that " the Family " so often objected.   Curll, however, knew his business.   Why should not the public assist in what was intended for its entertainment ?   And did the Gentry require payment ?   It did not.   Obviously this was the cheapest and certainly the quickest way to produce " Lives."   Besides, why wait until half a dozen other booksellers had had time to produce other and possibly fuller versions ?   A good title-page covered a multitude of omissions.

Moreover, a " Life " was not the only kind of book that could grow in this gradual way.   With a little trouble and some imagination quite a small library could be produced from the slenderest materials.   There would first appear, say, a few verses by an anonymous scribe. In a few weeks' time a commendatory account of their alleged author might be printed.   The two pamphlets would then be issued together, though still separately paged, as *Poems on Several Occasions, with Some Account,* etc.   In a little while a " preface " would lend added importance to the work, and when some kind member of the public was good enough to send a five-line letter about it to Curll, it would be printed at the end, and the *Poems on Several Occasions, with Some Account,* etc., would become *The Poetical Works of* . . .   Finally, when the author died, his Last Will and Testament would provide a useful twenty pages or so, which being incorporated with the *Poetical Works* could very fitly be re-issued as " *The Whole Works,*" or, better still, *The Life and Times.* . . .

There was also the important question of names.

Some years were to pass before Curll invented a Mr. J. Gay and a Mr. J. Addison who had little in common with the admirable writers bearing those names, but already he was making tentative experiments in that direction. He would print a new man's work, but a glance at the title-page might lead you astray, for the only name to be found there might be that of a writer of the very first class. Yet he would not be guilty of actual fraud, for a closer examination would show you that the words " By Mr. CONGREVE," or whoever it might be, printed in such bold type on a line by themselves, referred not to the anonymously issued poem which filled twenty-nine pages out of thirty, but to some trifling paragraph or quatrain on a similar subject, that was printed (without permission) on the last page. Nor, indeed, was that the only way in which you could be fooled. If a new book does not happen to please the public, one naturally concludes that its contents are unattractive. Not so Curll. If a book of his did not please, why should the text be blamed ? Surely the title-page must be at fault. Very well. A new and entirely different and altogether more attractive title-page must be provided.

Which, not unnaturally, led to considerable recrimination.

Suppose, too, that one of your " best-selling " authors publicly announced that a work of his, advertised to appear shortly, was unauthorized. What could be done ? There was a simple means of dealing with so unwelcome an obstacle. When Prior objected to a second collection of his poems being printed by Curll, he said so in print. Whereupon James Roberts, acting for Curll as he so often did, inserted the following ingenious notice in the papers :

" Whereas a nameless Person has taken the Liberty to make use of Mr. Prior's name, and pretended that he had his Order for so doing : This is therefore to assure the Publick, that a Book entitul'd *A Second Collection of Poems* . . . are Genuine, and publish'd from his own correct Copies : The two last Poems in this Collection

being Satyres, Mr. Prior has never yet publicly own'd
them. . . ."

It was no reply to poor Mr. Prior, but it served its
purpose well enough.

II

We come to Curll's so-called first big publicity campaign.

Here there has been some confusion, and at the risk
of giving too much importance to a trivial, though
amusing, affair, I propose to examine it in detail.   In his
admirable article in the *Dictionary of National Biography*,
Mr. Tedder draws attention to the fact that the bookseller sold patent medicines in his first shop, and adds :
" He had not long been in business when he began a
system of newspaper quarrels with a view to force
himself into public notice.   Having published a quack
medical book known as *The Charitable Surgeon*, he got
up a fictitious controversy about its authorship in *The
Supplement* newspaper."   This statement, however, needs
considerable emendation.

The story of that newspaper campaign begins several
years before Curll set up for himself.   Somewhere about
the time of Queen Anne's accession a certain John Marten,
who had begun his career as a barber's apprentice and
in the usual way metamorphosed himself without tiresome examinations into a " surgeon," advertised to the
world his qualifications for dealing with the various ills
then (and still in some quarters) known as the pox.   His
particular claims to attention lay in the fact that he
deprecated, or pretended to deprecate, the use of
mercury in its cure.   In 1704 he issued a small treatise on
the subject which was more noticeable for its personal
abuse of rival practitioners than anything else.   But
apparently it sold well, and a seventh edition was
ultimately reached.[1]

---

[1] Incidentally, criminal proceedings seem to have been taken against Marten
in 1709 on account of certain bawdy additions to this book, but he was found
not guilty, and continued to practise.

MATTHEW PRIOR.
(From the painting by Hudson, after Richardson, in the National Portrait Gallery.)

[*To face p.* 26.

Amongst the rival quacks mentioned by name in this book, one was especially singled out for violent attacks. This was a Mr. John Spinke, who described himself—with what right I do not know—as a " Licensed Practitioner in Physick and Surgery," or, less dangerously though more cryptically, as "Med. Lond." Like his detractor, Mr. Spinke had begun as a barber, but, unlike him, never attempted to disguise his humble origin. Unlike Marten, moreover, he believed mercury to be the most useful " drug " in the treatment of all venereal ills. He, too, had his successes, and even at times of acute financial distress continued to advertise his own merits with a commendable lack of undue modesty.

Naturally he could not afford to ignore altogether Marten's attacks, but it was not until Curll's desire to increase what may be termed the therapeutical side of his business led him to commission a " medical " book, that Spinke really showed his claws. When it came, his counter-attack was all that counter-attacks should be. In two or three pamphlets—they are written, by the way, with such vigour and wit that one is led to suppose they were the work of some practised literary hand—he not only reduced his enemy to impotent silence, but caused Curll to regret his entrance into the medical arena.

The affair was brought to a head with the publication by Curll [1] of a quack treatise on the pox with a gorgeously alluring title-page. The author modestly described himself as " T. C., Surgeon," but, whoever he really was, I cannot think that he was responsible for the title-page, which could have been drawn up by nobody except Curll himself. With that title-page in front of you, indeed, you might almost have been reconciled to the pox. . . . Now this pamphlet had little good to say of the curative value of mercury, and it professed to tell you how to cure yourself at home without the unwelcome inquisitiveness of relations and by the use of the simplest preparations, all of which, by a curious coincidence, could be purchased at Mr. Curll's shop. It also contained an attack

[1] April, 1708.

on an unnamed quack " now remov'd from *Tom's* Coffee-House, *Ludgate*, to the dark Passage in Milk-Street, the moſt private place . . . in London." As it happened, Mr. Spinke's financial resources were not so great at the moment as they might have been, and he had retired to that particular " dark Passage."

I do not suppose that either Curll or his " surgeon " expected any counter-attack. They knew that Mr. Spinke had lately been sojourning in the Fleet prison, and a man who was hiding himself away in a dark passage could hardly be in a position to make much trouble. But early in 1709 there appeared a much-advertised pamphlet called *Quackery Unmask'd*, which not only attacked the lateſt edition of Marten's treatise and its author in the moſt amusingly virulent fashion, but contended that Curll's " conceal'd Quack " and " John Marten, Surgeon " were one and the same.

This little book makes joyous reading. It is so splendidly frank. It accuses Marten of being the bawdieſt scoundrel—reprinting, of course, the bawdieſt passages in that gentleman's work—and shows up his colossal ignorance of the elements of medicine. (I wish that I could reprint Mr. Spinke's wittieſt *mot*, which has ironical reference to Mrs. Marten's lucky choice of a husband, but that muſt not be.) At the end there is a " scourge " of Curll's " surgeon." Who, he asks, is this myſterious T. C. ? Timothy Cheat-you-all ? But whether he be surgeon or soap-boiler, tinker or tailor, it is certainly curious that his curative methods should be almoſt identical with those of the egregious Marten : so curious, indeed, that Mr. Spinke has felt impelled to inveſtigate the matter. He sent a man, he tells us, to see T. C., Surgeon, but T. C. remained annoyingly invisible. He purchased some of T. C.'s Generative Drops and found them " surely the same as Mr. Marten's Love Drops that will, he tells you, enable the moſt *saturnine*, *frigid*, *old* and *debilitated* Person to perform ſtrange Things in Venery." In any case, he asks, could there be found two more worthless, more ridiculous and more harmful books than Mr. Marten's treatise and Mr. Curll's *Charitable Surgeon*? Mr. Spinke was in no doubt of the only possible reply. It was in the negative.

Such an attack, strengthened as it was by the newspaper advertisements, could not be ignored. Curll immediately issued an announcement [1] assuring the world that Marten was not the author of *The Charitable Surgeon* and had no acquaintance either with its author, or, until the previous evening, with himself. This, I fancy, must be regarded as an extreme form of showman's licence. As for the misrepresentations of the book in question, it would be beneath Mr. Marten's dignity to take further notice of any " ignorant Pretender " who lived in a dark passage. Unfortunately Spinke showed no intention of retiring from the field. He persisted in his assertion that Marten, with the help of " the learned and ingenious E. Curll, Bookseller " was the " conceal'd Quack," and—could either he or Curll deny it ? Why, moreover, if it were an honest book (and what other kind would E. Curll publish ?) should they wish to deny it ?

In his reply Curll was less judicious than usual. He said nothing about his own author, but attempted to make fun of Spinke's parade of scholarship. His mathematical learning, he asserted, was lamentable, " and for his grammatical, though he pretends in his Book to understand Greek, I have five Guineas in my Pocket, which if John Spinke can *English* so many Lines out of any School-Book, from *Sententia Puerilis* to Virgil, he shall be entitl'd to. 'Tis Money easily earn'd, and will pay the rent of his House in the *dark Passage* for a Year, and buy him Ingredients to make Pills and Powders . . . to last for that time. And for his Assistance in that great Task, all the Dictionaries in my Shop shall stand by him ; and if he does not perform it some time this Week, he must expect to be enroll'd for a Scholar."

One imagines that most men in Spinke's position would have laughed, and said nothing. That, I fancy, is

[1] *Post Boy*, April 5th, 1709.

what Mr. Marten would have done, for although his own books were generously sprinkled with Latin, he paid an assistant—his advertisement for a young scholar to do just this work had been unearthed by Spinke—for all such embellishments. Spinke, however, was out for blood. He promptly accepted the challenge, and although a little embroidery suggests itself, there is no reason to doubt his version of the ludicrous business. He walked round to the Peacock—he had met Curll, he tells us, on two previous occasions—" duly English'd " the five lines from Virgil, " and then offer'd to do the same in any Latin School-book in his Shop, or in the Greek Testament," and " demanded the 5 Guineas." But it is one thing to be playful in a newspaper advertisement, and quite another to be taken at one's word. Curll refused to pay over the money, and Spinke went to law. " Then, indeed," he informs us, Curll " by his Attorney, paid not only the said *five* Guineas to my Use, but also 14*l*. 2*s*. and 6*d*. *Costs* of *Suit*, to Mr. Thomas Carwood, who was my Attorney in that Case. And," he adds, " I have not since heard of any Latin that he wants to have *English'd*."

But there was more to come. A second edition of *The Charitable Surgeon* was just now ready to be put on the market—doubtless this fact has led to the supposition that the whole affair was an advertising fake—and Spinke learnt that the sheets had been sent by Curll to be " revis'd and corrected " by Marten. He suggested that it might be " for the Satisfaction of the Publick "—Curll's favourite opening—to seek " a *Certificate* under the Hand of Mr. *Smith*, by *Exeter-Change*, his Master, signifying, that he serv'd him honestly during the whole of the Time for which he was bound 'Prentice to him."

The precise significance of this suggestion is not known, but it certainly implies a doubt as to Curll's good behaviour in his 'prentice days. I should not be in the least surprised to find that there *had* been trouble, although this is the only reference to its possibility. Curll himself said nothing in reply, and allowed Marten to have what in the newspapers at any rate was the laſt word. But it was not a very biting laſt word, and Mr. Spinke had every reason to crow.

Now, if matters had ended there, I should be inclined to agree with Mr. Tedder, but they did not. The second edition of *The Charitable Surgeon* duly appeared, but it does not seem to have been successful, and in his search for novelties, Curll invented more " conceal'd Quacks." He announced *A New Method of Curing* . . . one manifeſtation of the pox, but decided that it would hardly pay him to be selling two books on much the same subjeçt. Commenting on this façt in the second edition of his *Quackery Unmask'd*, the indefatigable Spinke expressed his opinion that Curll's policy was the right one. " For about two months," he relates, " we heard no more about " this second produçtion. Then it was re-advertised, and the sheets " sold by Mr. Woodward . . . and Mr. Baker . . . to whom, upon Enquiry, I was inform'd *E. Curll* convey'd them." While, however, on its firſt appearance the *New Method* was oſtensibly the work of " E. N., Surgeon," its title-page was soon altered, and " W. Warren, Surgeon," became the author. And you are not surprised to learn that there was a fairly well-known medical man called George Warren in praçtice at the time. Spinke continued his inveſtigations, and did not hesitate to publish them. The *New Method* was pulled to pieces, and proved to be the work of a man wholly devoid of medical knowledge.

" Some may perhaps be apt to inquire," he wrote, " to what Purpose any man who is not a Surgeon . . . should compose it. I answer, We have in and about this *Town* many poor Schollars who are willing to *scribble* any Thing that either a *Printer* or Bookseller will pay them for ; and I suspeçt that this *Traçt* was compos'd by some such Person, and publish'd by him that purchas'd the Copy, purely with a Design to get Money by the Sale of the Book. But whether it was so or not, *E. Curll* can (I believe) beſt inform you. However, in Case you shall think fit to make any Enquiry of him, I desire you (he being my good Friend and Benefactor) to do it after a very obliging and Gentleman-like Manner, least, putting him into a Passion, he would look *nine Ways at once* "—a nasty allusion to Curll's pronounced squint—" and tell you as many L - - s into the Bargain."

To this further attack no verbal reply was made, but Curll did not give up the fight.   Yet a third book of the kind made its appearance.   *The Generous Surgeon* was published at the Peacock, but only after Curll had left it for larger premises.   Its ostensible proprietor was one William Dolphin.   Unfortunately it was not sufficiently dissimilar from its predecessors.   Spinke pounced again, and played his final card.[1]   Those beautiful Drops and those inimitable Pills, with whose help the worst pox in the world could be conquered—what did they contain ? Alas for poor Marten and his mercury-hating *confrères* ! Quite an appreciable quantity of the detested metal was to be found in their composition.

A deliberate fraud ?   Certainly not.   That was the last accusation that Mr. Spinke would dream of making.   It must just have happened that Mr. Marten's great scientific knowledge had failed him at the critical moment.   He did not know mercury when he saw it.

There was nothing to be said.   All the " conceal'd Quacks " disappeared.   There was no further allusion to the dark passage.   True, for a while Curll seemed unwilling to leave medicine to look after itself.   He advertised a " Pulvis Anti-Ictericus . . . a never-failing Remedy against the Yellow Jaundice or such Distempers as proceed from a vitiated Gall."   He asserted that by its wise use " those who for years have been faint, weak, and look'd like Gipsies, have recovered Health and Complexion."   But there seems to have been a strange dearth of people who looked like gypsies, and in a very short time the bookseller wisely washed his hands of the whole unsavoury business.[2]

---

[1] Against Curll, that is to say.   He continued to attack Marten when the seventh edition of his *Treatise* appeared.

[2] In 1731, however, he was still flirting with " cures."   " There is now made

The View from the "Dial and Bible."

[*To face p.* 33.

III

If, however, his " surgeons " were failing him badly, Curll's publications in general were meeting with success. Early in August, 1709, he moved into a larger house inside Temple Bar. This was the *Dial and Bible* against St. Dunstan's Church, which had formerly been occupied by Andrew Bosvile, a well-known bookseller of the time, and his first book issued from the new shop was a volume of Shakespeare's Poems which completed Rowe's illustrated edition. This was a good beginning, but scandal is an easier " seller " even than Shakespeare, and he was soon being attacked for reviving the century-old " Case " of Bishop Atherton, about which the less said the better. It is to be noticed, however, that sundry advertisements appeared which were calculated to heighten public interest in this unfortunate prelate. It was said that distinct proof of his innocence had been established—proofs which anybody could examine for himself if he chose to go to the General's Head near Somerset House. No doubt many people did go, and the book was more than once reprinted, but Curll was forced to defend his position, and made a poor show. The real reason for his publication lay in the fact that there had recently been a number of criminal cases in London of a similar nature : the alleged reason was the fear lest Britain's innocent youth should be led astray by an ignorance which could so easily and so cheaply—the whole Atherton Case for a shilling !—be removed. . . .

At the *Dial and Bible* there was room for a lodger, and it was indirectly due to one of these lodgers that Curll made an enemy very much more powerful, though

Publick," ran a notice of his in the *St. James's Evening Post* of June 24th, " Dr. Radcliffe's Draught for the Gout." Apparently the recipe had been given by the famous doctor to " a Gentleman who was Steward to the late Lord Craven." The steward, knowing a good thing when he saw it, had it " made up " and did business with Curll, who charged half a guinea a bottle.

Again in 1738 he seems to have been agent for a quackish doctor called Alexander Stuart, though he was on safer ground when he sold William Beckett's medical books.

Also, of course, one or two of the books which brought him to grief were described as " medical " books. Here Curll does not stand alone.

considerably less able to annoy him, than Mr. Spinke. In March, 1710, he published Swift's *Meditations upon a Broomstick and Somewhat Beside of the Same Author's* as a sixpenny pamphlet, and in his own copy of the little book, now in the British Museum, he tells us how the manuscript came into his hands. It was given him " by John Cliffe, Esq. ; who had them of the Bp. of Kilalla, in Ireland, whose Daughter he married & was my Lodger." The book enjoyed a success and was soon being reprinted and sold at twopence. It was followed by the first of the many " Keys." In some way Curll learnt that a fifth edition of *A Tale of a Tub*, the first to contain the Author's Apology and Wotton's Notes, was about to appear. He issued a *Complete Key*, compiled, he tells us, from notes given him by a certain Ralph Noden of the Inner Temple. In a preface, too, he gave his reasons for printing them :

" As these *Notes* were communicated to me purely for my own Use, so had I never the least Intention of making 'em public : But finding what various Opinions are entertain'd of the Authors, and Misrepresentations of the Work to which they belong, inasmuch that Mr. Wotton has added to his *Reflections upon Learning* some score Remarks, in which he represents the *Book* as a design'd Satyr upon the *Church of England*, and even to ridicule the Doctrine of the Trinity, upon which score these Papers now appear, plainly to demonstrate, that the true Intent and Aim of the Authors was not to ridicule all Religion, but to assert and defend the Purity of our Church's Doctrine, which Mr. *Wotton* and his Party would insinuate they have aspers'd, and to display the Innovations of *Rome* and Fanatical Hypocrisy in their proper Colours."

He speaks, you notice, of " the Authors," and one of the notes describes the *Tale* as " perform'd by a couple of young clergymen who having been domestic chaplains to Sir William Temple thought themselves obliged to take up his quarrel." The two clergymen were Swift and his cousin Thomas, and while Swift was credited with *The Battle of the Books*, it was to Thomas that the *Tale* was ascribed.

Swift, who had taken such pains to preserve his anonymity, was naturally furious. In a letter to Benjamin Tooke, his own bookseller, he expressed his disgust. " I have just now had your last," he wrote, " with the Complete Key. I believe it so perfect a Grub Street piece, it will be forgotten in a week. But it is strange that there can be no satisfaction against a bookseller for publishing names in so bold a manner. I wish some lawyer could advise you how I might have satisfaction ; for at this rate, there is no book, however vile, which may not be fastened on me. I cannot but think," he added, " that that little parson cousin of mine is at the bottom of this," and no doubt he was, though whether Curll had ever met Thomas Swift is not known. " I shall," he concluded, " at the end, take a little contemptible notice of the thing . . . and I dare say it will do you more good than hurt." The " little contemptible notice " duly appeared in a postcript to his Apology, where attention was drawn to " a prostitute bookseller " who " has publish'd a foolish paper . . . with some account of the author ; and with an insolence which, I suppose, is punishable by Law, hath presumed to assign certain names." There was, however, no satisfaction to be got, as Swift was admitting to Stella ten months later. " That villain Curll," he informed her, " has scraped up some trash, and calls it Dr. Swift's Miscellanies, with the name at large, and I can get no satisfaction of him. Nay, Mr. Harley told me he had read it, and only laughed at me before Lord-Keeper, and the rest." In 1716, too, he was obliged to confess to Pope that nothing had been done. " I had a long design," he wrote then, " upon the ears of that Curll, when I was in credit ; but the rogue would never allow me a fair stroke at them, although my pen-knife was ready drawn and sharp." Nor, indeed, did he forget the " most infamous bookseller of any age or country " in his verses *On the Death of Dr. Swift*, written in 1731.

> " Now Curll his shop from rubbish drains :
> Three genuine tomes of Swift's remains !
> And then, to make them pass the glibber,
> Revised by Tibbalds, Moore, and Cibber,
> He'll treat me as he does my betters,
> Publish my will, my life, my letters :
> Revive the libels born to die ;
> Which Pope must bear, as well as I."

Curll may have been " insolent " to the great man in
making unauthorized use of his name, but his little preface to the *Complete Key* was certainly not inimical in tone.
You may, of course, look upon it, with its pious talk of
the Church, as the merest catchpenny device. Not for
one moment do I believe that there had ever been any
intention in his mind of allowing Noden's notes to
remain unprinted for all time in a drawer. On the other
hand, it is fully in keeping with Curll's curious character
that he should be genuinely keen to speak of the *Tale*
and its moral as he did. At this time, at any rate, he was
a keen supporter of the Church of England. Papists and
Dissenters he hated like poison. Moreover, it was not
only by the regular publication of religious works—
some of them of more than temporary renown—that he
showed his feelings. It may be said, I know, that a man
who deals in the kind of stuff for which Curll is best
known, invariably finds it expedient to assume the
saintliest demeanour. Regularly will he be found in his
place in church, and if there is a vigilance committee in
his village or town, he will be its most zealous supporter.
Curll, however, never made any such pious pretence,
but when, for instance, the whole country divided itself
into two camps over the Sacheverell impeachment, the
part he played in the controversy cannot be wholly
ascribed either to his love of money or to his desire to
remain in the public eye.

The name of Sacheverell was on everybody's lips. He
had dared to say that the Church was in danger through
Whig neglect, and the moribund Whig ministry was ill-
advised enough to bring him to trial. Pamphlets for and

against him streamed from the press, and it was only to be expected that Curll, ever keen to take advantage of the latest sensation, should add to their number. In point of fact he issued some half-dozen or more. But —and this is the important point—he himself wrote at least four fairly long essays bearing upon the question, and so far from trumpeting their merits in his advertisements, he had every one of them anonymously published. You may say that as the Whigs had not yet been defeated this was only the result of his natural caution, but I do not think so. I fancy he was perfectly sincere. He was so painfully sincere as to be almost unreadable. Unhesitatingly I acquit him of religious hypocrisy.[1] Here, too, I may draw attention to a passage in Thomas Amory's very interesting and too little read book *John Buncle*, which, in addition to giving us a vivid picture of Curll, has something to say on this point. "He was not an infidel, as Mrs. Rowe misrepresents him in one of her letters to Lady Hartford (afterwards Duchess of Somerset). He told me it was quite evident to him that the scriptures of the Old and New Testament contained a real revelation : there is for it a rational, a natural, a traditionary, and a supernatural testimony, which rendered it quite certain to him. He said he no more doubted the truths of the Christian religion than he did the existence of an independent supreme Creator ; but he did not believe the expositions given by the divines. . . ."

The first of these tracts was *The Case of Dr. Sacheverell. Represented in a Letter to a Noble Lord*. It was addressed, Curll relates, to the Duke of Bedford, and it attempted to "demonstrate . . . that the *Dissenters Moderation* is now turned into the utmost Revenge, and the *Toleration* endeavour'd to be Usurpt into a *Dominion*." It was obviously written in a hurry, and as hurriedly printed. Numerous misprints are to be found on every page. Its language is flowery, and its sentences sometimes so long

---

[1] Were it not for the fact that he wrote his name and certain notes in his own copies of the four little books which came into George III.'s hands and so to the British Museum, we should never have known that he was their author.

and so involved that, as in Thucydides, the verb is occasionally loſt altogether.   It cannot be said to have demon-
ſtrated anything except its author's good intentions, and
it is replete with what, even in his day, muſt have been
well-worn platitudes.   Nevertheless it is not devoid of
intereſt.   It shows Curll in the light of a shrewd observer
of life, not afraid of boldness in its proper place, but
counselling a clear-headed caution.   Of all vices, he
thinks, that of unreasoned prejudice muſt be held to be
moſt dangerous to the community, and his attack upon
it covers such a very wide field that Sacheverell himself is
in danger of being completely forgotten.

" Where a Man's Nature," he is declaring in one place,
" is wrought up with Impetuosity and Fire, the Spirit
will assert it self in Boldness and Ambition, in Rage and
Rashness, in Turbulency and Choler.   This will make all
his Counsels sanguine and precipitate, his Aɛtions un-
advis'd and unſteddy."   For which regrettable ſtate of
affairs prejudice is almoſt invariably to blame.   It is, too,
an ubiquitous vice—not only the result of ignorance and
affeɛtation, but also the effeɛt of public cuſtom and
education.   Those " in a lower Sphere " think and aɛt
" as they are direɛted at Second-hand.   Others, that are
engag'd in a Tumult and Hurry of Business scarce give
themselves Leisure to retire into their Thoughts ;   to
ſtate their inward Accounts. . . . Their Minds are so
full with the subſtantial and engaging Concerns of this
Life, that they find little Room for those of the next."
And how many shrink from that necessary though " disagreeable " scrutiny of themselves !   As for the blessings
that men enjoy, one ſtands firſt :   it is " a firm adhesion
to, and unshaken Perseverance in, the Doɛtrine of This
BEST OF CHURCHES, which no Seducing Prejudice can
pervert."

Well, well.   It is all rather different from Curll's usual
pronouncements, but—religious traɛts of all ages have
had an atmosphere peculiarly their own. . . .

Another of his contributions was *A Search after Principles*, of which he says : " This I wrote at Farmer Lam-

bert's, at Banstead, in Surrey, whither I went with Mr. Gosling," a brother-bookseller with whom for a while he was in close partnership. Here a dialogue is carried on between one Timothy up from the country and Philatheus a townsman, and here, too, there is a plea for loyalty to the Church, this time combined with an attack on the new sect of " Freethinkers " who, he thinks, will prove such a danger to the State. But not even all Churchmen are free from blame : they are too apt to be led astray, or fancy that regular attendance at Morning Service is all that can be required of them. There are even folk, we are told, so lost to all sense of proportion as to suppose that " Seeing a Play on a *Saturday*-Evening, or Reading a few Pages out of *Petronius Arbiter*, is a sufficient Preparation for Receiving the Sacrament."

In his *Considerations Humbly Offer'd* to Bishop Burnet, that self-satisfied Whig who took such a prominent part in the impeachment, Curll kept more strictly to the point, and showed that the Bishop's views on certain important matters of doctrine had not always been the same. This pamphlet " by a Lay Hand " reached a second edition, though its author was less fortunate with his *Impartial Examination* of two of the episcopal speeches at the trial " wherein a very gross Mistake committed by my Lord of Norwich is justly reprehended."

I do not know whether any of the other Sacheverell tracts that the bookseller issued were written by him, but these four should not be passed over in silence. They serve to introduce Curll as an author. Henceforth hardly a year went by without his list containing at least one book which had been written wholly or in part by himself.

IV

There came plans on a more elaborate scale.

In 1712 a second shop was opened in Tunbridge Wells.[1] The lists of new books advertised in the London

---

[1] Possibly the one which had belonged to Richard Smith " at the upper end of the Walks."

newspapers became longer, and particular attention was paid to their appearance. " An Elzevir Letter "—a favourite of Curll's—stood for neatness and legibility at a time when not many booksellers worried themselves overmuch about typographical matters. There were large paper copies " for the Curious " and " cutts " engraved in profusion. Also there came certain new " features." A primitive *Who was Who* came into existence. Last Wills and Testaments were printed in some abundance, greatly to the public liking, and allowed Dr. Arbuthnot to make his oft-repeated remark that a new terror had been added to death. There were more *Keys*, more translations from the racier classics, and original ventures such as " the Reasons why " Her Majesty had created So-and-So a peer. (What a pity we have none of them now !) Amongst the books of which no publisher need have been ashamed were several of antiquarian interest—Crull's *Westminster Abbey* was the first of them —and the Hon. Roger North's *Discourse of Fish and Fish-Ponds*. At the same time there were others, notably *The Cases of Impotency and Divorce*, for years one of his " best-sellers," and some novels of not too reputable a type.

And people said things. They said that Curll was going too far. I can see the bookseller's slightly crooked smile at his growing notoriety. What hypocrites these good folk must be ! Did not everybody take the warmest interest in other people's unfortunate love affairs, even though they pretended to be shocked ? Of course they did. Then why all this fuss ? There was no law compelling them to *buy* his " top-shelf " books, was there ? Interfering busybodies ! In later years, when even his political " services " could not save him from official interference, he was lavish with his excuses and explanations, but at this time he was content to give the public what it wanted. Yet in the first edition of his *Impotency* volumes, he did print one sentence calculated to explain his position. " The Publication of Books of this Nature," he wrote, " has all along in the

THE HON. ROGER NORTH.
(From the painting by Lely in the National Portrait Gallery.)

[To face p. 40.

Republic of Learning, been looked upon as a laudable Design. . . . The Censurers of these Performances are generally our Reforming Zealots ; who, as Dr. South observes, instead of esteeming Godliness to be a great Gain, make a great Gain of Godliness." Incidentally, the inclusion of the worthy Robert South's name in this passage is typical of his methods : he rarely missed an opportunity of making use of some celebrity of the extremest respectability, who might all unexpectedly find himself mixed up in the most deplorable affair, and in such a manner as to make contradiction or explanation almost worse than silence.

With this increase in his business Curll found it convenient to keep several hack-writers more or less permanently in his employment, and for this he was often, though, as it seems to me, unjustifiably, attacked. It was said that he treated his minor poets and his translators like dogs. Pope accused him of actually starving one of them, William Pattison, to death. This was so far from being the truth that it was Curll himself who nursed the young man—he was only twenty-one when he died—during the whole of his last illness. And while there is ample evidence that he was punctilious in paying his hacks and even generous in the sums that he gave them—there is a manuscript list of such payments to be seen—there is none that he bullied them or kept them on short commons. It may be that they were forced to assume all sorts of strange identities at Curll's behest, and to be included amongst their number may have been a sign of urgent financial distress, but they were little worse than other booksellers' hacks, and one or two of them achieved more than a modest renown.

It is true that Dr. George Sewell, one of his best-known " hirelings " died in poverty, but for that Curll himself cannot be blamed, for the unfortunate doctor had ceased to work for him several years before. Sewell's history is interesting. He studied medicine at Leyden, and practised in London. Moving to Hampstead, he saw his practice ruined by rivals, and was forced to change his profession. A ready pen and some facility for writing passable verse brought him to Grub Street and Curll, for whom he did a great deal of miscellaneous work. The production of his tragedy *Raleigh*, however, and a chance of doing political work under Walpole, caused him to leave the bookseller, and brought him a second and final time to ruin.

Another writer of whose pen Curll made frequent use was the historian and dramatist John Oldmixon, a rather quarrelsome person, it would seem, but a man of considerable ability. (I confess I prefer him to many a more polished historian, even with all his mistakes.) It is probable that a number of anonymously produced pamphlets on matters of current interest which have never been ascribed with certainty to any particular author were his work.

Amongst the translators first place must be given to the pompous John Ozell, a Leicestershire man of whom Chalmers says : " It was his misfortune to undertake works of humour and fancy, which were qualities he seemed not to possess himself." In his own opinion, however, he was Britain's foremost translator, and a vague testimonial from " the whole Bench of Bishops " was trotted out at every available opportunity. Swift ironically speaks of him as " an illustrious writer," and Pope, who naturally pilloried him in the *Dunciad*, also attacked him in *The Translator :*

> " Ozell, at Sanger's [1] call, invoked his muse—
> For who to sing for Sanger could refuse ?
> His numbers such as Sanger's self might use.
> Reviving Perrault, murdered Boileau, he
> Slander'd the ancients first, then Wycherley ;
> Which yet not much that old bard's anger raised,
> Since those were slander'd most whom Ozell praised. . . ."

He must have had a fair knowledge of three or four languages, but one is not surprised to find that when Johnson was writing his *Lives of the Poets*, the egregious fellow was wholly forgotten.

[1] Egbert Sanger, Curll's first regular partner.

Two other of Curll's " minions " may be mentioned here. It was Pope who first drew public attention to the " wretched " condition of his hacks, and it was Amory who made him tell Buncle that " his translators in pay lay three in a bed at the Pewter Platter Inn, in Holborn, and he and they were for ever at work to deceive the public." But it was Richard Savage—himself at one time forced to accept work at Curll's hands—whose *An Author to Let* has probably done as much as Pope to damage the bookseller's reputation as a taskmaster. " I was employed by Curl," he makes his Iscariot Hackney relate, " to write a merry tale, the wit of which was its obscenity. This we agreed to palm off upon the world for a posthumous piece by Mr. Prior. However, a certain lady, celebrated for certain liberties, had a curiosity to see the real author. Curl, on my promise that if I had a present, he should go snacks, sent me to her. I was admitted while her ladyship was shifting ; and on my admittance, Mrs. Abigail was ordered to withdraw. What passed between us a point of gallantry obliges me to conceal ; but after some extraordinary civilities, I was dismissed with a purse of guineas, and a command to write a sequel to my tale. Upon this I turned out smart in dress, bit Curl of his share, and run out most of my money in printing my works at my own cost. But some years after (just at the time of his starving poor Pattison) the varlet was revenged. He arrested me for several months board, brought me back to my garret, and made me drudge on in my old dirty work. 'Twas in his service that I wrote Obscenity and profaneness, under the names of Pope and Swift. . . . I abridged histories and travels, translated from the French what they never wrote, and was expert at finding out new titles for old books. . . . Had Mr. Oldmixon and Mr. Curl agreed, my assistance had probably been invited into Father Bohour's logick, and the critical history of England. . . . My pamphlets," he adds, " sell many more impressions than those of celebrated writers ; the secret of this is, I learned from Curl to

slap a new title-page to the sale of every half hundred ; so
that when my bookseller has sold two hundred and fifty
copies, my book generally enters into the sixth edition."

Allowing for a little embroidery, this is probably not
too far from the truth, and I am inclined to think that it
has reference to Charles Gildon, whose literary career
was even more lamentable than Sewell's. As a young
man Gildon had been comfortably off, but in spite of a
certain social and literary success, he had been forced,
about 1709, to come under " the tyranny of Curll." He
lived, says his lateſt biographer, " in a garret in Chancery
Lane, and his nightly drudgery by candlelight began to
affeċt his eye-sight." By 1718 he had become completely
blind, a faċt which Pope muſt have had in mind when he
wrote :

> " Yet then did Gildon draw his venal quill ;
> I wished the man a dinner, and sate ſtill."

If I am right in my supposition that Savage had Gildon
in mind when he wrote his *Author to Let*, Curll's slightly
less dramatic, but intriguing, version of the affair with
the lady " celebrated for certain liberties " and obviously
Mrs. Manley of *Atalantis* fame, is to be found in his
preface to the 1725 edition of her *History of her own Life
and Times*. It is inſtruċtive both as showing how soon
well-known people were coming to look upon Curll as a
difficult cuſtomer, and also as illuſtrating the bookseller's
habit of keeping any letters that might ultimately be of use.

" In the year 1714," he writes there, " Mr. Gildon,
upon a Pique, the Cause of which I cannot assign, wrote
some Account of Mrs. Manley's Life, under the Title of,
The Hiſtory of Rivella, Author of the Atalantis. Of this
Piece, Two Sheets only were printed, when Mrs. Manley
learning it was in the Press and suspeċting it to be what
it really was, A severe Inveċtive upon some Part of her
Conduċt, she sent me the following Letter ;

" Sir,
" As I have never, Personally, disobliged, I have no
reason to fear your being inexorable as to any Point of

FRONTISPIECE TO "THE WHOLE ART OF FISHING," ISSUED
BY CURLL IN 1714

[To face p. 44

Friendship, or Civility, which I shall require of you, provided I make it your own Interest to oblige me. If the Pamphlet you have advertised be not already published, I beg the Favour of you to defer it 'till I have spoken to you : Please to send me Word, what Hour after Four o'Clock this Day, you will be at Home, and I will call at your House : If you should not be at Home when this Note comes, pray send me a Line or Two when I shall wait on you, which will very much oblige

" Sir

" Your humble Servant,

" D. MANLEY.

" Tues. Mar. 1714
past 12 a Clock
" Direct for me, at Mr. Barber's on Lambeth Hill."

" I returned for Answer to this Letter," he continues, secretly charmed, one supposes, at the idea of so well-known a lady proposing to come to his house, " That I should be proud of such a Visitant. Accordingly, Mrs. Manley, and her Sister, came to my House in Fleet Street, whom, before this Time, I had never seen, and requested a Sight of Mr. Gildon's papers. Such a Request, I told her, I could not, by any Means, grant, without asking Mr. Gildon's Consent ; But, upon hearing her own Story, which no Pen, but her own, can relate in the agreeable Manner wherein she delivered it, I promised to write to Mr. Gildon the next Day ; and not only obtained his Consent to let Mrs. Manley see what Sheets were printed, but also brought them to an Interview, by which Means, all Resentments between them were thoroughly reconciled. Mr. Gildon was, likewise, so generous, as to order a Total Suppression of all his Papers ; and Mrs. Manley, as generously resolved to write The History of her Own Life and Times, under the same Title which Mr. Gildon had made Choice of. The Truth of which will appear by this Letter.

" Sir
" I am to thank you for your very honourable Treat-

ment, which I shall never forget: In Two or Three
Days, I hope to begin the Work.

"I like your Design of continuing the same Name and
Title: I am resolved to have it out as soon as possible:
I believe you will agree to print it as it is writ: When
you have a Mind to see me, send me Word, and I will
come to your House; for if you come upon this Hill, *B.*
will find it out; for God's sake let us try if this Affair
can be kept a Secret. I am, with all Respects,

"Sir,

"your most obliged humble

"Servant,

"D. MANLEY.

"Wednesday Noon
15 Mar.

"P.S. I have Company, and Time to tell you only,
That your Services are such to me, that can never be
enough valued. My Pen, my Purse, my Interest, are all
at your Service: I shall never be easy, ' till I am grateful.'

"About a Week after," relates Curll, who must have
been thoroughly enjoying himself, "I received the
greatest Part of the Manuscript, with the following
Letter.

"Sir,

"Judge that I have not been idle, when I have sent
you so much Copy. How can I deserve all this Friendship from you? I must ask you to pity me; for I am
plagued to Death for want of Time, and forced to write
by Stealth. I beg the Printer may not have any other to
interfere with him, especially because I shall want Time
to finish it with that *Eclat* I intend. I dread the Noise
'twill make when it comes out; it concerns us all to keep
the Secret. I design to wait on you, to tell you part of
that extream Acknowledgment, which, my Heart tells
me, is due to so sincere a Friend.

"Yours, &c.

"D. M."

" While these Memoirs were in the Press," he concludes, " I had the Favour of several other obliging Letters from Mrs. Manley, in one of which she says, ' Though the World may like what I write of others, they despise whatever an Author is thought to say of themselves.' This being the sole Reason of her throwing it into the Disguise of a Translation, and insisting, that it should be kept a Secret during her Life-time ; I hope what is now produced will be allowed to be a sufficient Proof of her being the Genuine Author."

A hint of polite blackmail in the background ? Not a bit of it. An illustration, rather, of the fact that it was not always the bookseller who ordered translations from the French of " what they never wrote."

V

I have mentioned *John Buncle*, and here it may be well to insert Amory's further account of Curll. The bookseller's appearance cannot have been attractive. " He was in person very tall and thin, an ungainly, awkward, white-faced man. His eyes were a light grey, large, projecting, goggle and purblind. He was splay-footed and baker-kneed." In another passage he is called " a debauchee to the last degree. . . . As to drink, he was too fond of money to spend any in making himself happy that way ; but at another's expense he would drink every day till he was quite blind and as incapable of self-motion as a block." Well, this is the only mention, so far as I know, of his drinking propensities, but Amory should know. He lodged with Curll for a while.

There is information, too, in *John Buncle* of the bookseller's social activities. Throughout his life, you will find him acquainted with the unlikeliest people, and there can be no doubt that he was what is called " good company." " As Curll knew the world well," says Amory, " and was acquainted with several extraordinary characters, he was of great use to me at my first coming to town, as I knew nobody nor any place.

He gave me the true characters of many I saw; told me whom I should avoid and with whom I might be free. He conducted me to the playhouses and gave me a judicious account of every actor. He understood those things well. No man could talk better on theatrical subjects. He took me likewise to Sadler's Wells, to the night-cellars, and to Tom King's, the famous night-house at Covent Garden. As he was very knowing and well known at such places, he soon made me as wise as himself in these branches of learning; and in short, in the space of a month I was as well acquainted in London as if I had been there for years. My kind preceptor spared no pains in lecturing. But what of all things I thought most wonderful was the company I saw at the Sieur Curll's. As he was intimate with all the high whores in town, many of them frequented his bookshop to buy his dialogues and other lively books. Some of these girls he often asked to dine with him, and then I was sure to be his guest. . . . "

A good liver, then, this theatrically-minded bookseller who could play kind preceptor to other young men besides Amory " of a literary turn." Both Oxford and Cambridge came to know him well, and he was even toasted by the poetical clubs. An expelled under-graduate, in particular, was likely to be guided towards his shop, and at least two of these—Nicholas Amhurst and John Durant Breval—largely owed their careers to him. A dangerous fellow, perhaps, but—successful. An impertinent rascal, but entertaining. An unpopular man, except perhaps in the theatres and taverns, but the kind of man that few people would care to have for an enemy. A not very respectable person, but genuinely keen on books. A careful man of business, though not afraid to print the first works of young poets at his own expense. A possible drunkard and debauchee, but well able to look after himself, unless, perchance, somebody tired of mere verbal philippics and ventured to use an entirely novel form of attack.

In 1716 somebody did.

CHAPTER THREE

Ye Poets ragged and forlorn,
 Down from your garrets haste ;
Ye rhymers, dead as soon as born,
 Not yet consign'd to paste ;

I know a trick to make you thrive ;
 O, 'tis a quaint device :
Your still-born poems shall revive,
 And scorn to wrap up spice.

Get all your verses printed fair,
 Then let them well be dried ;
And Curll must have a special care
 To leave the margin wide.

Lend these to paper-sparing Pope ;
 And when he sets to write,
No letter with an envelope,
 Could give him more delight.

When Pope has fill'd the margins round,
 Why then recall your loan ;
Sell them to Curll for fifty pound,
 And swear they are your own.

Swift.

I

HITHERTO there had been angry words in abundance, but nothing more. The Law had not been broken, and if a few authors were fuming against this upstart in Fleet Street who refused to be intimidated by their legitimate abuse, nobody had thought to adopt any more drastic method with him. And as for the knocks, had they really been felt ? On the contrary, they had been turned to good purpose. Abuse of the really great is almost the most piquant morsel that can be offered to an emotional public, and when Curll did fight it was with one eye on the exchequer. So Gay was not far wrong when he wrote :

> " Were Prior, Congreve, Swift and Pope unknown,
> Poor Slander-selling Curll would be undone."

But it was only to be expected that a more drastic method against him would ultimately be attempted, and it was left to Alexander Pope, a great poet though by no means a great man, to inaugurate the new form of attack.

Curll was making enemies all his life, but of all of them none was more bitter than Pope, and none stooped to such contemptible (and unpoetical) tricks. For more than a quarter of a century they were at war, and if at times there was comparative calm in the trenches, the fiercest of battles was liable to break out at any moment. At the end, as usual, both parties claimed to be the conqueror, but, although the bookseller received several hard blows, even Pope's own biographers are obliged to give any victory there was to Curll.

The quarrel rose suddenly. Pope, of course, was not unaware of Curll's reputation, or of the way in which he had treated his friend Swift. He may even have connected Curll with Thomas Burnet's attack on his intended translation of Homer in 1715, but nothing happened until March, 1716. In that month there was published a small volume of satirical pieces, which most critics now assign severally to Gay, Pope, and Pope's then great friend, Lady Mary Wortley (Montagu), though the lady maintained that she was their sole author. Several points about the grotesque affair that followed remain obscure, but as far as I can gather from the various versions here is what actually occurred.

Towards the end of 1715 a Mr. Joseph Jacobs, " late of Hoxton," as Curll tells us, and " the Founder of a remarkable Sect called The Whiskers," gave to Oldmixon " three poems at that time handed about, entitled The Basset Table, The Toilet and the Drawing Room," which were said to be Lady Mary's work. Oldmixon showed them to Curll, who immediately perceived their

LADY MARY WORTLEY MONTAGU.
(From the painting by Richardson.)

[To face p. 50.

commercial value if published under Lady Mary's name. The unauthorized use, however, of so great a lady's name might be attended with danger, and with his usual caution, he not only shared the risks of publication, but arranged for another bookseller's name to appear on the title-page. It was agreed that any profits there might be from the sale of these *Court Poems,* as they were called, should be divided equally between Oldmixon, John Pemberton, at this time Curll's most regular partner, and Curll himself. As for James Roberts, who had been chosen as the ostensible proprietor, one can only hope that he was paid a good fee for the use of his name. But in the earlier part of the new year, news of the intended publication came to the ears of Pope. He, it is to be noted, never admitted that he had written any of the verses, though this, as we shall see, meant little enough, but whether he was acting on his own, or on Lady Mary's behalf, he discovered that Curll was taking a hand in the business, and " threatened " him—how or in what way is not known. This was enough for Curll. It gave him a clue. The verses might or might not be Lady Mary's work, but the great Mr. Pope must have had something to do with their composition. And so when the book was actually published on Monday, March 26th, two days after Lintott had announced that the second volume of Pope's *Iliad* was ready, no author's name appeared on the title-page, but an anonymous and not very grammatical preface contained a clear hint about the authorship.

At St. James's Coffee House, it was there stated, the poems were very generally attributed to a Lady of Quality. At Button's, however, " the *Poetical* Jury brought in a different Verdict ; and the *Foreman* strenuously insisted upon it, that Mr. Gay was the *Man.*" Whereupon an umpire was called in, " a Gentleman of distinguished Merit, who lives not far from *Chelsea,*" and he was in no doubt at all. " Sir," said he, " Depend upon it, these Lines could come from no other Hand, than the laudible Translator of Homer." And thus, finished the prefacer, "having impartially given the Sentiments of the *Town*, I hope I may deserve Thanks, for the Pains I have taken, in endeavouring to find out the *Author* of these valuable Performances : and every body is at Liberty to bestow the Laurel as they please."

An intriguing little introduction : but there was an additional touch of romance attached to the book, inasmuch as it was announced—by showman's licence—that the poems had been " *Publish'd faithfully, as they were found in a Pocket-Book taken up in* Westminster-Hall, *the last Day of the Lord* Winton's *Tryal*" for high treason, about which everybody was then talking, and on account of which, by the way, Curll himself was to be in serious trouble very soon. Great interest was duly aroused, and the little book sold very well.

What followed it is difficult to believe. Pope at once asked his own publisher Lintott to introduce him to Curll, and on the Wednesday morning the three of them met—it was the only occasion when Pope and Curll did meet—at the Swan Tavern in Fleet Street. They chatted for half-an-hour or so, they drank together, though not from the same bottle, and on returning home Curll was exceedingly ill. And this was no accidental illness, for Pope had contrived to add an emetic to Curll's glass of sack.

Curll himself gives us an account of the business. At the Swan, he relates—and although twelve years were to pass before his account was printed,[1] there seems no no reason to doubt its accuracy—" my brother *Lintot* drank his half Pint of *Old Hock*, Mr. *Pope* his half Pint of *Sack*, and I the same quantity of an *Emetic* Potion, but no threatnings past. Mr. *Pope*, indeed, said, *that* Satire *should not be printed* (tho' he has now changed his mind). I *answered* They should *not be wrote, for if they were they would be printed. He replied, Mr. Gay's Interest at Court would be greatly hurt by publishing these* Poems. This

---

[1] In *The Curliad.*

was all that passed in our *Triumvirate*. We then parted, *Pope* and my brother *Lintot* went together, to his Shop, and I went home and *vomited* heartily." [1]

Surely a childish trick, and without excuse. Yet in one of Pope's letters one does find some sort of an excuse. Writing to Caryll on April 20th of this year, he says : " *Item*, a most ridiculous quarrel with a bookseller, occasioned by his having printed some satirical pieces on the Court under my name. I contrived to save the fellow a beating by giving him a vomit. . . ." But what beating ? Were Lady Mary's powerful friends engineering some corporal punishment ? We do not know. Thirteen years later, in a note to the *Dunciad*, Pope once again mentioned the incident, but had nothing to say of the beating. On the contrary, he took credit to himself for having not only threatened the bookseller, but afterwards punished him for his temerity.

This, however, was not all. In the letter to Caryll, after mentioning the " vomit," he goes on to say that the history of the affair " has been transmitted to posterity by a late Grub Street author. I suppose Lewis[2] has sent you the pamphlet which has much entertained the Town." Swift also mentions this pamphlet in a letter to Pope. " I can hardly believe the relation of his being poisoned," he writes, " although the historian pretends to have been an eye-witness ; but I'll beg pardon, sack might do it, although ratsbane would not.[3] I never saw the thing you mention as falsely imputed to you ; but I think the frolics of merry hours, even when we are guilty, should not be left to the mercy of our best friends, until Curll and his resemblers are hanged."

And who was the " late Grub Street author " ? Swift had guessed. It was Pope himself.

---

[1] " My purgation was soon over, but yours will last (without a timely repentance) till, as the Ghost says in Hamlet, with all your imperfections on your head, you are called to your account, and your offences purged by fire." Curll to Pope, 1735.

[2] The Catholic bookseller.

[3] Does this suggest that Swift had once made a similar attempt to get the " satisfaction " he wanted so much ?

II

Let us have a look at this curious pamphlet, which, for all its ludicrous satire, gives an intimate picture of Curll and his methods of business. It muſt have been written almoſt immediately after the praćtical joke had been played. It was called *A Full and True Account of a Horrid and Barbarous Revenge by Poison, on the Body of Mr. Edmund Curll, Bookseller ; with a faithful Copy of his Laſt Will and Teſtament* " [1], and begins thus :

" Hiſtory furnisheth us with Examples of many Satyrical Authors who have fallen Sacrifices to Revenge, but not of any Booksellers that I know of, except the unfortunate Subjećt of the following Papers, I mean Mr. *Edmund Curll*, at the *Bible* and *Dial* in Fleetſtreet, who was Yeſterday poison'd by Mr. *Pope*, after having liv'd many Years an Inſtance of the mild Temper of the *Britiſh* nation.

" Every Body knows that the said Mr. *Edmund Curll*, on Monday the 26th Inſtant, publish'd a Satyrical Piece, entituled *Court Poems*, in the Preface whereof they were attributed to a *Lady of Quality*, Mr. *Pope*, or Mr. *Gay ;* by which indiscreet Method, though he had escaped one Revenge, there were ſtill two behind in reserve.

" Now on the Wednesday ensuing, between the Hours of 10 and 11, Mr. *Lintott*, a neighb'ring Bookseller, desir'd a Conference with Mr. *Curll* about settling the *Title Page* of *Wiquefort's Ambassador*, inviting him at the same Time to take a whet together. Mr. *Pope* (who is not the only Inſtance how Persons of bright Parts may be carry'd away by the Inſtigation of the Devil) found Means to convey himself into the same Room, under pretence of Business with Mr. *Lintott*, who it seems is the Printer of his *Homer*. This Gentleman with a seeming Coolness, reprimanded Mr. *Curll* for wrongfully ascribing to him the aforesaid Poems : He excused him-

[1] Fo. Sold by J. Roberts, J. Morphew, R. Burleigh, J. Baker, and S. Popping (all at one time or another partners of Curll). Price Three Pence. The text here printed is taken from the 1716 edition. When Pope reprinted it in his *Miſcellanies*, several correćtions and emendations were made.

A FULL and TRUE

ACCOUNT

OF A

Horrid and Barbarous

REVENGE by POISON,

On the Body of

Mr. *EDMUND CURLL*, Bookſeller;

With a faithful Copy of his

Laſt *WILL and TESTAMENT*.

Publiſh'd by an Eye Witneſs.

So when Curll's *Stomach the ſtrong Drench o'ercame,*
(Infus'd in Vengeance of inſulted Fame)
Th' Avenger ſees, with a delighted Eye,
His long Jaws open, and his Colour fly;
And while his Guts the keen Emeticks urge,
Smiles on the Vomit, and enjoys the Purge.

Sold by *J. Roberts, J. Morphew, R. Burleigh, J. Baker,* and *S. Pop-ping.* Price Three Pence.

self, by declaring, that one of his Authors (Mr. *Old-mixon* by Name) gave the Copies to the Press, and wrote the *Preface*. Upon this Mr. *Pope* (being to all appearance reconcil'd) very civilly drank a Glass of Sack to Mr. *Curll*, which he as civilly pledged ; and tho' the Liquor in Colour and Taste differ'd not from common Sack, yet was it plain by the Pangs this unhappy Stationer felt soon after, that some poisonous Drug had been secretly infused therein.

" About Eleven a Clock he went home, where his Wife observing his Colour chang'd, said, *Are you not sick, my Dear ?* He reply'd, *Bloody Sick ;* and incontinently fell a vomiting and straining in an uncommon and unnatural Manner, the Contents of his vomiting being as Green as Grass. His Wife had been just reading a Book of her Husband's printing, concerning *Jane Wenham*, the famous Witch of *Hartford*, and her Mind misgave her that he was bewitch'd ; but he soon let her know that he suspected *Poison*, and recounted to her, between the Intervals of his Yawnings and Reachings, every Circumstance of his Interview with Mr. *Pope*.

" Mr. *Lintott* in the mean Time coming in, was extremely affrighted at the sudden Alteration he observed in him : *Brother* Curll, says he, *I fear you have got the vomiting Distemper, which (I have heard) kills in half an Hour. This comes from your not following my Advice, to drink old Hock as I do, and abstain from Sack.* Mr. *Curll* reply'd, in a moving Tone, *Your Author's Sack I fear has done my Business.* Z——ds, says Mr. *Lintott*, *My Author !—Why did not you drink old Hock ?* Notwithstanding which rough Remonstrance, he did in the most friendly Manner press him to take warm Water ; but Mr. *Curll* did with great Obstinacy refuse it ; which made Mr. *Lintott* infer, that he chose to die, as thinking to recover greater Damages.

" All this Time the Symptoms encreas'd violently, with acute Pains in the lower Belly. *Brother* Lintott, says he, *I perceive my last Hour approaching, do me the friendly Office to call my Partner, Mr.* Pemberton, *that we may settle our Worldly Affairs.* Mr. *Lintott,* like a kind Neighbour, was hastening out of the Room, while Mr. *Curll* rav'd aloud in this Manner, *If I survive this, I will be revenged on* Tonson, *it was he first detected me as the Printer of these Poems,* and *I will reprint these very Poems in his Name.* His Wife admonish'd him not to think of Revenge, but to take care of his Stock and his Soul : And in the same Instant, Mr. *Lintott* (whose Goodness can never be enough applauded) return'd with Mr. *Pemberton.* After some Tears jointly shed by these Humane Booksellers, Mr. *Curll,* being (as he said) in his perfect Senses though in great bodily Pain, immediately proceeded to make a verbal Will (Mrs. *Curll* having first put on his Night Cap). . . ."

With all the details of this will we need not concern ourselves. The sick man prays for forgiveness " for those indirect Methods I have pursued in inventing new Titles to old Books, putting Authors Names to Things they never saw," and " publishing private Quarrels for publick Entertainment." Anything of his that may seem malicious is due to charity, he having made it his " Business to print for poor disconsolate Authors whom all other Booksellers refuse." And Mr. Pemberton is begged " to beware of the Indictment at Hicks's-Hall for publishing Rochester's bawdy Poems," " that copy otherwise " being his best legacy to his " dear Wife and helpless Child." The squib ends with the arrival of Mr. Oldmixon.

" *Ah ! Mr.* Oldmixon (said poor Mr. *Curll) to what a Condition have your Works reduced me ! I die a Martyr to that unlucky Preface. However, in these my last Moments, I will be just to all Men ; you shall have your Third Share of the* Court Poems, *as was stipulated. When I am dead, where will you find another Bookseller ? Your* Protestant Packet *might have supported you, had you writ a little less scurrilously. There is a mean in all things.*

" Then turning to Mr. *Pemberton,* he told him, he had several *Taking* Title Pages that only wanted Treatises to be wrote to them, and earnestly entreated, that when they were writ, his Heirs might have some Share of the Profit of them.

"After he had said this he fell into horrible Gripings, upon which Mr. *Lintott* advis'd him to repeat the Lord's Prayer. He desir'd his Wife to ſtep into the Shop for a Common-Prayer-Book, fetch'd a Groan, and recommended to Mrs. *Curll* to give Forty Shillings to the Poor of the Parish of St. *Dunſtan*'s, and a Week's Wages Advance to each of his Gentlemen Authors, with some small Gratuity in particular to Mrs. Centlivre."

The final paragraph relates the means whereby "the poor Man" is unexpectedly relieved, though "it is judged by Sir *Richard Bl——e*, that the Poyson is ſtill latent in his Body, and will infallibly deſtroy him by slow Degrees, in less than a Month. It is to be hoped the other Enemies of this wretched Stationer, will not further pursue their Revenge, or shorten this small Period of his miserable Life."

III

It was not to be supposed that Curll would be content to do nothing, and little time elapsed before the counter-attack had been launched. Firſt, however, there appeared a disclaimer from Oldmixon.[1]

"Whereas Mr. *Lintot*, or Mr. *Pope*, has publish'd a false and ridiculous Libel, reflecting on several Gentlemen, particularly on myself; and it is said therein, that I was the publisher of certain Verses call'd *Court Poems*, and that I wrote the Preface; I hereby declare that I never saw a great part of those Verses, nor ever saw or heard of the Title or Preface to them till after the Poems were publish'd.

"Witness, E. Curll.   J. Oldmixon."

This reads a little curiously, but may be quite true. After handing over the verses, Oldmixon may not have

---

[1] *Flying Poſt*, April 3rd.

worried himself further about them, and Curll himself, I don't doubt, wrote the preface.

Four days later the attack proper began with a mock advertisement of a " Second Part of Mr. Pope's Popish Translation of Homer." The subscribers, it was announced, had made great complaint that so far there had been no pictures issued with the work, which omission Mr. Curll proposed to make good by giving them " a spacious MAP of Trojan Tents and Rivers finely delineated. Translated into *Copper* from the Wooden Original." Not a very good beginning, but in a postscript it was announced that in the following week an " Excellent New Ballad, call'd The Catholick Poet, or Protestant Barnaby's Lamentation," would be issued with the promise that

> " Tho of his Wit the Catholick has boasted,
> Lintot and Pope by turns shall both be roasted."

Accordingly another advertisement was inserted " to prevent any farther Imposition on the Publick " to the effect that Homer was to be defended from his latest " pretended " translator. It would be proved that Mr. Pope neither understood the original nor the author's meaning, and that in several places he had " falsified it on Purpose." *The Catholick Poet* naturally took a little time to prepare, but, meanwhile, Curll had procured a copy of some other satirical verses " To the Ingenious Mr. Moore, Author of the Celebrated Worm-Powder," by Pope, and issued them on May 3rd with the impudent notice that " all his Writings for the Future, except Homer, will be Printed for *E. Curll.*"

This led, a week or two later, to the appearance of MOORE' WORMS FOR THE LEARNED MR. CURLL, BOOK-SELLER ; *Who, to be reveng'd on Mr. Pope for his poisonous Emetick, gave him a Paper of Worm-Powder, which caused that Gentleman to void a strange sort of Worms.*

A few verses may be given. (They are not likely to be reprinted elsewhere !)

" Oh Learned Curll ! thy Skill excells
    Ev'n *Moore's* of *Abchurch-Lane*—
He only *Genuine Worms* expells,
    To crawl in Print for Gain.

From a Wit's Brain Thou mak'st Worms rise,
    (Unknown in the *Worm-Evil*)
Fops, Silkworms, Beaus, and Butterflies,
    With that old Worm the *Devil.*

Ev'n *Button's Book-Worms* shall, with these,
    (Like these with Dust decay'd)
In *Grub-street Rubbish* rest in Peace,
    Till *Curlls* their peace invade.

For Booksellers vile Vipers are,
    On Brains of *Wits* they prey ;
The very *Worms* they will not spare,
    When *Wits* to *Worms* decay . . .

Ah Curll ! [1] how greedy hast thou fed
    (E'er *Worms* gave Food to thee)
Upon the late Illustrious *Dead,*
    With Worms of thy Degree.

Why did the Venom [2] of a Prude
    Allure thy vicious Taste ?—
Safer Thou'dst feast on *Maggots Crude*
    Or with Tom D'Urfey fast.

For see ! thy meagre Looks declare,
    Some Poison in thee Lurks.
Let Bl[ackmo]re ease thy restless Care—
    Or who shall print his *Works ?*

[1] Famous for printing the Lives and Last Wills of Great men.
[2] The Court Poems printed by Mr. *Curll.*"

It was not until the last day of the month that *The Catholick Poet* (the work of Oldmixon, it would seem, and not, as was supposed at the time, Mrs. Centlivre's) appeared, and when it did it was accompanied by a vitriolic *True Character of Mr. Pope and his Writings.* This was the work of John Dennis, who excused his mention of Pope's deformity which, he handsomely admitted, was not the poet's fault, on the ground that the " little Monster " had upbraided other people's calamities even when, as in Curll's case, he had been responsible for them.

At the same time it was announced that " These Town Diversions " would " be continued Weekly, so long as the Pope-*ish* Controversy is on foot." And they doubt-less would have multiplied exceedingly, had not the disastrous affair of the trial of Lord Winton just then intervened.[1]

On his part, too, Pope was not idle. Some time in June he issued the second of his three squibs against Curll. In *A Further Account of the Most Deplorable Condition of Mr. Edmund Curll, Bookseller*, purporting to be by an-other hand, but included by Pope in his Works, the satire is distinctly coarser than that to be found in its predecessor. The bookseller's symptoms have now become much more alarming. In fact it would seem that poor Mr. Curll, though still alive, is losing his senses. At first he is only " speaking civilly to his customers, singeing a pig with a new purchased label "—what this refers to I have not a notion—" and refusing two and ninepence for Sir Richard Blackmore's Essays." But later, when his frenzy increases, he attacks his best friends, dines on "nothing but copper-plates," and, in general, behaves in a scatalogical manner that is wholly unprintable. Mrs. Curll, poor soul, desires the prayers of various congre-gations, and beseeches Mr. Lintott's assistance. Her husband's violence has now become terrific, and she is afraid to write much, for she can " hear the rap of Mr. Curll's ivory-headed cane upon the counter. . . ." " He is coming in," she concludes her letter, " and I have but just time to put his son out of the way for fear of mis-chief."

Fortunately there comes a lucid interval, during which Curll orders " a general summons to all his authors " who forthwith parade.

Instructions, however, have first to be given to a porter as to how these gentlemen are to be found. So " the historian "—presumably Oldmixon—must be fetched from " a Tallow-chandler's in Petty France, half-

[1] See next chapter.

POPE BEATING CURLL. BY HOGARTH
An enlargement of the picture shown in the first state of
The Distressed Poet

[*To face p.* 60

way under the blind arch." At a music-house in Moor-
fields, two translators will be discovered in bed together.
Then at a tavern in Vinegar-yard, there will be a " schoolmaster with carbuncles on his nose "—I cannot identify
him further than as a Mr. B—— —and " at a black-
smith's shop in the Friars, " a Pindaric writer in red
stockings." This was Ambrose Philips, the poet, the
" simple Macer " of Pope's own verse. Mrs. Centlivre
herself—" the Cook's wife " : her husband was Yeoman
of the Mouth and later Master Cook to George I.—is
to be found in Buckingham Court. As for " the beetle-
browed critic " at the Mint—John Dennis—and " the
purblind poet at the Alley over against St. Andrew's
Holborn "—Charles Gildon—the porter need not be
particular to fetch them, unless there is time on his
hands.

" All these gentlemen," continues the historian,
" appeared at the hour appointed in Mr. Curll's dining-
room, two excepted ; one of whom was the gentleman
in the cockloft, his landlady being out of the way "—and
so unable to produce the necessary ladder—" the other
happened to be too closely watched by the bailiffs.

" They no sooner entered the room, but all of them
shewed in their behaviour some suspicion of each other ;
some turning away their heads with an air of contempt ;
others squinting with a leer, that shewed at once fear
and indignation, each with a haggard abstracted mien,
the lively picture of scorn, solitude, and short commons.
So when a keeper feeds his hungry charge of vultures,
panthers, and of Libyan leopards, each eyes his fellow
with a fiery glare : high hung, the bloody liver tempts
their maw. Or as a house-wife stands before her pales,
surrounded by her geese ; they fight, they hiss, they
gaggle, beat their wings, and down is scattered as the
winter's snow, for a poor grain of oat, or tare, or
barley. Such looks shot through the room transverse,
oblique, direct ; such was the stir and din, till Curll
thus spoke. . . .

" Ah, gentlemen ! What have I not done ? what have

I not suffered, rather than that the world should be deprived of your lucubrations ? I have taken involuntary purges, I have been vomited, three times have I been caned, once was I hunted, twice was my head broken by a grenadier, twice was I tossed in a blanket ; I have had boxes on the ears, slaps on the chops ; I have been frighted, pumped, kicked, slandered, and beshitten.[1] . . . I hope, gentlemen, you are all convinced, that this author of Mr. Lintot's, could mean nothing else but starving you, by poisoning me. It remains for us to consult the best and speediest methods of revenge."

Many proposals are put forward, but although everybody agrees that something ought to be done to the very annoying Mr. Pope, no definite agreement is arrived at, and after being sworn at indiscriminately by Curll, they are banished to his Tunbridge shop. . . .

Though it belongs to a later date,[2] it may be convenient to mention here Pope's third and last squib : *A Strange but True Relation how Mr. Edmund Curll . . . out of an Extraordinary Desire of Lucre, went into 'Change Alley, and was Converted from the Christian Religion by Certain Eminent Jews ; and how he was circumcised, and initiated into their Mysteries.*

" It having been observed to Mr. Curll," he there recounts, " by some of his ingenious authors (who I fear are not overcharged with any religion), what immense sums the Jews had got by bubbles, &c., he immediately turned his mind from the business in which he was educated, but thrived little, and resolved to quit his shop for 'Change-alley. Whereupon falling into company with the Jews at their club at the sign of the Cross in Cornhill, they began to tamper with him upon the most important points of the Christian faith, which he for some time zealously, and like a good Christian,

---

[1] As we shall see, Curll was duly tossed in a blanket within a very short time, and no doubt he was constantly being slandered, but as for the other misfortunes there is no evidence to show whether they belong to actual fact or, what is more probable, to Pope's vivid imagination.

[2] I am uncertain as to its date. Possibly 1717.

obstinately defended. They promised him Paradise, and many other advantages hereafter, but he artfully insinuated, that he was more inclinable to listen to present gain. They took the hint, and promised him, that immediately upon his conversion to their persuasion he should become as rich as a Jew."

Whereupon a certain necessary operation was made—with untoward results. . . .

IV

The final blow, however, of this first round had still to be delivered, and although Curll's name is not mentioned in this connection, there is little doubt that his was the hand to strike it.

In the *Further Account* some surprise may have been occasioned at the time that so worthy if second-rate a scribbler as Sir Richard Blackmore had been pilloried with the rest. But in June of this year there had been published, ostensibly by Mrs. Burleigh, but really by Curll, whose name appeared on subsequent editions, *Mr. Pope's Version of the First Psalm.* This was an indecent and blasphemous parody, never, of course, meant for publication, but undoubtedly Pope's own work. Blackmore had seen it, and rebuked the author as " godless," though without mentioning his name. The pamphlet is brought to Swift's notice in a letter from Pope dated June 20th. " I have begun to take pique," he writes, " at the Psalms of David, if the wicked may be credited, who have printed a scandalous one in my name." He adds a facetious reason for not discouraging the report of his authorship too much, but in actual fact he " had the hardihood," to use Mr. Elwin's words, to insert the following advertisement in the *Post-Man* of July 31st :

" Whereas there have been publish'd in my Name, certain scandalous Libels, which I hope no Persons of Candor would have thought me capable of, I am sorry to find my self obliged to declare, that no Genuine Pieces of mine have been printed by any but Mr. Tonson and Mr. Lintot. And in particular, as to that which is entitul'd, A Version of the first Psalm ; I hereby promise a Reward of three Guineas to any who shall discover the Person or Persons concerned in the Publication of the said Libel, of which I am wholly ignorant.

"A. Pope."

Purposely this is not too clear, but in any case Pope had gone too far. As Lintott is made to say to Pope in Breval's *Confederates* issued in the following year :

" You may with Curll your quarrel now repent ;
Or else to him you might for Help have sent :
But he with Ballads will debauch the Town,
And cloud your small Remainder of Renown."

Mrs. Burleigh also advertised, and without claiming the three guineas' reward, announced her willingness to show the *Version* in Mr. Pope's own handwriting to anybody who cared to come to her shop.

This advertisement remained unanswered.

ALEXANDER POPE IN 1716
From Smith's engraving of Kneller's portrait

[*To face p.* 64

CHAPTER FOUR

UNPLEASANT ADVENTURES AT WESTMINSTER (1716)

> Much had piratic Mun by pamphlets got,
> For print he would, if authors would or not.
> By vengeful boys decoyed, he takes ten flights,
> From blanket, loftier than from Grub Street Hights.
> Nay more : ſtretch'd out at length on maple board,
> Feels boyish pains in rigid schools abhorred,
> Impatient of the rod, *Ye Dogs uncivil,*
> He cries, *By . . . I'll sue you to the Devil.*
> Lashes loud threats extort : in greater ſtore,
> The threats flie out, the wretch is lashed the more.
>
> *Carmina Quadragesimilia.*

I

THERE were several reasons why the Earl of Winton's trial should be exciting more than ordinary intereſt. He alone of the peers impeached for the part they had played in the '15 rebellion had refused to plead guilty and throw himself on the King's mercy. He was, moreover, a peculiar man—some believed him to be a little mad—and he had succeeded in delaying his trial more than once. When it was aĉtually begun on March 15th, he was not permitted to be heard by counsel. He was found guilty, but succeeded in escaping from the Tower.

On April 10th, Jacob Tonson announced that as "ordered by the House of Peers" he would have ready in a few days' time *The Trial of George Earl of Wintoun,* a shilling pamphlet in every way official and complete. On the same day a Mrs. Sarah Popping announced (juſt below one of Curll's attacks on Pope) *An Account of the Tryal of the Earl of Winton* at twopence, but being well aware of the danger of upsetting the peers—on one occasion at leaſt she had been taken into cuſtody for an injudicious publication—declared that her own version of the trial had been " Translated from the French Original published in Amsterdam." No doubt the public was grateful at the opportunity of obtaining details of so intriguing a trial for twopence, but the peers could not overlook what they regarded as a serious breach of privilege.   Translation or not, the pamphlet must be suppressed.   Three days after its appearance formal complaint was made in the House of Lords and the luckless Mrs. Popping taken straightway into custody.

As it happened she was ill at the time—so ill, we learn from the House's *Journal*, that she was in no condition to be brought to the Bar.   " A Person," however, was attending at the door who could explain how the pamphlet had come to be printed.   " Whereupon *Elizabeth Cape* was called in ; and examined, upon Oath, at the Bar, touching the said printed Paper," and announced that although Mrs. Popping's name might appear on the title-page, she was by no means its " onlie begetter."

We may gather what she said from the sinister sequel.

" Ordered, that the Gentleman Usher . . . do forthwith attach the Bodies of *John Pemberton* and *Edmund Curl*, Booksellers in Fleet Street . . . and keep them in Custody until further Order."

And so for the first time Curll lost his liberty.

Three days later Mrs. Popping presented a petition for release : " That being ill at the Time the said Paper came to her Hands, her Sister, who is not acquainted with such Things, had published it before the Petitioner knew any Thing of it, and praying in regard they have fully declared all they know about the Booksellers concerned in it, that the Petitioner may be discharged without Fees ; her Condition and the Profits she has by Publication not being able to bear it."   After several postponements she and the two booksellers were summoned to the Bar and " severally examined," and you are not altogether surprised to learn that while Mrs. Popping and Pemberton were immediately discharged without paying fees, Curll was ordered to be kept in

custody. It was he, of course, who had conceived the
idea of a translation from the French " what they never
wrote," and he, no doubt, who had attempted to safe-
guard himself and his partner by using a sick woman's
name.

His printer, one Daniel Bridge of Paternoster Row,
was also " taken up," and the two of them remained in
prison until May 2nd, when they were examined at the
Bar. Their replies to questions cannot have been too
satisfactory—Bridge admitted that he had had the
" copy " from Curll—for they were sent back into
Black Rod's custody, whence on May 6th they wisely
issued the humblest of petitions. Being ignorant of the
Standing Orders of the House in regard to such things,
they said, they " did inadvertently cause to be printed "
the offending pamphlet, but expressed " their hearty
Sorrow for their Offence," at the same time praying " in
regard they have Families, which must inevitably be
ruined unless this House have Compassion on them,
that they may be discharged from this Confinement."
" Inadvertently " strikes me as being not quite the right
word, but the peers seem to have considered that three
weeks' loss of liberty would meet the case, and on May
10th Curll and his printer on their knees were reprimanded by the Lord Chancellor and allowed to go free.

It was not perhaps a very serious business, but it was
a slight foretaste of what was to come.

II

No more than two months were to pass before Curll
was again in trouble, but neither the " Pope-ish " controversy nor his experiences in the custody of Black Rod
could prevent him from working hard. New books
appeared every week, and new plans were constantly
maturing. In particular there was the antiquarian series,
and two letters of his, belonging to this period, show at
once to what pains he would put himself in the endeavour
to obtain the best " copies " and the fact that for all his

reputation as a piratical bookseller, he did not lack friends amongst University scholars.

Both these letters were written to the well-known Ralph Thoresby, and they had reference to a proposed new edition of Erdeswicke's *Survey of Staffordshire*, which Richard Rawlinson, of manuscripts' fame, was just then preparing. I give them in full.

"May 22, 1716.

"Worthy Sir,

"The Life of Archbishop Tillotson is not yet done ; so soon as it is, both that and Radcliffe shall be faithfully sent you. Messrs. Gales desire your acceptance of their service. Mr. Rawlinson, of St. John's College in Oxon., has sent me up a copy of Mr. Erdeswicke's Survey of Staffordshire, which was put to the press this day. He is told, Sir, that you have a good copy of this valuable Manuscript, and entreats the favour of you that you will be pleased to lend him yours to collate with his own : all imaginable care shall be taken of it, and it shall be faithfully returned to you in a fortnight's time. This he hopes for from you, as you are a lover of antiquities, and a promoter of learning ; and your speedy answer to this request will very much oblige him, our club of antiquaries, and more particularly, Sir, your obliged humble Servant, E. CURLL."

Precisely what the club of antiquaries may have been I do not know, but Curll was genuinely keen on all matters of the kind, and one may share his satisfaction at Thoresby's reply, which allowed him to play the part of collator himself.

"Friday, June 1, 1716.

"Sir

"I have just received your obliging letter, wherein you are so kind to promise me the loan of your copy of Erdeswicke. The greatest care imaginable shall be taken of it, and I herewith send you a note of my hand for the safe return of it in a month's time. I must desire you, Sir, to send it to me by the very first opportunity (I will pay the carriage), because I have this day received the first printed sheet back from Oxford, and will not let it be worked off till I have collated it with your manuscript, with which I will return you two printed Copies. I will deliver Dr. Radcliffe's Life to whosoever you order to call for it. As to Collins, I know nothing of his residence; the last time I saw him, he told me he was promised to have a place in the Custom House.

"I am, Sir, your obliged humble Servant

"E. CURLL.

"June 1, 1716.

"One month after the date hereof, I promise to return, free from all damage, to Mr. Thoresby, or his order, his manuscript copy of Erdeswicke's Survey of Staffordshire, together with two printed copies of the same work.

"Per E. CURLL."

III

It would have been well for Curll had he confined his attention at this time to antiquarian books. In that case he would not have been given an emetic by Pope, reprimanded by the Lord Chancellor after three weeks in custody, or—whipped by the boys of Westminster School.

This last misfortune, I confess, seems to me to have been ill-deserved. To print, even without permission and not wholly free from false concords, a Latin oration spoken by a schoolboy is surely more of a compliment to the boy than anything else. To-day, it may be, we should call the whole business a " rag," and perhaps it was a " rag " then, but if so it went too far. You may wonder that Curll should have troubled to print any such oration, but he did print it, and suffered for it, both physically and by the jeers of the scribes.

On July 8th the famous Dr. Robert South died at the age of eighty-three. He was a worthy and learned old man, whose support of Dr. Sacheverell six years before had doubtless roused Curll's particular interest in him. His refusal of a bishopric did not prevent his being buried in Westminster Abbey, and it was at the first part of his funeral on July 16th that John Barber, the then Captain of Westminster School, delivered his oration over the corpse in the College Hall.

Ten days later Curll issued this oration in Latin and English as a sixpenny pamphlet. Undoubtedly Dr. South had enjoyed a great reputation, and it may be that young Barber's panegyric was of more than usual merit. (I confess that I was content to look at its title-page.) In any case the bookseller, who was already projecting the usual "Life," thought it worth his while to print the thing, and could have had no idea of the untoward result.

It is not known for certain how exactly the "rag" was engineered, but it would seem that a letter of thanks was sent from Westminster to the *Dial and Bible*, in which a polite invitation was extended to its proprietor to visit the school. To Westminster, accordingly, Curll went on August 2nd, and for the second time within three months was obliged to go down on his knees and ask pardon.

"Mr. Edmund Curll," Pope was writing gleefully to Teresa Blount in a few days' time, "has been exercised in a blanket, and whipped at Westminster School by the boys, whereof the common prints have given some account." Chalmers mentions a "humorous letter, copied by Mr. Nichols in Atterbury's Correspondence from the *St. James's Chronicle*, and dated Aug. 3," and this is presumably the letter signed T. A. which appeared in *The Original Weekly Journal* of the same week.

"King's College, Westminster, Aug. 3, 1716.

" SIR,

" YOU are desired to acquaint the Publick, that a certain *B——er* near *Temple-Bar* (not taking warning by the frequent Drubs that he has undergone for his often pyrating other Men's Copies) did lately (without the Con-

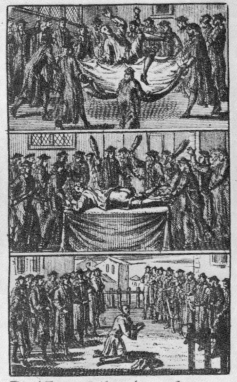

Ibis ab Excuso Missus ad astra Sago.
Æthereas, lascive, Cupis Volitare per Auras,
I, fuge, Sed poteras Tutior esse domi.

CURLL AT WESTMINSTER SCHOOL
(From the Frontispiece to *Neck or Nothing*, 1716)

[*To face p.* 71

sent of Mr. *John Barber* present Captain of *Westminster* School) publish the Scraps of a Funeral Oration, spoken by him over the Corps of the Reverend Dr. *South*. And being on *Thursday* last fortunately Nab'd within the Limits of *Dean's Yard* by the King's Schollars, there he met with a College Salutation : For he was first presented with the Ceremony of the Blanket, in which, when the Skeleton had been well shook, he was carry'd in Triumph to the School ; and after receiving a Grammatical Correction for his false Concords ; he was Reconducted to *Dean's Yard*, and on his Knees, asking Pardon of the aforesaid Mr. *Barber* for his Offence ; he was kick'd out of the Yard, and left to the Huzza's of the Rabble.

" I am, Sir, Yours, T. A."

It would seem, by the way, that the masters were not too displeased at this display of youthful exuberance. At this time the head usher was Samuel Wesley, an elder brother of John, and related in some way to the half-crazy but most entertaining bookseller, John Dunton. He is supposed to have been the author of *Neck or Nothing* : *A Consolatory Letter from Mr. D-nt-n to Mr. C-rll Upon his being Tost in a Blanket*, which was printed as a fourpenny pamphlet a week or two later. This satire in verse contains a frontispiece which shows Curll being tossed in the blanket, held down and beaten on a table, and on his knees begging pardon in Dean's Yard. Some of its lines may be given here.

After addressing his " Dear Mun " as " a Glorious Confessor," the supposed Dunton wonders a little that his usually cautious " brother " could have stepped unsuspiciously into such an obvious trap. He asks :

> " Could none of thy Poetick Band
> Of Mercenary Wits at hand,
> Foretell, or ward the coming Blow,
> From Garret high or Cellar low ?
> Or else at least in verse bemoan
> Their Lord, in Double Sense cut down ?

Or waſt Thou warn'd, and couldſt believe }
That Habit fitted to deceive,
That corner's Cap, and hanging Sleeve ? }
What Proteſtant of sober Wits
Would truſt Folks dreſt like Jesuits ?
And couldſt Thou, *Mun*, be such a Sot
As not to smell a Powder-Plot ?
And looking nine Ways couldſt not spy
What might be seen with half an Eye.

" What Planet rul'd that luckless Day,
When Thou, by Traitors call'd away,
Thy haſty hapless Course didſt ſteer
To fatal Flogging *Weſtminſter ?*
For Hat and Gloves You call'd in haſte,
And down to Execution paſt.
Small need of Hat and Gloves, I trow ;
Thou might have left thy Breeches too !
Perhaps thy Soul, to Gain inclin'd,
Did gratis Copies think to find ;
Or else, miſtaken Hopes, expeſted
To have at leaſt the Press correſted.
Correſtion they designing were
More difficult but better far ;
Tho' whatsoe'er the Knaves intended,
Thou 'rt but correſted not amended.
No ! let it ne'er by Man be said,
The Pirate's frighted from his Trade :
Tho' vengeful Birch should flea his Thighs, }
Tho' toss'd from Blankets he should rise, }
Or ſtand faſt nail'd to Pillories ! " }

His bowels yearn, he goes on to say, at the sight of a
brother ſtationer made to smart for mere " copy-ſteal-
ing," for has he not himself issued fifteen hundred
pamphlets or more, " a Plagiary in every one " ? And
yet, although misfortunes of many kinds have attended
his efforts, he has never had cudgels nor birches raised
againſt him. Indeed any such assault is clearly againſt
the Law, and not even Cuſtom gives any such " Tyran-
nous Prerogative." There follows a detailed account of
the dreadful affair :

" Inhuman Punishment, inflicted
By Stripling Tories, Rogues addicted

> To arbitrary Constitution ;
> 'Twas Rome ! 'twas downright Persecution :
> I sweat to think of thy Condition
> Before that barb'rous Inquisition.
> Lo ! wide-extended by the Crowd,
> The Blanket, dreadful as a Shrowd,
> Yearns terrible for Thee, poor *Mun*,
> To stretch, but not to sleep upon.
> Glad wouldst Thou give thy Copies now,
> And all thy golden Hopes forego ;
> Some Favour from their Hands to win,
> And 'scape but once with a whole Skin :
> Yet vain, alas ! is thy Repentance.
> For *Neck or Nothing* is thy Sentence :
> How doest thou lessen to the Sight,
> With more than a Poetick Flight ?
> I ken Thee dancing high in Air,
> With Limbs alert, and quiv'ring there :
> So, whizz'd from Stick, I've seen to rise
> A Frog, sent sprawling to the Skies,
> By naughty Boys, on Sport intent,
> Caught Straggling from its Element."

Such a scene, indeed, must appeal to the graver, who will be invited to hand down the affair to posterity. Mr. Curll must be shown suspended in the air like Mahomet, though this, alas, had been beyond his powers in Dean's Yard.

> "Whate'er thine Effigy might do,
> Thy Person could not hover so.
> Happy at *Westminster* for Thee,
> Cou'dst thou have hung by Geometry ?
> But, ah ! the higher Mortals soar,
> So Fate ordains, they fall the lower ;
> With swifter Rapidness down-hasting,
> For nothing violent is lasting.
> With greater Force thy Forehead came,
> Than Engine, or than batt'ring Ram ;
> Nor Blankets interposing Wooll
> Could save the Pavement or thy Scull. "

After which, of course, there comes the inevitable allusion to Pope's " vomit " :

> " This sure might seem enough for once, Oh !
> This tossing up, and tumbling down so ;

And well thy Stomach might incline
To spue without Emetick Wine :
Their Rage goes farther, and applies
More fundamental Injuries.

Like Truant, doom'd the Lash to feel,
Thou'rt dragg'd, full sore against thy Will,
To School to suffer more and worse,
No Wonder if you hand an Arse
As thy Posteriors could foresee
Their near-approaching Destiny.
The School, the direful Place of Fate,
Opes her inhospitable Gate ;
Which ne'er had yet such Rigour seen,
No ! not from *Busby*'s Discipline.
And first of all, the cruel Rabble
Conduct Thee, trembling, to a Table :
Thy wrigling Corps across they spread,
Two guard the Heels, and two the Head.
The rest around, a threat'ning Band,
With each his Fasces in his Hand,
Dreadful as *Roman Lictors* stand.
So oft a four-leg'd Cur I've known,
By hind Legs, and by fore kept down
To be dissected, while Physician
Stands o'er with Weapon of Incision.
The Scene they order to disclose ;
' Strip, pull his Breeches o'er his Hose :
' Nay, farther, make the Coast yet clearer,
' Tho' near the Shirt, the Skin is nearer.

So said, so done, they soon uncase
Thy only penetrable Face,
The Breech, the Seat of Bashfulness.
As hence we gather by its Caring,
So very rarely for appearing ;
Not oft its pretty self revealing,
Devoid of Sight, but not of Feeling :
And now upon thy Rump they score Thee
And pink thy fleshy Cushions for thee.
Come hold him Fair, we'll make him know
What 'tis to deal with Scholars —— Oh !
Quoth *Edmund* : —— Now, without Disguise,
Confess, quo' they, thy Rogueries.
What makes you keep in Garret high
Poor Bards ty'd up to Poetry ? ——
I'm forc'd to load them with a Clog,
To make them study —— Here's a Rogue

Affronts the School, we'll make Thee rue it :
—— Indeed I never meant to do it ! "

And then there follows that oft-quoted couplet :

" No ? didst Thou not th' Oration print
Imperfect, with false Latin in't ? "

Curll cannot deny this awful accusation, and begs
pardon, that being about the only thing that a man in his
unfortunate predicament can expediently do. This, however, is not enough for the boys.

" No, Sir, have a care,
False Latin's never pardon'd here ! "

The bookseller promises to amend his ways, and asks
his tormentors to handle him like gentlemen. This they
proceed to do, pointing out that his betters have often
enough been forced to undergo much the same form of
correction :

" And with a Lash, as is their Fashion,
Finish'd each smart Expostulation."

The poem ends with some good advice and a nasty
reminder that others besides the writer are likely to take
notice of so unusual a business :

" Hast thou not oft enough in Court
Appear'd, and often smarted for't ?
And dost thou not, with many a Brand,
Recorded for a Pirate stand ?
Glad that a Fine could pay th' Arrears,
And clear the Mortgage of thy Ears.
Then what Relief dost hope to draw,
From that which still condemns Thee, Law ?
And if from Law no Help there be,
I'm sure there's none from Equity :
Lay Hand on Heart, and timely think,
The more Thou stir'st, the more thou'lt stink :
And tho' it sorely gauls Thee yet,
Well as thou canst, sit down with it :
And since to rage will do no Good,
Pull in thy Horns, and kiss the Rod,
And while thou canst, retreat, for fear
They fall once more upon thy Rear.

Tho' 'tis vexatious, *Mun*, I grant,
To hear the passing Truants taunt,
And ask Thee at thy Shop in jeer,
Which is the Way to *Westminster?*
Oh! how th' unlucky Urchins laugh'd,
To think they'd maul'd Thee fore and aft:
'Tis such a sensible Affront!
Why *Pope* will write an Epick on 't!
Bernard will chuckle at thy Moan,
And all the Booksellers in Town,
From *Tonson* down to *Boddington.*
Fleet-street and *Temple-bar* around,
The *Strand* and *Holborn*, this shall sound:
For ever This shall grate thine Ear,
Which is the Way to *Westminster?* "

CHAPTER FIVE

CURLICISM EXPOUNDED (1717–1724)

Is there a bard whom Genius fires,
Whose ev'ry thought the god inspires ?
When envy reads the nervous lines,
She frets, she rails, she raves, she pines,
Her hissing snakes with venom swell,
She calls her venal train from hell,
The servile friends her nod obey,
And all Curll's authors are in pay.

                                        Gay.

I

MR. WESLEY'S advice was not taken. There was no drawing in of horns for some years. On the contrary, there came even more impudent tricks, even more scandalous books, and, by consequence, a more or less continual rumbling and rumpus in the newspapers. How often Curll was actually sued in the Courts at this time I do not know. We are told of no further assaults by poets or schoolboys or presumably jealous grenadiers. But never before had the lists of new books issued from the *Dial and Bible* been so extensive—and peculiar. Some of the " translators in pay " and some of the " hireling poets " had disappeared, but there were others to take their place. The accommodating Sewell had had enough of it, but there was a useful new man in the person of Nicholas Amhurst, just then smarting from his treatment at Oxford, and John Breval, also a University man with a grievance, showed signs of becoming a writer of parts. There were, in addition, men like Robert Samber, who could generally be trusted to nose out some tasty French morsel for home consumption, and like the mysterious Thomas Foxton who came to play general editor. A still more mysterious fellow who called himself Philalethes invented the " blurb " and appeared almost daily in print. (But he, as a matter of fact, was anybody, including Curll, who happened to be on the spot at the appropriate moment.)

In the Curllean gallery, too, a Mr. J. Gay had made his appearance.

Dear, gentle Gay, of *Beggar's Opera* fame ? No, indeed : another Mr. J. Gay, who possessed about as much flesh and blood as Curll's various surgeons. . . .

In 1716 Gay had not achieved anything like the amazing success on the stage that was ultimately to be his, but he was already becoming popular as a poet. His *Trivia* had appeared at the beginning of the year, and people were talking about him. A new poem bearing his name was fairly sure of a ready sale. Such a poem appeared in the summer. It was called *The Petticoat*,[1] and many people bought it, I imagine, as Gay's work. Its ostensible publisher was Burleigh, and it professed to be the work of Mr. J. Gay, but in this case J. stood for Joseph, and it continued to stand for Joseph for many years. Pope mentions the phantom in the *Dunciad* :

> " Curl stretches after Gay, but Gay is gone :
> He grasps an empty Joseph for a John."

The Petticoat was the work of one Francis Chute, who, however, soon relinquished all claims to the pseudonym. But Joseph was too useful to be killed off like a mere surgeon, and John Breval, willingly or unwillingly, stepped into his shoes.

It may have been a clever move, but it was not without danger, for people were talking again. There had been too many such moves. Once, perhaps, they had been fairly diverting, but now they were more than tiresome : they were inexcusable. And nothing would stop the fellow. Besides, one or two of his recent books had been very muddy indeed. Curll, they repeated, was going

---

[1] Subsequently called *The Hoop Petticoat*, and often, though erroneously, considered to be Breval's work.

too far. Something would have to be done. But—
what ?

Another attack came, this time from an unexpected
source—from Daniel Defoe, as a matter of fact, in his
most venomous mood.

It took the form of a trouncing in the *Weekly Journal*,[1]
where the authorities were exhorted to take action, and
it has an additional interest in being, so far as I know,
the first printed article to mention the word coined
from Curll's name, which at one time seemed likely to
find a permanent place in the language. After calling
attention to the foul nature and purpose of some recent
publications, the writer points out that " there is indeed
but one Bookseller eminent among us for this Abomina-
tion, and from him the Crime takes the just Denomina-
tion of *Curlicism*.[2] The Fellow is a contemptible Wretch
a thousand ways : he is odious in his person, scandalous
in his Fame ; he is mark'd by Nature, for he has a bawdy
Countenance, and a debauched Mien ; his Tongue is an
Echo of all the beastly Language his Shop is fill'd with,
and Filthiness drivels in the very Tone of his Voice."

Then why, he goes on to ask, should such a man be
allowed to go unpunished ? Why is his " abominable
Catalogue " allowed to remain unsuppressed " in a
Country where Religion is talk'd of (little more, God
knows), whose Government is form'd by wholesome
Laws, where Kings obstruct not the Execution of the
Law : where Justice may, if duly prompted, take hold of
him : I say, *Mist*, what can be the Reason such a Criminal
goes unpunish'd ? How can our Stamp Office take
Twelve Pence a Piece for the Advertisement of his
infamous Books, publishing the continued increase of

---

[1] The attack was anonymous, but Lee has shown that Defoe was the writer.
[2] Which, however, is hardly the right word, as Ozell points out in one of
his newspaper quarrels with Woodward and Peele. They had accused him of
using the word " Blockheadism," upon which he retorted : " I have seen many
words in Print which are not in *Baily's* Dictionary. Curlicism for one, which I
am told was coin'd by this very Woodward to abuse an honester man than himself . . . tho' after all," he added, " it is but duncically done : for the true Cast
wou'd have been *Curlism* not *Curlicism*, unless his name had been *Curly* instead
of *Curll*."

lewd abominable Pieces of Bawdry, such as none can read even in Miniature, for such an Advertisement is to a Book. How can these refrain, in informing the Government what Mines are laid to blow up Morality, even from its very Foundation, and to sap the Basis of all Good Manners, nay, and in the End, of Religion it self."

He appeals to the Bishops, though he cannot hide his disgust at their supineness. "How much more like Preachers of Righteousness," he cries out, "had ye appear'd, if as far as it became you, ye had labour'd to establish our Youth in Virtue and Piety, and so suppress'd the spreading abominable Vices by the Agency of the Printing Press."

"In a Word, Mist," he concludes, "record it for Posterity to wonder at, that in Four Years past of the blessed Days we live in, and wherein Justice and Liberty are flourishing and establish'd, more beastly unsufferable Books have been publish'd by this one Offender, than in Thirty Years before by all the Nation; and not a Man, Clergyman or other, has yet thought it worth his while to demand Justice of the Government against the Crime of it, or so much as to caution the Age against the Mischief of it."

Distinctly outspoken: difficult to ignore. For reasons best known to themselves the Government took no immediate action, and although Bishops may have fulminated in pulpits and country curates warned their flocks against pornographical dissertations, several years were to pass before complaint was officially made to the Secretary of State. Curll himself, however, replied almost at once, and in the cleverest way, for he issued a pamphlet which, while ostensibly defending his activities, was in reality an alluring advertisement for the books most bitterly complained about. *Curlicism Display'd*, indeed, is probably his wiliest piece of belligerent writing.

Naturally he accepts the new word, welcomes it, in fact. What other bookseller could hope for so much publicity so cheaply acquired? Curlicism? Excellent!

EUNUCHISM

DISPLAY'D.

Defcribing all the different Sorts of

EUNUCHS;

THE

Efteem they have met with in the World, and how they came to be made fo. Wherein principally is examin'd, whether they are capable of Marriage, and if they ought to be fuffer'd to enter into that State.

The whole confirm'd by the Authority of Civil, Canon, and Common. Law, and illuftrated with many remarkable Cafes by way of Precedent.

Alfo a Comparifon between Signior *Nicolini* and the Three celebrated EUNUCHS now at *Rome*, *viz.* *Pafqualini*, *Pauluccio*, and *Jeronimo* (or *Momo*) : With feveral Obfervations on Modern EUNUCHS.

Occafion'd by a young Lady's falling in Love with *Nicolini*, who fung in the Opera at the *Hay-Market*, and to whom fhe had like to have been Married.

Written by a Perfon of HONOUR.

There are, who in foft Eunuchs place their Blifs,
And fhun the Scrubbing of a bearded Kifs.

                                   Dryden's Juv.

LONDON:

Printed for *E. Curll* at the *Dial* and *Bible* over againft St. *Dunftan's Church* in *Fleetftreet*, 1718. pr. 3 s.

ONE OF THE BOOKS WHICH LED TO DEFOE'S ATTACK.

[To face p. 81.

But how mistaken is that " super-annuated *Letter-Writer*," who asserts that it is of but " Four Years standing ! " " Poor Wretch ! " he continues, " he is a mere Novice in Chronology, and I do sincerely assure you, Mr. Mist, that CURLICISM (since it must be so call'd) dates its Original from that ever memorable *Æra* of the Reign of the first Monarch of the Stuartine Race." For what is the first book about which complaint has been made ? Lord Essex's divorce-case, as printed in one of the *Impotency* volumes. But who drew up the report of that case ? No less a person than Dr. George Abbot, then Archbishop of Canterbury ! And had not such a case more than a sensational interest ? Of course it had ! " Had your learned Correspondent . . . been ever so little conversant in our *English* History, he would have found that the abovemention'd Case engag'd the Politicks of the greatest Statesmen, and the Casuistry of a Monarch himself." The Archbishop, then, is clearly to blame—but how stupid ! For take a look at the most engaging features of this singular case. Are they not extraordinarily amusing ? Curll's readers, at any rate, are given full opportunity to take such a look, for the liveliest passages are printed in detail.

And as for the other books, he goes on, are they really so bawdy ? Complaint has been made about a little volume on Eunuchs. But eunuchs exist, do they not ? You can enjoy their singing, if you like, any night at the Opera. Surely they are entitled to some consideration ? Moreover, if private vice exists, as Mr. Curll understands it does, is it not better to be open and frank about it and to explain to the young the dangers that beset them ? (One feels almost sorry for the bookseller that the psychoanalists had not yet come to provide him with a whole new vocabulary.) And how is a layman to judge the value of a purely medical work like Meibomius's *Treatise of Flogging* ? But of course the whole attack is a piece of pure malice, which can be easily refuted. He is *not* the inventor and producer of books " on such subjects as were never before known to be brought under the Pen," as you can prove for yourself by browsing awhile in any old library. Books are *not* bawdy which treat " only of Matters of the greateſt Importance to Society," conduce " to the mutual Happiness of the *Nuptial State*," and are " directly calculated for Antidotes and againſt *Debauchery* and *unnatural Lewdness*." For which reasons, he adds with delicious candour, " I shall not desiſt from printing such Books, when the Occasion offers, nor am I concern'd or asham'd to have them diſtinguish'd by the facetious Name of Curlicism." Indeed, he admits that he would never have replied to the attack " had not an Opportunity thereby offer'd it self to me of publishing to the World the Contents at large of these several Pieces. . . ."

A final paragraph outlines a counter-charge. Why had this attack been made ? Purely on grounds of morality ? Mr. Curll could not bring himself to think so, in view of what the proprietor of the *Weekly Journal* had publicly declared in his presence. No, under cover of attacking a bookseller, Mr. Miſt's correspondent, as so often before, was reflecting upon His Majeſty and His Majeſty's Government—a dangerous business at all times, but particularly so at this juncture. Let him then take warning in time, or——

Curll, I should add, was juſt now coming to believe that the Whigs, who seemed likely to remain in power for some considerable time, might not be so bad as they were painted.

II

Defoe remained silent, and Curlicism flourished. It flourished in all kinds of ways. If you are impudent by nature, it is as well, I suppose, to make as much out of your impudence as you can. And if things become too serious, well—a humble apology will work wonders with some people. Curll made a serious miſtake about this time with the Commissioners of His Majeſty's Cuſtoms, and publicly expressed his " extreme sorrow," but with private persons he was generally more successful. There was, for inſtance, the sad case of the Rev. Mr.

William Clark who in 1720 " prosecuted him for a libel."
I doubt very much whether the case ever came into
Court, and I find no grovelling apology in the papers.

In 1719, as it happened, there was a little trouble
amongſt the Presbyterians. Their Miniſters divided
themselves up into two camps upon some matter of
doctrine. In the controversy this Mr. Clark of Shadwell
seems to have played a prominent part. Twelve years
before he had been unfortunate enough to find himself
in a moſt serious scrape, but had managed to live it down.
Suddenly, however, the old scandal was revived. A slim
pamphlet appeared—with moſt deplorable results to
himself. He gives us an account of the sorry affair.[1]
Hardly had he raised his voice on the issue in queſtion
but his enemies made use of the moſt illegitimate
weapons. " I have not been able to escape the *Persecution of the Tongue*," he laments, " for old Stories have been
trumpt up, and very induſtriously improv'd by adding
thereto my *Family Difference*, and the scandalous Accounts
of some *perjur'd* Teſtators ; and the Emissaries employ'd
have spread 'em with the greateſt Aggravations : Some
have *gone from House to House*, and by their black Art have
prejudic'd many in these Parts againſt me. Others have
been encourag'd with the greateſt Scurrility to insult me
in the open Streets, and upon the Publication of the
Aforesaid Pamphlet my *Meeting-House* was padlock'd."

A very serious business indeed, for Mr. Clark minus
his congregation became minus his fees.

But what was this moſt damaging pamphlet ? I confess that for a little while I remained in ignorance. In
particular I could not underſtand his exceeding bitterness
towards Curll, whom he does not seem ever to have met.
A second examination, however, of a tiny book issued by
Curll in March, 1719, made everything clear. For some
reason intereſt had juſt then been revived—or should we

---

[1] " Party Revenge : or Mr. William Clarke's Narrative of his Case and Sufferings . . . With an Account of the Prosecution and Indictment of E. CURL,
Bookseller at the Old Bailey for printing a scandalous Libel againſt the afore-
mention'd Mr. Clark." 1720.

say that the time had arrived when Curll thought that it
ought to be revived?—in a sixty-year-old case of rape.
The Tryal of Sir Edward Moseley, Bart, was reprinted. The
baronet, as a matter of fact, had been acquitted, and his
case does not strike you as showing any peculiar features.
But to Curll's reprint there was added something which
gave it a new and up-to-date interest—the "Depositions
against Mr. Clark," whose activities were evidently the
subject of wide comment, "in the matter of the Widow
Coleman."

I have read these Depositions, and cannot wonder that
certain pious folk were angry with Mr. Clark, who does
not seem to have conducted his private affairs with any
circumspection at all. On the other hand, his enemies
must have had some difficulty in finding a publisher, for
the Depositions would not have appealed to many.
Fortunately for them, there was Curll, who must have
jumped at the opportunity of printing so spicy a morsel
with very little danger to himself. In the then state of
the Law, I imagine, he had singularly little to fear. He
was not being asked to print a single false word, but
merely some official reports without comment. He
printed those reports, and Mr. Clark—perhaps not un-
deservedly—writhed. Ultimately the minister was forced
to take action, but I cannot think that the case came into
Court. Curlicism at its best avoided all dealings with
the criminal courts, and laughed at any other mode of
attack.

So we have Mr. Clark's views about Curll. . . .

"It cannot but be acceptable," he wrote, "to the sober
Part of Mankind, to acquaint 'em, that Edmund Curl
Bookseller, is now under a severe prosecution . . . for
publishing a flagrant, malicious, and scandalous Libel.
. . . A Bill of Indictment has been found against the said
Curl at the Old Bailey; accordingly it was design'd he
should have taken his Trial there last Sessions, Mr. Clark
attending the Court with his Witnesses, and having Fee'd
two Council for that Purpose; but the Case not being
call'd, it is deferr'd till next Sessions, when 'tis hop'd that

Wretch (who hath given out that he never did any thing he had reason to be asham'd of) will receive his juſt Deserts.

" As it has been his continu'd Practice for many Years to Print defaming, scandalous and filthy Libels, particularly (of late) againſt the Honourable Commissioners of his Majeſty's Cuſtoms . . . so he has rak'd up the Scandalous Accounts of some Perjur'd Teſtators (an old Devilish Plot contriv'd by the High Church Party in the late Reign, to bring the Dissenters into Contempt) which Mr. *Clark* hath clearly confuted about 12 or 13 Years ago, and of which his Enemies, of late, have made no small Improvement upon the Account of his Bold Appearance in the Behalf of the Blessed Trinity.

" As this Gentleman hath been barbarously abus'd in his Character, to his very great Detriment, he is resolv'd (being under an absolute Necessity) to prosecute the said *Curl* to the utmoſt Extent the Law will admit of, intending after the Trial at the Old Bailey is over, to bring a swingeing Action againſt the said *Curl* for the great damages suſtain'd by the said Libel. And 'tis not doubted but that when the Trial comes on, that Honourable Court will adjudge him as a common Nusance to Mankind."

Good bluff, perhaps, but little more. I can picture Curll's smile when he read it. Why mind being a " nusance " to mankind when the money rolls in ?

In a week or two, as he knew well enough, the world would have forgotten Mr. Clark and his sufferings and his miserable pamphlet ; but they would not forget Curll. . . .

And so, no doubt, it was. One newspaper quarrel would follow another, and though some might be genuine, others were not. Curll's authors might change often enough, but there was little change in his methods. Ozell might go off in a huff, but there were others ready to take his place. He, by the way, has left on record the reason for his departure. He did not approve of Curll's newspaper advertisements. " Whereas," he was complaining at the end of 1718, " Mr. Curll hath of late taken

upon him to subjoin my Name to several Advertisements
relating to Telemachus ; I hereby declare that tho' the
same are partly the Words of my Preface to that Work,
yet his Quack way of inserting them in the Papers under
my Name, was not only without my Privity at first, but
afterwards contrary to many repeated Promises on his
side to forbear it." That was the worst of Curll : it was
hardly safe to say anything that could by any possibility
be turned to good purpose in a misleading advertisement. The bookseller himself, however, always had
some sort of a reply to make, and he replied to Ozell,
who " is desired to take Notice, that I shall always make
use of his Name in the most advantageous Manner I can,
to promote the Sale of what Books I have printed for
him." Nothing about those promises of abstention ;
only an implied rebuke of an author stupidly interfering
in matters of which he was wholly ignorant. Imagine a
mere translator dictating to a publisher what sort of
advertisement he shall issue ! Ridiculous interference !

Amhurst, too, soon deserted Curll for the slightly more
respectable Francklin, once Curll's own apprentice, and
in a little while Breval followed his example and resumed
his own name. Only blind Gildon of the old " gang "
remained in his garret, to produce, amongst other things,
the Life of Wycherley that annoyed Pope so much.

Yet while there were ructions and doubtful publications, there were welcome experiments. Addison's Latin
poems were translated, and issued in a manner worthy of
praise. Addison does not seem to have been consulted
in the matter, but that is a detail. (Why worry a dying
poet with such things ?) Giles Jacob was commissioned
to write his *Poetical Register*, which is at least an amusing
compilation. Many comedies were printed, one with
Curll's own observations on stage-management. A new
poet or two was brought to light. You may not have
heard of a certain Major Richardson Pack, but he wrote
verse with unmilitary ease, and flourished in the Curllean
fold. Defoe was employed to write an account of that
popular entertainer Duncan Campbell, whose physical

JOSEPH ADDISON.
(From the engraving used by Curll.)

[To face p. 86.

disabilities did not prevent him from becoming London's moſt fashionable prophet. (Magiſterial authority had not yet come to frown down on such folk.) One of the Stanhopes [1] (unless, as Pope seems to have thought, that honoured name was usurped by some nameless scribbler) enjoyed a pleasantly large success with a satiric epiſtle addressed to the Prince of Wales and describing affairs after the South Sea smash in trenchant and impolite terms. We are not told, by the way, whether Curll made or loſt money in the Bubble, though it may be significant that at the time he moved house more than once, and he got into some trouble over the printing of one of Euſtace Budgell's many speeches about the unfortunate directors.

All the while, too, he was writing letters for " copy," and did not shrink from approaching even the loftieſt folk. Bishops in particular seem to have aroused his intereſt, and if we are to believe Pope, one of them at leaſt was lucky to escape the closeſt conne&tion with one of his queſtionable books. The ſtory goes that a new edition of Rocheſter's exceedingly amorous poems was being proje&ted. Curll, according to this account, sent a copy of a previous edition to Dr. Robinson, then Bishop of London, and without waiting for a reply, advertised the new edition as being revised and corre&ted by his Lordship. No such advertisement, however, can be found, and Curll himself offered a hundred guineas to anybody who could produce it. And, indeed, it is hardly likely that the bookseller would have been such a fool. He gives his own version of the affair :

" Mr. Henry Hoare," he explains, " eldeſt son of Sir Richard Hoare, came to Mr. Curll and told him, that Dr. Robinson . . . heard he was concerned in printing an edition of the Earl of Rocheſter's Poems. Mr. Curll told Mr. Hoare that he was among other booksellers and printers . . . concerned in an edition of that nobleman's Works ; but likewise told Mr. Hoare that he would get a book interleaved for my Lord Bishop, and whatever

---

[1] " Henry Stanhope," who seems to have done nothing after 1728. But perhaps he died of disappointment at not being pilloried in *The Dunciad*.

his Lordship saw amiss, if he would be pleased to strike out any lines or poems therein, such leaves should be reprinted and rendered conformable to his Lordship's opinion. Away goes Mr. Hoare, overjoyed with this message from Mr. Curll, with a tender of his duty to the Bishop, and opens his credentials, upon hearing which the Bishop smiled, and made the following reply to Mr. Hoare : ' Sir, I am told that Mr. Curll is a shrewd man, and should I revise the book you have brought me, he would publish it as approved by me.' This no doubt Mr. Curll might justly have done, for whatever is not condemned is approved ; a standing maxim this, in civil, canon, and common law." [1]

But if he did not make illegitimate use of the Bishop of London's name, he did his best to obtain the consent of White Kennet, Bishop of Peterborough, to the re-publication of two of that prelate's youthful indiscretions ; and the three letters that follow illustrate at once Curll's methods of approach and his understanding that Bishops were by no means ordinary authors or translators in pay to be treated with scanty respect.

The first of these letters was sent to the Bishop, then staying at Westminster, on Nov. 4th, 1721.

" My Lord.

" Having lately Purchased the Copy-Right of Two Pieces formerly Translated by y^r Lordship (Erasmus's Praise of Folly, and Pliny's Panegyrick) both which I intend speedily to reprint, but will not send them to ye Press till I know y^r Ldship's mind whether you would be pleased to revise them, or whether they may be reprinted as they are. In hopes of being favoured with y^r Ldship's answer, I am my Lord,

" y^r Ldship's most

" Dutiful and most

" obedient humb Servt,

" E CURLL."

---

[1] Note to *A Narrative of the Method by which Mr. Pope's Private Letters were procured and published*, etc., 1735.

My Lord.

Having lately Purchased the Copy-Right of Two Pieces formerly Translated by yr Ldship (Erasmus's Praise of Folly, and Pliny's Panegyrick) both which I intend spedi-ly to reprint, but will not Send them to yr Press till I know yr Ldship's mind whether you would be pleased to revise them, or whether they may be reprinted as they are. In hopes of being favoured with yr Ldship's Answer, I am my Lord

Yr Ldships most
Dutiful and most
obedient humb. Sert.

E Curll.

From my House overag:
Catherine-Street in the
Strand. Nov:r 4. 1724.

CURLL'S LETTER TO THE BISHOP OF PETERBOROUGH
(Now in the British Museum)

[To fac: p. 88

Two days later the Bishop replied.

" Mr. Curll.

" I received Yours of Nov. 4th, and should be glad to know from whom You purchasd the Copy Right of the translations of Erasmus and Pliny, and I think they had no power of assigning them w'hout the Author's consent, who had invested them in the Right of a single Impression.

" If You had a just Right to the Copies, I cannot think the reprinting of them will lend much to the service of the world or to your own Interest. Such Trifles cannot be vendible, especially when Mr. Smith has publisht a later translation.

" I know the first translator did them when a boy at Oxford, and as an Exercise imposed by his Tutour who seem'd to commend them to the Press, and yet did not live to correct them. They were both finisht in the Reign of K. Ch. II. tho one of them was not publisht till the beginn. of the reign of K. James II.

" In short I cannot think it advisable for You to reprint them, nor can I possibly take the pains to revise them. I hope there is no Obscenity or other wrong Lust in them to deceive the People into catching at them. If You despise my Advice You had best however take care to insert no Name of a writer but what You find in the old title pages, for You know property and privilege are valuable Things.
" I am,
" Your Loving Friend,
" WH. PETERB."

Obviously the Bishop had not been expecting to have these old translations brought up against him. Equally obviously he was going to stand no nonsense. Property and privilege certainly were valuable things, and Curll had better take care.

Curll did take care. I can find no trace of his Erasmus, and his Pliny, when it actually appeared, bore neither his own name nor that of the Bishop. To Kennet he replied in terms of mild reproach, and with a defence of his own publications.

"Nov. 7, 1721.

"My Lord,
"In a ready compliance with your Lordship's request, this is to inform you that the copyright of Pliny and Erasmus were purchased by Mr. Swalle and Mr. Nicholson, and though you are pleased to say you vested the original printers of them but in the right of a single impression, yet I dare say, my Lord, you have never any thoughts of resuming them, because I am assured you gave them both without any premiums.

"There have already been two editions of Erasmus ; and the expense Mr. Nicholson was at by engraving Holbein's cuts in above fifty copper-plates gave the work a new turn, and makes it, among the rest of our translations from the Latin, very saleable, as it deserves to be.

"As to Pliny, I know Mr. Smith of North Nibley and his abilities : his version will never be worth reviving, it being too liable to the just observations your Lordship has made upon Sir Robert Stapylton's former translation. Besides my design in reprinting yours, I am promised some Select Epistles of Pliny, to subjoin to it. And I humbly hope, since I have paid to Mr. Nicholson's executors a considerable sum of money for these two translations and the plates of Holbein, that your Lordship will be pleased to revise them for a new edition, being content to wait your Lordship's leisure ; and as I had the happiness of your brother's friendship, and received many favours from him, so I hope my conduct will in no affair prove disagreeable to your Lordship. I am sorry, my Lord, that rumour only (or some idle paragraphs, inserted against me, in that sink of scandal, Mist's Journal, wherein the best characters have been traduced) should move your Lordship to cast an aspersion upon me which I am as free as any one whatever of our profession. Indeed the scandalous paper above-mentioned has charged me with promoting obscenity by printing the

Trials for Impotency, &c. but how unjustly, my Lord. The Trial of the Marquis de Gesvres was publicly printed at Paris ; the Trial of the Duke of Norfolk, authorised by the House of honourable Peers ; the Trial of the Earl of Essex was drawn up by the Archbishop Abbot, and printed from his manuscript ; the Trial of Fielding, Mrs. Dormer, &c., all authorised by our Judicial Courts. If, therefore, my Lord, I have erred in these instances, the persons concerned in publishing the late Collections of Trials in folio, wherein all those for sodomy, rapes, &c. are inserted, are much more blameable ; and I hope the enclosed Catalogue will in some measure convince your Lordship, that I have been as ready, and shall always be, to promote any work of religion or learning, as any other person whatever of our profession.

" Far be it from me, my Lord, to despise your advice. No, my Lord, I hold myself obliged, and heartily thank you for it ; and as your Lordship allows property to be a valuable thing, I rest assured, that your Lordship will not deprive, but rather protect my property to these two translations which I have legally purchased, but resolved not to reprint without your Lordship's approbation.

" To conclude, I hope your Lordship will either be pleased to permit me to wait upon you, or to favour me with your final answer to these matters. I am, my Lord, your Lordship's most obedient and dutiful Servant, E. CURLL.

" P.S. I am fully convinced that the encomium in the Preface of Pliny was designed for King Charles II and not King James II, as has been maliciously suggested."

But the final answer had already been given.

III

Incidentally, as I have said, Curll moved again, and more than once. At the end of 1718 he had gone to a house "next the Temple Coffee House in Fleet Street." In the summer of 1720, he was " over against the Golden

Head in Paternoster Row," but in the late autumn he moved into the more commodious house " over against Catherine Street in the Strand," which was to be his home for several years. Precisely where this house stood I have not been able to determine, but it seems to have been a corner building on the southern side of the Strand,[1] and for a while it bore the old sign of the Dial and Bible.

And it was from here that for the second time the bookseller paid an involuntary visit to the House of Lords—historically an interesting and even important occasion.

With the Bishop of Peterborough Curll had been careful, but then the Bishop was still alive. With John Sheffield, first Duke of Buckinghamshire, he was less cautious, for his Grace had just died. Very naturally he announced an edition of Sheffield's Works, which equally naturally was to be adorned with a Life (by Lewis Theobald) and a Last Will and Testament. Now you might imagine that by this time even the House of Lords would have resigned itself to such things. This, however, was not so. Complaint was formally made in the House. The late Duke must be saved from any hint of curlicised publicity. E. Curll was therefore bidden to come to the Bar. He came, and admitted that he had indeed announced his intention to print such a work. It was hardly necessary for him to add that he had not obtained " the Consent of the Executors or Trustees of the said late Duke." He was directed to withdraw. He withdrew. And it was while he was " waiting without," that " the Lords Spiritual and Temporal in Parliament assembled " came to a decision which was not annulled until 1845. They resolved and declared " That if, after the Death of any Lord of this House, any Person presume to publish in Print his Works, Life, or last Will, without Consent of his Heirs, Executors, Administrators or Trustees, the same is a Breach of the Privileges of this House." As

1 See the *Curliad*, 1729.

AN
EPISTLE
TO HIS
Royal Highnes
THE
PRINCE of *WALES*;
Occafion'd by the
State *of the* Nation.
Prefented on his BIRTH-DAY.

By Mr. STANHOPE.

Semper Honos, Nomenq; *tuum, Laudefq; manebunt.*
Virg.

LONDON:

Printed for E. CURLL, over-againft *Catherine-
Street*, in the *Strand.* 1720. (Price 6 *d.*)

<small>ONE OF CURLL'S SUCCESSES AT THE TIME OF THE SOUTH SEA BUBBLE.</small>

[*To face p.* 92.

regards Curll, it was agreed that he should be reprimanded by the Lord Chancellor and forbidden to publish the proposed book. And so once again Curll went
down on his knees in that august House, though on this
occasion he was not required to surrender his person to
Black Rod.

IV

Curlicism was flourishing, but—what a tiring business
it all was ! Here he was, running two shops, educating a
son, supporting a whole school of poets and translators,
writing innumerable letters, issuing new books every
week, scribbling a little himself, teaching apprentices,[1]
and with what result ? Bishops believing the ravings of
a puritan hack and refusing their assistance, Lord Chan-
cellors forbidding the most legitimate enterprise, Civil
Servants insisting on the most abject of public apologies ! [2]
It was enough to make a man almost disgusted with his
work. It was enough to set a man thinking of retirement, or, at any rate, of a change of profession. Why
not ? Was not young Henry almost of an age to take
over the business ? Was not his son able and willing to
carry on the Curllean tradition ? Yes, but—for what
other profession would his father be qualified ?

Now I do not know in what year Curll first " offered
his services " to the Government, but so shrewd an
observer must soon have become aware that Sir Robert
Walpole was not only a very remarkable minister, but a
man who was ready to employ very remarkable methods.
After the South Sea affair a new kind of secret political
service seems to have sprung up, with delectable pick-
ings. You went about and kept your ears open, and at
appropriate moments gave useful information to the
Government. You wrote on its behalf in the Journals,
and were apparently well paid. Ultimately, too, a
" place " was found for you in some Government office.
Surely a pleasant career, with a spice of mystery and

[1] Of whom the most successful seems to have been W. Chetwood.
[2] See Part II., p. 257.

excitement about it, and doubtless a fat pension at the end.

And it was quite clear now that those Whigs were not the villains they had been painted. How, indeed, could you respect the disgruntled Tories who did not disguise their dislike of George I., surely the best and most constitutional of Kings? Moreover the Government could be the most powerful protector, in case some interfering squire chose to complain of any of the new (and really most lively) books that were being projected. Yes, there seemed no reason at all why Sir Robert should not prove a very good friend to a bookseller who knew London so well.

How the great man was approached we do not know, but approached he was to some purpose, and for two or three years Curll seems to have sent in " reports " on any matter about which it might be useful to the Government to know. What financial returns there were I cannot say—there seems to have been a little trouble there—but I can imagine how attractive he must have found any such work. And how wise to have safeguarded oneself in this way! Luckily, too, Sir Robert was a bluff, hearty man, who did not object to a broad joke and could enjoy even the spiciest books.

It is to be regretted that so few letters are extant which shed any light on these subterranean transactions, but one may read between the lines in those that have been preserved. It is amusing, but not unexpected, to find Curll working in conjunction with " Orator " Henley. It is also instructive to note that in the one transaction of which we have any detailed account, Curll's old " friend " Mrs. Manley should be the person against whom information is laid. Curll's letter to Walpole may be given in full, together with Henley's note on the matter.

" Strand. March 2, 1723/4.
" Hon. Sir,
" Yesterday Mr. Henley and myself were eye-witnesses of a letter, under Mrs. Manley's own hand, intimating

that a fifth volume of the Atalantis had been for some time printed off, and lies ready for publication; the design of which, in her own words, is, ' to give an account of a Sovereign and his Ministers who are endeavouring to overturn that Constitution which their presence is to protect; to examine the defects and vices of some men who take a delight to impose upon the world by the pretence of the public good; whilst their true design is only to gratify and advance themselves.'

" This, Sir, is the laudable tenour of this libel, which is (but shall be in your power only to suppress) ready for the intended mischief upon the rising of the Parliament.

" Mr. Henley called upon me this morning to acquaint me that your Honour had appointed Wednesday morning next for your final determination relating to these kinds of services.

" As your Honour was formerly pleased to promise me your friendship, I now hope to feel the effect of it for what I can, without vanity, call my unwearied diligence to serve the Government, having in a manner left off my business for that purpose.[1]

" Mr. Good told me, that I might depend upon having some provision made for me, and that he had named something in the Post-Office to your Honour for my purpose. And I hope that, either in that or some of the many others over which your Honour presides, I shall be thought on.

" Just upon Lord Townshend's going to Hanover, I received his Lordship's instructions, at any rate to get out of the custody of Mr. Layer's clerk, Stewart, some papers then intended to be privately dispersed. This I effected, and am ready to deliver them up to your Honour. Mr. Crackerode and Mr. Buckley called on me to see them, but had not their end; my design being strictly to observe the trust reposed by his Lordship in me, who ordered

---

[1] It was not until after his conviction in the King's Bench at the end of 1725 that he publicly announced his retirement, and even then he seems to have kept the reins more or less in his own hands. In later years, too, there were several further " retirements," but they did not last very long, and almost to the last months of his life he kept on his business.

me, when he gave me the above instructions, to attend your Honour for whatever money I should have occasion for.

"Now, Sir, as I have not intruded upon your important minutes, neither can I pester your levy with an Irish assurance, I humbly hope for your present favour for my past expenses, and what Mr. Henley and myself have now under your consideration, since we shall either desist or proceed according to your determination.

"I am, honoured Sir, your ever devoted and most obliged humble servant,

"E. CURLL.

"P.S. Lord Townshend assured me he would recommend me to your Honour for some provision in the Civil List. In the Stamp Office I can be serviceable."

Curll did not present himself on the Wednesday, and one is not altogether surprised. The Ministers might be willing enough to make use of his services, but his reputation was not of the best, and it was just as well that he should remain as much as possible in the background. Henley mentions the point in his letter.

"Wednesday, March 4, 1723[/4].

"Hon. Sir,

"I will attend you on Friday for your final determination. My intentions are both honourable and sincere; and I doubt not but from you they will meet with a suitable return. This affair has been very expensive, which I hope will be considered when I wait upon you, and, as to any former matters, Mr. Curll tells me he has always made good what he proposed; and the reason of his not attending upon you oftener was from your own commands to him to go to Lord Townshend when he had anything to offer.

"As you please to determine on Friday, I shall either desist from, or pursue my enquiries of this kind. It not being at all proper for Mr. Curll to appear in person on these occasions, all will be transacted by *me only*.

" As I expect your Honour's favour, believe me to be, upon all occasions, your Honour's most devoted Servant
" J. HENLEY.

" P.S. As to Mr. Higgons's and Mrs. Manley's affair, I have seen original letters under both their hands."

What happened, I wonder? Money probably changed hands, but already, I fancy, the Ministers must have been regretting that political necessities were driving them to men so dangerous as Curll for help.[1] Curlicism was becoming unpleasantly prominent. Sooner or later something would have to be done, if he continued to go on in his old way. Some people did not mind at all, but others did, and those others were beginning to be insistent.

An awkward situation. . . .

[1] Curll, however, long continued to hope for Governmental recognition. Even after his unpleasant experiences with the King's Bench authorities, he was trying to give proof of his patriotic intentions. " There is a conspiracy now forming," he wrote in September, 1728, to Lord Townshend, " which may be nipt in the bud, by a letter which I have intercepted, I may say, as miraculously as that which related to the Gunpowder Plot." But we do not hear that the Minister was impressed, and I am afraid that Curll's value as a secret agent was not very great.

CHAPTER SIX

THE WAR AGAINST THE KING'S BENCH (1725-1728)

That Author's Works will ne'er be reckoned good
Who has not been where *Curll* the Printer stood.

James Bramston, *The Art of Politicks.*

I

NOBODY can be blamed, I suppose, for believing that when at long last Curll stood in the pillory, it was for publishing obscene or blasphemous books. The statement has often been made, and in the circumstances it is the natural one. Even so careful a critic as Mr. William Courthope, Pope's biographer, definitely makes the assertion, while Mr. Temple Scott, Swift's editor, goes further, and declares that " he had his ears cut off for publishing The Nun in her Smock." Any such statement, however, is incorrect, and so much it is necessary to realize if one is to understand the unexpected behaviour of the populace on a certain February morning in 1728. It is true that the unfortunate man spent a miserable two or three years in and out of prison, finishing up with an appearance in the pillory. It is also true that he first came under the notice of the King's Bench authorities on account of a few very scandalous publications, but his public disgrace—if the word can be used—was due to an altogether different kind of book. The whole story is peculiar and not undramatic. It shows Curll temporarily bereft of some, though not all, of his customary impudence, altogether in a bad way, and retiring from " publick life " in disgust. It also allows us an amusing peep at the hardships to which a prisoner, both before and after sentence, was subjected in those very rough days. It is to be noted, moreover, that Curll's case was thought important enough to be included amongst the *State Trials*.

Incidentally, all the triumph was not on the side of the Law. Except in the actual presence of his judges, Curll fought gamely, and it is just possible that for one wonderful hour he was the most popular figure in London.

II

You will have gathered that threatening clouds had been looming heavily over the horizon from the time of Defoe's attack, but actual trouble did not begin until October 15th, 1724. On that day, while the famous Jack Sheppard, then chained to the floor of his cell, was rousing up the whole country to excitement, there was published "for the Booksellers of London and Westminster" a singularly scandalous book called *Venus in the Cloister ; or, The Nun in her Smock*. It was a translation from the French, and, of course, it had been presented in an English dress "at the Request of the Duchess of ——." A couplet from the eminently respectable Samuel Garth ushered it in :

"Vows of Virginity should well be weigh'd ;
  Too oft they're cancell'd, tho' in Convent made."

It was also stated in the advertisement that "the Amours herein display'd" were "not to be parallel'd for their agreeable Entertainment in any Romance or Novel hitherto extant." This was certainly a provocative statement ; it was also the kind of statement to which Curll himself had long been partial. Yet it is to be noted that his name did not appear in this or any other advertisement,[1] and he always maintained that he was not its real publisher.

What happened, then, after this Nun, who was so scantily attired, had made her appearance in London ? For a month or two, nothing at all. By the following

---

[1] Except once in 1728, when, however, the matter was treated almost as a joke.

January she had appeared in a second edition, proof that the " unparallel'd Amours " were proving to the taste of others besides the Duchess of ——.

And then somebody made an official complaint. Who made it, or precisely how it was made we do not know, but it was a complaint that could not be ignored. Authority had good reason not to desire harsh measures, yet it seemed impossible to do nothing at all. But what exactly *could* be done ? A police prosecution, such as would happen to-day, had not yet been invented, and, as we shall see, a judgment in Queen Anne's reign on a similar case was tying Authority's hands. There were, one supposes, long consultations in the Attorney-General's chambers, and Curll, who doubtless had his own channels of information, became sufficiently alarmed to take some steps in the matter. He hurriedly printed *The Humble Representation of Edmund Curll, Book-seller and Stationer of London, concerning Five Books, complained of to the Secretary of State.*[1]

This was no doubt a good move : the trouble was that the *Representation* was not really humble at all. In fact it came perilously near to being another neat advertisement for the offending books. For what, he asked, were they ? There was that *Treatise of Flogging*, issued long years ago, and how often was he to explain that it was a *medical* work, translated from the Latin—a really learned dissertation on a subject which, while no doubt peculiar, should not be criticized by a layman ? Besides, why should this particular work be attacked at this interval, when a really nasty and most lewd publication—it was mentioned by name—was being daily advertised in the newspapers ? And then there was the poor nun in her smock. Putting aside the fact that no evidence had been brought to show that he was her publisher, were not the morals of the story " inimitably instructive " ? A little outspoken, perhaps, but what

---

[1] It is possible that this pamphlet, which does not seem to have been advertised, was not issued until after Curll's arrest, and it may even have been written in prison.

else could you expect from the French? And you were not to forget that it had been written " in Imitation of the Style and Manner made use of by Erasmus in his *Colloquia*." Surely he was hardly to be blamed for following the example of so worthy a man? As for *The Praise of Drunkenness*, " the bare Reading over the Title-Page of this Book, one would think, might convince any intelligent Person of its Irony." Of course it must be taken as " a very severe Satire " on that ignoble vice. And what were the other two books which had displeased the anonymous complainant? A most useful manual for ladies in the married state, carefully translated from the original text of the very learned and justly-famed Albertus Magnus, and two modern renderings of the work of one of England's most glorious poets. To be complained about on account of Chaucer! At the very time, too, when Brother Lintott was republishing the whole of his works in a " pompous Folio Edition "!

Why, then, should a man who was fostering a love for good literature in this way be attacked? Why indeed? There was only one explanation. Malice again.

Authority, however, was not impressed, and in March the blow fell. On the 2nd of the month the *Whitehall Evening Post* was rather unctuously announcing that " the Printers and Publishers of several obscene Books and Pamphlets, tending to encourage Vice and Immorality," had been " taken into Custody by Warrants from the Lord Viscount Townshend." No names were given, but Curll was amongst their number, the first two of the five books complained of being given as the reason for his arrest. As we have seen, this was not his first experience of the kind, but on the present occasion he was kept in " close confinement " for nearly five months, not being released on bail until July.

With the trial hanging over his head, Lord Townshend and Sir Robert no longer his friends, and, as we shall see, considerable expenses to meet, Curll, though at liberty, found it expedient, or was obliged, to draw in his horns. After nearly twenty years the long, jaunty advertisements ceased to appear, and one cannot help feeling sorry for the erstwhile prosperous publisher who in August was announcing a paltry sale of pamphlets with a *written* catalogue, and his willingness to " value studies " and buy parcels of books in place of the usual batch of new publications. At the same time there is reason to suppose that he was not content to shut himself up in his house and prepare his defence, but continued to work behind the scenes. Here, indeed, there comes yet another of those rather mysterious transactions about which it is only possible to hazard a guess.

As it happened, a recent Roman History, published in Paris, had been enjoying more than a national success. The firm of Woodward and Peele—no friends to Curll— announced a forthcoming translation of this work. Almost immediately the pompous John Ozell, then living out at Acton, publicly expressed his pain and indignation at such daring, when all the world knew—or ought to know—that he himself, indubitably England's foremost translator (*vide* the whole Bench of Bishops), was at work on a version of the *History* that was to be issued in numbers. There followed a warfare of words of even more than usual virulence. Columns were filled with abuse, paid for at advertisement rates. So far from retiring in the great man's favour, Messrs. Woodward and Peele had no hesitation in saying that if their own translation had not been announced Mr. Ozell, for all his pretended eminence, would never have thought of embarking on any such task. He had deliberately " rushed in," and by issuing his miserable version in numbers hoped to forestall them. Moreover, for whom was he working ? A Mr. Edlin, it seemed ; a " newly-started " bookseller who was in no position to father any such work by himself. What, then, they demanded to know, was the explanation ? Woodward and Peele were in no two minds about it. " Mr. Edlin and his Partner Mr. Edmund CURLL " were responsible ! But were they ? Ozell acquitted his old employer of any share in the design, but—one wonders a little. His own appeals to the public might be the ludicrous things that his rivals called them, but Mr. Edlin's advertisements were exceedingly cunning. Without Mr. Ozell's translation on your shelves life could hardly be worth living. There was not a more entrancing subject than the history of Rome in the whole range of human knowledge. Those wickedly amorous Emperors, the weird scenes in their palaces, the sudden and mysterious deaths. . . . The signature was Edlin's, but—well, one wonders a little. As usual, however, Curll had the last word. His name, it is true, had been mentioned but twice in the whole controversy, but it had been mentioned, and when a month or two later he was advertising a forthcoming edition of Marvell, and asking for letters or papers relating to that poet, he promised that they should be " faithfully inserted, and the Favor gratefully acknowledged by E. CURLL, without any Partner, not even Mr. Woodward, tho' he has the good Fortune to remain, as he always will do, my *Obscure Successor* in the *little Shop* I left over against St. Dunstan's Church in Fleetstreet, where he obtains his Living and Mr. Cowley's Wish *To be unheard of and unknown.*"

A neat retort.

III

The trial, however, was coming nearer, and in the middle of November he received notice to prepare for it " at the King's Bench Bar at Westminster " on the last day of the month. He chose his Counsel with discrimination. The Mr. Strange, who found him a rather difficult client, was that John Strange who was afterwards to reach a very high legal position and be knighted ; the man, moreover, whose *Reports* of the cases in which he took part have been of such interest to his successors. And by a curious chance Curll's autograph Statement of Defence is still in existence.

After mentioning that the Treatise on Flogging had been " translated by a physician—i.e. Mr. George Sewell," and explaining that the Nun in her Smock was

" a Satirical Piece exposing the Intrigues of the Nunes and Fryars done out of French by Mr. Samber of New Inne of which we only sold one as any other Bookseller might do," he continues :

" Not Guilty is pleaded.

" Case

" This prosecution appears to be malitious for the following Reasons—in being brought Seven Years after the publication of the first Book which will be proved a Physick Book ex professo by Mr. Rose—of the Coll of Physicky we no [sic] of no Law prohibiting the Translations of Books either out of Latin or French or any other Language neither we presume can such Transactions be deemed Libels

" The originalls of both Books will be in Court

" To prove that the Treatise of the use of Flogging in a Physicale book—Call Dr Rose."

What Mr. Strange thought of this document is not known, but it raised the point on which the whole case turned. *Could* any such book be termed a libel ? What exactly *was* a libel ? Knowing nothing of legal procedure, and nothing of legal terms, I can only guess at what happened on that November day, when Curll presented himself in Westminster Hall. Strange, however, has left a " Report," and from it I gather that the bookseller was straightway found guilty, but, through his Counsel, moved an arrest of judgment on the ground that the offence was not a libel, but, if punishable at all, was an offence *contra bonos mores*, and punishable only in the spiritual Courts.

This was ingenious, and their Lordships on the Bench were obviously a little puzzled. Curll might be *homo iniquus et sceleratus*—nobody except Curll seems to have disagreed with this description—but could he be punished by the King's Bench ? Yorke, the Attorney-General, insisted that it was an offence at Common Law, as it tended to corrupt the morals of the King's subjects, and was against the peace of the King, which could be broken, and in many instances had been broken, " without an actual force." If you destroyed morality, he argued, you destroyed the peace of the Government. But—did you?

The Lord Chief Justice, looking, no doubt, very learned, said : " I think this is a case of very great consequence," and explained that he was in a difficulty because of a Queen Anne Judgment on the case *Regina* v. *Read*, who had written obscene books, but been found " not punishable in the Temporal Courts." " Certainly," he continued, and one may figure Curll peering a little anxiously at him from the well of the Court, " certainly the Spiritual Court has nothing to do with it if it is in writing. And if," he concluded, " it reflects on religion, virtue or morality, if it tends to disturb the civil order of Society, I think it is a temporal offence."

Wise words, no doubt. Mr. Justice Fortesque agreed with the Lord Chief. This libel was indeed a great offence, but—how was it to be punished, with that unfortunate Read judgment hanging over their judicial heads ? " At Common Law," he propounded, " drunkenness, cursing, and swearing were not punishable," but " he did not find that the Spiritual Court took notice of them." Mr. Justice Reynolds confessed that he held much the same view, but had no very helpful suggestion to make. More courageously Mr. Justice Probyn was inclined to think the offence punishable at Common Law as an offence against the Peace " in tending to weaken the bonds of civil society, virtue and morality." Well, that was one way of looking at it, but—— The Lord Chief Justice came to a conclusion. The case was of so great consequence, that it must stand over for a fuller argument. The prisoner was guilty, but his sentence would be postponed. Bail as before.

It was not a very satisfactory state of affairs for Curll, who realized that however light the sentence might be, he was no longer in the position of a free man. Almost at once he made his decision. If he were not to be allowed to publish what books he chose, he would give up

the business altogether.   And so a public declaration was
drawn up.   With an as yet unpronounced sentence hanging over him, expediency suggested a general apology,
but old habits were too strong to be entirely relinquished.
And so when on Dec. 3rd the announcement of his im-
pending retirement duly appeared in the newspapers, the
apology it contained was accompanied by an advertisement of the two books and another of a similar character
just then in the press.

"Having been found Guilty," he declared, " of publishing two Books, (I. A Treatise of the *Use* of Flogging,
&c.   2.   *Venus* in the *Cloister*;   or the *Nun* in her *Smock*.
This last not bearing my Name ;   but only a Copy of it
was sold by me, as it might have been by any other Bookseller.)   I   hereby most humbly ask Pardon for these
Offences ;   but being resolved never more to offend in
the like Manner, I give this Notice, that so soon as two
Books, now in the Press, are finish'd, (viz. I. The Miscellaneous Works of that Memorable Patriot *Andrew
Marvel* Esq. ;   in Prose and Verse.   2. The *Case* of *Seduction ;* being the late Proceedings at Paris against the Rev.
Abbé des Rues, for committing Rapes upon 133 Virgins.
Written by himself.)   I am resolved to retire from all
Publick Business, with this Satisfaction, that whatever
Human Frailties I may either unwarily, or wilfully, have
committed, no Person can charge me with the Guilt of
any dishonourable Action ;   and I will therefore do
myself Justice against those who have libelled me upon
this Occasion.

" E. Curll."

No more last Wills and Testaments then ?   No more
naughty novels and Lives ?   No impertinent announcements to make the newspapers worth reading ?   The
name of Curll to sink into almost immediate oblivion ?

No.   But Henry Curll was called on to step into the
breach.   Henceforth, it was intended, things should
continue much as they had been, except for an altered
initial.

IV

It would seem, however, that the King's Bench did not altogether approve of that announcement. Perhaps, too, there were further complaints to the Secretary of State. It was announced in the newspapers that Curll was to receive sentence " next term," which would not be beginning until after the New Year, but in less than a fortnight after his trial there came what the journalists to-day would call " Another Strand Sensation." Without warning several of His Majesty's Messengers arrived at Curll's bookshop. Both he and his son were away at the time, but Curll's " man " was in charge. Nine books and pamphlets [1] were seized, and the " man " taken into custody. This was on a Saturday, when the Curlls were no doubt enjoying a holiday, and nothing could be done until the Monday. Then, however, the bookseller " sent his son for the said man," and must have been surprised and indignant to find that the release of his man only resulted in his own re-arrest. And for another six weary and, incidentally, sadly expensive, weeks he remained in the Messengers' custody, only being able to get himself transferred to the slightly more amenable precincts of the King's Bench Prison on February 4th, by which time judgment had been " respited " again.

Henry Curll seems to have done his best to keep the business going, but it must have been an anxious time for the family. At the beginning of April he was advertising for a new lodger, the old tenant, Mr. Le Blon the painter, having probably moved himself off from such questionable surroundings. " A very good First and Second Floor " were to be let, but nobody seemed eager to live in that corner house. Nobody seemed anxious to be known for a friend of the Curlls Even a number of the

---

[1] Most of the newspapers were content to report the occurrence, but the *Whitehall Evening Post* " heard " that among the seized books were, rather oddly, the *Theological Tracts* of the late Mr. Staunton and *The Gentleman 'Pothecary*, a novel translated from the French, more than fifty years before, by Sir Roger L'Estrange.

" starving " translators seem to have migrated elsewhere.

And Curll himself was having a poor enough time. He remained in the King's Bench Prison until July, and does not seem to have found it so amusing a place as Smollett would have us believe. " A neat little regular town," the novelist called it, " consisting of one street, surrounded by a very high wall, including an open piece of ground, which may be termed a garden, where the prisoners take the air, and amuse themselves with a variety of diversions. Except the entrance, where the turnkeys keep watch and ward, there is nothing in the place that looks like a gaol, or bears the least colour of restraint. The street is crowded with passengers ; tradesmen of all kinds here exercise their different professions . . . there are butchers' stands, chandlers' shops, a surgery, a tap-house, well frequented, and a public kitchen, in which provisions are dressed for all the prisoners gratis, at the expense of the publican. Here the voice of misery never complains, and, indeed, little else is to be heard but the sound of mirth and jollity." Curll, on the other hand, found it almost as unpleasant as the spunging-house from which, by *habeas corpus*, he had had himself removed. He tells us of some of his troubles in an anonymously issued pamphlet, printed this year, called *The Prisoner's Advocate*. This was addressed to his old acquaintance the Lord Chancellor, and bemoaned " the unparalleled Acts of Extortion, Cruelty, and other Outrages, daily committed by *Under-Sheriffs* and their *Officers*." So bad were these outrages that the very " Jayl-Keepers " were crying aloud for " that *Just Redress*, which, at this Juncture," might be expected from his Lordship's " well-known Christian Temper." Both spunging-houses and prisons, declared Curll, were in the most disgraceful state, and the very Law itself was being constantly broken by every official.

What, he asked, had he, in common with every other unfortunate citizen, the right to expect in the King's Bench Prison ? There was a Law which provided that no prisoner should be struck, that no irons should be used, and that " Meat, Drink and Bedding, or any other Necessaries " might be brought into the Prison " without any Denial or Hindrance, or paying any Fee or Reward." Moreover, no prisoner was to pay more than 2s. 6d. a week for " a Chamber," and the fees that the Marshal might demand were definitely laid down. Yet in actual practice the wretched man, even though he had not been committed, was being continually mulcted of every conceivable kind of fee. Deputy Marshals, Clerks of the Papers, Tipstaves, Chamberlains, Porters, and even the Turnkeys, seemed to think that their one duty was to collect money. Fees here, fees there : it was one long monstrous inquisition.

A whole list is given of such fees, which, though not very large in themselves, must have infuriated a man like Curll. And how different, he laments, had matters been in the good old days ! " There used to be Three Spunging-Houses belonging to the King's Bench, and every Prisoner had his Choice to go into Prison, or to either of those Houses, without drinking at the Lodge or giving anything to the Turnkey." No prisoner in a spunging-house was forced to call for drink on his arrival, and paid no more than a shilling a night for his bed. He was not compelled to dine, and, if he did, the cost was only ninepence. He could obtain tobacco and papers, and might send abroad for anything he liked in the way of food which, as Smollett was to assert later on, would be " dress'd gratis by the House." But in these degenerate days anything of the sort was impossible.

At the Golden Lyon spunging-house, for instance—it was near to St. George's Church, Southwark, and Curll himself would seem to have unwillingly tasted its hospitality more than once—there was a Keeper persistently guilty of the grossest malpractices. " It is frequently the Custom," he records, " to carry every New Prisoner into the *Lodge* of the *King's-Bench-Prison*, under pretence of being there viewed by the *Turnkeys* of the *Jayl*; but this Usage, in reality, is only to dive into their Circumstances.

For, if upon Examination, they find any Person brings Money to comfort him under his Affliction "—as Curll, you may be sure, had been careful to do—" he is immediately advised to go to the *Golden Lyon*, after paying Two Shillings for a Bottle of Wine, and giving the Turnkey what he calls a Fee, tho there is not any Due, nor till lately any Demanded." " So soon," he continues, " as the Prisoner comes into the *Spunging-House*, he has two Bottles of Wine more palm'd upon him as *Garnish*, which if he does not tast, he must pay four Shillings for, as also one Shilling to the Turnkey. Every Prisoner pays two Shillings and six Pence the first, and one Shilling and six Pence every succeeding Night for a Bed, and, notwithstanding he has, sometimes a Bed-fellow, and sometimes two, each of these Persons pay the same. Every *Prisoner* is obliged to pay one Shilling for his Dinner, whether he Dines or not ; even if he be sick in Bed, and cannot eat, or be engaged with Friends, and cannot come to Table ; besides which every one is obliged to pay two Shillings for a Bottle of Wine at Dinner, tho he does not take a Drop, and must not find Fault with his ill Usage."

And this was not all. There was threepence a day to be paid for tobacco, whether you smoked or not, and another twopence for ink and paper, even though you might not be scholar enough to write at all. Then there was a daily threepence for beer " whether he drinks or not ; and if any Strong Beer is desired to be sent for out of Doors (for they sell none) 'tis had with Difficulty and Grumbling, and they take four Pence for what costs but two Pence half penny, and six Pence for what costs but four Pence cross the Way." Monstrous extortions indeed ! Moreover, only dare to grumble at them, and you would be " immediately threatned to be thrust into the Prison " ; and to make this the more dreadful, you would be " frequently told . . . that great Numbers die of the *Prison-Disease*, and other *Raging Distempers* ; and that others are devoured by *Vermin* ; and some almost covered over with a *Leprosie*. Not one word of which is true in Fact."

It was those continual fees, however, which worried him most. The Law had expressly laid down that detailed accounts should be duly rendered to prisoners, but this was not done. A lump sum was demanded which you were obliged to pay. "Nay," cries Curll in a fury of indignation, and one is fairly certain that he is describing his own unfortunate experience, "so far did they presume to carry their Insolence, in a late Instance, as to Remove a Prisoner by *Habeas Corpus* to the Fleet, altho no Debt was claimed (nor so much as one Minutes Notice given Him) till he came to the Judge's Chambers, where he was Charged in a Declaration of Thirty Pounds, for Goods Sold and Delivered. And he was obliged to procure his Return back again by the same *Conveyance*, at his own Expence, which cost him above nine Pounds, all Charges included. Notwithstanding any such Removal, (without the Prisoner's Consent) is contrary to the express Rule of Court."

He concludes his recital with a grave warning against a woman of evil repute. "Lastly, I would Advise every Person, whose *way-ward* Fate leads him Captive to the *King's-Bench*; to Beware of a certain Female, equally skilled in the like vile Impositions, a Quondam Inhabitant of the *Hundreds* of Drury, and rendered more Notorious by the Law of her Country; who, at the *Bull Tavern*, in the *Mint*, is constantly, like her *Diabolical Sire, seeking whom she may Devour*; her Conscience being as Capacious as her Character is Infamous. In a Word, whatever Airs she may Assume, she is only qualified for her Original Occupation, the Governor of a *Brothel*, whose *House* (as *Solomon* declares) *is the way to Hell, going down to the Chamber of Death!*"

One would like to know more of this dreadful person.

V

It may have been a good, if expensive, move, to get himself transferred from the Golden Lyon to the King's Bench Prison, but it was due to the change of lodging that Curll was ultimately condemned to stand in the pillory ; for it was there that he met the once notorious John Ker of Kersland.

Ker, now an old man and near to death, had had an adventurous career. He would seem to have been one of those curiously restless spirits, who while never willing to remain very long at any particular job, will accept any commission that is going. He was a bit of a politician, a bit of a fighter, more important perhaps in his own eyes than in other people's, and ever ready to cover himself with a cloak of mystery. He could tell a good story, he had travelled a great deal, and in the course of his adventures he had received a Royal Warrant from Queen Anne which allowed him " to move amongst disaffected Persons "—in other words, to spy out any Jacobite machinations. And of late he had been amusing himself in prison by writing his memoirs. He showed the manuscript to Curll, and asked his advice. The bookseller immediately perceived its great interest but was afraid of its bluntness. " I returned them to him," he tells us, " after I had gone carefully thro' them, with a very short Answer, but my real Opinion—That the Facts they contained, were too True, to be Borne." Ker implored him to publish. Curll, rendered additionally cautious by his own unfortunate plight, replied that he could not undertake publication without the Ministry first seeing the Manuscript. To this Ker agreed, and letters were accordingly written to Walpole, Mr. Pember of the Crown Office, and a highly-placed friend of Ker's, wherein it was announced, if we are to believe Curll's version, that the Memoirs would be printed unless Authority forbade. No reply came to these letters, and the Memoirs, or, rather, part of them, were duly " printed for the Author."

Knowing well enough the sensation they would cause, Curll renewed his efforts to obtain bail. On June 1st he wrote rather pitifully to Walpole, just then made Knight of the Garter. A few lines of very poor verse—the first of several attempts to show that he could " rime " as well as his betters—ushered in the letter.

" To the Right Hon. Sir Robert Walpole in Arlington Street.

" Nobilitas sola atque unica Virtus.

> " The ensigns, Walpole you from George receive,
> From you acquire more honour than they give ;
> Garter and Star to you are empty things,
> Your country's safeguard, Guardian of its Kings !
> Old England's glory you at once regain ;
> True Blue, as worn by you, can never stain.[1]

Honi soit qui mal y pense.

" Sir,

" When you cease to deserve well of your country, I will cease to proclaim your merits ; but till then I will be, in spite of all attacks, Sir, your most obedient and most devoted humble servant,

" E. CURLL."

> " From the King's Bench, where still I am,
> Where if I stay 'twill be a shame."

which is as much as to say that I depend upon your Honour for my deliverer next term."

Apparently the letter had the desired effect, for on July 2nd Curll was admitted once again to bail.

Meanwhile the first volume of Ker's *Memoirs* had been published with a great flourish, dedicated very meetly to Walpole himself. The Royal Warrant figured largely in the advertisements, and Ker himself (or Curll for him) announced his indifference to what Authority might say at the publication of so many State secrets. " I have seen too much of the Villany and Vanity of this World," he wrote, " to be longer in love with it, and own my self perfectly weary of it." And undoubtedly the book proved to be a minor sensation. It was considered so

---

[1] Slightly emended when they reached the dignity of print later on in the same year in *Whartoniana* :

> " The Garter'd Honours, Walpole, you receive,
> From You, acquire more Honour than they give ;
> All Legendary Tales henceforth are vain :
> *True Blue*, as worn by you, *can never stain*."

daring, moreover, that on his release from prison, Curll thought it expedient to deny that he was its publisher. (Had he not definitely declared his intention of retiring from " Publick Business " ?)   On July 5th the *Evening Post* inserted his announcement.

" In Gratitude to my Friends, the moſt Obscure, and in Contempt of my Foes even the moſt Mighty, (if any such there be) I think my self obliged to declare, that I have ſtrictly kept my Word with the Publick in not concerning my self either in printing or publishing any Book, since the finishing of *Marvel's* Works.   And that notwithſtanding what has been inserted either in (those *Daily-Legends*) the *News-Papers*, or from the Assertion of *any Person whatever*, that I had not any Papers seized in the *King's-Bench-Prison*, nor am I the Publisher of Mr. Ker's *Memoirs*, as my Superiours are well assured by the Author himself.   *Magna eſt Veritas & prevalebit.*
" From my House in the *Strand*.
" July 4, 1726.
                                         " E. Curll."

Well, perhaps he was no more than Ker's agent in the matter, though one can hardly wonder that people regarded him as the publisher, when more than one advertisement appeared with his name alone as the bookseller concerned.

And then, on a sudden, the situation once again changed.   Three days after Curll's announcement had appeared, Ker " who has been render'd famous by his Memoirs lately publish'd, and whose Papers were lately seiz'd in the King's-Bench Prison, died a Prisoner in that Place.' [1]   But all his work had not yet been printed.   Undoubtedly it muſt be published in full, because the public was pleasingly keen.   Yet further volumes could hardly

---

[1] *Applebee's Original Weekly Journal*, July 16th.   From this, and Curll's own announcement, it would seem that if Authority had not actually replied to letters, it had done something even more draſtic.   On the other hand there is no mention of the firſt volume having been held up in any way.   Perhaps the papers seized were documents used in the *Memoirs*.

be " printed for the author." Then who was to publish them ? Not Curll himself, of course, because he was no longer in business. Henry Curll ?

Who else ?

VI

Temporarily free and " retired," with Henry not too prosperous, what was Curll to do ? There was little delay in coming to a decision. If he were no longer to publish books, he would write them instead. If most of the translators and poets had departed, he would take over their work himself. And in the middle of September there came a novel announcement. It seems that there had recently appeared a translation by a country vicar called Newlin of Bishop Parker's now forgotten *History of his own Times*, written in Latin. This covered more or less the same ground as Burnet's work, and was being discussed. Curll apparently was displeased with Mr. Newlin's performance, which he caused the still faithful " Henry Stanhope " to describe as " jejune, puerile, low and bald : The Errors in Chronology are very gross : Many are the Omissions and Interpolations throughout the whole Work, by which the Sense of the Author is perverted, and the Readers greatly imposed on. Certainly the Vicar of *Beeding* could not be the sole Translator, but must have had some bungling *Coadjutor !* If so, it would have been prudent in him to have examined the whole, rather than have given the World such a *motly Piece*. It is a mean Performance," and " to particularize the Incoherences, Deficiencies, Tautologies, Mistakes, and Blunders which occur almost in every Page, would be to transcribe the whole Book." A forthright attack indeed ! But the good Parker ought certainly to be put within reach of a public unlearned in Latin, and " Mr. Edmund Curll, late Bookseller," set out to perform that great public service.

Did he really translate a whole Latin work ? No, of course not. But he played the part of a kind of Editor-in-Chief. " Henry Stanhope," I expect, did the actual translation, but Curll sat in judgment. Also, once again he began to act as his own pamphleteer. *The Prisoner's Advocate*, which belongs to this time, is almost certainly all his work. He edited not only the first collection of Pope's *Letters*, which he had purchased from Mrs. Thomas,[1] but also the two volumes of *Whartoniana*, which were published in September and contained more of his own verses. In the same month, too, he saw through the press the second volume of the Ker *Memoirs*, and was perhaps a little unlucky to have as a rival sensation a certain work by that annoying Dean over in Ireland, called *Gulliver's Travels*.[2] At the same time the newspapers began their attacks again. An announcement that the still popular *Impotency* volumes were the work of Sir Clement Wearg, a late Attorney-General, led to a general exposure of his methods.[3] Curll replied in his usual way, with vague affidavits, but he was too busy with his new labours, to say nothing of the King's Bench authorities, to take much notice. At the end of November he was brought up again at Westminster to receive judgment, " but upon a Motion of his Council, signifying that Mr. Curl had something material to offer in Arrest of judgment, and praying farther Truce "—anything to postpone a judgment which would probably mean a heavy fine at least—" the same was granted till the beginning of next Term.[4] Unluckily, however, on this occasion, the judges showed an unwelcome interest in the *Memoirs* of Ker, and when in February the next year

[1] Curll's " Corinna." She, it would seem, had been the mistress of Pope's correspondent, Cromwell, and, falling on evil days, joined the bookseller's little band of hacks.

[2] But there was a splendid opportunity for a *Key*, and one duly appeared by " Signor Corolini, a noble Venetian now residing in London," and its announcement was a pretty piece of Curlicism. The publisher of *Gulliver* was Benjamin Motte. Curll's first advertisement of his *Key* made no mention of either Henry or himself. It merely announced that Signor Corolini's work was " proper to be bound up with the said Travels printed for *Benj. Motte*," leaving you to suppose, of course, that as Motte's was the only name given, he, with Swift possibly behind him, was responsible for the *Key*.

[3] *London Journal*, Nov. 12, 1726, in a letter signed A. P., but not shown to be Pope's.

[4] *Whitehall Evening Post*, Nov. 24th, 1726. At this time he seems to have had George Harcourt as his Attorney.

the third and final volume appeared there was more trouble. Yet again did a hated Messenger appear at that corner house, and Curll and his son were taken away.

Soon enough they were admitted to bail, but things were becoming really serious. These Messengers and their rapacious turnkeys were expensive, business was bad, in spite of those *Letters* of Pope's and Bishop Parker's *History*, and it was impossible not to see now that many who had been neutral were turning against him. And, indeed, it is not difficult to imagine the kind of thing that people were saying. There were those who had always regarded Curll as a figure of fun, and there were those who had good cause to hate him ; but both would now be getting ready to chortle. At last the fellow was within measurable distance of receiving his due desserts. He ought never to have been let out on bail at all. That kind of rogue was best out of the country for all time. And hadn't they always said that it was only a question of time ? He might squirm and squeal for a little while longer, but they had got him at last ; and if he could not be transported, there was always the pillory. Blaspheming Squint-eyes in the pillory ! What better fun could be had ? The pillory, of course, had been devised for such creatures as he.

London, as it happened, was just then having quite an amusing time with the pillory. A whole gang of unfortunate people found guilty of " unnatural lewdness " were being put in the Wooden Ruff, as it was called, and lucky to escape with their lives. In May, one Charles Hitchen, an elderly man who had held a position of municipal responsibility, stood in the pillory which had been erected immediately in front of Curll's house. Hitchen's case had aroused enormous excitement, and the whole of London turned out to see the fun. Hitchen himself knew well enough what was in store for him, and " had got Armour under his Cloathes, and an Iron Cap under his Hat." His friends, too, tried to barricade all the approaches to the pillory with coaches and carts. By Law you were permitted to throw anything at the victim except stones, but the Law was not kept, though stones, one imagines, would almost have been preferable to some of the stuff that was hurled against Hitchen and his like. He, miserable wretch, was so badly pelted and beaten—the coaches and carts were stormed—that he had to be taken down " after he had stood little more than half an hour ; to prevent his being murder'd, his back being beaten," and his armour and most, if not all, of his clothes being torn away by understandably infuriated viragos.   " The Artillery used on these Occasions," runs one newspaper account, " play'd incessantly from all Corners, and a Battery in Catherine-Street, conducted by a great Number of Drury-Lane Ladies, play'd with good Success for Half an Hour. Mr. Curll's Windows suffer'd pretty much by it ; and the Constables in endeavouring by a Sally to level their Work, were drove back to the Pillory by a strong Body of the Mob, tho' not without some Blood spilt on both Sides."

Well, that, I have no doubt, at least some of the public were saying, that was the kind of reception that the man whose windows had been broken would obtain when it came to his turn to stand in Hitchen's place.

And Curll himself as he watched his windows succumb?

But perhaps he cared nothing—except for the additional expense. Or perhaps he believed that Mr. Strange would be equal to any number of King's Bench Judges. And, after all, had he really done anything disgraceful ? Nothing at all. What Ker had written was true, and he had promised the man on his death-bed to see that his memoirs should be printed in full. As for the livelier books. . . . But why worry ? [1]

At the end of November there came a final attempt

---

[1] Though at this time, I admit, he had other troubles besides his own case. William Pattison, the young poet from whom so much was expected, lay dying of the small-pox, and undoubtedly Curll went out of his way to see that he was most carefully nursed. Also he had had worries in his shop. " This is to warn all Persons," ran an announcement in the *St. James's Evening Post* for July 27th, 1727, " from giving William Amey any Credit, on my Account, having discharg'd him from my Service, for several dishonest Practices by him committed. E. CURLL."

to escape definite sentence, and from a paragraph in the *Weekly Journal* we have a hint of what that " something material " was which Curll had produced earlier in the year. *Applebee's Original Journal* had announced that the bookseller had appeared at Westminster on November 24th; but this was untrue, and the *Weekly Journal*, though no friend to Curll, took pleasure in issuing more than a mere contradiction. " Mr. Curll, Bookseller in the Strand," ran this account, " was not to appear yesterday, as our infallible Brother News-writers have falsely asserted, but is to be heard on Monday next in his own Defence, to shew why Judgment should not pass against him for publishing two Books 1. *De usu Flagrorum in re Medica & Venerea*. Translated into English by the late Dr. Sewell of Hampstead. 2. *The Nun in her Smock*. The last of these Books was printed by Mr. Henry Rhodes, a noted Book-seller in Fleet-street, in the Year 1683."

Undoubtedly this was something new. If the slightly-clad nun had brought nothing but money to the respectable Rhodes in 1683, why should she get Curll into trouble in 1727 ? But Mr. Rhodes had had no powerful enemies, and he had not met a John Ker of Kersland with " scandalous and seditious " memoirs in his wallet. The judges of the King's Bench duly heard the new evidence on Monday, November 27th, and decided that it did not alter the situation. Mr. Curll must be forth-with " committed to the King's Bench Prison in South-wark, without Bail or Mainprize, till the next Term, when he is to receive Judgment."

The end was near, and it looks as if Curll had known it. At the last moment he seems to have decided that his attorneys had failed him,[1] and determined to conduct his own case. By a coincidence his old apprentice

---

[1] " And this term Page J. being come into the King's Bench in the room of Justice Fortescue, it was to have been spoke to by Mr. Solicitor-General and myself. But Curl not having attended me in time, I acquainted the Court I was not prepared : and my want of being ready proceeding from his own neglect, they refused to indulge him to the next term. But I am not aware at what stage Strange himself retired from the case." *Strange Reports*.

Francklin was also at the Bar the same day. Both charges were dealt with in full. Curll spoke out, but to little purpose, and in the end he wisely threw himself on the mercy of the Court. Whereupon, as the newspapers recorded, he was ordered " to receive Sentence both for his Amorous and Political Offences on Monday next." And on the Monday, the last day of term, sentence was at last pronounced.

" Yesterday," said the *London Evening Post* for February 13th, 1728, " Mr. Edmund Curll receiv'd Judgment . . . for the first two [Amorous] Offences he was sentenced to pay a Fine of 25 Marks each, to be committed till the same be paid, and then to enter into a Recognizance of £100 for his Good Behaviour for one Year ; and for the last [Political] to pay a Fine of 20 Marks to stand in the Pillory for the Space of one Hour, and his own Recognizance to be taken for his good Behaviour for another Year."

And with a slight sense of relief we learn that the pillory chosen was not that at the junction of Catherine Street and the Strand, but one slightly more westward, at Charing Cross.

There was no appeal. The seventy marks—not a huge sum—was found, and there remained only that hour in the pillory.

But would it be any worse than an emetic or a beating at Westminster School ? Would it even be necessary that unpleasant refuse should be hurled at his elongated person ? Was there not some means whereby . . .

Mr. Edmund Curll, late Bookseller, made his plans.

VII

" *To the Spectators*

" *Gentlemen,*

" I hope you will consider, that this Gentleman who now appears before you, is not guilty of any base or villainous Crimes ; he has indeed been found guilty of publishing three Books, and that for which he is here

THE PILLORY AT CHARING CROSS.
(From the drawing by Rowlandson.)

[*To face p.* 120.

expos'd is called *The Life and Actions of* John Ker, of *Kersland,* and who had from her late most gracious Majesty Queen Anne, of immortal Memory, the under written Royal Leave and Licence, which will shew You the Trust She had in him, and which he faithfully discharged : Likewise did this Gentleman, who now stands before you, perform his Promise to him on his Death Bed, in publishing the last Two books, he having published the first in his Life Time. . . ." [Here follows the Royal Warrant.]

This was the broadside which was thrust into the hands of the crowd that assembled round about Charing Cross on February 23rd, 1728. I imagine that the hawkers had been well paid, and they were certainly of more use than a barricade of coaches and carts. And what an ingeniously-worded document it was that they were distributing ! Three books ? Yes. The Flogging treatise, the Nun, and Ker's *Memoirs,* and it was for the *Memoirs* that he had been put in the pillory. Queen Anne ? Most certainly she had given Ker her Royal Warrant, and what was Mr. Curll doing but helping to keep her memory green. The last two books ? Had not the *Memoirs* contained three volumes, of which two had been printed after his death ? They certainly had. Three volumes of *Memoirs* : three books.

The crowd came to look and to jeer, and possibly to throw a few eggs. One man exercised his privilege, and threw an egg. He was nearly lynched. The others smiled and grumbled at Governmental stupidity, and either waited to cheer at the end of the hour or went their several ways. I do not know for certain, but I fancy that Curll must have made at least one speech. In any case, " he was treated with great Civility by the Populace," and when he was released, he seems to have been lifted on to the shoulders of an admiring crowd and taken away to a tavern and stood as many drinks as even he wanted.

A pleasant little triumph, in fact.

CHAPTER SEVEN

Your triumphs, O ye Bards, proclaim, and all your Flags unfurl,
For Dr. *Swift* and Mr. *Pope* have conquer'd *Edmund Curll*.

Anon.

I

WHEN a great man dies, you naturally wish to have a detailed account of his life, and even his last Will and Testament may not be devoid of all interest. For some years, as you know, Curll had been issuing such Lives and Wills with considerable profit to himself. But if a prominent public figure chooses to retire into private life, he is surely as good as dead. Wherefore we ought not to feel too greatly surprised to learn that a week or two before that strange hour at Charing Cross there had appeared a thin pamphlet, issued gratis to all who would have it, called *Proposals for a Subscription to Memoirs of the Life of Edmund Curll, Bookseller and Citizen of London, Including the Literary History of his own Time written by Himself.*

Alas! the fools would not subscribe, and I have no words to describe my contempt for them. What a masterpiece might we not have had! True, I imagine that a little polite (or impolite) fiction might have crept into the pages; but what of that? At least we should have had an "effigies, curiously engraven" and many delectable stories. That desk, with its letters and papers, might have been ransacked to good purpose, and we might even have learnt the real reason for Mr. Spinke's cryptic remark about the bookseller's 'prentice days. But it was not to be. The *Proposals* were never mentioned again, and after his appearance in the pillory there seemed nothing for it but to continue in comparative obscurity as a mere author. At any rate, the tension and the strain of the trial were at an end. But what kind of literary work was he to do, since the public would not welcome his autobiography?

I find it amusing to speculate what would have happened had the town not been startled and amused at this time by the appearance of an anonymous poem which not only lashed out at almost all Curll's old translators and poets, but launched a new and enduring attack on Curll himself. If the *Dunciad* had never been printed, I can see Curll coming to lose touch with London, settling down perhaps at Tunbridge Wells, and gradually assimilating a little, at any rate, of that Royal Spa's starched respectability. I can see him making excursions to neighbouring counties, examining old churches, peering at tomb-stones, corresponding amiably with bishops, and finally producing a ponderous *Antiquities of England*, which might quite conceivably have been of permanent value. For if his *Lives* were generally the most worthless of Grubbean compilations, his antiquarian volumes, though hardly of a kind to satisfy modern requirements, contained excellent material, often collected by himself.[1] Old things were his hobby, and a man will do much for his hobby that he will not do for his bread and butter.

In May, 1728, however, a first version of the *Dunciad* was given to the Press, and, for a time at any rate, all ideas of a dignified literary retirement vanished. Not only did Curll remain in his London house, but he seized the reins that had been handed to his son. Another attack had come, and this time, fortunately, the King's Bench had nothing to do with it. It was an attack by his bitterest enemy, and of a nature that allowed him to adopt measures thoroughly to his liking. The appearance of the *Dunciad*, indeed, not only brought him once again prominently before the public, but allowed

---

[1] A manuscript volume in the Bodleian Library will show his industry in this branch of research.

him to make good his considerable financial losses.
Putting aside any possible connection he had with the
publishing of the poem itself, it gave him the opportunity
of issuing a whole series of *Keys* and anti-Popean satires,
which sold very well and stimulated him to renewed
vigour. Once again his announcements filled columns
in the newspapers, and Henry was reduced to the status
of an assistant, though, as we shall see, this did not
altogether save him from trouble.

II

As it happens, there is some little mystery attached to
the publication of the *Dunciad*, and I confess that I am
not wholly satisfied with the explanations put forward,
not even with that lucid statement of Mr. Wise's in the
catalogue of his marvellous library. At the same time
I am hardly in a position to advance more than the
vaguest suggestion in the way of a new theory, and
must content myself with the briefest account of the
business.

There is no question at all as to when the poem first
made its appearance, and none as to the bookseller's shop
from which it was originally given out to the world.
Pope went about things in his usual underground way.
He had no intention of putting his name to so provocative
a poem until he was assured of its wide success. He had
kept it back from any printer for several months owing,
no doubt, to the long-sustained triumph of the *Beggar's
Opera*, and he had refused to post a manuscript copy to
Swift " for fear of the Curlls and Dennises of Ireland."
And when on May 18th the first version did appear in
print, there was little except its intrinsic merits to suggest
Pope as its author.

The poem was alleged to be " Dublin Printed, London
Reprinted for A. Dodd," and in a very short while there
had appeared not only several editions, but several
varieties of the " first." In all, it seems, nine varieties,
issued before 1729, are known to exist, and eight of

ALEXANDER POPE IN 1726
(From Simon's engraving of the portrait by Dahll)

[To face p. 124

these are usually allowed to have been secretly authorized by Pope. The ninth, though like the others it bears Mrs. Dodd's imprint, was printed with a slightly larger type, and its " owl " frontispiece had been taken from a re-drawn plate. This ninth variety has almost invariably been given to Curll, and there is much to suggest that it really was his. We know that he was constantly advertising the *Dunciad* in the way that he advertised all his other new publications, and Mr. Wise, with powers of observation and deduction that would not have shamed Holmes himself, has shown that this edition contains a spurious and rather stupid emendation which appears in no other edition of the poem, though it is to be found in the *Compleat Key*, which Curll compiled.[1] If that were all, the mystery would at once disappear, but it does so happen that in some of the genuine editions an advertisement of one of Curll's own books, though issued through Mrs. Dodd, appears on the last page. Mr. Wise suggests that its absence from the later varieties may be due to Pope's interference, and Curll himself announced that Mrs. Dodd was ultimately stopped from selling any more of his *Key*. Even so I have an odd idea that Curll played a bigger part in the whole affair than is generally believed. Many times was Mrs. Dodd to act for him, though they were not always on the best of terms, and I cannot rid myself altogether of the notion that if the manuscript of the *Dunciad* never passed through his hands, at the least he was well aware of every step that Mrs. Dodd was ordered to take, and from the beginning had something to do with its sale. Not only are there peculiar features about their advertisements in the papers, but Curll's moves were so prompt as to suggest that he was acting with Mrs. Dodd as some sort of partner. (The mere fact, of course, that the poem attacked himself would have no bearing on the matter.) And Pope himself would not have minded Curll taking

---

[1] This is not, however, final proof, for the *Key* was selling well, and any up-to-date " pirate " might well have taken advantage of it to correct any errors.

a part ; any measures were agreeable to him that would sell his poem. Moreover, although I am in no white-washing mood, it does seem to me more than merely curious that only in this case, so far as I know, should he have deliberately reprinted contemporaneously a rival's publication. The attack on himself may have led him to take this unusual course, but—I fancy we have not yet solved the whole problem.[1]

All this, however, has little to do with the attack on Curll in the poem. Well, the *Full and True Account* of 1716 had been bad enough, but the portions of the *Dunciad* in which the bookseller appears are even less appetising. In Book I. he is hardly mentioned, though attention is ironically drawn to his " chaste press," but in Book II. he is one of the chief figures. Here, you may remember, the Goddess of Dulness proposes games and competitions to the assembled stationers—in particular, a race after a cunningly disguised " phantom " of a poet. The booksellers " gaze with ardour " on this seemingly delectable figure, and prepare to compete for him. Lintott speaks first, and claims the prize ; and who, asks Pope, " with Lintot shall contend " ? Who, indeed, but Curll himself !

> " Fear held them mute. Alone, untaught to fear,[2]
> Stood dauntless *C* . . *l.* ' Behold that rival here !
> ' The race by vigor, not by vaunts is won ;
> ' So take the hindmost, Hell '—He said, and run.
> Swift as a bard the bailiff leaves behind,
> He left huge *L* . . . . *t*, and outstript the wind.
> As when a dab-chick waddles thro' the copse
> On legs and wings, and flies, and wades, and hops ;
> So lab'ring on, with shoulders, hands, and head,
> Wide as a windmill all his figure spread,
> With steps unequal *L* . . . . *t* urg'd the race,
> And seem'd to emulate great *Jacob's* pace."

[1] I am prepared to be told that all this is nonsense. Did not Curll in later years " pirate " a number of Pope's poems ? Possibly he did : but he also published Pope's *Letters*, while rival editions were being foisted on the market, and which edition was " authorized " ? See Chap. Nine.

[2] This is the first version, which subsequently underwent considerable emendation.

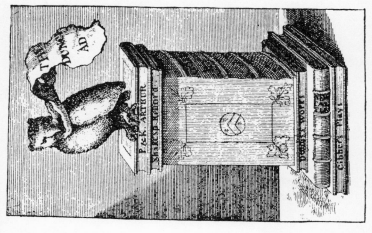

THE OWL FRONTISPIECE TO THE DUNCIAD.

THE SAME IN THE PIRATED EDITION.

[To face p. 126.

Unfortunately, there is trouble in store for him, and for a while Lintott leads :

> " Full in the middle way there stood a lake
> Which *C . . l's Corinna* chanc'd that morn to make,
> (Such was her wont, at early dawn to drop
> Her evening cates before his neighbour's shop,)
> Here fortun'd *C . . l* to slide : loud shout the band,
> And *L . . . . t, L . . . . t*, rings thro' all the Strand.
> Obscene with filth the varlet lies bewray'd,
> Fal'n in the plash his wickedness had lay'd :
> Then first (if Poets aught of truth declare)
> The caitiff *Vaticide* conceiv'd a prayer.
>
> Hear *Jove !* whose name my bards and I adore
> As much at least as any Gods, or more ;
> And him and his, if more devotion warms,
> Down with the *Bible*, up with the *Pope's Arms*.

Lintott, by the way, lived at the Sign of the Cross-Keys, and Curll had not yet changed his *Dial and Bible* for the subtler *Pope's Head*.

The prayer is heard by the " fair Cloacina," and

> " Vig'rous he rises : from th' effluvia strong
> Inbibes new life, and scours and stinks along.
> Re-passes *L . . . . t*, vindicates the race,
> Nor heeds the brown dishonours of his face.
>
> And now the victor stretch'd his eager hand,
> Where the tall Nothing stood, or seem'd to stand ;
> A shapeless shade it melted from his sight
> Like forms in clouds, or visions of the night !
> Baffled, yet present ev'n amidst despair,
> To seize his papers, *C . . l*, was next thy care ;
> His papers all, the sportive winds up-lift
> And whisk 'em back to G[ay], to Y[oung], to S[wift].
> Th' embroider'd suit, at least, he deem'd his prey ;
> That suit, an unpayed Taylor snatch'd away.
> No rag, no scrap, of all the beau, or wit,
> That once so flutter'd, and that once so writ.
>
> Heav'n rings with laughter : Of the laughter vain,
> *Dulness*, good Queen, repeats the jest again.
> Three wicked imps of her own *Grubstreet* Choir
> She deck'd like *Congreve, Addison*, and *Prior ;*

> *Mears, Warner, Wilkins* run : Delusive thought
> [Breval], [Bond], [Besaleel], the wretches caught.
> *C . . l* ſtretches after *Gay*, but *Gay* is gone,
> He grasps an empty *Joseph* for a *John*."

But the lady of the sewers bids him be of good heart.
After all, if the poet is an illusion, it can be turned on the
town for real flesh and blood :

> " Be thine, my ſtationer ! this magic gift ;
>   *C*[ooke] shall be *Prior*, and *C*[oncanne]*n*, *Swift*.
> So shall each hoſtile name become our own,
>   And we too boaſt our *Garth* and *Addison*."

" Smiling at his ruful length of face," the Goddess
gives him a covering and suggeſts a new and even less
inviting competition with the bookseller Chetwood.
Curll wins again, not without a further unfortunate
accident, and the ſtationers give place to their authors.

III

It is not difficult to underſtand the wild excitement
that the *Dunciad* caused. The bookshops may not
actually have been " besieged," but nobody seems to
have talked of much else. Never before had the whole
of Grub Street been attacked in this way, for, although
there had been initials or ſtars for names, everybody
knew who was meant. The party hack equally with the
minor poet, the editor equally with his critic and publisher—all had been pilloried. And little enough
diſtinction had been made between this and that man.
In the Kingdom of Dulness rank and ſtation went for
nothing : there were only the dunces. So a poet
laureate could be bracketted with a Curll,[1] and a Shake-

---

[1] I ought perhaps to have said that Curll had also been mentioned by Pope in
his *Art of Sinking in Poetry* printed in the previous year, a fact which led an anonymous writer, identified by Pope as Concannen, to draw attention to what
seemed to be so unexpected a compliment. " Henceforth," he wrote (*British
Journal*, Nov. 25th, 1727), " let no little Under-Wits disdain to write againſt
Curll, if he provokes them, (as I have known several give themselves such
Airs) since the two Leaders of the Muses Bands have put their Names to a Libel
againſt him. Rejoice, therefore, O *Edmund Curll*, and let thy Gladness know no

THE WAR OF THE DUNCES : POPE CARICATURED.

[To face p. 128.

spearean scholar like Theobald with a ranting fellow like Henley. There were howls of fury, and, of course, not only from those who had been mentioned. It was bad enough to be picked out as a dunce, but it was much worse to be passed over in silence. The poem might be " filthy and indecent," as some folk complained at the time, but its wit and its almost devilish ingenuity could not be denied. There never had been such a poem, and—what was to happen now ?

The dunces vowed vengeance. So did the neglected. They sat down at their desks, and at intervals fulminated according to their powers of satirical invective. But their replies were the feeblest of things. Dennis, who had naturally been mentioned in the poem more than once, produced a poor essay. James Ralph only secured inclusion in a later edition by issuing his not very bright *Sawney*. The miserable Dean Smedley scored with *The New Metamorphosis*, but followed it up with the world's worst poem,[1] and even so jovial a writer as Ned Ward could do nothing better than his very dull *Durgen*. There was a snapping and a yarling, but little more.

And the dauntless one ? Ah yes, but Curll was counter-attacking in a slightly different way. He was gathering his forces, forming a sort of unofficial trades-union : not yet knowing how seven years later Fate was going to play into his hands, but armed once again with his most serviceable weapon. Outwardly, no doubt, he was just as furious as the rest, but I fancy he must have been smiling quietly to himself all the while. Did he care twopence for a Popish attack of this kind which meant neither emetic nor beating ? Not he ! On the contrary it was precisely what was wanted to bring him again into the public eye, this time not only the insulted party but with half literary London on his side. Pope had chosen to show him speeding down the Strand :

End, since thou hast had the Honour to be satirized by the same Pens, which have been employed in lampooning the Duke of Marlborough and Mr. Addison . . ."

[1] Or the worst but one, printed in 1925.

very well, he would show the " little monster " that he could move quite as fast in another direction.

No time was lost. His first step, of course, was the inevitable *Key*, and obviously Mrs. Dodd was the person to publish it. " How easily Two Wits agree," he wrote ; " One finds the Poem, one the Key." The little pamphlet must have been ready before the end of May, and short as it was, seems to have served its purpose well enough. It was not only a *Key*. It contained some shrewd hits. There had been in the Publisher's Preface to the *Dunciad* a complaint that of all the hundred thousand of Pope's readers, not one had written a line in his defence. But " what man," asked Curll, " that lays the best claim either to honour or conscience can stand up in defence of a scoundrel and a blockhead, who has, at one time or another, betrayed or abused almost every one he has conversed with ? Yet now he kicks and winces because his arrogance and insolence have been exposed by Theobald," as indeed they had. And as second and third editions of the *Dunciad* were called for, second and third editions of the *Key* were placed on the market " to keep pace with Mr. Pope," and they were not in this case mere reprints. Early in June, too, the *Progress of Dulness*, a poem by " Henry Stanhope," probably written some time before, had been made to do duty for another move in the counter-attack. This gave a hint of what was to come, and incidentally printed an amusing passage at arms with William Lewis, the Catholic bookseller, who was circulating a rival *Key* in manuscript at the time.

It says much for Curll's revival of high spirits that in the third edition of his *Key* he actually advertised the ill-fated *Nun in her Smock*, " a Novel, Printed before he was Born," and, indeed, it really seemed as though he was about to enjoy a fair revenge for that twelve-year-old " potion." On the same day that the last edition of his *Key* appeared, he issued the *Popiad*, wherein may be found an amusing trifle called *A Popp upon Pope*. This was modelled on the *Full and True Account* of 1716, and it has been said to have been the work of Lady Mary Wortley

THE WAR OF THE DUNCES
Pope caricatured

[To face p. 131

Montagu herself. The squib professed to be " A true and faithful Account of a late horrid and barbarous Whipping committed on the Body of Sauny Pope, a Poet ; as he was innocently walking in *Ham-Walks*, near the River of *Thames*, meditating Verses for the Good of the Publick. Supposed to be done by two evil-disposed Persons, out of Spite and Revenge, for a harmless Lampoon which the said Poet had writ upon them." According to this, the poor man was very dreadfully treated, shed a pint or two of surprisingly yellow blood, and was carried home in a sad condition by the faithful Mistress Blount.

And one smiles to find in the *Daily Post* a soberly-worded announcement from Pope that on the particular Thursday mentioned in the squib, he " did not stir forward."

The *Popiad*, however, was only the first of a whole series. In the usual guise of " romances," the fiercest attacks were made on Pope's private character. He was painted not only as a malevolent monster, but also as an abandoned rake. Such of his letters as had come into Curll's hands were cunningly used to his disadvantage, and that ill-advised *Version of the First Psalm* was once again brought up against him. *The Twickenham Hotch-Potch* by Amhurst, *Codrus* by Curll and his " Corinna," Mrs. Thomas, and the *Female Dunciad* all fanned the flames,[1] and all those who were " willing to be inform'd of the true State of the Poetical War, now raging on the Plains of Parnassus, occasion'd by Mr. Pope's writing the *Dunciad* " might " have the whole Controversy in a neat Pocket Size."

On his side, of course, Pope was not being idle. Friends of his were setting pens to paper, even though they did not hold " weekly clubs " as the dunces were said to be doing under Curll's direction. A year or two

---

[1] Not, however, the Curll-like *Character of the Times*, with which he had nothing to do. " The said Pamphlet," he tells us in the *Curliad*, " I refused, upon the many Errors I perceived in it, only on a cursory View of the Manuscript, at *Hurt's* Coffee-House in my Neighbourhood."

later Savage was able to gather quite a respectable number together. And, spurred on by Swift, Pope himself was preparing the *Variorum* edition of his poem, which, when it appeared in the following year, was as heavily laden with literary matter as was the ass in its frontispiece. The " pretentious " quarto was published by Mrs. Dodd in conjunction with Gilliver, and almost immediately a pirated edition " printed for A. Dob " came out. A. Dob, moreover, offered to give gratis a list of the various corrections that Pope had been making in the course of the last ten months.

Who was A. Dob ? Curll in a new disguise ? I do not know. Nobody knows. On the whole I am inclined to think not. I prefer to believe that there was a working agreement with Mrs. Dodd. In any case Pope's notes on the various dunces renewed the excitements, and there followed threats of libel actions and further " reprisals."

Curll himself came in for a fair measure of attention. " We come now," wrote Pope with fine irony, " to a character of much respect, that of Mr. Edmund Curl. As a plain repetition of great actions is the best praise of them, we shall only say of this eminent man, that he carried the trade many lengths beyond what it ever before had arrived at ; and that he was the envy and admiration of all his profession. He possessed himself of a command over all authors whatever ; he caused them to write what he pleased ; they could not call their very names their own. He was not only famous among these : he was taken notice of by the State, the Church, and the Law, and received particular marks of distinction from each." I do not quite understand this reference to the Church, but would not be surprised to find that Curlicism had been the subject of more than one sermon " printed at the desire of the auditors."

As to his inclusion in the *Dunciad,* " it will be owned," continues Pope, " that he is here introduced with all possible dignity ; he speaks like the intrepid Diomed ; he runs like the swift-footed Achilles ; if he falls, 'tis like the beloved Nisus ; and (what Homer makes to be the chief of all praises) he is favoured of the Gods ; he says but three words, and his prayer is heard ; a goddess conveys it to the seat of Jupiter : Though he loses the prize, he gains the victory ; the great Mother herself comforts him, she inspires him with expedients, she honours him with an immortal present (such as Achilles received from Thetis, and Aeneas from Venus) at once instructive and prophetical : after this he is unrivalled and triumphant.

" The tribute our author here pays him," he concludes, " is a grateful return for several unmerited obligations : many weighty animadversions on the public affairs, and many excellent and diverting pieces on private persons, has he given to his name. If ever he owed two verses to any other, he owed Mr. Curll some thousands."

Polite enough, if not quite true. Curll replied in what is the most interesting of all the pamphlets that he wrote. This was the *Curliad*, described as " a Hypercritic . . . with a farther Key." After reading it several times, I regret more than ever that its author did not ignore the ill-success of his *Proposals* and issue his autobiography in the usual way. For, although there is little enough in the *Curliad* that is not repetition or abuse, there are passages here and there of genuine autobiographical interest. It is here that he gives his account of the *Court Poems*, here that he mentions his apprentices by name, and here that he tells of his meeting with Ker. From this pamphlet, too, we get a hint that " Henry Stanhope " may really have been William Bond, a Norfolk man with several poems to his credit besides the *Epistle* and the *Progress of Dulness*, that Chute and not Breval wrote the *Hoop Petticoat*, and that Mrs. Centlivre had had nothing to do with *The Catholick Poet*. Here, too, he points out what is undoubtedly true, that the fulsome letter from Cleland, which had introduced the enlarged *Dunciad*, had really been written by Pope.

Nor was he content with mere prose. At the end there

come several couplets which made amusing enough reading.[1]

> " Of some, so very hard the Fate, and Luck is,
> *Gay* has no Pension, tho' his Friend 's a Dutchess.
> *Hibernian* Politicks, O *Swift*, thy doom,
> And *Pope* now owns, he did translate with *Broome*.
> Drawlers, like *Savage*, fix on him their hopes,
> Thinking that Rhime and Sneer will make them *Popes*.
>   Thus easy, 'tis, in Parody to shine,
> *Pope* shares the *Dunciad*, and the *Curliad* 's Mine ;
> Alike, too, next the Road, our Houses lye,
> Backward he views the Thames, and so do I."

IV

The war of the dunces dragged itself on, and Curll continued in the van of his troops. Otherwise there is little to say. Without the most minute analysis of the *Dunciad* itself, any detailed account of the various sorties and feints would be impossible, and it will be enough to point out that a pike amongst minnows does much as it likes. The *Dunciad* immortalized several scribblers who could not have hoped for the honour, and it left Pope in a position that only his own vanity could make even temporarily insecure. And if he triumphed over the dunces, I supposed he triumphed over Curll as well.

Financially speaking, however, I should say that the bookseller had the best of the bargain. . . .

The excitement had hardly died down before Curll was once again thinking of retirement. This time, however, there were no signs of disgust at unmerited treatment, but rather a desire for peace. It was, I feel, as a now prosperous tradesman becoming tired of the racket and asking for nothing but to be allowed to indulge his hobby, that the bookseller made public his intentions.

---

[1] I have been asked whether Curll really wrote the various verses bearing his name, which are scattered through his later publications. There is certainly no positive proof that he did, and nothing would have been easier for him than to " order " a verse or two from one of his hacks. On the other hand there is no contemporary suggestion that he did anything of the kind, and I see no reason to suppose that he put his name to what he did not write. After all, it is not very difficult to do a little rhyming on occasion, and if his grammar was sometimes a little peculiar, Curll could certainly write.

Scanty though it is, there is evidence that even at his busiest times he liked to get away from the hurry and bustle of London. There was his country-shop, of course—I do not know in what year, if at all, it was given up [1]—but it was not always business that took him away. For all his love of the theatre and rowdy companions, he liked to potter quietly in far-away places and forget for a while how much he adored money. The showman's job may have its excitements, but it makes big demands. Curll had now been in business for twenty-one years, of which the last three had been unpleasantly volcanic. He wanted a rest, and why—with a son to succeed him—should he not have it ?

How old Henry may have been at this time I do not know, but his marriage had probably taken place, and I fancy that for a short while he had started a separate business.[2] He had taken his father's place during the various " confinements," and was to do so again now, but he was never allowed to " reign " for very long, and I cannot bring myself to believe that he was an altogether satisfactory person,[3] even from the Curllean standpoint. More than once was Curll obliged to " come back " and find new partners outside the family circle, and if no book ever appeared " printed for E. and H. Curll," it was not, I imagine, the father's fault.

This brings me to another mysterious affair, about which, I confess, I know nothing beyond what may be gathered from the satire in verse that commemorates it. In some way it seems, Henry Curll had been inveigled into paying a visit to—of all places—Westminster School. Exactly when he went there I do not know, but it was during the war of the dunces, and his visit may possibly have had something to do with it. I would even have nothing to say against the suggestion that Mr. Pope or one of his supporters had not been wholly ignorant of the invitation. Go, however, to Westminster Henry did,

---

[1] He was still its proprietor in 1740.

[2] In Henrietta Street, 1726.

[3] He, too, announced, at least once, that he was leaving off business. (*Post Boy*, Aug. 7th, 1730.)

and found a reception almost identical with that which had been accorded his father twelve years before.

It sounds peculiar, and yet how else are we to understand the anonymous sixpenny pamphlet, issued by Moore in 1728, called *Hereditary Rights Exemplified ; or, a Letter of Condolance from Mr. Ed . . . d C . . . l to his Son H . . . y, Upon His Late Discipline at Westminster ?*

Conceivably Wesley is the author again, but this time there is no newspaper account to pave a way for the satire. We come upon the thing suddenly, and must make of it what we can. The poem opens with a short explanation : Hal is to hear no " sage lectures of Morality," but to receive real condolance on this second murderous attack on the family. " I little thought," says he,

> " in Perils past,
> When tost, and buffetted, and lash'd ;
> When maul'd again a second time
> in Cut (no matter for the Rhyme,)
> Where I appear'd engrav'd on high,
> With Legs long scrambling in the Sky ;
> With Nock indecently made bare,
> Expos'd for ever to the Air :
> And Kneeling down in Self-defence,
> Forc'd to dissemble Penitence ;
> I little thought on my Heir Male,
> The Rod descending to entail."

And, with us, he wonders

> " Was it thy Choice, *Hal*, or thy Fate,
> Made Thee thy Father imitate ? "

Surely, he thinks, it would have been enough had Hal stolen Copy in the good old way, and not considered that tradition also demanded a Westminster castigation. Filial piety could really be taken too far. However, the thing had been done, and they, to be sure, are not the only sheep to be branded :

> " Thy Breech with Gashes equal scotcht ;
> Answers to mine like Tally notcht ;
> And if thy Trowzers they unfurl,
> Men strait will smoke Thee for a . . . "

Yet matters are not so bad as they might be, for if Hal should suffer transportation, he is in no danger of being lost—the Curllean brand now being known the world over.

In the future, however, there need be no further trouble. Hal is now qualified to print *any* sort of book, even though it deals with flogging.

> " Thou might'st be timorous at first,
> But Fortune now has done her worst :
> Nor need'st Thou Publishing with-hold,
> Tho' *Pope* should rave, or *Swift* should scold."

There follows some useful advice :

> " The Printing-Trade goes well enough,
> Since I and *Dunton* left it off ;
> And trust me, Thou can'st never do,
> As Bookseller and Author too ;
> They're inconsistent ! chuse Thee whether,
> But never aim at both together.
> If I may counsel, *Hal*, depend
> Solely for Wit upon thy Friend.
> Let that thine Author's Province be,
> For thine, 'tis only Piracy.
> Steal all comes near Thee, Bad or Good,
> Thou'lt pick a pretty Livelihood.
> No matter how Thou fobb'st the Town,
> How coarse the Paper, or how brown ;
> No matter tho' the wretched Stuff,
> Is not like *Lintot's* wiping Proof.
> Tho' Patience 'self it would enrage,
> To foul ones Fingers with thy Page.
> What tho' Thou rak'st in every Nook
> Of private Life, or Pocket-Book ?
> Like me still careful to display,
> The Deeds of Mid-night in Mid-day ?
> Let Losers into Passions break,
> (As Losers may have leave to speak !)
> The Rascal swings that steals a Purse,
> A scabby Sheep, or found'red Horse ;
> While he goes scotfree with his Prey,
> Who steals our Fame or Friend away :
> So let them talk, while we that win
> May laugh, tho' not in a whole Skin."

Westminster, nevertheless, is a place of peculiar danger, where a man cannot call even his tail his own, and therefore

> "I charge Thee on my Blessing, *Hal*,
> Come not near *Westminster* at all . . .
> If e'er Thou hop'st again to vent,
> A Man's Last Will and Testament ;
> If e'er Thou hop'st the Pence to see,
> From long black Strokes and Blasphemy ;
> If e'er Thou hop'st to 'scape with Ears,
> From House of Commons, or of Peers ;
> Never, ah never, Boy, come near
> That fatal flogging *Westminster*."

Tradition is all very well, but there are times when it may conveniently be broken. If Hal should have children, they must be told that Westminster is strictly out of bounds. For

> "If we from Father down to Son,
> Are whipp'd from Generations on,
> A C . . . .'s Backside can ne'er have Peace,
> That stirs within the Liberties ;
> And what at first was thought a Crime,
> Will mellow into Right by Time."

Finally, of course, there is the choice of authors, and here there is surely one who may occupy the first place.

> "Lastly, to finish all thy Woes,
> May'st Thou ne'er publish Verse or Prose,
> But what prefixt, the Name shall bear,
> Of *E . . . . d C . . l*, late Bookseller."

Well, it seems to me that Henry had excellent opportunities. But, perhaps, like his father, he was rather too fond of having a good time. He certainly did little enough. The war of the duncesdied down, and Edmund slipped away—but only for a while. Before the end of the year they were wanting him back, and not only as author.

The good showman, I suppose, like the poet, must be born and not made.

CHAPTER EIGHT

A WIT, A WILKS, AND A WILL (1729–1733)

> . . . Ribaldry and Scandal lawless Reign.
> Thus shall you gain the Profit you pursue.
> And *Curl* get money by the Copy too.
> > ? James Miller, *Harlequin Horace.*

I

THERE was a little trouble over a Life of Congreve.

The great man had died at the beginning of 1729, and his Will really was curious, for he had left the bulk of his fortune not to his needy relations but to no less a person than the young Duchess of Marlborough. Naturally Curll was not satisfied to print even so spicy a Will: he must needs issue a Life. For his author he invented a Mr. Charles Wilson, who seems to have been our old friend Oldmixon, and his faithful " Corinna " obliged with some singularly inaccurate details of Dryden's family and funeral. Much, of course, was made of the dramatist's relations with the Duchess and Mrs. Bracegirdle, and Congreve's short novel *Incognita* was reprinted to give due substance to the book. Rumours flew round the town that the *Life* was to be even more scandalous than most of Curll's things, and endeavours were made to prevent its publication. Arbuthnot, amongst others, seems to have sought out Curll and demanded to be shown his " papers." Precisely what happened we do not know, but the book duly appeared in August, 1729,[1] " In Opposition to all Ridiculous Messages and Threatnings."

And at Michaelmas Curll went away—to Oxford

---

[1] " Printed in the Year 1730," and without Curll's name.

amongst other places. He had advertised that his house would be to let on that date—Henry, I fancy, had already migrated to Clement's Inn—and offered to sell his books at very low rates. The house was apparently either sold or let to a mysterious Mr. Leventhorp, who may or may not have been a bookseller, and London, no doubt, prepared itself to sustain the loss of one of its favourite butts. But something went wrong. While Mr. Rawlinson and his friends were entertaining their brother antiquarian at the University, the antiquarian's son was not, it would seem, doing his duty. The reins were but slackly held, if they were held at all, and Hal showed no intention of taking parental advice.

There was nothing to do but to postpone all ideas of a definite retirement. Curll returned to London, found a new house, and in November was announcing a fresh start.

No longer, you gathered, were there to be curlicised books. No longer was there to be a *Dial and Bible.* The visit to Oxford must have inculcated in him a new and commendable desire for pure learning. And so at his "Literatory," as he called it, a house with "two green Spires, next Door to Will's Coffee-House in Bow Street, Covent Garden," there were to be issued only such books as his University friends would approve of. Even so famous an antiquarian as Brown Willis would recommend him, and endeavour to make the public understand to what great expense the bookseller had been put with such works.

Mr. Brown Willis certainly gave Curll his recommendation. The publisher, he said, of no less than twenty valuable volumes of antiquities "deserves to be encouraged by us all, who are Well wishers to this Study." And "no Bookseller in Town," he added, had been "so curious as he."

Alas! even in a Literatory, with learned Oxford Fellows urging you on, antiquarian volumes are not the most paying of propositions, and in a very short while there came a sad lapse. Here was Curll, back again in a

London shop, with a public demanding the same old things, wanting impotency cases and scandalous memoirs —the Congreve was going very well—and paying little attention to tomb-stones and vaults. Here were the theatres and the taverns, only waiting to hear more of his amusing theatrical chatter, and—what on earth was he doing in a Literatory?

For a while he seems to have hesitated. Perhaps he hoped that Henry would show some signs at any rate of his own particular flair; but Henry did nothing. Once again he played with the idea of retirement. He even sold his rights in a number of books to one Wilford, a bookseller in St. Paul's Churchyard. And then, on a sudden, he decided upon another course of action. He went into temporary partnership with the new tenant of the Catherine Street house. A new sign was painted, and the *Congreve's Head* came into existence. Plans were immediately made for more lively translations from the French, more pamphlets about divorce and other exciting adventures of that kind, and all ideas of a permanent retirement vanished.

II

It was about this time that the *Grub Street Journal* began its seven years' career. Pope denied that he had anything to do with it, but soon enough it became an open secret that he, and no other, was the power behind the editor's throne.[1] And naturally the dunces, Curll amongst them, came in for a deal of attention.

---

[1] In a dialogue between Pope and the Ordinary of Newgate, which is to be found in Burnet's *Achilles Dissected, Being a Compleat Key of the Political Characters in that New Ballad Opera, Written by the late Mr. Gay* (1733), the poet is made to say:

> "Mischief's *my dear Delight*—*not* Satan's more:
> *But touch me*, and no Statesman is so sore.
> I rave, I foam, my utmost Venom hurl,
> And in the *Grubstreet-Journal* libel *Curll*.
> By *Popiads*, *Keys*, *Court-Poems*, I'm become
> Of Ridicule, his universal Drum;
> And shall continue thus my *whole Life long*,
> The grievous Burthen of his *merry Song*."

In an early number it was pretended that a literary club of an exclusive kind was being formed, and soon enough applications for membership of this Grub Street Society, as it was called, were supposed to have been received by its secretary, " Mr. Bavius," from various people who considered that they had a right to belong. Amongst these, of course, was one who signed himself KIRLEUS, and his letter asking to be appointed official bookseller to the Society makes very nice reading.

In this case the applicant acknowledges that a " natural backwardness and modesty " had been a great disadvantage to him on many occasions, but he has managed to publish *all* sorts of books. Some of these, he admits, will be found to be without his name, but there are " a great many cases in which it is not at all proper either for an Author, or a Bookseller, to put his name to the book he publishes." In fact, he can prove that he has printed as many under fictitious names as under his own. He proceeds to give some little account of a not unadventurous career. An escape from poison had been providential, and at Westminster he had been treated in a barbarous and inhumane manner " without the least regard to the sacred ground on which the College stands, or to the Vicinity of the Abbey, the King's most ancient palace, and of the Court of Judicature." In the House of Lords, he mentions, he has been attacked by Atterbury and others, though " that which gave me the most sensible affliction was, that by their false representations they were at last able to draw upon me a prosecution from the Government, to which I had always been so well affected. So that instead of admitting me into a share in printing the Gazette, Votes, &c. for my good Services, as I had just reason to suspect, I was advanced to a station to which, tho' very conspicuous, I had no ambition to aspire." Then, too, it must be realized that he is no ordinary bookseller, but has himself " written many *Things* both in prose and verse, which have been well received by the Town." He will not actually ask

CURLL (TWO-FACED) with HIS BAND OF AUTHORS
(From a caricature in the *Grub Street Journal*, 1732)

[*To face p.* 143

for admission to the Society as its Author, but thinks that so learned a society could very well accept him as its Bookseller.

The matter is duly considered, but, as in the *Dunciad*, there are other stationers to be considered, all now eager to occupy so dignified a position. In particular there is Lawton Gilliver, Pope's own publisher, with a very good record. He is chosen as the rival candidate. Speeches are made by the committee appointed to conduct the election. It is pointed out that Mr. Kirleus " has not only reprinted all the lewd books he could collect in English ; but likewise taken care to get a great number translated out of foreign languages." And is not Curlism—the Society, you note, prides itself on etymological exactitude—is not Curlism his invention ? As against this, another member makes a brave endeavour to show that the most bawdy of books may really be printed as an antidote to lechery. Besides, surely a bookseller owes it to his family to *sell* a book, not to trouble himself about its contents ? This last speech might have carried the day but for the unfortunate name of the speaker. Pruriento, it seems, is not a very popular member of the committee. His arguments are discounted and Gilliver is duly elected.

Naturally Kirleus is bitterly disappointed. He is also angry. He is so angry that he attacks the Society in print. He is accused by Mr. Bavius of being the author of a letter to the *Daily Journal* of May 23rd. A bad business : but the Society will overlook the strange outburst inasmuch as he has " lately cleared his Literatory of Books of Antiquities," which every right-minded man will admit are wholly outside his province.

Whether Curll wrote the angry letter in the *Daily Journal* I do not know, but he had no cause to welcome the *Grub Street Journal*, with its policy of almost continual pin-pricks. In June, 1730, for instance, he was being attacked again in a set of verses which he was supposed to have written himself. The last of these may have touched him on a tender spot :

> " To shine in verse is all my aim :
>   My fondeſt wish, my daring hope,
> Is but to emulate the fame
>   Of Waller, Dryden, or of Pope."

At a later date, too, he was being twitted about his advertisements, which had now resumed their jauntieſt garb. It was pointed out as worthy of note that though at the top of a column an announcement of his " might be design'd for the Direction of the Soul," the ones below it would generally be " for the Diversion of the Body." At the same time Mr. Bavius was sorry to see a really fine Curlism of that kind being coolly purloined. " The original Art of Advertising," said he, " was ſtolen from Mr. Curll's Literatory, by Grub-Orators and Hyp-Doctors, by Paper-Mongers, by Pamphleteers," and the like, and it was a sad business to see his indubitable rights in " that ingenious and profitable Art " being " mimicked " in this way by such Jackanapes.

And once there appeared a kind of monſtrous carica-ture—a rarity in the journalism of that day—and of three adjacent plates, two were concerned with Curll. Bavius's letter-press draws attention to a point about the bookseller's activities which would puzzle anybody who did not remember his greed for money. " The same bookseller," he writes, explaining the middle plate, " has frequently printed at his own charge, religious and impious, godly and lewd books. This sufficiently juſtifies the application of the figure with the two faces.—In the attitude in which he is placed, he may be supposed as giving his orders to his slaves the printers who work like horses, grunt like hogs, and fawn upon him like dogs. Or else he may be considered as giving directions to his authors, to write poetical, political, hiſtorical, theological, and bawdy books ; which authors are properly presented by the gentlemen who have the heads of a dog, a horse, a swine, and are accordingly treated by him like spaniels, hackneys and hogs." In the other plate Curll is shown as a monstrous devil, and Bavius does not spare him. " The devil," says he, " seems to

CURLL IN HIS LITERATORY
(From a caricature in the *Grub Street Journal*, 1732)

[*To face p.* 144

denote a particular bookseller, stripped of all ornaments of puffs, advertisements, and title-pages, and *in propria persona*, putting up his own and other people's copies, books some of pious devotions, others of lewd diversions, in his literatory."

Not a pleasant " effigies "—in the next number Bavius was being exhorted not to frighten his readers again with such horrors—but to me, at any rate, most interesting. Who else would they have caricatured in this way ? Very few writers ; certainly no other bookseller. You could pretend to ignore this rogue of a Curll, but he was still going strong. You could fine him, and put him in the pillory, but you could not put an end to his activities. And no matter what sort of attacks you made on him, with cudgels or whips or pens dipped in the bitterest ink, the result was just nothing at all.

I can see Curll framing the unlovely things and hanging them up in his shop.

III

There were to be further attacks from the Bavian fold,[1] but in the meantime Curll was preparing for other changes. Throughout the earlier part of 1731 Leventhorp seems to have worked with him. During that time he invented yet another biographer, by name William Egerton, who produced *Faithful Memoirs* of the celebrated and deservedly popular Anne Oldfield, and I see no reason to doubt that Mr. Egerton and Mr. Curll were one and the same. So much, indeed, was clearly implied by the writer who fourteen years later was attacking Curll's *Memoirs of Pope*. At the end of May, however, the mysterious Leventhorp disappears, leaving his partner alone. But Curll had had enough of the Catherine Street house, and in August the *Congreve's Head* was removed to " Burleigh Street, over against the Savoy in the Strand." From one of his advertisements we learn

---

[1] As, for instance, Mr. Bavius's comment on the death of Booth, the actor, " I hear, Mr. C——l designs to kill him again by writing his life," which, however, he did not do.

that the new house adjoined Exeter Exchange, and was "the Fourth House on the Left Hand," and it was from here that he issued his much-abused life of "that eminent comedian" Mr. Robert Wilks.

In this case it would seem that he was caught napping. True, there was a most interesting new case of impotency at the time to demand his attention, but it is strange that he should have allowed not one but two biographers to forestall him. The first of these Lives was the work of one Slow, and was published by Warner on October 15th, 1732. The second, which reached a third edition before the end of the year, was the work of Daniel O'Brien, and was published by Rayner. This last must have roused Curll's particular anger, for it professed to give all the actor's "Adventures among the Ladies." But he had his revenge, for when his own Life appeared on November 7th, he was able to print two testimonials from the comedian's family. Writing from Bow Street, the widow condemned the two "false and scandalous Pamphlets," both of which were "greatly injurious" to Mr. Wilks's memory, and Knapton, the actor's brother-in-law, lodging in "Charing-Cross-Meuse," not only attacked the "silly Pamphlet said to be writ by one O'Bryan (if there be any such Person)," but acknowledged that he had given to Mr. Curll all his recollections of the great man.

Now if you look at the title-page of *The Life*, you cannot fail to be pleased. The vignette of Wilks himself is a triumph of contemporary engraving. But, alas! if you are unwise enough to read on, you will find very little indeed about the actor. It was the old story: some sort of a Life at all costs. Here, as it happened, Curll was only third in the field, but even so he could do nothing more than hash up a few biographical details culled from the newspapers and quotations from books already printed. It is really curious, this complete inability on Curll's part ever to add anything to our knowledge of a man to whom he was playing biographer. But was it perhaps mere laziness? He did declare once

THE
LIFE
OF
That Eminent COMEDIAN
ROBERT WILKS, Esq;

Farewell! O born with ev'ry Art to Please,
Politeness, Grace, Gentility and Ease.

Quantum mutatus ab illo.

LONDON:

Printed for E. CURLL, in BURGHLEY-*Street*,
in the *Strand.* 1733.

that in his opinion the duty of a biographer was " to give a faithful recital of what others had written," but his tongue must have been in his cheek as he wrote those words. He knew well enough what people thought of his *Lives*.[1] In the case of Wilks, moreover, you would suppose that after all his theatre-going and all the hours spent in taverns and ale-houses, he must have accumulated a whole store of diverting information. Did he not talk well on theatrical subjects ? Nobody better. Yet the Wilks book contained nothing at all that was novel or amusing, and he received a thoroughly well-deserved trouncing for it in the *Grub Street Journal*.

" Tho' we have often refused, tho' offered a gratuity, to insert puffs in recommendation of books ; yet we could not refuse to publish *gratis* the following *Contents* of the *Life of that eminent comedian* Robert Wilks Esq ; written by a much greater comedian ; and of which the world has not taken that notice which it deserves.

---

[1] In 1734 there appeared *The Life of Mr. John Dennis* . . . NOT written by Mr. Curll.

" The reader, by caſting his eye upon this table, will
be surprized to see the *Life* of so great an actor, drawn
within the narrow compass of 8 pages ; for which he
cannot surely grudge to pay 1s. 6d. having 4 pages of his
laſt will and teſtament, and 66 of useful digressions into
the bargain."

A similar table could be drawn up with reference to
his *Life of Gay* which quickly followed. The " approbation " that accompanied its publication cannot have
travelled much further than the advertisement columns
which report its exiſtence. And yet, you know, he wrote
endless letters to those who could have helped him, had
they chosen to do so. " Curll," wrote Arbuthnot to Swift
at this time, " who is one of the new terrors of death,
has been writing letters to everybody for memoirs of
his life. I was for sending him some, particularly an
account of his disgrace at Court, which I am sure might
have been made entertaining, by which I should have
attained two ends at once, published truth, and got a
rascal whipped for it. I was overruled in this." Of
course he was overruled. But what a pity that a man
who could take such pains to decipher a tombſtone or
an inscription should prefer, when the lives of men were
concerned, the pen-knife [1] to the pen, and be satisfied
with an engraving or two !

Or were scissors in use at the time ?

THE
LIFE
OF
Mr. *JOHN GAY,*

Author of the BEGGAR's-OPERA, *&c.*

POETS have an unquestion'd Right to claim,
If not the Greatest, the most lasting NAME.
                                        CONGREVE.

LONDON:
Printed for E. CURLL, in BURGHLEY-*Street,*
in the *Strand,* 1733.

THE LIFE OF GAY " RECEIVED WITH APPROBATION "
                              [*To face p.* 148

IV

It is one of Curll's most distinctive qualities that he lost few opportunities of appearing in a *cause celèbre*. I do not say that he actually appeared in many, but if there was a chance of a little extra notoriety, he took it. And in 1733 there occurred an opportunity which does not often arise. In the course of his ordinary business he printed the last Will and Testament of a distinguished man, and the Will turned out to be forged!

London was intrigued, and rather shocked, when it heard the details of the Will of old Matthew Tindal, the deist. Tindal had long been a public figure, and for a theologian his career had been singularly picturesque. He had a nephew, the Reverend Nicholas, the translator of Rapin, and Nicholas was a most respectable person. To everybody's surprise, however, and very much to Nicholas's annoyance, the bulk of the old man's small fortune was left to Eustace Budgell, Esq., "that his great talents may serve his country."

Well, testators have a knack of doing peculiar things, but this was very peculiar indeed, for, as far as was known, Budgell had no real claims. On the other hand he was in dire need of money.

His had been a chequered career. He was a cousin of Addison's, and had been politically associated with him. He had contributed to the *Tatler* and the *Spectator*, and written squibs which had got him into trouble. In the South Sea affair he had lost the bulk of his fortune, and spent the rest in unsuccessful attempts to enter Parliament. He was a clever, unbalanced person, with a pen that could be venomous, and of late he had endeavoured to increase his importance in the eyes of the public by running a weekly paper called *The Bee*. Incidentally he knew Curll, and disliked him. In July of this year a definite attack on the bookseller had appeared in his paper. Here any "brother Scribbler" in search of a title-page for his work had been invited "to come to an apartment five stories high, at Timothy Stitchum's, a collector of old Cloathes in Rag Fair," where he would be furnished " with a very taking one . . . at a moderate price." If he desired, moreover, he could also obtain " a large quantity of taking Title-pages, serious, comical, or political on both sides, &c : Some dozens of last Wills and Testaments and Lives of remarkable persons not yet dead (all these bespoke by Mr. Edmund Curl), many last dying speeches and confessions of men as yet unhanged, stores of doleful ditties, horrid murders, and Cases of Impotency." It was not, however, until Tindal's death that there was a definite row between them. The old man died on August 16th, and almost immediately " the Honourable Mrs. Price," who, it seems, had actually written out the Will, sent to " Orator " Henley sketches of his life and to Curll a copy of the very extraordinary Will.[1] This the book-seller issued before the end of the month, and was immediately obliged to reprint. He followed it up with the usual hastily-compiled *Life*, and Budgell was exceed-ingly annoyed that his private affairs had thus been made public. He was even more annoyed when Nicholas declared his intention of contesting the Will on the ground that it was forged. Budgell accused Curll of printing—of course without authority—the most scurri-lous falsehoods, and the bookseller, perceiving the true state of affairs, and, incidentally, the chance of no little profit to himself, lost no time in inaugurating a great newspaper campaign.

On September 20th he inserted in the *Daily Journal* some letters which must have been sufficient to show the world that he had not, on this occasion at any rate, been writing without authority.

" Cold Bath Fields, Sept 15, 1733.
" Mr. Budgell's Certificate, relating to a Six-penny Pamphlet printed for Mr. Curll by the Appointment of the Hon. Mrs. Price and himself.
" I do not deny but the Copy contain'd in this

1 Curll had previously issued a life of her husband.

Pamphlet is a *True Copy of Dr. Tindall's* Will ; and that the Facts mention[ed] in the same Pamphlet are like wise True.   (Bee. No. 29.)

" EUSTACE BUDGELL.

" The Facts mention'd in this Pamphlet, Mr. Budgell himself told me, at Lady Price's Chambers, under a Promise of Secrecy ; but now seems concern'd, I did not name my Appointers, which in Justice to myself I hear [*sic*] Testify.

" E. CURLL.

" To the Lady Price
" *Madam,*
" I enclose the Paper I promised, and wish it may be of an Use to (Mr. Curll) the Person your Ladyship is pleased to favour.

" I am, Madam,
" *Your Ladyship's*
" *Most obedient humble Servant*
" Wednesday   EUSTACE BUDGELL
" 29 Aug. 1733.

" The Paper herein mention'd was a List of some Anonymous Pamphlets wrote by Dr. Tindall, and which are inserted in his Life.

" E. CURLL.

" *Extract of a Letter from the Rev. Mr. Tindal to Mr. Curll.*
" *Sir,*
" I receiv'd yours, and am oblig'd to you for your good Intentions.
" If —— would give you the *True Account of the* Will, it would be the most diverting : but I fear that must remain a Secret as yet.   I am, Sir,
" *Your humble Servant,*
" N. TINDAL.

" To Mr. Budgell.

" *Sir*,

" I will shortly show the World who beſt underſtands the Arts of Imposing upon and Cheating both private Persons and the Publick.

" This Affair between you and I shall (in your own moſt elegant Phrase) make a good deal of Noise, before I have done with you. I expeᴄt your True Answer.

" E. Curll."

This was bold enough. It forced Budgell to make some sort of a reply. He issued a rival version of the Will, with his own account of what had happened between himself, Mrs. Price and Nicholas Tindal, but by this time the public were beginning to form their own conclusions, and on this occasion they sided with Curll The attacks were continued for some time as Curll had promised they should be, and he was not prosecuted for libel. No doubt it would be very difficult to prove the Will a forgery, but—people were talking about it, and that meant that they were talking about Curll, and buying his *Life of Tindal*, and—what more was required ?

I fancy that the matter was never aᴄtually proved one way or the other, though there seems little doubt about Budgell's guilt. At any rate he was done for. He never recovered from the scandal that Curll was so largely inſtrumental in making public, and four years later drowned himself in the river.

But then, as the bookseller would probably have told you, he had always been a lunatical fellow.[1]

[1] The *Grub Street Journal*, of course, had much to say of the matter. On Oᴄt. 25th, 1733, Bavius published another plate, " The Art of Trimming emblematically displayed," which was thus described : " The wig upon the block represents *The laſt will and teſtament* of the late great Dr. Tindal, bequeathing to Euſtace Budgell, Esq. *two thousand one hundred pounds, that his* great talents *may serve his country*. A Will, I think, is very properly adumbrated by a wig ; because the sense of the one, and the hair of the other, proceed from the brain ; and the former is made up in form, in an artificial manner, by the will-maker, as the latter by the wig-maker. And as the wig, which any person wears, is seldom made by his own hair ; so it often happens, that a *Will* is not made of the persons own head, under whose name it passes : but this cannot be the case here— . . . This block, head, and wig, are placed between two figures

The ART of TRIMMING emblematically diſplayed.

CURLL, EUSTACE BUDGELL, MRS. PRICE AND THE TINDALS
(From a caricature in the *Grub Street Journal*, 1733)
[*To face p.* 152

which, by some part of their dress, appear plainly to be of two different sexes, and to be very busy in combing, powdering, and setting out the wig ; which therefore I take to be designed for the honourable Mrs. Prise, who wrote the will ; and the honourable Mr. Curl who first published it.—The next two figures, towards the right hand, stand for Eustace Budgell, Esq ; and the reverend Mr. Nicholas Tindal. We are to suppose the former to have been comforting the latter under the disappointment of his expectations from the will of his uncle. (See Illustration.) ”

CHAPTER NINE

> C——l raves, and is poison'd, he'll tell ye,
> Pray tye the poor man in his bed ;
> He has long had a Pope in his *Belly*,
> And now he's flown up to his *Head*.
>
> *Grub Street Journal*, 1735.

I

LIKE other harmless pursuits, bibliography has its excitements and thrills. Mysterious problems present themselves, and even crime is not absent. The weirdest yarns loom up on a sudden from nowhere in particular, and with a little luck you may find yourself in the midst of a wholly unbelievable business, with false clues abounding and innocent men being accused of all sorts of misdemeanours. You may even have the joy of experiencing at the end of a long and tiresome investigation that crash of surprise upon the production of which the detective-story writers so naturally pride themselves.

Now the almost incredible affair of Pope's Letters has been told of in detail more than once, but it will bear retelling, more particularly as I shall be viewing it from Curll's own standpoint. It is a complicated story, on the long side perhaps, but of quite astonishing interest. Both Pope and Curll wrote their own accounts of the strange business. Contemporary scribblers filled columns of more or less abusive comment, though without leaving us with more than the vaguest and most unsatisfactory records. Dr. Johnson found himself in a quandary when he came to write of the matter, and Warton was either unable or unwilling to venture very far into the maze of contradictory statements. Isaac D'Israeli wrote a narrative of the " extraordinary transactions," but even so enthusiastic a bibliographer as he failed to clear away very much of the general confusion. It was left to Mr. Ashton Dilke in the eighteen-fifties, and Mr. Elwin, writing some fifteen years later, to clear up the mystery and give to the world a story that must be almost unparalleled in the history of letters.

I confess that I am in some little difficulty as to how best the queer story should be retold. One does not want to be worried with too many documents and letters, but on the other hand it is hard to know what to omit. It will be best, I suppose, to follow Curll himself through the various phases and allow the story to look after itself. As far as the main facts go, the thing is simple. Here you have Pope and Curll once again engaged in the fiercest of battles—the distinguished poet with highly-placed friends ready to do his bidding, and the not very " eminent " bookseller, several times imprisoned, ever sailing too near the wind, and very generally dubbed liar and scoundrel. On the face of things, you might think that the opponents were singularly ill-matched. And yet in this third round, at any rate, there is no doubt at all as to whom the honours must be given. For although in a sense Pope may be said to have succeeded in his general design, it was Curll who stepped out of the ring with the insolence of victory. It was Curll who was found to have spoken the truth, Curll whose cunning had been equal to that of all his opponents, Curll who wiped out all old-standing insults.

Let us look, then, into this singular matter.

II

The preliminaries are worthy of the closest attention.

You will remember that during his fight with the King's Bench, the bookseller had secured from Mrs. Thomas a bundle of letters written by Pope to one of his earlier friends. These had sold very well in their printed form, and naturally he was not averse from obtaining more. Unfortunately for him Mrs. Thomas had no others to dispose of, and he was hardly in a position to seek Pope's own co-operation. But he did not despair. However much he might hate the "little monster," there was no doubt that a great deal of money could be made out of him, and towards the end of 1732 he seems to have conceived a new idea which might mean an even greater financial return. The *Lives* of dead men of eminence had been one of his surest successes—recently had not his *Life of Gay* been receiv'd with acclamation ? [1]—but why not the Life of a man still alive ? Announcements of so novel a departure might well bring him more letters, and in any case if he acted in this instance as his own biographer, the dunces at least would have good cause for satisfaction. Accordingly he inserted an advertisement in the newspapers, and waited for results. One, at any rate, was not long in coming. The *Daily Journal* for March 30th, 1733, contained the following statement :

"THE SECOND Time of Asking. (There is now Actually in the Press) The Life of Mr. Pope. Containing a faithful Account of him and his Writings. (Founded upon a Plan deliver'd by himself to Mr. Jacob, with two Guineas, to insert it in his Lives of the Poets) Embellish'd with Dissertations and Digressions, Notes and all Kinds of poetical Machinery, in order to render the Work Compleat. Nothing shall be wanting but his (universally desired) Death. Any Memoirs, &c, worthy his Deserts, if sent to Mr. Curll, will be faithfully inserted.

"N.B. Pursuant to my former Advertisement in this Paper, I received on Wednesday last, some Anecdotes relating to *Mr. Pope's Behaviour when he went to School to one Bromley, a Popish Renegado. They were communicated by a Gentleman, who declares, that he was Schoolfellow with Mr.*

---

[1] Or so he said. It was the usual compilation with a page of biography and fifty of quotations.

THE "LITTLE MONSTER"
(From a print in the British Museum)

[To face p. 156

Pope, and the late D. of Norfolk at the same Time, in Devon-
shire Street, Bloomsbury. The Fact is very remarkable, as it is
a Proof of that Natural Spleen which conſtitutes Mr. Pope's
Temperament (as my Lord Bacon observes of all Deformed
Persons) and from which he has never yet deviated.

" As I intend to write this Life in a Chronological Method,
I desire those Gentlemen, who are willing to do Mr. Pope's
Character Juſtice, to be ſpeedy in transmitting what Memoirs
they intend, that they may be placed in their proper Order of
Time ; and shall be faithfully inserted in the Words of the
Writer.

" Burghley-Street in the Strand,

" E. CURLL.

" March 30, 1733."

The anecdotes mentioned (but not described) had come
in a letter dated March 27th, and signed E. P. This letter
which, like those that followed it, was carefully preserved
by Curll, contains some of the sentences printed above.
Who E. P. may have been we do not know—though
Curll in one place hints that he was a peer—and the
letter is only intereſting as mentioning Pope's satirical
powers even at school and the punishment infliċted upon
him for attacking his maſter in so unusual a way. It was
not apparently followed by others from the same hand.
As it happened, too, Henry Curll was showing some
little energy at the time, and his father seems to have
gone away and allowed the new scheme temporarily to
lapse. In Oċtober, however, another letter, this time
signed P. T., was delivered at the Burghley-Street house.
In this P. T., underſtanding that Mr. Curll proposed to
issue Pope's Life, desired to correċt one or two errors
about the poet's descent which were current, and
hinted that if the bookseller would agree to print
nothing libellous, further intereſting memoirs might be
forthcoming. Mr. Curll was invited to insert a notice in
the *Daily Advertiser*, if he wished to receive such memoirs
and would comply with P. T.'s conditions.

Such a notice duly appeared. " E. C. hath received a

letter, and will comply with P. T." Evidently a cautious fellow, this P. T., but possibly a useful man. He might need careful handling, but if he had, as seemed possible, some spicy details, they would go very well into an initial chapter which, though it was by no means " Actually in the Press " was in the bookseller's head—the next best place.

P. T. sent his second letter on Nov. 15th. Here it was hinted that P. T. himself had no reason to love Pope any more than did the bookseller, but it must be clearly understood that extreme secrecy was necessary. The least false move might lead to all kinds of trouble. More important, however, was the news that there had recently fallen into P. T.'s hands a collection of Mr. Pope's letters " which being more considerable than any yet seen, and opening many scenes new to the world, will alone make a perfect and the most authentic memoirs of him that could be." And if Curll would insert the advertisement that was enclosed, the letters themselves should indubitably be forwarded on.

A pleasantly mysterious business, but there were features about it which Curll did not like. In the collection of letters, it seemed, there were letters to and from peers, and, as the bookseller had good reason to know, the peers could be the nastiest gentry to deal with. Besides, he was being asked to announce that " the Originals will be shown at E. Curll's when the book is published." Perhaps, after all, it would be as well to have nothing to do with P. T., or at least to wait until something more was known about him. If the letters themselves had accompanied the draft of the advertisement, well and good, but they had not yet been seen. They might not be genuine. They might even not exist at all. There were several folk who would be quite equal to baiting a trap for him. Much better do nothing at all. When P. T. wrote again to know why the advertisement had not appeared, Curll did not reply.

After all there was really no hurry, and at the time he was about to launch out in a new direction. While keeping on his shop in Burghley Street he opened in March,

1734, a " Printing Office " in Rose Street, apparently at
the Covent Garden end, and, with Wilford as partner and
spasmodic assistance from Henry, conducted for a while
a two-sided business. New editions of old books
streamed forth, the idea of having the life of a living man
written was carried into execution with Walpole, there
were side-issues like the selling of real estate and pictures,
and—well, Pope could wait. The letter from P. T. with
the suggested advertisement was put away in a drawer
and forgotten.

Then one day in March, 1735, Curll tells us, "upon
regulating some papers in my scrutoire . . . this advertisement came to my hands, and reflecting within myself
that the resentment between Mr. Pope and me, though
from the first ungenerously taken up by him, had continued much too long, being about eight years"—he
might have said twenty—"I was willing to lay hold of
an opportunity for proposing an accomodation." Admirable Curll! What might not happen with Pope on your
side ? But was the search in the scrutoire so fortuitous as
he would here have us believe ? I fancy not.[1] Two days
before, he had been lampooned again in the *Grub Street
Journal*. " A Lover's Auction " had been playfully announced. All kinds of love letters were to be sold, but the
auctioneer made one stipulation. " N.B. E——d C—l
is to take notice, that he won't be admitted to be a bidder
at this sale : lest the world should suspect the genuineness
of these Letters, if they should ever come to be published."
Here, surely, was a reminder. The papers were fetched
out of their drawer, the " universally desired " death of
the poet was forgotten, and a letter sent to Twickenham
with the advertisement and P. T.'s last note.

---

[1] In another place he says that he was " directed " to forward the P.T. papers
to Pope. But at whose direction ? Elwin suggests that as he seemed uncon-
scious of having contradicted himself " he may have been influenced by some
concurring advice." The biographer had not apparently noticed the " Lover's
Auction " in the *Grub Street Journal*. I admit, however, that the letter to Pope
was " singularly opportune," and it may be, as Elwin and Dilke suggest, that
there were those about the bookseller who were not unfriendly to Pope. They
may even have arranged the attack in the *Journal*, and drawn his attention to
the last few words.

" Rose-ſtreet, March 22, 1735.

" Sir,

" To convince you of my readiness to oblige you, the enclosed is a demonſtration. You have, as he says, disobliged a gentleman, the initials of whose name are P. T. I have some other papers in the same hand relating to your family, which I will show you if you desire a sight of them. Your letters to Mr. Cromwell are out of print, and I intend to print them very beautifully in an octavo volume. I have more to say than is proper to write, and if you will give me a meeting, I will wait on you with pleasure, and close all differences betwixt you and yours.

" E. CURLL.

" P.S.   I expect the civility of an answer or message."

Pope did not reply by letter, but inserted an announcement in the *Poſt-Boy* and two other papers.

" Whereas A. P. hath received a letter from E. C., bookseller, pretending that a person, the initials of whose name are P. T., hath offered the said E. C. to print a large collection of Mr. P.'s Letters, to which E. C. requires an answer, A. P. having never had, nor intending to have, any private correspondence with the said E. C., gives it him in this manner. That he knows no such person as P. T., that he believes he hath no such collection, and that he thinks the whole a forgery, and shall not trouble himself about it."

Well, well. That was clear enough, though not perhaps the " civility " required. Afterwards the poet gave an explanation of his brusqueness which at any rate was plausible enough. " Mr. Pope's friends," he wrote or dictated, " imagined that the whole design of E. Curll was to get him to look on the edition of Cromwell's letters, and so to print it as revised by Mr. Pope. . . . Or if there was any such proposal from P. T., Curll would not fail to embrace it, perhaps pay for the copy with the very money he might draw from Mr. P. to sup-

press it, and say P. T. had kept another copy." Meanwhile there was Curll in much the same position, though
minus the suggested advertisement, and not unnaturally
he was cross. What Pope called an "impertinent
answer" was printed next day :

"Whereas A. P., poet, has certified in the *Daily Post
Boy,* that he shall not trouble himself at all about the
publication of a large collection of the said Mr. P.——'s
letters . . . this is to certify, that Mr. C. never had, nor
intended to have, any private correspondence with A. P.,
but was directed to give him notice of these letters. Now
to put all forgeries, even Popish ones to flight, this is to
give notice that any person, or A. P. himself, may see
the originals, in Mr. P——'s own hand, when printed.
Initials are a joke ; names at length are real.

> "No longer now like suppliants we come,
> E. C. makes war, and A. P. is the drum."

Rather bold ? Yes, but there was a reason. An hour
or two after he had seen Pope's announcement in the *Post
Boy* of the previous day, the mysterious P. T. had cropped
up again with a communication which contained an
entirely new proposal about the letters. He had seen
A. P.'s rejoinder, he wrote, "and did not expect you of
all people would have betrayed me to Squire Pope ; but
you and he both shall soon be convinced it was no
forgery, for since you would not comply with my proposals to advertise, I have printed them at my own
expense, being advised that I could safely do so. I would
still give you the preference if you will pay the paper and
print, and allow me handsomely for the copy. But I shall
not trust you to meet and converse upon it," he added,
"after the suspicion I have of your dealings with Master
P., unless I see my advertisement of the book printed
first, within these four or five days. If you are afraid of
Mr. P., and dare not set your name to it as I proposed at
first, I do not insist thereupon, so I be but concealed. . . .
It makes a five shilling book."

Excellent ! But did P. T. really suppose that a wise old bird like Edmund Curll would agree to buy even printed sheets without a sight of the originals ? A pretty fool he would look if he were to issue the book without proof that its material was authentic. Why did not P. T. cease being so mysterious and show him the originals ? Then there need be no further delay. P. T., however, remained coy. He did not seem eager to produce any originals. Would not a sight of the printed sheets be sufficient ? If so, Curll had only to come to " the Rose Tavern, by the Playhouse, at seven in the evening, April 22nd," when " one " would show him a copy of the book. Very well, Curll would go, though the meeting committed him to nothing. He told P. T. that he would go, pointing out, however, that the price asked—£75—was rather high.

And then P. T. made a queer mistake. At the last moment he put Curll off, and the reason he gave was sufficiently odd. "I received a countermand," Curll informs us, " that he thought he had lost his wits by making such an appointment, and seemed in a terrible panic lest Mr. Pope should send some of his Twickenham bravoes to assault us ; but how Mr. Pope was to know of this meeting was the cream of the jest. I sent him word that I commiserated his fears, but as to my own part I did not at all dread any assassination whatever from Mr. Pope, even though it were a poetical one."

How, indeed, should Pope learn of this meeting, unless perchance P. T. and Pope were in communication ? *Were* they in communication ? But surely P. T. had said that he had quarrelled with the poet ? They were on very bad terms. He had been going to forward all sorts of spicy details about the little man. But—had anything of the sort come ? No, so far there had been nothing *against* Mr. Pope. True, the letters had not yet been seen, but—one is not surprised to find the bookseller becoming very suspicious. And when, a week later, P. T. offered to send a set of the printed sheets to Curll's own house at eight o'clock in the evening, Curll refused to meet him. Instead, he left a letter for the man who should call. "I have never met with anything," he wrote, "more inconsistent than the several proposals of your letters. . . . April 21, you put off this meeting, fearing a surprise from Mr. Pope. How should he know of this appointment unless you gave him notice ? I fear no such besettings either from him or his agents. . . . You want seventy-five pounds for a person you would serve ; that sum I can easily pay, if I think the purchase would be of any service to me. But in one word, sir, I am engaged all the evening, and shall not give myself any further trouble about such jealous, groundless and dark negotiations. An honourable and open dealing is what I have always been used to, and if you will come into such a method, I will meet you anywhere, or shall be glad to see you at my own house, otherwise apply to whom you please."

An offhanded ending, but if I am right, Curll's suspicions that Pope himself was not wholly ignorant of these P. T. transactions were rapidly changing to a certainty. It would not be the first time that the poet had taken unusual precautions in the matter of a new publication. But if Master Pope was hiding in the background and really wanted his letters published by Curll, there must be some very queer reason. Or *was* it a trap ? It behoved him to go very warily indeed.

P. T., however, was not to be put off. On May 3rd he took a big step forward. He announced that in four days' time his messenger would be coming at eight o'clock in the evening with fifty sets of sheets, complete except for a title-page, and suggested that the bookseller might safely advertise publication for May 12th. Presumably he had also agreed to give Curll a glimpse of some, at any rate, of the originals. " Accordingly," Curll tells us, " on the 7th of May, R. S., a short, squat man, came to my house, not at eight, but near ten at night. He had on a clergyman's gown, and his neck was surrounded with a large lawn barrister's band. He showed me a book in sheets almost finished, and about a dozen original letters, and promised me the whole at our next meeting."

We know who this R. S. was. As the controversy reached an acuter stage, he was called " the Rev. Mr. Smythe," but his real name was James Worsdale. He was " an indifferent painter," but " a man of some humour in personating a character, for he performed ' Old Lady Scandal ' in one of his own farces. He was also a literary adventurer, for, according to Mrs. Pilkington's Memoirs, wishing to be a poet as well as a mimic, he got her and her husband to write all the verses which passed with his name ; such a man was well adapted to be this clergyman with the lawyer's band." [1] Curll, of course, required no long time to understand the importance of what he was being asked to buy, and prepared straightway to make a big splash. At the same time it was necessary to remain very strictly on guard. When P. T. asked for the return of his own letters to the bookseller, Curll, none too keen to part with what might be valuable evidence in case of trouble, put Worsdale off with an excuse. Some of the letters, he said, had been taken out of town—possibly to Peckham, where about this time he took a " country " house—though he promised to send a messenger for them. [2] All would be well, he announced, if he were treated in an honourable way. And, indeed, there seemed little likelihood now of things going wrong. The edition was being printed off, the price for the sheets had been lowered, and the risk to himself was but small. There were no letters printed actually *from* peers, though many *to* them, and they could hardly object to being mentioned. Moreover, if Pope himself knew of the transactions, any danger from that quarter might be discounted.

By May 8th all the sheets—600 sets, it was said—had been printed off, and " Mr. Smythe " was telling Curll

[1] D'Israeli, *Quarrels of Authors*. There are many more details about him in Mrs. Pilkington's *Memoirs*.
[2] He did return them, as promised, but only after he had taken very careful copies.

that " the old gentleman," as he described P. T., was
" vastly pleased." On the 10th, Curll was being assured
that no other bookseller should be given the opportunity
of selling one single copy. And, according to P. T.'s
instructions, on May 12th an agreeably pompous advertisement duly appeared in the *Post Boy*, containing a list
of persons to whom Pope had written " with the
respective answers of each correspondent "—a statement,
by the way, which is not so precise as it might seem to
be. Fifty copies of the *Letters* were ready for sale, and
they were sold off at once. Worsdale, very busy playing
carrier, had promised more for the afternoon, and bade
Curll stay at home. Accordingly he remained indoors,
" and about one o'clock R. S. sent for me to the Standard
Tavern in Leicester Fields, where I paid him ten pounds,
and gave him a negotiable note for fifteen pounds,
payable in a month as he desired. We had not been
together half an hour, before two porters brought to
the tavern five bundles of books upon a horse, which
R. S. told me had come by water. He ordered the
porters to carry them to my house, and my wife took
them in. They contained but 38 books in each bundle,
making in the bundles 190 books."

Not by any means the whole edition, you see, not
even the numbers that had been promised, but at least
the long-drawn-out transactions had led to some tangible
result. P. T. might or might not be in league with Pope,
R. S., with his barrister's bands was certainly not " the
Rev. Mr. Smythe," but Mr. Pope's *Letters* were on the
market. And if they bore no bookseller's name on their
title-page, all the world would know soon enough that
they could only be obtained at one shop.

III

Immediately there was trouble.
Hardly had the five bundles been taken into Curll's
house, when Black Rod's Messengers arrived and
impounded the lot. Curll himself and Wilford, as

publisher of the *Post Boy*, were summoned to attend at
the Bar. And why? Complaint had been made in
Parliament that amongst the letters were some which
were either from peers or reflected upon them. Who had
made the complaint? A certain Lord Ilay. On his own
initiative? No : apparently at the instigation of somebody else. But who?

Dr. Johnson was in London at the time. He tells us
that it was Pope himself. There can be no doubt whatever about the truth of his statement. Unquestionably
the books had been seized as a result of Pope's complaint
to certain noble lords.

Then, had Curll been wrong? Had P. T. really been
playing a lone hand? And were the peers after all going
to be nasty?

The two booksellers duly appeared at the Bar, and
were asked to explain. They explained. Whereupon
the complaint was referred to a committee, which would
meet in two days' time, when Black Rod was ordered to
attend with some of the books.

Now mark what followed. Curll returned home, and
the next morning received a letter from " Mr. Smythe."
As soon as he had heard of " the misfortune," he wrote,
he had " posted off to P. T.," who " said if you had been
more cautious than to name lords in your advertisement,
this need not have happened." Rather cool of P. T.,
considering that it was he who had drafted the advertisement and insisted on its insertion ; but no matter, there
was more important news. " Mr. Smythe " had discovered that the rogue of a printer " had delivered your
last parcel imperfect ; but I will bring you both these
sheets, and the whole impression, the very first day they
can be safely delivered you."

Imperfect? In what way? Curll did not know, for
he had hardly had time to open the bundles ; but I think
he had a shrewd suspicion. I think that to his mind the
almost simultaneous arrival of the 190 copies and the
Messengers from Black Rod would seem to have been
more than a peculiar coincidence. But " Mr. Smythe "

had other instructions to give. " As it is plain," he continued, that " Pope's whole point is only to suppress the books, and find out who gave the letters, you will certainly disappoint him in both, if whatever questions the Lords ask, you will answer no more than thus—that you had the letters from different hands . . . and that as to the originals, many you can show now, and the rest you can very speedily." " The Lords," he concluded, " cannot stop the books above two or three days, if at all . . . and P. T. . . . apprehending injunctions in Chancery might suppress the book, had already printed another title and preface, which throws the publication entirely off you, and might be safely vended in that case. In short, if you absolutely conceal all that has passed between P. T., me, and yourself, you win the old gentleman for ever. For his whole heart is set upon publishing the letters, not so much for this volume, as *in ordine ad* to much more important correspondence that will follow."

More letters, then, if he followed instructions ! But— whose were the instructions ? If Mr. Pope had instigated the enquiry in Parliament—and of that neither P. T. nor himself was in any doubt at all—what were you to think ? Surely no man in his senses would deliberately attempt to suppress his own book ?

On the 14th Curll went again to the House of Lords. The Committee sat, Lord Delawarr in the chair. " After debate in relation to the method of proceeding, the Earl of Ilay acquainted the Committee that he had one of the books at home which was bought at Mr. Curll's ; and that in the 117th page there was a letter to Mr. Jervas which contained, as he apprehended, an abuse of the Earl of Burlington, and his lordship desired that the book laid before the Committee might be looked into for that letter ; but the said book being in sheets, and the pages not to be easily turned to, Mr. Curll was called in, and directed to take the said sheets and fold an entire book, which he having done accordingly, he brought the same and delivered it to the lord in the chair, and then he

withdrew." [1] The letter to Jervas was not to be found.
Curll was recalled, and asked how he came to insert
an advertisement which mentioned letters from peers.
" Says the advertisement was sent him ; he was to take
a copy of it, and put it in the paper. He does not know
from whom it came, but the person who sent it sub-
scribed himself P. T. . . . He is directed to look in
the book which was delivered to the Committee, and
asked whether that book contained the whole of what
he published and sold in pursuance of his advertisement.
Says this book was more than he published, for this has
a preface and title-page, which he never saw before he
came to the Committee." But surely his advertisement
had been definite enough ? Yes, but it was his ignorance
that must be blamed : " he only meant, by correspondents, such persons as had answered the letters ;
and says there is not any letter of any lord printed in
the book. He read every line of the book before he
purchased it." Very well, but what of the copy that my
Lord Ilay had bought in his shop ?

The Committee had better order Black Rod to give
some more copies to the clerk, to see whether the
Jervas letter could be found, and adjourn until to-
morrow.

So far, so good. " Mr. Smythe " wrote at once to
Curll with " hearty congratulations " and further instructions. He had " sure information " that the books
would be restored on the morrow, and the old gentleman was charmed with Mr. Curll's behaviour ; " only
thinks it wrong that he hears you owned the books were
sent to your wife by an unknown hand. This may
induce inquiry and suspicion of some dark transaction,
and be thought shuffling. The Lords will think you
more sincere, and it will have a better air, to say you had
the originals and copies from different hands, and that
some you paid for, some were given you, and you
printed them in your own right. You can suffer no more

---

[1] *Journals* of the House of Lords.

for printing than for publishing them, and the Lords cannot touch a hair of your head."

In this letter, too, for the firſt time, there was a hint as to how some of the letters had come into P. T.'s hands.

" If you observe all the old gentleman's directions," Curll was told, " you will soon be fully acquainted both with his person and designs. In the meantime, to show you he will take off the mask, and clear the *myſterium magnum* you complain of, I have his leave to tell you these things, which he would have writ to you himself, but that his arm is now disabled by rheumatism. He is no man of quality, but conversant with many, and happening to be concerned with a noble lord, a friend of Mr. Pope's, in handing to the press his letters to Wycherley, he got some copies over and above. This incident put firſt into his head the thought of collecting more, and afterwards finding you did not comply in printing his advertisement, he went on with it by himself ; found Cromwell's answers in the same lord's possession, with many others, which he printed as near as possible to correspond with the letter and paper, &c. The alterations he made in some paragraphs, &c., were necessary, the same things being repeated in other letters, either of this or the next volume,—particularly the original of the letter to Mr. Walsh is in his hand."

Wycherley and a noble lord ? Curll, I think, smiled again to himself. It was all rather vague—the information that he had been given, but—what did the reference to Wycherley suggeſt ? Nothing definite perhaps, and yet——

I can imagine him re-reading that letter several times, and I can imagine in what spirit he dashed off his reply to " Mr. Smythe " early next morning. " I am juſt again going to the Lords," he wrote, " to finish Pope. . . . My defence is right. I only told the Lords I did not know from whence the books came, and that my wife received them. This was ſtrict truth, and prevented all further enquiry. The Lords declared that they had been made Pope's tool. . . . Lord Delawarr will be in the chair by ten this morning, and the House will be up before three. I depend that the books and the imperfections will be sent, and believe of P. T. what I hope he believes of me."

To finish Pope! A large order, but, as Elwin says, "he verified his boast. In place of adopting the advice of P. T., he showed the letters which contained it." He answered all questions without trouble, and seems to have enjoyed every moment of the enquiry. Benjamin Motte, writing to Swift a little later, said that "Curll was ruffled for them [the letters] in a manner as, to a man of less impudence than his, would have been very uneasy." Johnson tells us that "Curll appeared at the Bar, and, knowing himself in no great danger, spoke of Pope with very little reverence. *He has*, said Curll, *a knack of versifying, but in prose I think myself a match for him.*" Delicious moment! No unfriendly Lord Chancellor this time to bid him go down on his knees, but an audience of peers, angry with Pope, and willing to believe his own account. And "a knack of versifying"! The phrase could not have been bettered. It was superb. I only wish that we had the whole speech verbatim.

And, of course, the Committee could arrive at only one conclusion. No Standing Order of the House had been infringed. The books must be returned to their owner.

I have no doubt that they sold very quickly indeed.

IV

The preliminaries were over : what was the position ? It was surely a peculiar one. Two sets of books had been delivered, and they were not the same. The identities of both P. T. and "Mr. Smythe" remained hidden, but everything—not least the fact of the books arriving by water—pointed to their being in secret league with the little poet out at Twickenham. It was he, however, who had fathered the House of Lords enquiry, where only one lot of books had been examined, and the enquiry had led to the bookseller's complete vindication. As for the public, what did it think? I imagine that at this time the whole affair was put down to another of Curll's peculiar tricks. Naturally, Mr. Pope would be furious at such unwarranted use of his private correspondence, and so he had complained to the peers. As for these mysterious folk with initials—trust Curll to invent some advertising trick of that sort! Soon enough the real truth would emerge, and—meanwhile there were some very interesting letters to read.

The real truth did not emerge in its entirety until more than a hundred years had gone by, but there were dramatic developments within a very few days. Mr. Pope announced that he had heard of P. T. and the clergyman, who had printed a book parts of which could only have been procured from his library—you note the admission—and offered twenty guineas to either of these persons if they would discover the whole affair. And if either of them could prove that he had acted " by direction of any other, and of what person," he should receive double that sum.

Moreover, on the very day after his speech to the peers Curll had received a letter which showed a complete change of front on the part of P. T.

" I have seen P. T.," wrote the mock-clergyman to him, " from whom I hoped to have had the MSS. But I found him in a very different humour from what I left him. He says you did not follow the instructions he sent you, in not owning the printing . . . further, we are certainly informed that you have named me as the hand that conveyed them. This you have said, that I was a clergyman belonging to C. Church in Southwark. Judge you whether we can think of you as you have reason to think of us, whether this be honourable usage, after you had known what P. T. had done, and what a sum he had paid to get you the whole impression. P. T. had reason to think you would betray him as soon as you had it. Judge, too, if you have done wisely to hazard, by your blabbing, the loss of a future copy of immense value, which I much doubt he will let you have." And then followed a demand for £20 before the missing sheets would be supplied.

So they were threatening him, were they? Threatening to give the sheets elsewhere because he had insisted on speaking the truth in the House of Lords! And who had been betrayed? How could he have betrayed a man whose name he did not know and an elderly shadow? His reply was, as Pope's own biographer calls it, " lofty and defiant."

" Rose-street, past three, Friday, May 16, 1735.
" Sir,
" Ist, I am falsely accused. 2. I value not any man's change of temper; I will never change my *veracity* for falsehood, in owning a fact of which I am innocent. 3. I did not own the books came from *across the water*, nor ever *named you ;* all I said was, that the books came *by water.* 4. When the books were seized, I sent my son to convey a letter to you ; and as you told me everybody knew you in Southwark, I bid him make a strict enquiry, as I am sure you would have done in such an exigency. 5. Sir, *I have acted justly* in this affair, and that is what I shall always think wisely. 6. I will be kept no longer in the dark ; P. T. is *Will o' the Wisp ;* all the books I have had are imperfect ; the first fifty had no titles nor prefaces ; the last five bundles seized by the Lords contained but thirty-eight in each bundle, which amounts to one hundred and ninety, and fifty, is in all but two hundred and forty books. 7. As to the loss of a future copy, I despise it, nor will I be concerned with any more such dark suspicious dealers. But now, sir, I'll tell you what I will do : when I have the *books perfected* which I have already received, and *the rest of the impression*, I will pay you for them. But what do you call this usage? First take a note for a month, and then want it to be changed for one of Sir Richard Hoare's. My note is as good, for any sum I give it, as the Bank, and shall be as

punctually paid. I always say, *gold is better than paper*.[1]
But if this dark converse goes on, I will instantly reprint
the whole book ; and, as a supplement to it, all the
letters P. T. ever sent me, of which I have exact copies,
together with all your originals, and give them in upon
oath to my Lord Chancellor. You talk of *trust*—P. T.
has not reposed any in me, for he has my money and notes
for imperfect books. Let me see, sir, either P. T. or
yourself, or you'll find the Scots proverb verified, *Nemo
ne impune lacessit*.

> " Your abused humble servant
>
> " E. CURLL.

" P.S. Lord O—— and Lord Delawarr I attend this
day. I will sup with you tonight. Where *Pope* has one
lord, I have twenty." [2]

This letter had its effect. If there was one thing that
P. T. wished to avoid at this stage, it was to have his
letters in print. When " Mr. Smythe " wrote again,
there were no more complaints, but a promise that the
rest of the impression should be delivered by the following Thursday. " For I am really tired with this capricious
temper of the old gentleman ; he suspects his own
shadow. I shall leave it to your generosity to consider
me for the copy. I am just sent for to him, and told he is
in a good humour."

But Curll had had nearly enough, and when information reached him that copies of the *Letters* were being
offered surreptitiously to another bookseller, he did not
wait for that Thursday, but at once took the public into
his confidence.

It was done in the grand style. A manifesto to the
Peers of Great Britain was issued. Always would he
remember the justice and honour that their lordships

---

[1] There seems to have been a little misunderstanding on Curll's part with
regard to P. T.'s financial proposals. I presume the trouble had arisen over
P. T.'s desire to remain an enigma.

[2] When Cooper reprinted this letter in Pope's own account of the affair the
postcript was slightly different. Curll tells us that he actually spent the evening
with Lord Haversham. I think the peers must have enjoyed his speech.

had done him. Mr. Pope had said that an evasion was a lie guarded : he was, no doubt, a very modest man, but the peers were to understand that there were times when you could be too modest, hiding away in a background. As for himself, he proposed to publish in a very few days a new edition that should contain all those portions which had been removed from the copies examined by their lordships, and in order to detect, if possible, the contrivers of the gross imposition that had been practised he proposed, by way of supplement, to print all the letters he had received from E. P., P. T., and R. S. Finally he intended to hang Mr. Pope up in effigy, " for a sign to all spectators of his falsity and my own veracity, which I will always maintain."

Magnificent Curll ! But this was not enough. The booksellers must be warned not to poach on his preserves. There was another manifesto for them. If they dared to sell a single copy of the *Letters*, reprisals would be taken in the event of their printing any additions which might not be in his edition.

Here, then, was the clearest assumption of copyright. I do not say whether he was justified or not in uttering the threat, but, at any rate, there it was, and war had been declared.

Almost immediately the conspirators counter-attacked. In a jointly-signed statement, P. T. and R. S. expressed their astonishment at such insolence on the part of Edmund Curll. " We hereby declare," said they, " that neither P. T., much less R. S. his Agent, ever did give, or could pretend to give, any Title whatever, in Mr. POPE'S LETTERS, to the said Edmund Curll, and he is hereby challenged, to produce any Pretence to the Copy whatsoever—— We help'd the said Edmund Curll, to the said Letters, and join'd with him, on Condition he should pay a certain Sum for the Books as he Sold them. . . . Besides which, P. T. was persuaded by R. S., at the instigation of Edmund Curll, to pay the Expense of the whole Impression . . . therefore every Bookseller will be indemnify'd every way, from any possible Prose-

Mr POPE's
Literary Correspondence

For Thirty Years; from 1704 to 1734.

BEING,

A COLLECTION of LETTERS,

Which paſſed between him and

Several Eminent Perſons.

VOLUME the Firſt.

LONDON:

Printed for E. CURLL, in *Roſe-ſtreet, Covent Garden.*

M. DCC. XXXV.

THE FIRST EDITION OF THE LETTERS PRINTED BY CURLL.

[*To face p.* 174.

cution, or Molestation of the said Edmund Curll. And whereas the said Edmund Curll threatens to publish our Correspondence, and as much as in him lies, to betray his Benefactors, we shall also publish *his Letters to* us, which will open a Scene of Baseness and foul Dealing, that will sufficiently show to Mankind his Character and Conduct."

Quite so : but was it not a little odd that P. T. and R. S. should feel themselves able thus publicly to apportion out copyright as they liked, without consultation with Mr. Pope ? Would they be any better entitled than Curll to play the part of aggrieved proprietors ? Undoubtedly, however, the *Letters* themselves were having " a good press." They were having a splendid press. It was announced that " the clergyman concerned . . . hath discovered the whole Transaction." It was announced that an edition of the *Letters* would be published without the " impertinences " of Mr. Curll. It was announced that Curll could have no rights at all. There were all sorts of rival editions. There was a narrative of how the letters had been procured by Curll [1] and another narrative by himself.

And the *Letters* sold. They continued to sell.

And Pope himself ?

Nothing further was said about the twenty guineas. But I may point out that on May 12th he had mentioned the *Letters* to his friend Caryll. " But what makes me sick of writing is the shameless industry of such fellows as Curll, and the idle ostentation, or weak partiality of many of my correspondents, who have shown about my letters (which I never writ but in haste, and generally against the grain, in mere civility, for almost all letters are impertinent further than *Si vales, bene est ; ego valeo*) to such a degree that a volume of 200 or more are printed by that rascal. But he could never have injured me this way, had not my friends furnished him with the occasion by keeping such wretched papers as they ought to have burned."

---

[1] Written by Pope, and full of misrepresentations.

Rather a curious passage to find in a letter from Pope dated May 12th, 1735, for on that day he was most busily engaged with James Worsdale in arranging for large bundles of books to be taken down Thames to Curll.

V

I shall not retrace the steps taken with such infinite care by both Dilke and Elwin to show that P. T. was Pope and no other. It will be enough to give in the roughest outline Pope's own activities in the matter of the *Letters* as revealed by their activities. Pope himself, of course, admitted nothing, but even in his own day it was fairly well understood that if he had not himself engineered the whole business, he was well aware of every step in the negotiations. " It seems," wrote Johnson, " that Pope, being desirous of printing his letters, and not knowing how to do, without imputation of vanity, what has in this country been done very rarely, contrived an appearance of compulsion, that when he could complain that his letters were surreptitiously published, he might decently and defensively publish them himself." There you have the whole thing in the proverbial nutshell. But neither Johnson nor any of his contemporaries, including Curll, ever understood with what astonishing pains the whole fabrication had been built up.

It had been a good move to pick on Curll as the intended victim. " He was an enemy, and could be denounced when he had been deceived. He had printed the letters to Cromwell without the consent of the poet, and it would readily be credited that he had repeated the act. He was not nice in his notions of honour, and he might be expected to catch at an offer, however discreditable, which promised both profit and revenge." [1] Unluckily for his posthumous reputation, he had underestimated the bookseller's ability to take very good care

---

[1] Elwin. Introduction to Pope's *Works*. 1871.

of himself except when the King's Bench authorities were his enemies. . . .

The desire to see in print his letters, carefully edited and if necessarily re-written by himself, was an old one. In 1729 he had had copies made of selected (and edited) portions of his correspondence, and bound them into a volume which he asked his friend Lord Oxford to house in his library. This, he said, was " in case either of the revival of slanders, or the publication of surreptitious letters, during his lifetime or after, a proper use might be made of them." In 1733 Curll's announcement of an intended *Life of Pope* gave him the idea of inventing the shadow P. T.[1] who should approach the bookseller with such material as it would suit him to have printed. Curll had proved rather more cautious than might have been expected, but in 1735 came his letter, whether by chance or design we do not know, and full advantage of it was taken.

And here is the interesting point. Earlier in that same month Pope had written to Lord Oxford for the loan of " the bound volume of copies " which he said he wanted to consult. It was sent him, and probably never returned. Undoubtedly it was not required for a mere consultation, because the originals were in his own possession : but the copies had been already edited, and they were wanted for the edition he had in mind to offer Curll. His refusal to reply in his own person to Curll's letter other than by means of a newspaper announcement now becomes clear. Writing as P. T. he offered the sheets. Curll's excessive caution was annoying, particularly as it led indirectly to that stupid mistake about a feared attack from Twickenham bravoes, but the carefully planned complaint in Parliament—Lord Ilay, by the way, was a friend and neighbour of the poet's—might be calculated to counteract its possible bad effect. Pope must have known that it would fail to inculpate Curll, but " he wished to stimu-

---

[1] " Were it not absurd to pretend to decipher initials, P. T. might be imagined to indicate the name of the owner, as well as his place of abode." D'Israeli, *Quarrels of Authors.*

late indignation, and divert suspicion from himself without interfering with the success of his work, and he conducted the prosecution with so much care to ensure defeat that we may readily credit the assertion of Curll "that the lords declared they had been made Pope's tools." [1] Unfortunately Curll refused to obey orders—on this occasion he even refused to "equivocate pretty genteelly "—and showed R. S.'s incriminating letter to the Lords. It was an awkward business, and led to the "twenty guineas" advertisement which was forced out of the poet, now that it had been shown that certain of the Wycherley letters had been taken bodily from an older book for which he had been responsible. After Curll's announcement, moreover, of his intention to print the "initial" correspondence, there was nothing for Pope to do but to break off all negotiations with him, throw the letters on the market, and do what he could to blacken Curll by issuing a garbled "narrative" of the means whereby those letters had been obtained. He was lucky to forestall the bookseller in this way, but, as Elwin says, "the documents show that the lying and trickery rested with P. T., while the bookseller was veracious in his assertions and straight-forward in his proceedings." It was Curll's boast, he continues, "that falsehood had been his abhorrence throughout the discussion, and he drew vaunting comparisons between Pope's addiction to the vice, and his own detestation of it. His very failings in one direction had helped to sustain his virtue in another. He had too much effrontery to care to descend to duplicity, and it is impossible to read his many controversial manifestoes without perceiving that he was in general as truthful as he was impudent. In the instance of Pope's letters, there is the original blot, that he saw no discredit in publishing papers which he supposed to be purloined ; but he had already avowed the fact before the House of Lords, and the crime was more than shared by P. T. In everything else the acts and language of the

[1] Elwin, *Introduction*, p. xliii.

bookseller contrast favourably with the meanness and falsehoods of his correspondent." [1]

"As truthful as he was impudent." Well, not always perhaps, but certainly in these high days of his fame. I think, however, that he would have appreciated Mr. Elwin's words. The honours were his indubitably, even if the referee was rather late on the scene.

But, after all, did Pope, with his love of dark intrigue, care very much? Did he mind if a rascally bookseller chose to continue with his long-standing campaign of "libels"? Had he not succeeded well enough in his original purpose? And when Curll, with no more P. T.'s to help him, was obliged to dish up old stuff to make further volumes of *Mr. Pope's Literary Correspondence*, had not the poet what an ignorant public would think good cause to insert the following notice in the *London Gazette?*

"Whereas several booksellers have printed several surreptitious and incorrect editions of letters as mine, some of which are not so, and others interpolated; and whereas there are daily advertisements of second and third volumes of more such letters, particularly my correspondence with the late Bishop of Rochester, I think myself under the necessity to publish such of the said letters as are genuine, with the addition of some others of a nature less insignificant, especially those which passed between the said Bishop and myself, or were in any way related to him, which shall be printed with all convenient speed. A. POPE." [2]

VI

It is amusing, and something of a relief, to turn from the poet's astonishing behaviour to Curll's subsequent endeavours to make the most of what he had and to disgruntle his rivals. Anybody buying the five volumes which he issued as Pope's *Literary Correspondence*, will find

[1] Elwin, *Introduction*, p. liv.

[2] I am conscious of some glaring omissions in this section, particularly those which relate to the Atterbury letters, but the curious reader is directed to study Mr. Elwin's masterly *Introduction* in the first volume of his edition of *Pope.*

little enough, after the firſt two, of the poet's letters, but
he will find much about Curll himself and a whole series
of diverting attacks upon Pope. Some people might
choose to take the poet's word againſt his, but he, too,
had friends, and even his enemies would buy his books,
if only to see what new piece of effrontery he had printed
for their entertainment. And never before, I suppose,
had he been in so good a position to provide that entertainment.

The firſt volume of the *Correſpondence*, with its
" initial " supplement, had duly appeared, and it was
followed early in July by a second. Here there are certainly more letters to Pope, if not many written by him,
but—the main objeƈt of the book was to attack the poet,
and attack him it did with no mincing of words. Mr.
Pope, E. P., P. T., and R. S. were " all out of the question," and Mr. Curll was the sole editor. The contents
were " not ſtollen, either from Twickenham, Wimpole
or Dover-ſtreet ; but at the laſt place, while Mr. Pope
was dangling, and making *Gilliver* and *Cooper* his Cabinet-
Counsel, away goes Mr. CURLL, on the 12th Day of June
. . . and by the Assiſtance of that Celebrated Artiſt, Mr.
Rijsbrack, takes a full View of our Bard's Grotto . . .
and his Dog *Bounce*." (What a pity the press photo-
grapher had not yet appeared !) Anybody could see,
wrote the ſtill obliging Philalethes in an *Introduction*, that
Mr. Curll had " fully made good his Promise, to the
Lords, of being a Match for Mr. *Pope* in Prose." " And
he may really say," he concluded, " in regard to all the
Attacks which have been made upon him, *by this petulant
little Gentleman, eſpecially the laſt*, VENI VIDI VICI."

It was, however, in a letter " To Mr. Pope " that the
real attack opened. After penning a pleasant little essay
on the misfortunes of being deformed, Curll proceeded
to outline the proceedings of the laſt two or three months.
I quote from such passages as relate to incidents not
already dealt with in the " initial " correspondence.

" On the 12th of May laſt I published . . . your
Letters, and on the same day, upon your being told by a

gentleman, who saw you in the Court of Requests at Westminster, that it was pretty plain the letters published were no forgeries, you very pertly answered, ' So much the worse.' ' Yes,' replied the gentleman, ' so it is for you, Mr. Pope.' But this, by the bye, sir, was owning them to be genuine." In the Lords, too, he added, Pope had suffered a second defeat, for it had been he who had set in motion that previous attack on his proposed edition of Sheffield's works.

> " Therefore, confess you have a *Tartar* caught
> Be, once, sincere ; and frankly own your Fault."

There followed some good advice, couched in rhyme, and if these and the lines to be found in later volumes of the *Correspondence* were really by Curll, at least it may be said that he " had a knack at versifying."

> " And shall thy Verse to future Age pretend,
> Thou wert *Curll's* Enemy, but now his Friend ?
> That urg'd by thee, He turn'd the tuneful Art
> From Sounds to Things, from Envy to the Heart ;
> For Wit's false Mirror held up Nature's Light ;
> And prov'd the Air of Lying was not Right,"

which shows, at any rate, that he had read the *Essay on Man*.

Whatever might have happened in 1716, he continued, it was now his turn to punish, " and if I have not the Spleen of a warpt Poet, or a *Scots* Medicaster, I will find some other Prescription that shall, once more, as *Shakespeare* says, *harrow up your Soul*." Pope's behaviour, he considered, was on a par with that of a notorious thief who " by his egregious Shuffling " put Mr. Recorder *Lovel* into a violent passion. Sirrah, says he, you have got a Trick of *Denying* what you ought to *Own*, and of *Owning* what you might as well *Deny*. An' please your Honour, quoth *Culprit*, that's the Way *not to be hang'd*. However, impudent Jack was tuck'd up by a fresh Fact proved upon him that very Sessions.

> " Thus if with small, great things may be compar'd,
> Kind Fate, at length, may wait on Thief and Bard."

" Ananias and *Saphyra*," he concluded with fine scorn,
" felt the Divine Vengeance for one Lye ; what then do
your Confederates expect, or justly ought to dread, for
so many as have been told about the Publication of your
Letters ?   The Plot is now discover'd : *Lawton Gilliver*
has declared that you bought of him the Remainder of
the Impression of *Wycherley*'s letters, which he printed,
by your Direction, in 1728, and have printed Six Hundred
of the additional Letters, with those to Mr. *Cromwell*, to
make up the Volume.   Yet still it must be given out that
a Nobleman has been robb'd, and his innocent Servant
must be discarded, to support *Your most flagrant Falshood*.
This, Sir, is *Eating* Shame and *Drinking* after it.   Therefore, if you have any Remorse of Conscience, take Dr.
Arbuthnot's Last Advice, *Study more to* Reform *than*
Chastise, and begin with making yourself the Precedent."

How pleasant to see Curll occupying this high moral
platform !   How pleasant, too, to find him not at all cast
down at the division of the spoils !   In this same volume
occurs the following set of verses :

" CURLL TRIUMPHANT ; AND POPE OUT-WITTED

"Pope, meditating to disgrace
    Those, whom his *Satire* jeers
Not long since to a wildgoose chace
    Entic'd *Great-Britain*'s Peers.

" He led 'em to pursue a Wight
    Egregious—*Curll* his name,
Who not surpriz'd, and in no Fright,
    By this pursuit reap'd Fame.

" He undeceiv'd the *Nobles* all,
    More cou'd he ask or hope ?
While *Pope* had thus contriv'd his Fall,
    He triumph'd over *Pope*.

"The *Vomit* foul, the *Dunciad* keen,
    Vex'd *Curll*—but all admit,
Tho' *Pope* twice *shew'd he had most Spleen*,
    Curll once *has shewn most wit*."

And of course there was a reference to that forty
guineas. A little bill was subjoined :

THE
LIFE
OF THE LATE
RIGHT HONOURABLE
GEORGE
Lord CARPENTER.

SOLDIERS have an undoubted Right to claim,
The greatest Honours, and most lasting NAME.

LONDON. Printed for E. CURLL, 1736.
" AN EXCELLENT VIGNETTE."

[*To face p.* 183.

" Mr. Alexander Pope, Debtor to Mr. Edmund Curll.

To an *Advertisement* in the *Post-Man*, promising Three Guineas to discover the Publisher of his Version of the *First Psalm*	3	3	0
To a Promise of Ten Pounds, on producing one of Bishop *Atterbury*'s Letters .	10	0	0
To discover the *Publishers* of Mr. *Pope's Letters*	42	0	0
Total . . .	53	3	0

Meanwhile Curll's entire business had been transferred to the "printing office" in Rose Street, Covent Garden, and here the new sign of *Pope's Head* was set up. No enemy, indeed, can ever have been of such financial assistance as was Pope to Curll, and the "honour" was surely deserved. The various editions of the *Letters* were still selling merrily, and before the end of the year Curll was advertising a third volume. By this time, however, it had been very generally discovered that all his talk of new materials was but a trick. There might be new material, but not much of it was Pope's. The *Grub Street Journal* bade him beware in a quatrain that was not very polite :

> " C . . l, let me advise you whatever betides,
>   To let this third Volume alone ;
>   The Second's sufficient for all *our* backsides,
>   So pray keep the Third for your *own*."

Out it came, however, with an introductory dialogue, written presumably by Curll—he was doing most of his own " hacking " just now, and I do not blame him, for it must have been much the cheapest way—and suggesting that he might, if he liked, have emulated his " brother " Dodsley, and " scribbled farces " for the stage. Brocade enters the bookshop and informs Curll that he has clearly imposed on the town : for how much of Pope's work had there been in his last volume ? Very little indeed.

Quite so, agrees the bookseller, but " some of my Customers, whose Judgment is much esteemed among their
Acquaintance, have said that Mr. *Pope's* share in this
Second Volume is the very worst Part of the Book." At
this expression of opinion Brocade is shocked, but Curll
remains impenitent. This *is* the kind of book for which
the public asks, and nobody will deny that if it is not all
Pope, the new volume is most entertaining. For will
not Brocade find, in addition to a whole series of most
curious " political " letters from various great statesmen,
a Memorial to that very great lady, the Duchess of
Ormonde ? Will he not have the opportunity of reading of that strange genius the late Mr. Thomas Hearne,
an even greater antiquarian than his biographer ? No,
no, Brocade has no cause to complain—and a copy of
Volume Three will be five shillings, please.

Nevertheless I am afraid that this third volume did not
meet with the success of its predecessors. There were
indignant cries. This, surely, was going too far. The
Grub Street Journal said little, but it printed the following
letter :

"Jan. 8. 1735[/6].

" I have read in your Paper a Letter, dated Oct. 28
complaining of C—— a Bookseller, as guilty of imposing
on the Publick in certain Volumes published with the
Title of Mr. P——'s *Literary Correspondence*. As I take
this to mean a reflection on the *candid* Mr. E—— C——,
I beg leave to say a few words in defence of that eminent
Stationer ; who, far from attempting to impose on any
one, hath ingenuously prefix'd *his* Name to every Book
which he hath publish'd ; besides a pretty Picture of the
Initial Letters E. C. curiously interwoven in Cyphers ;
and who cannot be said to have deceived any *one* Purchaser. Since who is there in the Kingdom that sees Mr.
C——'s Name in the Title Page, and is not from that
circumstance enabled to form a perfect judgment of the
Book.

" I am your humble servant,

" D. D."

Yet a fourth volume, of much the same kind, appeared in the following year, and a fifth and last in 1737. From this I take Curll's letter " to my Subscribers encore " and his longest set of verses, and leave the *Correspondence* to look after itself.

" Gentlemen,

" Having, as you All know, honestly Purchased the First Volume of Mr. Pope's Literary Correspondence of his Agent the Reverend Mr. Smith ; Published and paid my Respects to my Benefactor in the Second ; Dispatched Brocade and Tim Lancet in the Third ; and, Got rid of the Shifters in the Fourth ; I now come to give you a just Account of the Contents of this Fifth Volume.

" Beside, what is here presented to You, I have Several other very valuable Originals in my Custody, which, with these, were Transmitted to me from Ireland. And this Volume will be closed with whatever additional Letters Mr. Pope shall think fit to insert in his Works in Prose, now printing in Quarto,[1] Price a Guinea ; but the Controversy between Me and Mr. Pope will never be ended till the Eyes of one of Us are closed (I mean by Death, not by Dr. Taylor) : if mine are open longest, to the last Volume of Literary Correspondence shall be prefix'd A faithful Account of Mr. Pope's Life and Writings, with a True Copy of his Last Will and Testament, if he makes one.[2]

" I am, Gentlemen,

" Your obliged

" Humble Servant

" E. Curll.

" 5 Nov.

" 1736."

---

[1] Curll had made good his threat to take all measures to protect what he called his own copyright. At this time he was engaged on a law-case with Dodsley and others, the details of which, however, are not too easy to understand.

[2] See Chap. Ten.

His verses took the form of a " Parodie " on the Imitation of the Second Epistle of the Second Book of Horace, which Pope had recently issued.

> " Pleasingly, Sir, you *Horace* still pursue ;
> And I as pleasingly still follow you.
> Dear Mr. *Pope* your Own, not Countrys Friend,
> You rapture as with ev'ry Verse you send ;
> But turn your *Frenchman* and his *Boy* adrift,
> And with one Shirt let Man and Master shift ;
> Let 'em at *Blois* their Services record,
> Such Raggamuffins ill befit a Lord.
> The Town still judge you in a proper light,
> Whether Lampoons or Letters you indite ;
> *Sober Advice* from *Horace* you have giv'n,
> Yet disavow it in the face of Heav'n.
> To this and other Points your[e] quite excentric,
> Till you put in the Claim, then All's Authentic.
> The Case being stated thus 'twixt you, and I,
> You've here the Instance, now let me apply.
> Two Years ago, by Jesuitic-Arts,
> I was, poor Culprit, Game for Men of Parts ;
> But whether I have been the Hunt or not,
> I'll frankly leave to *Wilcox* and to *Motte*,
> Your New Associates, Brothers of the Quill,
> Who push'd the Fate of your Depending Bill,
> The One was Typographically bred,
> T'other to any Craft can turn his Head.
> But what have *Tonson, Lintot, Lawton*, done
> That you to Brindley, Corbet, Dodsley run ?
> 'Tis kind indeed a Liv'ry Muse to aid,
> Who scribbles Farces to augment his Trade.[1]
> Where *You* and *Spence*, and *Glover* drive the Nail
> The Devil's in it if the Plot should fail.
> From you to ask a Verse can be no Crime,
> The only thing you're good for is to Rime.
> The Story you of Anna's Days have told,
> Of a Pot-Valiant Soldier poor and old,
> May serve at *Chelsea-College* for Chit-Chat,
> Each Invalid there knows what you'd be at.
> And if such pretty Stories you'll rehearse,
> A Jest-book will sell very well in Verse.
> It was for *Lintot*'s Gold that you begun
> To rime from Greek the Wrath of *Peleus*' Son.

---

[1] Robert Dodsley had begun his career as a footman. He had written *A Muse in Livery* and one or two successful farces.

Rest to your Father's Soul : who from a Lad,
Taught you the Art to know the Good from Bad.
All Laws by Those who smart are thought unjust,
Thieves only swing poor Souls for Breach of Trust.
The Pious hopes of Papists still will fail,
Whilst *Brunswick* Rules and *Hardwick* holds the Scale.
Thro' Life you may enjoy true Peace of Mind,
Poet's-Convict, are neither Tax'd nor Fin'd.
With what your Muse brings in *per annum* clear,
No Prince or Peer alive, will interfere.
Repose, or scribble, be assur'd that Time,
Will part ev'n you and me, and snatch your Rime.
And ev'ry Wheel of the Satyric Mill
That turns your daily Libels must stand still.
You never can Relapse, for want of Grace
Is stampt upon your Soul where'er the Place.
Before the Lords whene'er your Case comes on,
If Pop'ry be the Theme you'll be undone.
And much you'll suffer, if you don't in Bounds,
Keep in your spleenetic, ill-manner'd Sounds.
Let me with *Arbuthnot* your Friend advise,
Study to mend Mankind but not chastise,
Much you can flatter when the Whim does bite,
This all your Patrons know to whom you write.
This Maxim's true, all Mankind will reject,
Malevolence, not Treat it with respect.
There liv'd *in primo Georgij* they record,
Sev'ral Large-Paper-Dupes, and each a Lord ;
Who in the Senate-House, and in their own,
Thought you an *Homer*, *Milton* but a Drone.
Howe'er 'tis granted that in bounds to roll,
You can make Thoughts keep Measure with the Soul.
    Thus, for your Sake, Sir, I have play'd the Fool,
As Boys make random Verses when at School,
And when you offer any thing that's New
Wagging must be my Quill, and so Adieu.
" E. Curll."

CHAPTER TEN

THE OLD FELLOW STILL IN GRUB STREET (1737–1747)

Peace be with Curl—with him I wave all strife,
Who pens each felon's, and each actor's life.

Richard Savage, *On False Historians*.

I

EVERYBODY knows that the rowdy youngster with leanings towards theoretical anarchism as often as not ends his days as the stateliest Tory. In the same way the ex-rake will deceive himself into believing that wisdom alone has been responsible for putting a period to his earlier excesses. It is all very pleasant, and you expect an old gentleman to be decently mellow. A quiet twinkle in the eye, a twitch at the lips, perhaps a deprecatory wave of the hand—you know that it was not ever thus, and feel that all is just as it should be.

Well, it may be regrettable, but I can find no change in the elderly Curll. True, he recedes appreciably from the public gaze, and I dare say a fair proportion of his time may have been spent, peacefully and respectably, in his Peckham garden. We know, too, that he " died penitent." But almost to the end of his days he seems to have carried on in much the old way, ever nosing round —I can think of no better words—for private papers and letters, routing out scandals, occasionally indulging in a newspaper squabble. His new books are much fewer in number, but they become " curiouser and curiouser." Finally there is his masterpiece of impudence, the *Memoirs of Pope*. I find nothing in the way of a desire for a rather different reputation, and there are no new respectably solid " antiquity " books. The old impudence persists, and the old underground methods : inci

BOOKS

Printed for *E. CURLL,*

At *POPE's-HEAD,*

In *Rose-Street,* *Covent-Garden.*

HE Philological Works of the Learned Dr. *Burnet,* Mafter of the *Charter-Houfe.* In Five Volumes, 8*vo.* viz. I. *Archæologiæ Philofophicæ:* Or, the Ancient Doctrine concerning the *Originals* of *Things.* Faithfully tranflated into *Englifh* from the *Latin,* with Remarks thereon. By *Thomas Foxton* of *Witham,* in *Effex,* Gent. PART I. Being a Critique on the *Mofaic* Creation, 8*vo.* Price 3 *s.*

II. The *Second Part* of *Archæologiæ Philofophicæ.* Containing a Theory of the *Vifible World*; by way of Commentary on his *Theory of the Earth,* with Remarks by Mr. *Foxton.* To which is added, *The Immobility of the* Earth demonftrated, *by Reafons drawn from the eftablifhed Rules of Phyfics, Mechanics, and Geometry: Proving the* Earth *to be in the Center of the Univerfe*; *and that all the* Celeftial Bodies *perform their* Diurnal Motions *round the* Earth, *and not round the* Sun; *in Oppofition to the* Solar Syftem. Written in *French* by Monfieur *Ionchere.* Made *Englifh* by Mr. *Morgan.* Price 3 *s.*

III. *Doctrina Antiqua de Rerum Originibus:* Or, An Enquiry into the Doctrines of the Philofophers of all Nations, concerning the ORIGINAL of the WORLD. Tranflated by Mr *Mead* and Mr. *Foxton.* To which is prefix'd, An Account of the Life and Writings of Dr. *Burnet.* Price 6 *s.*

IV. *De Statu Mortuorum & Refurgentium Tractatus.* A Treatife of the STATE of the DEAD, and of THOSE that are to RISE. Tranflated from Dr. *Burnet's*

A

THE 1735 CATALOGUE.

[*To face p.* 188.

dentally, too, his weakness for bishops. When Warburton became Bishop of Gloucester and the literary executor of Pope, there were several youthful lucubrations of his that he naturally wished should be wholly forgotten. The rights in one of these, an enquiry into the causes of prodigies and miracles, were offered to Curll, and he bought them. Warburton has left on record the fright he was in when the usual letter asking for " corrections " reached him. " A few years before Curll's death," he told his friend Hurd, " he wrote me a letter to acquaint me that he had bought the property of *my excellent Discourse* ; and that as it had long been out of print, he was going to reprint it ; only he desired to know if I had any additions or alterations to make, he should be glad of the honour of receiving them. The writer, and the contents of his letter, very much alarmed me ; so I wrote to Knapton, to go to the fellow, and buy my own book of him again, which he did ; and so ended this ridiculous affair, which may be a warning to young scribblers." And I do not doubt but that there were others who found themselves in much the same predicament. There had been no illegality, but—how annoying to have the fellow playing grave-digger in this way ! Bishops, too, have to be extra-careful about such things, even though laymen can take risks. A few of such lesser folk, I imagine, told Curll to publish and be damned, for by this time they would have realized that the world knew the kind of book that was likely to be issued from *Pope's Head* in Rose Street, but even they cannot have felt too easy. You never *quite* knew—where Curll was concerned.

Yes, I am afraid that the bookseller was rather a nasty old man. Perhaps it was his way of showing disappointment. He had had his successes, but I do not suppose that at any time he was a really rich man. Besides, there was Henry, who had not fulfilled expectations. I have an idea that Henry wanted to have his father's good time without sharing his father's capacity for hard work. He did very little indeed, and faded out before his time. In

which year he died I do not know—probably 1740—
but he does not seem to have been greatly regretted. In
1742 Curll added a codicil to his will, and being by this
time a tried rhymer, put it in verse :

> " I have no relatives, my son is dead,
> He left no issue, and his wife 's rewed ;
> Therefore no legacies at all I leave,
> But all I've got to my dear wife bequeathe."

We catch a glimpse of him about this time in Lætitia
Pilkington's *Memoirs*. The lady had fallen on rather evil
days, and was in dire need of money. She had written
to John Barber, that printer-friend of Swift's who became Lord Mayor of London, for assistance which was
only proferred after she had exerted a little Curllean
pressure. It came to nothing, but people must have
known of her difficulties, for one day she received a
strange visitor.

A short time after her disappointment with Barber,
she tells us, " my Landlady told me, there was an ugly
squinting old Fellow, who said he had Business of the
utmost Consequence, and must speak to me ; I bid her
shew him up, and found he answered her Description ;
he asked me, was my Name *Meade?* I said, yes ; why
then, said he, I am come to inform you, that there is a
Legacy of five hundred Pounds left you by one Mr. *Clark*,
who died last Week at *St. Edmonsbury*, but the Lady I
was ordered to enquire for is Mr. P——n's Wife ; are
you the Person ? I told him the Direction was very right,
but that I neither was related to, nor even acquainted
with any Person of the Name of *Clark*, from whom I had
the smallest Reason to hope for such a Favour : Nay,
Madam, returned he, as you have changed your Name,
why may not he ? Upon this, he shewed me a Letter, to
my Fancy authentic, wherein I was desired, if living, to
wait on Counsellor *Clark* in *Essex-Street* in the Strand,
who had Orders to pay me the Money, on Proof I was
Mrs. *Pilkington*.

" I knew not what to make of all this ; I was in hopes

the fickle Goddess, who is well represented standing on a Wheel, was, for once, in a Good Humour with me, and was resolved to make me amends for her former Caprice, or, to speak more seriously, that the Supreme Almighty Being, that Power, who

> *Builds Life on Death, on Change Duration founds,*
> *And gives th' eternal Wheels to know their Rounds,*

had taken Compassion on my Sufferings.

" While I was lost in musing on this odd Adventure, the old Fellow asked me very gaily, if I would give him my Company to *Richmond*, and take a Dinner with him ? I told him I never went abroad with persons I did not know, especially Men ; he told me, he was very capable of being serviceable to me, and that it was also in my Power to be so to him ; in what, Sir ? Why, I have received from Ireland, from your Husband, the Life of Alderman *Barber*, wherein there is an Account of the Amours of *Cadenus* and *Vanessa*, to which the Alderman was privy, and related them to Mr. P——n : Now I have been informed you have some Letters of the Dean's, which may embellish the Work ; and also a true Character of the Alderman, written by his Chaplain ; I will make you a handsome Consideration for them, if you will give them to me to publish.

" This Discourse surprized me almost as much as the first ; I therefore begged he would not hold me any longer in Suspence, but let me know who I conversed with ? He answered his Name was *Edmund Curl*, upon which, in spite of Vexation, and the Disappointment of my new-born Hope, I could not forbear laughing at the fine Scheme he had laid, to trick me out of any valuable Manuscripts I might possibly possess ; so making him a Courtesy, I said, Farewel, Legacy !

" I should not trouble the Reader with this Story, but that I have been charged with writing the Life of the Alderman ; and, as I shall answer it to God, I never even saw it in my Life, not but Curiosity would have engaged me to read it, especially as I heard it was very

well wrote ; but at the Time it was published, I was a
Prisoner in the *Marshalsea*, and really had not a Crown
to spare for a Book.

"As Mr. *Curl* swore heartily, that his Letter, with
regard to the Legacy, was genuine, I went the next Day
to Counsellor *Clark* ; there was indeed an old Gentleman
of his name newly dead, at *St. Edmonsbury*, who had
Children and Grandchildren, Heirs at Law, sufficient to
inherit his Fortune, and, as it happened, he died inteſtate.

"However I comforted myself that Mr. *Curl* had not
made a Fool of me, as he has done of many a better
Writer, and secured me a Prisoner in his poetical
Garret. . . ."

There, I suppose, you have the real Curll. He hears
that a lady is in misfortune. He believes that she has
valuable papers. He knows that she is a poetess of some
little standing, and a friend of Swift's. He gains admittance by an inexcusable trick, and knowing that her
reputation is none of the beſt, immediately suggeſts a
little outing to Richmond. He takes the natural rebuff
as a matter of course, and proceeds to business. Nothing
comes of it, and off he goes. But something might have
come of it, and who can say that he did not go to great
pains to make his forthcoming Life of Alderman Barber
a model of biographical care ?

II

If, however, he was unsuccessful with Mrs. Pilkington,
he had rather better luck with her old patron Swift. At
this time Faulkner was projeċting an edition of the
Dean's works, and had ready a volume of his letters.
Any new " literary correspondence " of Pope's was now
beyond Curll's reach, but a whole colleċtion of the
Dean's letters would be a prize indeed. Somehow he
managed to get hold of an advance copy of the Dublin
book, and with a single addition of his own, reprinted
it as *Dean Swift's Literary Correſpondence* with something
of his old-time flourish. Pope himself had not been

JONATHAN SWIFT
Engraved by Andrew Miller from the portrait by Francis Bindon

[*To face p.* 192

forgotten and certainly not forgiven, and in the usual impudent preface there came a further attack.

" A Late honourable Writer," he wrote, " has most judiciously remarked, that, it is a Liberty peculiar to Libellers, to turn Truth into Lyes by False insinuations. The Public have seen many Instances of this kind verified by Alexander Pope, Esq ; in the Conduct of several of his Performances.

" As to the present Case, it is well known, that the Dublin Edition of these Letters is Lawful-Prize here, and whatever we print is the same there.   The safe Hand to whom Dean Swift delivered them, conveyed them safely to Us ; so that all the Pretences of sending a Young Peer to go in Search of them, or the Attempts by an old Woman to suppress them, was arrant Trifling.   Many false Insinuations therein are fully refuted in our Notes ; and we have also given a Clavis to the whole. . . .

" Mr. Pope's mean Artifice of taking eight Old Pieces and one New one, for the Sake of a Guinea, or even Half-a-one, is scandalously mean, and may be thus justly reprehended :

" Pope will at length, we hope, his Errors own,
'Tis Curll *diverts*, but Pope defrauds the Town."

Well, he certainly had something to offer this time—eighty-eight letters, no less.   There were not many notes ; but to one at least attention may be drawn.   Writing to Swift on November 28th, 1729, Pope had written : " I smile to think how Curll would be bit, were our Epistles to fall into his Hands, and how gloriously they would fall short of every ingenious Reader's Expectations."   Curll, I think, must also have smiled when he read the words. His comment was short.   " Booksellers, as well as Books," says he, " have their Fate.   I am content with mine."

Just so : and one imagines that he was even more content with his Fate when at the end of 1744 he had fulfilled an old promise and compiled—with or without help I would not care to say—a life of his bitterest enemy. There could be no more emetics and no more Dunciads now, for Pope was dead, and he let himself go. When the *Memoirs* appeared, they filled more than seven hundred pages !

Imagine it ! Seven hundred pages of a Curllean Life, with nothing that was new, and little that he had not himself said many times before ! Not a page that could be of the slightest value to posterity, except, perhaps, as a warning. Amongst the hundred worst books the *Memoirs* must be given a high place—though not, I hasten to add, so much for what they contain as for what they are alleged to be. If Curll had called them *A Miscellany of Excerpts from Many Pieces in Prose and Verse Printed (Generally more than Five Times) during the Last Forty Years, with Some Account of the Various Attacks made upon Mr. Pope*, nobody could have objected : but when he asked the world to accept his work as a *Life* of anybody, he stepped on to the highest rung of the ladder of misrepresentation.

It is amusing to observe what precautions were adopted to hide his own connection with the work, which when it appeared in two very neat volumes on January 8th, 1745, bore all the outward marks (except one) of being thoroughly official and of the most superlative importance. The title alone was sufficiently impressive : *Memoirs of the Life and Writings of Alexander Pope*, but there was a novel addition to the advertisement. All unexpectedly the Royal Arms appeared at the top, with the announcement that " By Virtue of a Patent under His Majesty's Royal Signet " William Ayre, Esq. had been granted " our Royal Licence for the Sole Vending the said Work, for 14 Years, and so the Master, and Wardens and Company of Stationers are to take Notice." Heavens ! how could they help taking notice ? Obviously here was the most important book that had been published since Shakespeare's First Folio, and if the Bishop of Gloucester, whose modest announcement of a forthcoming work of a similar nature had appeared only the day before, thought that he could hope to rival it, he must be vastly mistaken.

And yet there was one small factor about this regal production which was slightly puzzling. "William Ayre, Esq."? Curious : one did not seem to have heard the name. He must necessarily be an intimate private friend of the dead poet, and possibly averse from the public's gaze, but—had he written anything before ? And had he been mentioned in any of those numerous volumes of Mr. Pope's Letters with which the town had been deluged ? It was very singular, but not the smallest reference to the gentleman could be found. Then who was he ? The *Memoirs* themselves might provide a clue : better buy the two volumes and see.

So they bought, and saw. . . .

Fortunately for us, at least one purchaser was sufficiently angry to put his thoughts into print. The author of *Remarks on 'Squire Ayre's Memoirs* signed his initials, J. H., but gave no further clue to his identity.[1] He addressed his *Remarks* to " Friend Edmund " and included " Authentic Memoirs " of the bookseller's own life. And here you have the last attack on Curll during his lifetime.

Naturally the disgruntled buyer is first of all concerned with the title-page of " this surprising Performance." " You," says he, " who, it must be own'd, are as good a Judge of Title-Pages (however little you concern yourself about the rest of a Book) as any Man, I mean of Title-Pages that will bring Customers, must have known that the whole *English* Language could not have furnished you with a Set of Words more proper to engage a Multitude of Purchasers than *Memoirs of the Life of Mr. Pope.*" He concedes, however, the great wisdom shown in concealing real names. " So well," he admits, " have you in this Affair top'd your Part, as the Phrase is, so much outdone your usual Self, by the bold Venture of the Royal Patent, that I acknowledge even myself who know you so well, to have been over-reach'd by you in this, to have bought the Work without the least suspicion of your being concern'd in it."

[1] " Orator " Henley, do you think ?

The name of Mr. William Ayre, he continues, is strange ; but then so was the name of an earlier William —the Mr. Egerton who wrote of Mrs. Oldfield, and in that connection perhaps it has escaped Friend Edmund's notice that " the Gentlemen of the *Pegasus* at *Grubstreet* begin one of their Memoirs in these Words : *An Abridgement of faithful Memoirs of the Life, Amours,* &c *of Mrs.* Anne Oldfield, *by* William Egerton, *Esq ; alias* Edmund Curl, *Bookseller.*"

As for these 'Squires, he thinks, surely the world could do with a few more of them, for their views on biography are so refreshingly original. No knowledge of your subject required, and no silly qualms about a little inaccuracy here and there. " I cannot but lament their not having become sufficiently numerous in the Days of the *Dunciad,*" for in that case " I doubt not they would have set foremost in the Rank of Fame, and that *Curl's* 'Squires had made a much greater Figure there than his *Pindars* and his *Miltons.*"

The patent, however, was a really brilliant idea. It reminds him of a story told of King Charles II. His Majesty was invited to witness the daring exploit of a fellow who could climb up the outside of a church to the topmost point of the steeple. He witnessed the performance, and, on the suggestion that its hero should be given some suitable reward, gave him a patent that prevented anybody else mimicking his feat.

But of course the book had been written only for " the dear Thirst of Gain," and 'Squire Ayre had had to be born in order to prevent the " loud Laugh " which would have greeted an announcement that Edmund Curll was the author. Serious criticism, too, is out of the question for such " an injudicious Jumble of Extracts " and such fatuous praise for old dullards. Yet there is one feature about it that calls for comment. " How came you," he asks, " among all these Characters . . . so long, so tiresome, and unnecessary, how came you to be so short and so imperfect in that one so greatly interesting and so necessary, that of your dear Friend, and, without a Figure, inseparable Companion Mr. *Edmund Curl?*" A bare half page! Surely this is the most inexcusable neglect?

And so we are given the " Authentic Memoirs " of Curll himself. Unfortunately they are little more than the old Popian satires rewritten. The bookseller, he solemnly declares, " shew'd an early Inclination to Letters, and Plagiarism," finding " Bawdry " much to his liking. At the age of twelve he compiled a Life of the parson of his parish, " and not judging it safe to appear as the Author of it, he hir'd a lubberly Boy of a neighbouring School, to write it over his own Hand, and say he had been the Author of it." His grandmother had sent him off to become a bookseller, and already in his 'prentice days he had carried the Trade to greater lengths than it had ever been carried before. (What *had* happened in the days of Richard Smith ?) Afterwards— but I need not continue. J. H. has nothing new to tell us. Already, in 1745, however, we find a writer making the mistake of supposing that the bookseller had stood in the pillory for printing *The Nun in her Smock.*

Poor old Curll! I cannot think that 'Squire Ayre's masterpiece enjoyed much of a sale. There was no reply to J. H.,[1] and no second edition of the *Memoirs.* The book was not even advertised under another name. True, for a while, there came a little spurt of energy, and a few other books made their appearance ; but Curll, I fancy, must have been a tired man now. Perhaps his eyes were giving him trouble, and Pope was dead, and times were changing, and new rivals were springing up to seize the young poets as they came up to town from Oxford and Cambridge, and they were becoming stupidly strict about questions of copyright, and there was nothing particular that he wanted to do. He had lived his life, and been cursed and abused, and had a good time, and

[1] Though a bluffing attempt was made. " We hear that the Author of the *Remarks on 'Squire Ayre's Memoirs* . . . having therein grossly reflected on William Ayre Esq. ; and Mr. Edmund Curll, Bookseller, they are determined to prosecute him with the utmost severity the Law prescribes." *Daily Advertiser,* Feb. 4th, 1745. But what *could* be done ?

done all sorts of odd things, and made and lost money, and—who was ignorant these days of the name of Curll?

A very tired old man, I think. . . .

III

Is there anything more to be said? A neat vignette of the man to round off these chapters in the conventional way? No, that belongs to the biography proper. But there is one little discovery of mine that must be mentioned. It is a very pleasant discovery indeed. I do not know how or when the thing came about, but for some years at any rate they called one of those alleys that led off from the Strand *Curll's Court*.[1] I wish I knew at what date the compliment was paid him. After his death? I expect so. But I should like to think that Mrs. Curll was able to tell him about it as he lay dying, for in that case I can imagine him laughing as loudly as his ebbing strength would permit. But he would have been vastly pleased all the same. It is not everybody who has a Court named after him. . . .

He died, by the way, on a Tuesday, December 8th, 1747, and they buried him on the Sunday night.

One day I must look for his grave.

---

[1] *London and its Environs*, 1761.

PART II

THE BOOKS

A HANDLIST

(1706–1746)

I CAN imagine that the more scientifically-minded bibliographer will be infuriated by the handlist that follows. It is not complete, in parts it is vague, and some of the notes may be considered to be unnecessarily facetious. I shall not complain if he comes to believe that a little of Curll's impudence has descended on to his biographer, and I shall have nothing to say if he accuses me of " optimistic inaccuracy."

But Curll was a peculiar man, and so the handlist is peculiar. It is odd, to say the least of it, to find that a book which prints the names of half the second-rate booksellers in London on its title-page, and has nothing to say about Curll, should really be his publication. Yet such is often the case. It is odd to find books with title-pages wholly dissimilar turning out to be the same. Yet such is also the case. And at every turn come difficulties which I feel that no amateur like myself ought ever to be pitted against. The odds are too heavy.

Undoubtedly Curll advertised his books with marked regularity in the newspapers, but he rarely advertised a particular book in the same way for more than a very few weeks, and as often as not the books he advertised neither bear his name nor show any connection with him. He seems to have sold whole editions to other booksellers when he became tired of stacking them in his shop, and he bought old sheets which were given no more than a fresh title-page to become what on the face of it seem to be entirely new books. He would announce a book for publication " next week," and, as far as I can see, that would often be the end of it. He would publish old books as new, delightfully disguised in the advertisements, and if I do not happen to have seen them myself, I am reduced to the necessity of exercising such imagination as I happen to possess. There are entries, I admit, which are more than doubtful, but I pride myself on others which have really earned their place only after the most prolonged Sherlockian experiments. Incidentally you must not forget that in addition to Curll's playful habit of hiding behind some wretched pamphlet-seller, it would often happen that two rival publications (neither of them more than semi-legitimate) would appear in the same week, and lead to a wordy warfare, and it is not always possible to probe deeply enough to find out which was Curll's. (He was quite capable of sponsoring both!)

As a general rule, it may be taken that if nothing is said to the contrary, an entry was actually advertised by Curll as his. So often, however, he advertised but once, and that perhaps in some fifth-rate journal, that I dare say the gravest omissions may be discovered. (How jolly for the discoverers!) There are certain to be found editions with dates other than those here ascribed, for Curll was fond of altering his titles ; but what, after all, is a mere date—outside the auction-rooms? In the same way, the bookseller's habit of stitching two or more pamphlets together, and printing a general title, may have given birth to a whole library of books which seem to be altogether ignored in my list. And then there is the question of post-dating. You may look for a book in its proper year, and not find it. Do not despair. Look back : you may find it in the previous November or even July !

To be candid, I confess that at times I have simply " let things go." With the best will in the world, it is impossible, I have found, to say that this is Curll's and that is not. In fact, there have been moments when even I, who believe that for a hobby to be really engrossing it must be quite useless, have felt that I may have been wasting my time. For the boundaries of Curlland are misty and vague. I dare say that annoyance at the poor

view has led to hasty conclusions and even false statements. I may even have been guilty of " howlers."
(But what fun if I have !)

But I have formed one or two rules for myself. If a
bookseller's name in brackets follows a title, he is mentioned in a newspaper advertisement. If no brackets
surround him, he has actually been seen on a title-page.
The books are shown in a chronological sequence, and
if no advertisement has been found, they are grouped
together at the end of the year. I have included Henry
Curll's books and the books *about* Curll on the assumption that he was not uninterested in their sale, but I have
not printed all the " Lists of Books " that are so frequently bound in with his publications. Authors' names
appear first, except in the case of Wills, not because I
suspect the wills of having been forged, but because they
are so often found with a *Life* or *Remains*.

The usual abbreviations are used. P.B. Post Boy,
P.M. Post Man, F.P. Flying Post, D.C. Daily Courant,
D.J. Daily Journal, E.P. Evening Post, W.E.P. White-
hall Evening Post, S.J.E.P. St. James's Evening Post,
D.P. Daily Post, G.S.J. Grub Street Journal, G.A.
General Advertiser, G.E.P. General Evening Post,
L.E.P. London Evening Post, C. Craftsman, D.A. Daily
Advertiser, B.M. British Museum.

1706

Feb. 28.   *Bibliotheca Harrisoniana.* Catalogue of an auction held
at the Temple-Change Coffee-House. To be had gratis
of various booksellers, including " Mr. Curl at the
Peacock near St. Clement's Church."

      Possibly without his name, though on Mar. 1st only
Curll's name is given as the man who will supply the
catalogue.

Mar. 14.   *The Athenian Spy*, with the Way of a Man with a Maid.
The Second Edition. " Sold by J. Baker . . . And
Edm. Curll." *2s. 6d.* (D.C.)

      This is not the book of a nearly identical title, of
which a second edition was " Printed for R. H. and
Sold by Samuel Ballard " in 1709, but what it was I do
not know. Probably a top-shelf book, but only of

interest inasmuch as, so far as I know, it is the first book in which Curll " had a share."

June 22.   *A Letter to Mr. Prior.* Occasioned by the Duke of Marlborough's late Victory at Ramilly. " W. D. for E. Curll." Fo. 6*d.*
Publication apparently shared with Benjamin Bragge. (D.C.)

Oct. 24.   Catalogue of a Collection of Books . . . to be Sold at the Marine Coffee House.

Nov. 4.   [WARREN (REV. ROBERT)] *The Devout Christian's Companion.* (Charles Smith.) 2*s.* 6*d.* (D.C.)
Several times reprinted. A 2nd part afterwards added (q.v.).

Nov. 27.   *Bibliotheca Selecta.* Catalogue of an auction. (D.C.)

Dec. 18.   Catalogue of an auction. (D.C.)
CÆSAR. *Commentaries,* made English, by Capt. [Martin] Bladen. " Second Edition, Improv'd." " Printed for R. Smith . . . and sold by Charles Smith . . . and E. Curll." 8vo. Cuts.
The first edition had appeared in the previous year. Where the improvements are to be found remains a mystery, but Curll may have considered that the new title-page was sufficient improvement.
Not apparently advertised in the newspapers until 3rd July, 1707, when other booksellers' names are mentioned in place of the Smiths.

1707

Jan. 31.   PRIOR (MATTHEW). *Poems on Several Occasions.* Burrough, Baker. 8vo. 2*s.* 6*d.* (B.M.)
The first, though unauthorized, edition, now very valuable. Contains two poems afterwards disowned by Prior, but undoubtedly his. Various other booksellers' names appear in the advertisements. (See Text.)
Four books are advertised at the end of this volume as printed for the three booksellers, but they probably do not bear Curll's name, and I dare say he had nothing to do with them. They are :
A Collection of Divine Hymns and Poems. By the Earl of Roscommon and others. 8vo. 2*s.* 6*d.*
LLOYD (E.) *Sacred Miscellanies.* 12mo. 1*s.*
The Life of Leopold the late Emperor of Germany. 5*s.*
Prince Eugene ; An Heroic Poem on the Progress of the Confederate Arms in Italy. 6*d.*

Mar. 10.   *A List of Horse-Matches* to be run at Newmarket. (Morphew, Deard.) 2*d.* (D.C.)
Showing thus early Curll's healthy sporting instincts.

Mar. 12. Catalogue of the Library of Wm. Dormer, Gent.

? PETRONIUS. *Satyricon cum Fragmentis.* " Typis J. N. Impensis Galf. Wale . . . Edm. Curll." 12mo. 1s. 6d. Frontispiece and nine other plates added later.

The first edition actually printed in England, Curll thus forestalling his biographer by two hundred and three years. It is possible that Curll had an interest in Bragge's edition of *The Satirical Works*, made English by Wilson, Burnaby, and others, which appeared in the following year, but his advertisements are sometimes so vague that it is impossible to tell which particular book he means.

Mar. 27. [WARREN (REV. ROBERT).] *The Devout Christian's Companion.* The Second Edition. 2s. 6d. (London Gazette.)

Here, as elsewhere, the word " second " is probably to be taken in its Pickwickian sense.

June 16. *The Danger and Folly of Evil Courses ;* Being a Practical Discourse shewing the Base and Vile Nature of Sin. . . . 1s. 6d. (D.C.)

Which Curll no doubt read more than once.

June 16. S. (S.) *The Republican Conclave ;* Or, the Present State of Whiggism in England. . . . 1s. (D.C.)

At this time Curll was a good Tory.

July 16. Catalogue of an Auction of Books at Tom's Coffee-House. (P.B.)

Aug. 28. CASA (GIOVANNI DELLA). *The Compleat Accomplish'd Gentleman.* . . . Done from the Italian . . . and suited to our *English* Customs. 1s. 6d. (P.B.)

Possibly a reprint of *The Refin'd Courtier* printed for R. Royston in 1679.

? WILMOT (JOHN, EARL OF ROCHESTER) &c. *The Works.* . . . With a Collection of Original Poems. To which is prefix'd Memoirs . . . by Monsieur St. Evremont. The Second Edition. 8vo. 5s. Portrait. The publication was shared by Curll and Bragge, and there are two title-pages known, each bearing but one bookseller's name. Both editions advertise on the last page of text five books, none of which, however, is separately advertised by Curll. These are :

The Jilted Bridegroom.

WARD (EDWARD.) *The Secret History of the Calves Head Club.*

Memoirs of Robert Dudley, Earl of Leicester.

Life and Memoirs of Cardinal Wolsey.

Miscellaneous Works of George, Duke of Buckingham.

N.B. The words " Second Edition " do not neces-

sarily imply that Curll had had anything to do with a
" firſt " edition.

? TOLAND (JOHN). *Ed. A Philippick Oration* to incite
the English againſt the French . . . in Latin and English. Sanger, Chantry. 8vo. 3*s*. B.M.

No mention of Curll's name, but it is advertised as
partly his in *The Kit-Cats* (1708).

Oct. 9. *The Memoirs of the Marquise de Langallerie.* . . . Trans-
(dated   lated from the French. Burrough, Baker, Sanger. 8vo.
1708).   5*s*. B.M.

Oct. 9 CONANT (REV. JOHN). *Sermons on Several Subjects.* The
(dated   Fifth Volume [of six]. Burrough, Baker, Sanger, Cliff ;
1708).   Curll not mentioned. B.M. (Advtd. in D.C.)

Oct. 9 DU PERIER ( ). *A General Hiſtory of all Voyages*
(dated   *and Travels.* . . . Made English from the Paris Edition.
1708).   Sanger. 8vo. 6*s*. Frontispiece and four plates. B.M.
This book apparently came out in parts.

Nov. 8. *The Case of Sodomy*, in the Tryal of Mervin, Lord Audley.
J. Morphew only. 6*d*.

Issued both alone, and with John Atherton's Case.
Probably dated 1708.

? *Memoirs of the Royal House of Savoy.* . . . Translated from
an Italian Manuscript. 8vo. 1*s*.

Advtd. in *The Kit-Cats.* Possibly Sanger's name
only. ? dated 1708.

? GREENE (THOMAS). *A Funeral Poem* to the Memory of
the Rt. Hon. John Lord Cutts. 8vo. " Printed for
Edmund Curll, 1707." (Cat.)

1708

Feb. 5. D'AULNOY [D'AUNOIS] (Comtesse). *Secret Memoirs* of
the Duke and Duchess of Orleans. (Sanger.) (P.B.)
Portrait.

Preliminary advertisements were Curll's, but J.
Woodward's name appeared alone until April, 1709,
when Curll again advertised the book.

Woodward did not long remain a friend of Curll's.

Apr. 23. C. (T., Surgeon) [? JOHN MARTEN]. *The Charitable
Surgeon.* 12mo. 1*s*. and 1*s*. 6*d*. (D.C.)

I cannot resiſt making an exception in the case of this
book and giving the title-page in full. It runs thus :

The Charitable Surgeon : Or, The beſt Remedies for
the Worſt Maladies Reveal'd. Being a new and true
way of Curing (without Mercury) the several degrees of
the Venereal Diſtemper in both Sexes, whereby all
Persons, even the meaneſt Capacities, may, for an
Inconsiderable Charge, without Confinement or Know-

ledge of the nearest Relation, cure themselves easily, speedily, and safely, by the Method prescrib'd, without the help of any Physician, Surgeon, or Apothecary, or being expos'd to the hazardous attempts of Quacks and Pretenders. With a new discovery of the true seat of Claps in Men and Women, different from the commonly receiv'd Opinions of Authors. And a peculiar Method of Curing their Gleets and Weaknesses, whether Venereal, Seminal, or otherwise ; with some pertinent Observations relating thereto, never before taken notice of. Likewise the certain easy way to escape Infection, tho' never so often accompanying with the most polluted Companion.

May 14. [WARREN (REV. ROBERT).] *The Devout Christian's Companion*. The Third Edition. (Sanger.) (D.C.)

May 22. BLACKMORE (SIR RICHARD). *The Kit-Cats*. A Poem. Sanger. Fo. 1s. B.M.

Pirated by H. Hills in 1708 and 1709. 8vo.

June 1. BOILEAU-DESPREAUX (NICHOLAS). *Lutrin :* A Mock-Heroic Poem . . . Render'd into English Verse. To which is prefix'd some Account of Boileau's Writings, and this Translation, by N. Rowe, Esq. Burrough, Baker, Sanger. 8vo. 2s. 6d. Frontispiece. B.M.

June 21. " The new edition of Petronius Arbiter " is advertised. (D.C.) This may be the old sheets with a new title-page.

June 24. [TAVERNER (WILLIAM).] *The Maid the Mistress*. A Comedy. Sanger. 4to. B.M.

Feales issued a second edition in 1732, and a third in 1736, in his pocket series (in some of which Curll had an interest).

June 30. *The Natural Morality of Humane Souls* Clearly Demonstrated . . . Being an Explication of a Famous Passage in the Dialogue of S. Justin Martyr with Tryphon. With a Letter . . . by Henry Dodwell, M.A. Sanger. 8vo. 2s. 6d. B.M.

For some reason Curll says of this book : " The first book I ever printed." But this was in 1726.

July 5. JOSEPHUS (FLAVIUS). *The Jewish History* . . . Abridg'd from Sir Roger L'Estrange's Translation . . . with a Continuation . . . by J. Crull, M.D., F.R.S. Briscoe, Burrough, Baker, Sanger. 2 vols. 8vo. 12s. Frontispiece and maps. B.M.

A catalogue of the Library of the Rev. William Pierce, sold by Curll this month, may be found.

For the rest of the year he seems to have been away on a holiday.

1709

Jan. 6.　THEOPHRASTUS. *The Moral Characters* . . . Translated
. . . by M. de la Bruyere. The Fifth Edition, with large
Additions. (Sanger, Pemberton.) 8vo. 6s. (P.B.)

Jan. 27.　ROWELL (THOMAS). *A Specimen of a New Translation of
Sallust.*

　　Post Boy of this date announces that it will be delivered
gratis to any gentleman who wishes to compare it with
the one advertised by R. Sare to be " done by one John
Rowe (not Mr. Rowe, author of Tamerlain, &c.)." The
rival version had just appeared, but I cannot find further
trace of Curll's intended publication. Possibly the blame
is not mine.

Feb. 17.　HILL (THOMAS). *Nundinæ Sturbrigiensis,* Anno 1702.
(Typis J. Tonson ; impensis E. Curll.) 6d. (P.B.)

Feb. 20.　PEAD (D.). *Parturiunt Montes,* &c. Or Lewis and
Clement taken in their own Snare. A Sermon. 8vo.
1d. Superfine copies at 6d. B.M.

Mar. 10.　BLACKMORE (SIR RICHARD). *Instructions to Vander Bank*
(a Sequel to the Advice to the Poets). A Poem. (Sanger
only ; but the advertisement in the *Post Boy* has Curll's
and their joint publications in the same paragraph.)
　　Pirated this year by Hills. Mentioned in the *Tatler,*
No. 3.

Mar. 14.　WILMOT (JOHN, EARL OF ROCHESTER). *The Works* . . .
" The Third Edition, with Additions." 2 vols. 8vo.
5s (later 6s.). B.M.
　　" The Speech of Alexander Bendo " may be found
either in Vol. I. (separately paged), or at the end of
Vol. II., which contains poems by Lord Roscommon
and Swift's *Baucis and Philemon.*
　　In the text I explain why the publication of the two
volumes was slightly delayed.

Mar. 18.　HORNECK (PHILIP). *An Ode* Inscrib'd to his Excellency
the Earl of Wharton. (Round, Sanger, Collins, Atkinson, Baker.) (D.C.)

Mar. 18.　DE CERVANTES (MIGUEL). *The Diverting Works* . . .
now first translated from the Spanish by several Hands.
With an Introduction by the Author of the London Spie
[Edward Ward]. (Round, Sanger, Collins, Atkinson,
Baker.) (D.C.)

Mar. 29.　[PRIOR (MATTHEW).] *Poems on Several Occasions.* The
Second Edition. 4s. (P.B.)

Apr. 13.　*Epilogue* Spoken by Mrs. Barry . . . at a Representation
of Love for Love. Sanger. 2d. B.M.

Apr. 19.　GERHARD (JOHN). *The Christian's Support* under all

Afflictions : Being the Divine Meditations . . . Now render'd into Modern English. . . . By T[homas] Rowell. Sanger. 8vo. Frontispiece. 3s. B.M.

Apr. 19.   *Short Rules* to bring a Godly Life into Daily Practice. Sanger. 1d. or 6s. a hundred. (P.B.)

May 10.   C. (T. Surgeon) [? JOHN MARTEN]. *The Charitable Surgeon*. The Second Edition, with Additions. 12mo. 1s. B.M.

The additions are not nearly so amusing as they might be.

May 16.   WHIT[E]LOCK (BULSTRODE). *Memorials of the English Affairs*. Sanger, Pemberton. Fo. 12s. B.M.

For some reason Curll bestows a knighthood on the author. Perhaps he was aware that the historian had at one time been a member of Cromwell's House of Lords. The first edition had appeared in 1682. This reprint contains a preface by James Welwood, M.D. It was issued with much pomp " under Her Majesty's Royal Licence."

June 6.   [HOLDSWORTH (EDWARD).] *Muscipula, sive Kambromyo-maxia*. Sanger. 8vo. 6d. Frontispiece. B.M.

" This poem is now first printed with the Author's consent." (*Tatler*, 4th June.) " In some measure to pre-vent the like Imposition upon many other Gentlemen, I do publicly declare, That I never saw, nor am any way acquainted with Mr. Lintott, a Bookseller ; but that the several Editions he has printed of my *Muscipula*, were wholly without my Consent, and are very defective, mangled, and full of Faults. *E. Holdsworth*." (P.B., 7th June.) Lintott had advertised an edition on 23rd Nov., 1708, " proving the Welsh to be the Inventors of Mouse-Traps." On 10th Feb., 1709, Morphew had published another edition (with Poole) with an English version called *Taffy's Triumph*. It is satisfactory to record the fact that Curll paid the author five guineas for " a compleat copy " of his poem, and agreed to hand over fifty free copies to him. He afterwards re-issued the poem with a translation by Samuel Cobb.

In its day this poem enjoyed an astonishing success. It is often found bound up with one or other of the translations. Curll's edition has a vignette of a peacock on the title-page, and should possess a frontispiece repre-senting " the Cambrian Paradise."

The vignette of the peacock is not found again, for in August Curll moves to the *Dial and Bible* on the city side of Temple Bar.

?   BRIDGMAN (SIR ORLANDO). *Conveyances.* Vol. II.
(Sanger.) Fo. 8s.

Advertised in many of Curll's lists, and also in his
edition of Shakespeare's *Poems.*

Sept. 1   SHAKESPEARE (WILLIAM). *The Works.* . . . Volume
(dated   the Seventh, containing Venus and Adonis, Tarquin and
1710).   Lucrece and his Miscellany Poems, with Critical Remarks on his Plays, &c. ; to which is prefix'd an Essay
on the Art, Rise, and Progress of the Stage in Greece,
Rome and England [by Charles Gildon]. Sanger.
8vo. 5s., or on large paper 7s. 6d. "Adorn'd with
Cuts." B.M.

This was meant to supplement Rowe's first edition of
the Plays, issued by Tonson. It was not the only one of
the kind, as Lintott issued a similar volume. In Curll's
earlier advertisements the name of J. Baker was added to
those of Sanger and himself, but Baker seems to have
quarrelled with them, and issued advertisements of his
own, offering to print large paper copies " to make up
sets." These, however, must have been supplied by
Curll.

Nov. 15.   *Reflexions on the Idolatry of the Jesuits,* and other Affairs
relating to Religion in China. In a Letter from a Gentle-
man at the Hague to Dr. Francis Atterbury. English'd
from the Paris Copy. 6d. (D.C.)

? dated 1710.

Dec. 6   HARDINGE (G.). *Victory and Success from God Alone.* A
(dated   Sermon. 8vo. 6d. B.M.
1710).   " Printed at the Request of the Auditors." The author
was Vicar of Kingston.

Dec. 22   HOADLY (BENJAMIN). *The Foundations of the Present
(dated   Government Defended.* Sanger, Pemberton. 8vo. 1s.
1710).   and 1s. 6d. B.M.

Pirated in the following month. (*Tatler.*)

?   [OLDMIXON (JOHN).] *The History of Addresses.* By One
very near a Kin to the Author of a Tale of a Tub. 8vo.
" Printed in the Year 1709."

Part I. only. Attributed by some to Defoe.

?   " E. N. Surgeon " (later " G. Warren, Surgeon ")
[? JOHN MARTEN]. *A New Method* of Curing, without
Internal Medecines, that Degree of the Venereal Dis-
ease, called a Gonorrhea, or Clap.

Advertised before publication by Curll (see *Quackery
Unmask'd,* 2nd ed.), but sold first by Woodward and
Baker, and afterwards (with new title-page) by Isted.

It just scrapes into the list.

Auctions held on 24th Nov. and 12th Dec., 1709, may have had printed catalogues.

1710

Jan. 3.   BARNARD (NICHOLAS, Dean of Armagh). *Some Memorials of the Life and Penitent Death of Dr. John Atherton.* 8vo. 1s. B.M.

Advertised rather less delicately as "The Case of John Atherton, Bp. of Waterford, in Ireland, who was Convicted of the Sin of Uncleanliness with a Cow and other Creatures, for which he was Hang'd at Dublin."

The pamphlet is often found with *The Case of Sodomy*, with the title of either *The Case of Bishop Atherton* or *The Cases of Unnatural Lewdness* (q.v.). An " Advertisement " signed D. L. (*Tatler*, 14th Jan.) is probably by Curll himself, who makes a poor enough excuse for dragging before the public this very old scandal. Certain copies may be dated 1711, and include a reply to an attack against *The Cases.*

Jan. 31.   DUNTON (JOHN). *Athenianism* (or Six Hundred New Treatises in Prose and Verse). " Sold by J. Morphew, J. Woodward, and E. Curl." (P.B.) 6s.

Probably without Curll's name on the title-page.

Feb. 7.   *Bibliotheca Wickiana.* Being a Catalogue of the Library of the late Hon. Sir Cyrill Wick. 6d. (*Tatler.*)

? Feb.   *The Cases of Unnatural Lewdness.* 8vo. 1s. 6d. and 2s.

Originally this was a re-issue, with a new title-page, of the Audley and Atherton Cases. Subsequently a third case was added, with Curll's reply to the attack on him in *The Case of John Atherton . . . Fairly Represented* (1710), when the book sold for 3s.

Mar. 18.   The same. The Second Edition.

Mentioned in the preface to *The Case . . . Fairly Represented.*

Mar. 23.   [CURLL (EDMUND).] *The Case of Dr. Sacheverell.* Represented in a Letter to a Noble Lord. " Printed in the Year 1710." 8vo. B.M.

See text.

Apr. 6.   [SWIFT (JONATHAN).] *A Meditation upon a Broom-Stick, and Somewhat Beside ; of the Same Author's.* Harding. 8vo. 6d. B.M.

?   The same. Another edition. " E. Curll, 1710." 2d.

Apr. 6.   XENOPHON. *The Banquet.* Done from the Greek, with an Introductory Essay . . . by James Welwood, M.D. 8vo. 2s. 6d. (D.C.)

Apr. 6.   HIGDEN (WILLIAM). *A View of the English Constitution.*

The Third Edition. " Printed for S. Keble . . . and R. Gosling," but advertised by Curll. (D.C.) 8vo. 1s. 6d. B.M.

Apr. 6. " A Pocket Edition, printed with an Elzevir Letter " of the Petronius is announced. (D.C.)

Apr. 29. *The Spirit of Fanaticism*, Exemplify'd in the Tryals of Mr. James Mitchel . . . and Major Weir . . . By an Advocate of the Civil Law in Scotland. 8vo. 1s. B.M.

Mr. Mitchel was a Presbyterian Minister who was unwise enough to " assault " the Archbishop of St. Andrews. Major Weir was accused of every unpleasant crime under the sun. Somewhat naturally the account of their trials was included in *The Cases of Unnatural Lewdness* in its enlarged form.

? Apr. SACHEVERELL (HENRY). *Answer to the Articles of Impeachment*. 8vo. 6d.

" Printed in the Year 1710," and advertised by Curll in his *Impartial Examination*, but whether he was really the publisher I do not know.

? Apr. [CURLL (EDMUND).] *An Impartial Examination* of the Right Reverend the Lord Bishop of Lincoln's and Norwich's Speeches at the Opening of the Second Article of Dr. Sacheverell's Impeachment. 8vo. 4d. B.M.

See text.

? Apr. [CURLL (EDMUND).] *Some Considerations* Humbly Offer'd to . . . the Ld. Bp. of Salisbury. By a Lay Hand. Morphew only. 8vo. 6d. B.M.

See text.

? Apr. *The Reasons* of those Lords that enter'd their Protest in Dr. Sacheverell's Case. " Printed in the Year 1710." 8vo. 3d.

Advertised in *An Impartial Examination*.

The same in Fo. " to bind up with the Tryal," 4d., is similarly advertised, as are also the following two books :

Tracts Relating to the Impeachment of Dr. Henry Sacheverell. . . . With an Exact List of those Lords and Commons that voted for him. With his Effigies. " Printed in the Year 1710." 8vo. 1s. (The B.M. copy has no frontispiece, and none is mentioned on the title-page. But then it may not be the book that is advertised in the Curllean pamphlets.)

The Art of Confuting Scripture by History. The Third Edition. 6d.

? May. [CURLL (EDMUND).] *A Search after Principles*. In a Free

Conference between Timothy & Philatheus, concerning the Present Times. Morphew only. 8vo. 6d. B.M. See text.

June 17. [CURLL (EDMUND).] *A Complete Key to the Tale of a Tub.* With some Account of its Authors. 8vo. 6d. B.M. Reprinted in the *Miscellanies* of 1711.

July. [? MARTEN (JOHN).] *The Generous Surgeon.* (Dolphin only.) See text.

Aug. 5. *The Perjur'd Phanatick;* or the Malicious Conspiracy of Sir John Croke . . . against the Life of Robert Hawkins. (Morphew.) 1s. "on small paper." (*Tatler.*) A second edition, in folio, bears only Morphew's name.

Aug. 24. WISE (THOMAS). *The Faithful Stewards.* A Sermon. Gosling. 8vo. 3d. A small number "on a very fine paper" at 6d. B.M.

Aug. 29. KETTLEWELL (JOHN). *An Help and Exhortation* to Worthy Communicating. The Sixth Edition. Gosling. 8vo. 4s. Frontispiece. This contains one addition in the author's Profession of Faith, which might be had separately at 1d. Which seems to me a moderate price.

Sept. 16. [GILDON (CHARLES).] *The Life of Mr. Thomas Betterton.* . . . To which is added, The Amorous Widow, or the Wanton Wife. A Comedy. Written by Mr. Betterton, now first printed from the original Copy. Gosling only. 8vo. 3s. 6d. Portrait. B.M. The Comedy is separately paged. Strictly speaking, this was not the first time that it had been printed, but the words were retained from the title-page of its first edition in 1706.

? BETTERTON (THOMAS). *The Amorous Widow.* . . . The Second Edition. Sanger, Gosling. 4to. 1s. 6d. B.M. The edition is dated 1710. I am not certain whether it came out before or after the *Life.* The setting differs from that found with the *Life.*

Sept. 16. *The Debate at Large,* relating to the Word Abdicated, Anno, 1688. 8vo. 1s. (P.M.) Issued in connection with the interminable Sacheverell controversy.

Oct. 26. *Some Account of the Family of Sacheverell.* Morphew only (but with Curll's list at the end). 8vo. 6d. Portrait. B.M. Entered by Curll at Stationers' Hall.

Nov. 7 (dated 1711). LE CLERC (JEAN). *The Rights of the Christian Church adjusted.* . . . Translated from the French. Sanger. 8vo. 1s. B.M.

Ecclesiastical polemics.

Dec. 4. *The White Crow ;* or, an Enquiry Into Some new doctrines broach'd by the Bp. of Salisbury, in a Pair of Sermons utter'd in that Cathedral on the 5th and 7th days of November last, 1710 ; and his Lordship's last Restauration Sermon. " Printed in the Year, MDCCX." 8vo. 6d. B.M.

Entered at Stationers' Hall.

The same. " The Second Edition Corrected." " Printed in the Year of Grace, 1710." 8vo. 6d. B.M.

The word " more " is printed before " new doctrines " on the title-page.

A Dream ; or the Force of Fancy. A Poem. Containing Characters of the Company now at the Bath. 12mo. " For Edmund Curll : London 1710." (Cat.)

The Perjur'd Phanatick. . . . The Second Edition. " Printed for W. J. and Sold by J. Morphew, 1710." 1s. B.M.

Apparently not advertised before 25th June, 1711, and then by Mr. Hawkins, the aggrieved party, who announced that the book was to be bought at his house. Curll may have sold his interest in it. I imagine that Mr. Hawkins was rather a nuisance, but my imagination is not to be trusted.

Memoirs Relating to the Impeachment of Thomas, Earl of Danby [and Duke of Leeds]. With an Appendix of Original Papers. Morphew only. 8vo. 4s. B.M.

Originally advertised by Curll and Sanger, later by Gosling. Mentioned at the end of Le Clerc's *Rights of the Church.*

1711

Jan. 25. *Fanatical Moderation,* or Unparalleled Villany Display'd ; being a Faithful Narrative of the Barbarous Murder committed upon Dr. James Sharp . . . 1679. (Gosling.) 8vo. 1s. (P.M.)

I should not be in the least surprised to find that this book is *The Spirit of Fanaticism* with, or without, a new title-page. Whatever it was, Curll seems to have suggested that it was the work of Dean Hickes—his name may be on the title-page in some connection or other—and in the *Post Boy* of 12th Feb., 1713, the

Dean, a most respectable dignitary, declared that he was in no " ways privy to the publishing of the said Book, to which this Title is prefix'd with his Name."
Very few Deans loved Curll.

Jan. 30.   C[RULL] (J[OHN].)   *The Antiquities of St. Peter's* . . . *Westminster.* " Printed by J. N[utt], and Sold by John Morphew." 8vo. 6s. " Adorn'd with Draughts of the Monuments." B.M.
The advertisements show that Sanger and Pemberton were associated with Curll in the venture.

Feb. 8.   D'ORLEANS (F. J.).   *The History of the Revolutions in England* under the Family of the Stuarts. Translated from the French. (Gosling.) 5s. (P.M.)

Feb. 15.   *The Fall and Restoration of Man.* A Poem. 2d. (P.B.)

Feb. 22.   D'AUBEUF (AUBERT DE VERTOT).   *History of the Revolution in Portugal* in the Year 1640, whereby they freed themselves from the Spanish Yoak. 1s. 6d. (P.B.)
An enlarged account was issued in the following year by Samuel Buckley.

Feb. 22.   LE CLERC (JEAN).   *Reflections Upon what the World Commonly calls Good-Luck and Ill-Luck,* With Regard to Lotteries. Done into English. 2s. (P.B.)
Gillyflower had issued a translation in 1699.

? Mar.   *Bishop Atherton's Case Discuss'd :* in a Letter to the Author of a late Pamphlet, Intitul'd, The Case . . . fairly Represented. 8vo. 1s. B.M.
Generally found with *Some Memorials* or *The Cases of Unnatural Lewdness.*

? Mar.   [SWIFT (JONATHAN).]   *Miscellanies.* 8vo. 1s. B.M.
A manufactured volume made up of such of Swift's pieces as Curll had already printed, including also the *Key to the Tale of a Tub.* It must not be confused with Morphew's *Miscellanies in Prose and Verse* issued this month.

Apr. 21.   *Musæ Britannicæ,* e Poematis varii Argumenti . . . (Sanger.) " On an Elzevir Letter." 2s. 6d. (P.B.)
Contributors include " Mr. Holdsworth . . . Mr. Thomas Hill of Trin. Coll. Camb., the late Mr. John Philips, N. Rowe, Esq., Dr. South, Mr. Brocknell of Westminster."

May 5.   PETRONIUS. *Satyricon.* " A new and correct Edition . . . adorn'd with ten Cuts." 2s. and 2s. 6d. (P.B.)
A re-issue of the 1707 edition, with plates copied from a French edition, and a new title-page.

May 19.   *An Account at Large of what pass'd at the Old-Bayly* . . .

relating to the Tryal of Richard Thornhill, Esq. " Sold by J. Morphew." 8vo. 2d. B.M.

Thornhill was tried for the murder of Sir Cholmley Deering, Bart. Then, as now, murder trials were about the most important things that could happen, and " Edmund Curll and R. Goslin " accordingly took the precaution to enter this book at Stationers' Hall.

June 4.   *The Reasons Which Induced Her Majesty to Create . . . Robert Harley . . . a Peer.* With the Preamble to his Patent in Latin and English. Morphew only. 4to. 2d. B.M.

Two varieties. (*a*) Latin and English face each other. (*b*) Latin text on pp. 3–5, English on pp. 6–8.

Entered at Stationers' Hall by Curll and Gosling.

Falsely attributed to Swift.

July 14.   " Edmund Curll and R. Goslin then entered for their Copy More Secret Transactions relating to the Case of Mr. William Gregg, by the Author of the Former Part." Stationers' Company Book.

I have not seen this book. Its author may have been John Oldmixon, who this year published " A Letter to the Seven Lords of the Committee appointed to Examine Gregg," but on the other hand he may not.

? Sept.   *Memoirs Relating to . . . the Earl of Danby. . . .* The Second Edition. Advertised in the book immediately below.

Sept. 20.   *The Reasons Which Induced Her Majesty to Create . . . Sir Simon Harcourt a Peer.* With the Preamble. Morphew only. 4to. 2d. B.M.

Sept. 24.   The same for

Lord Dartmouth.   6d.

Lord Raby.   6d. (also 2d.).

Earl Ferrers.   6d.

Earl of Orrery.   6d.

Duke of Hamilton.   6d.

Often found bound together, with a general title-page.

There are confusing accounts of the prices, but in any case you will have to pay even more than sixpence, if you want them to-day.

All entered by Curll at Stationers' Hall.

Sept. 24.   *The Reasons Which Induced Her Majesty to constitute John Bishop Of Bristol Keeper of the Privy Seal.* Being the Preamble to his Patent. 2d. (*Spectator.*)

Oct. 9.   *The Medal : Or, a full and impartial Account of the late Proceedings of the Dean and Faculty of Advocates in*

Scotland. Morphew. 3*d*. "With an exact Draught of the Medal curiously engraven by Mr. Vertue." (P.B.)

About which, I confess, with due shame, that I know nothing.

Oct. 11.   *An Account of the Life and Writings of Mr. John le Clerc.*
. . . Sanger, Morphew. 8vo. 1*s*. 6*d*. B.M.

Nov. 9.   ? Catalogue of an Auction held in the Inner-Lower Walk of Exeter-Change. (D.C.)

Nov. 17.   WARD (EDWARD). *The Life and Notable Adventures of*
(dated   . . . *Don Quixote* . . . Merrily translated into Hudi-
1712).   brastick Verse. Vol. II. Norris, Bettesworth, Harding, Woodward, Gosling. 8vo. 5*s*. B.M.

Curll's name does not appear on the title-page of Vol. I., though he advertises it as on sale in his shop.

Dec. 1   DE MONTFAUCON (BERNARD). *The Travels* . . . from
(dated   Paris thro' Italy. . . . Made English. "Printed by
1712).   D.L." Sanger, Gosling, Lewis. 8vo. 6*s*. "Near 30 Cuts." B.M.

A Vindication of his Grace the Duke of Leeds from the Aspersions of some late Fanatical Libellers. 8vo. 6*d*.

? year. Advertised in the Harcourt preamble, and possibly part of the *Memoirs* with a new title-page.

The Case of Insufficiency Discuss'd ; being the Proceedings at Large, Touching the Divorce between Lady Frances Howard and Robert, Earl of Essex . . . for Impotency. "London : Printed for E. Curll . . . 1711." 8vo. 1*s*. B.M.

Subsequently incorporated into the *Impotency* volumes.

[OLDMIXON (JOHN).] *The History of Addresses*, With Remarks Serious and Comical. Part II. Baker only. 8vo. 1711.

1712

Jan. 8.   BOILEAU-DESPREAUX (NICHOLAS). *The Works* . . . made English . . . by several hands. Sanger. 2 vols. 8vo. 12*s*. Cuts. B.M.

Vol. I. contains "*The Life* . . . Written in French by Mr. Des Maizeaux" and translated by John Ozell, "*The Lutrin* . . . The Second Edition, London, Printed in the Year MDCCXI." (and possibly issued by itself), and *The Art of Poetry*. Vol. II. contains Longinus's *Treatise of the Sublime*, separately titled and paged (1712), and *Miscellanies, with a Discourse on Satire* (with title-page dated 1711).

A third volume was added later.

? Mar.   *An Impartial Enquiry into the Management of the War in Spain.* " Printed and Sold by J. Morphew." 8vo. 5*s.* B.M.

    Not advertised as Curll's, though the second edition is. Re-issued in 1726 with a new title-page, but not by Curll.

Mar. 20.   The same. " The Second Edition, corrected." " Printed for E. Curll." (P.M.)

Mar. 20.   [BRAGGE (FRANCIS).] *A Full and Impartial Account of the Discovery of Sorcery and Witchcraft, Practis'd by Jane Wenham* . . . with her Trial. Baker. 8vo. 6*d.* (P.M.)

Mar. 25.   The same. The Second Edition. (P.B.)

Apr. 12.   [BRAGGE (FRANCIS).] *A Defence of the Proceedings against Jane Wenham.* 8vo. 6*d.* (P.B.)

    Contains the Wenham Case, an " Account of the most general Objections against the Being and Power of Witches," and " The Tryal of Florence Newton in Ireland."

    Advertised as *Witchcraft further display'd.*

? May.   *An Agreeable Criticism of Paris and the French.* Done from the French. The Third Edition. 1*s.* Advertised in the preceding book. The second edition had been printed for Chantry in 1706.

June 28.   SEWELL (GEORGE). *The Patriot.* A Poem. Fo. 6*d.* B.M.

July 1.   QUILLETUS (CLAUDIUS). *Callipædia.* A Poem in Four Books. Made English by N. Rowe [and others]. Sanger. 8vo. 4*s.* Frontispiece. Large paper copies at 7*s.* 6*d.* B.M.

    The first book was the only one to be translated by Rowe, the others being done by Sewell, Cobb, and Draper.

    This had originally been announced on 5th April, 1708, when Bowyer had issued the Latin text. Lintott announced a rival version in English, and there followed a warfare of words. In the end Woodward got in first with somebody else's version. This, I fancy, must have been Morphew's *Callipædiæ,* to which is added St. Marthe's *Pædotrophiæ,* 1710.

July 15.   HOLDSWORTH (EDWARD). *The Mouse-Trap :* a poem. Written in Latin . . . made English by Samuel Cobb. Sanger. 8vo. 1*s.* (afterwards 6*d.*). Frontispiece. B.M.

Aug. 30.   *A Complete Key* to all the Parts of Law is a Bottomless Pit, and the Story of the St. Alb–ns Ghost. " The Fifth Edition, Corrected." 3*d.* (P.B.)

Aug. 30.   *Stanzas* written to my Lady Sunderland at Tunbridge Wells this Summer. 8vo. 2*d*. (P.B.)

? Sept.   *The Tunbridge-Miscellany* : Consisting of Poems, &c. Written at Tunbridge Wells this Summer. By Several Hands. 8vo. 6*d*. B.M.

This contains a page of " New Pamphlets Printed for E. Curll," wherein are mentioned :

The Junto. A Poem. 8vo. 6*d*. 1712.

A Defence of the Bishop of St. Asaph's Four Sermons, wherein his Preface is fully consider'd. 6*d*.

[KING (WILLIAM).] The Art of Cookery. 6*d*.

Which edition this was I do not know. Lintott had published one in 1708, and there were two " surreptitious " editions in the same year. One of these was " Printed, and are to be Sold by the Booksellers of London and Westminster."

Memoirs of the late Right Honourable John, Lord Haversham, with all his Speeches in Parliament. " Printed for J. Baker, 1711." 8vo. 1*s*. B.M.

[BRAGGE (FRANCIS).] *A Full and Impartial Account.* . . . The Fifth Edition. 8vo. 6*d*.

? summer.   A Catalogue of Books and Pamphlets, Printed for, and Sold by Edmund Curll. . . . 1712.

Oct. 28.   SUIDAS. *A very ancient, authentick, and remarkable Testimony* concerning . . . Jesus Christ. By Theodosius a Jew. Now made English. (Morphew.) 6*d*. (P.B.)

Dedicated to Robert Nelson, who was not pleased, as his announcement on 4th Nov. proves :

" Whereas there hath lately been publish'd a certain Legendary Story of an unknown Theodosius, concerning the Priesthood of Christ ; Translated out of Suidas. . . . Which the Translator hath taken the Liberty not only to dedicate to me, but to use my Name in the Title Page ; thereby giving occasion to think that I countenance the Authority of that Testimony. Now these are to certify, That the Person who publish'd that Pamphlet is altogether a Stranger to me, and that I was in no way acquainted with his Design, till I saw it in Print : For tho' the Passage produc'd may appear remarkable, yet I cannot think the Testimony either Ancient or Authentick."

And if I had read the book myself, I feel convinced that I should agree with Mr. Nelson, whose portrait I have often admired in the Bodleian Library.

Curll did not reply, but I don't blame him.

Dec. 6.   BROWNE (SIR THOMAS). *Posthumous Works.* Gosling.

8vo. 6s. Portrait and 23 plates. B.M. Large paper copies subsequently advertised at 12s.

Contains " Repertorium, or the Antiquities of the Cathedral Church at Norwich," an account of some urns found at Bampton, a letter from Sir William Dugdale, Miscellanies, and a Life of the author.

Sheets purchased by Mears and re-issued with a new title-page in 1723.

An Epigram on the Spectator. Broadside. Fo. " Printed for E. Curll, 1712." (Cat.)

The Reasons which Induced Her Majesty to create Samuel Massam Esq, a Peer. Also Reasons . . . for creating Charles Mountague a Peer [Halifax] in 1700. 2d. M.DCCXII. B.M.

Advertised in this are Reasons for so treating

The Earl of Strafford,

The Electoral Prince of Hanover.

A Collection of Preambles . . . with Remarks. 4to. 1s. (Cat.)

The same. The Second Edition. 4to. " For E. Curll, 1712." (Cat.)

The Secret History of the Gertruydenberg Negotiation. 8vo. 1s.

Advertised in the Massam preamble, and afterwards incorporated into *State Tracts.*

[CURLL (EDMUND).] *Some Account of . . . Dr. Walter Curll,* Bishop of Winchester. With a Sermon, preach'd (by him) April 28, 1622. 12mo. B.M.

The sermon has a separate title-page, and may be found alone. " A Sermon . . . by Walter Curll . . . Printed by John Bill, 1622. And Reprinted by E. Curll."

CRISP (H[ENRY]). *To the Honourable Matthew Prior, Esq.;* on his Promotion to the Commission of Her Majesty's Customs and first coming to the Board. A Poem. " E. Curll, 1712." 4to. (Cat.)

CHAUCER (GEOFFREY). *The Carpenter of Oxford;* or, The Miller's Tale. Attempted in Modern English. By Samuel Cobb. . . . To which are added, Two Imitations of Chaucer. . . . By Matthew Prior, Esq. Gosling, Pemberton. 8vo. 1s. B.M.

Separate title-page to the two Prior poems " Printed in the Year MDCCXII."

[OLDMIXON (JOHN).] *The Secret History of Europe.* [Part I.] " Printed for the Booksellers of London and Westminster." 8vo. 3s. 6d. B.M.

The same. Part II. "Printed for A. Baldwin. . . . 1712." 8vo. 4*s.* B.M.
But undoubtedly Curll's.

1713

Feb. 3. [SEWELL (GEORGE).] *The Clergy and the Present Ministry Defended.* (A Letter to the Bishop of Salisbury.) "Printed for J. Morphew." 8vo. 6*d.* B.M.

On Jan. 26th Curll had entered at Stationers' Hall " The Bishop of Salisbury's new Preface to his Pastoral Care, Considered with respect to the following heads, viz. 1. The Qualifications of the Clergy. 2. The Distinction of High and Low Church. 3. The Present Posture of Affairs." Whether the matter went any further I do not know. At this time he could not leave the Bishop alone.

Feb. 10. THEOCRITUS. *The Idylls.* With Rapin's Discourse upon Pastorals, made English by Mr. Creech. . . . Also the Life of Theocritus by Basil Kennet. The Second Edition. sm. 8vo. 2*s.* and 2*s.* 6*d.* Portrait. (*Eve. Post.*)

Curll's first issue.

Feb. 12. [SEWELL (GEORGE).] *The Clergy . . . Defended.* The Second Edition. 8vo. 6*d.* (P.B.)

Feb. 12. SEWELL (GEORGE). *The Life and Character of Mr. John Philips.* 12mo. 1*s.* (P.B.)

Feb. 19. SEWELL (GEORGE). *Remarks upon my Lord N[otting]ham's Observations on the State of the Nation.* 8vo. 6*d.* (*Eve. Post.*)

Mar. 12. C[RULL] J[OHN]). *The Antiquities . . . of Westminster.* With a Supplement by Charles Taylor, Gent. 8vo. 7*s.* 6*d.* (P.B.)

" N.B. The Supplement may be had alone, price 1*s.* 6*d.* in sheets, 2*s.* 6*d.* bound."

This " New Edition," as it was optimistically called, was being advertised as " The Second Edition " in 1715.

Mar. 14. SEWELL (GEORGE). *Remarks.* . . . The Second Edition. 8vo. (P.B.)

Mar. 14. [SEWELL (GEORGE).] *The Clergy . . . Defended.* The Third Edition. (P.B.)

Mar. 16. CHÉRON DE LA BRUYERE (LOUIS CLAUDE). *The Whole Works.* . . . Revised by the last Paris Edition. With an Original Chapter after Bruyere's Method. By N. Rowe. Pemberton. 2 vols. 9*s.* (P.B.)

Occasionally advertised, somewhat cryptically, as " The Gentleman's Library."

Mar. 31.   [BLAND (Capt.).] *The Northern Atalantis, or York Spy*, . . . Including Apple-Pye, or Instructions to Nelly, a Poem. Written . . . by the late Dr. William King. (Baldwin.) 1*s*. and 1*s*. 6*d*. (P.B.)

The same. The Second Edition. " Printed for A. Baldwin . . . 1713." 1*s*. and 1*s*. 6*d*. 8vo. B.M.

Apr. 5.   WEBSTER (   ) of Christ-Church, Oxon. *The Stage*. A Poem. 8vo. " Printed for E. Curll, 1713."

Begins : " Since all the Din of War begins to cease."

Curll announced this poem as having been " written last Summer, upon the following Occasion ; The Spectator's Account of the *Distrest Mother*, had rais'd the Author's Expectations to so high a Pitch, that he made an Excursion from College, to see that *Tragedy* Acted, and upon his Return, was commanded by the Dean to write upon the *Art*, *Rise* and *Progress*, of the *English* Stage, which how well he has perform'd, is now submitted to the Judgment of that worthy Gentleman, to whom it is inscrib'd (i.e. Joseph Addison)."

Now it happens that at the end of this year there also appeared REYNARDSON (FRANCIS) *Poems on Several Occasions*, " Printed for E. Curll, 1714," which, however, consists only of one long poem called *The Stage*. I have not seen this pamphlet, but I would not be surprised to find that it is the same as Mr. Webster's. I admit, however, that while Mr. Webster is described as of Christ-Church, Mr. Reynardson is " Late of Baliol." Perhaps the poems are quite different, and then we must deduce a little undergraduate rivalry, but I have an idea that there was only one poem, which Curll reprinted more than once in his miscellanies.

Apr. 7.   WARREN (ROBERT). *The Devout Christian Remembrancer*. . . . (Harding, Cliff, Bettesworth.) 1*s*. (P.B.)

Apr. 25.   SEWELL (GEORGE). *A Second Letter to the Bishop of Salisbury*. . . . Morphew. 8vo. 6*d*. B.M.

Apr. 30.   [SEWELL (GEORGE).] *Observations upon Cato*, a Tragedy by Mr. Addison. " Printed for A. Baldwin." 4to. "to bind up with the Play." 6*d*. B.M.

A manuscript note in the B.M. copy runs : " wrote by Dr. Sewell, & of wh^ch I sold 20[oo]EC."

George in these days was indefatigable.

?   [PHILIPS (JOHN).] *Ode ad Henricum St. John, Armig.* " Londini Impensis E. Curll." (Cat.)

Apr. 30.   PHILIPS (JOHN). *The Works*. 12mo. 1*s*. 6*d*. (P.B.)

Separately paged pieces, I expect, as in the later editions, and containing the Ode above.

May 2.   [SEWELL (GEORGE).] *Observations on Cato*. . . . The

Second Edition. To which is added, a Comparison between Cato and Cæsar, by Mr. [Richard] Steel[e]." (P.B.)

May 5. SEWELL (GEORGE). *First Letter to the Bishop of Salisbury ;* or, The Clergy . . . Defended. . . . The Fourth Edition. Morphew. 8vo. 6*d*. B.M.

May 12. *Whigg and Tory ;* or Wit on both Sides ; being a new Collection of State Poems. 2*s*. 6*d*. (P.B.)
Including contributions by Garth, Prior, &c.

May 14. PHILELEUTHERUS LIPSIENSIS (i.e. RICHARD BENTLEY). *Remarks upon a late Discourse of Free-Thinking* [by Anthony Collins] in a Letter to F. H[are]. D.D. The Second Edition. Morphew. 8vo. B.M.
The first edition, printed earlier in the year, bears only Morphew's name, and was not advertised by Curll.

May 16. SEWELL (GEORGE). Ed. *Sacred Miscellanies :* or, Divine Poems. 8vo. 6*d*. (P.B.)

May 23. [BARKER (JANE).] *Love's Intrigues*, or the History of the Amours of Basil and Galesia. . . . A Novel. Written by a Young Lady. Crownfield. 8vo. 1*s*. and 1*s*. 6*d*. B.M.
Dedication signed " J. B."
Apparently Curll's first novel, and almost what our grandmothers would have called " nice."

June 4. TASSONI (ALESSANDRO). *La Secchia Rapita : The Trophy Bucket*. A Mock-heroic Poem. Made English by Mr. [John] Ozell. 8vo. 1*s*. 6*d*. (P.B.)

June 4. *Biographia Collectanea ;* or Select Lives of Eminent Men, from the Year 1686, to this Time. 6*s*. (P.B.)
" Lately publish'd " according to the advertisement. Whether this is the actual title of the book I know not.

June 9. In an advertisement of Bulstrode Whitelock's History of England, i.e. *Memorials of the English Affairs*, Curll announces an "effigies" of the author, which had not been mentioned when the book came out in 1709. " Lately publish'd " on this date.

July 2. ANACREON and SAPPHO. *The Works*. . . . Done from the Greek by several Hands. Bettesworth. Sm. 8vo. 1*s*. 6*d*. and 2*s*. 2 plates. B.M.
This is the 1683 version by Cowley and others, with additions, and a preface signed G. S[ewell].

July 4. ADAMS (Dr. ? Samuel). *To the Queen upon the Peace*. A Poem in Latin and English. 4*d*. (later 3*d*.). (P.B.)

July 18. *The Student's Library*. 1*s*. (P.B.)
Which is only a catalogue of the books that Curll is selling, and may not be thus entitled.

Aug. 1.   *Stanzas to the Lord Treasurer, upon the Peace.* (P.B.)
Not priced in the advertisement, and consequently may belong to something else. But it does not seem to be Adams's poem.

Sept. 3.   *The Tunbridge Miscellany* for the Year 1713. . . . Written by several Hands. 6*d.* (P.B.)

July 19.   [NORTH (HON. ROGER).] *A Discourse of Fish and Fish Ponds.* " Done by a Person of Honour." 8vo. 1*s.* 6*d.* and 2*s.*, later 2*s.* and 2*s.* 6*d.* (B.P.)

Oct. 17.   PHILELEUTHERUS LIPSIENSIS (i.e. RICHARD BENTLEY). *Remarks upon a late Discourse of Freethinking.* . . . The Second Part. " Printed for J. Morphew and E. Curl." 8vo. 1*s.* B.M.

Nov. 17.   SAINT EVREMOND (CHARLES) DE MARQUETEL DE SAINT DENIS). *The Genuine Works.* . . with the Author's Life, &c. 3 vols. 8vo. (Churchill, Darby, Gosling, Round, Baker.) (P.B.)

Dec. 12.   SMALRIDGE (GEORGE). *Speech to the Upper House of Con-*
(dated   *vocation,* upon the Presentment of the late Prolocutor.
1714).   The Second Edition. " Printed for J. Roberts." 8vo.
6*d.* B.M.
Included in the author's *Miscellanies,* 1715.
The first edition, also dated 1714, was " printed for J. Roberts " too, but Curll does not seem to have advertised it.

Dec. 19.   WALKER (   ). *English Particles Latiniz'd ;* being a Compendious Improvement of . . . English and Latin Particles. Begun by a Gentleman of Sedbridge School, Yorkshire ; Completed by the Rev. Mr. Thomas Dyche. (Gosling, Pemberton.) 2*s.* (P.B.)
The Life of that Learned Antiquary, Sir William Dugdale. Published from an Original Manuscript. 8vo. 1*s.* B.M.
English Gratitude : or, the Whig Miscellany. " Printed for A. Baldwin, 1713." 8vo. 6*d.* B.M.
A list of books " Sold by A. Baldwin " is printed opposite the title-page : of these all but one are Curll's. The book is also included in one of Curll's lists, and it contains a poem which he printed.
[? CHURCHILL (R.).] *To his Grace the Duke of Marlborough,* on the Report of his Going into Germany. Pemberton. sm. Fo. (2 pp.) Dated 1713. 2*d.* B.M.
The Favourite. A Simile. Written by a Gentleman of Eton. sm. Fo. 2*d.*
Advertised at the end of the preceding pamphlet.

An edition had appeared in 1712, printed at Eton. Curll
may have put the poem on sale, or had it reprinted.

[WOODWARD (JOHN).] *An Account of some Roman Urns*,
and other Antiquities, Lately Digg'd up near Bishops-
gate. With Brief Reflections upon the Antient and
present State of London. In a Letter to Sir Christopher
Wren. " Printed for E. Curll, 1713." 8vo. 1*s.* B.M.

1714

REYNARDSON (FRANCIS). *Poems on Several Occasions*.
i.e. *The Stage*. See above.

Jan. 7. [SEWELL (GEORGE).] *An Introduction to the Life and
Writings of G[ilber]t, Lord Bishop of S[aru]m*. Being a
Third Letter. 8vo. 1*s.* B.M.

Jan. 21. DORIACK CHANCEL (A.). *A New Journey over Europe*.
" Printed for John Harding." 8vo. 3*s.* B.M.

Feb. 4. SEWELL (GEORGE). *Miscellanies in Prose and Verse*. 8vo.
4*s.* (P.B.)

Feb. 11. SMALRIDGE (GEORGE). *Two Speeches made in the Theatre
at Oxford*. Latin and English. 8vo. 6*d.* B.M.
Included in his *Miscellanies*.

Feb. 13. RISDON (TRISTRAM). *The Chorographical Description, or
Survey of the County of Devon*. 2 vols. 8vo. 7*s.* 6*d.* and
12*s.* on a superfine paper. B.M.
A list of subscribers is printed.

Feb. 23. [NORTH (HON. ROGER).] *The Gentleman's Accomptant*.
" Done by a Person of Honour." 12mo. 4*s.* and 5*s.*
" neatly bound and gilt."
In an advertisement issued in 1721 the name of the
author is indirectly divulged.

Feb. 25. *A Collection of Original Poems, Translations and Imitations*.
8vo. 5*s.* B.M.
The doubtlessly unwilling contributors include Rowe,
Prior and Swift. *The Stage* is also included, I presume
to its writer's content at being in such lofty company.
The pieces are separately paged. Some have title-pages
not of this date, but, as you have probably discovered
by this time, Curll had his own way of producing
miscellanies and things.

? ROWE (NICHOLAS). *Poems on Several Occasions*. 4to.
B.M.
Contains in front of the title-page " The Exception-
able Passage left out in the Acting and Printing of the
Tragedy of Jane Shore." It would.

Feb. 25. The same. The Second Edition. (P.B.)

Feb. 27. *The Whole Art of Fishing*. To which is added, **The Laws** of Angling. sm. 8vo. 2s. and 2s. 6d. Frontispiece, showing an angler at Windsor. (See illustration.) B.M.

Feb. 27. [NORTH (HON. ROGER].) *A Discourse of Fish and Fish Ponds.* 8vo. " Printed for E. Curll, 1714."

This is the same as the 1713 edition, with a new title-page and a leaf of errata. It is not the second edition.

Mar. 9. PHILIPS (JOHN). *The Works.* . . . To which are added, The Pastorals of Mr. Ambrose Philips. 8vo. 2s. 6d. Frontispiece.

Separately paged pieces, with a new title-page.

? Apr. YOUNG (EDWARD). *The Force of Religion;* or, Vanquish'd Love. Pemberton. 8vo. 1s. " A small number on superfine paper for such as are curious." 2 cuts. B.M.

Advertised as " speedily will be publish'd " in the *Post Boy* of 23rd March.

Apr. 8. MONTFAUCON DE VILLARS (NICHOLAS DE). *The Count of Gabalis :* Being a Diverting History of the Rosicrucian Doctrine of Spirits. . . . Done from the Paris Edition. Lintott. 8vo. 1s. B.M.

Philip Ayres had issued a translation in 1680.

Apr. 8. *The New Atalantis for the Year* 1713. 5s. (*Eve. Post*).

" The Publick is desired to take Notice, that this Book was not writ by the Author [Mrs. Manley] of the 4 Vols. of the Atalantis, publish'd by John Morphew ; the Author of those Volumes, having never seen this Book, nor knowing any thing of the Contents, will not be answerable for whatever may be display'd therein." (P.B., 15th April, 1714.)

Curll had never actually said that Mrs. Manley was the author of his publication, though her name had been dragged in very skilfully into his advertisements. Nobody could beat him at that sort of game.

Apr. 15. SHAKESPEARE (WILLIAM). *The Works.* Volume the Ninth. J. Darby, printer. K. Sanger, Pemberton. Sold by Tonson and others. 12mo. B.M.

SHAKESPEARE (WILLIAM). *A Collection of Poems*, in Two Volumes, being all the Miscellanies. . . . 2 vols. 8vo. " Printed by J. Darby for E. Curll."

The contents being the same as Vol. IX.

Apr. 27. BETTERTON (THOMAS). *The Amorous Widow.* The Third Edition. S. Keimer, printer. Gosling, Sanger, Bettesworth. 12mo. 1s. B.M.

The advertisement speaks of " an Elzevir Pocket Edition." Keimer was a Paternoster Row printer who specialized in theatrical books and issued some on his own account.

May 1. *Will with a Whisp; or the Grand Ignis Fatuus of London.*
Being a Layman's Letter to a Country Gentleman, concerning the Articles lately Exhibited against Mr. Whiston.
By a Gentleman formerly of Queen's College, Oxon.
(Woodward, Bettesworth, Gosling.) 1*s*. (P.B.)

May 4. SEWELL (GEORGE). *The Reasons For Writing against the Bishop of Salisbury.* 8vo. 4*d*. B.M.
It seems to me that they were certainly needed.

May 11. DILLON (WENTWORTH, EARL OF ROSCOMMON). *Poems on Several Occasions.* With others by the Earl of Dorset, Otway, Edmund Smith, Samuel Cobb, Prior and Swift. 12mo. B.M.

May 11. *The Life, Character, and Death of . . . Lady Jane Gray.*
Collected from the Best Historians. Very proper to be bound up with Mr. Young's excellent Poem, founded upon this Noble History [*The Force of Religion*]. " Printed for J. Roberts." 8vo. 6*d*. B.M.
Robert's list of books at the end contains only Curll's publications, and the book is repeatedly advertised as Curll's.

May 11. [CENTLIVRE (SUSANNA).] *The Wonder;* a Woman keeps a Secret. A Comedy. " Written by the Author of the Gamester." Bettesworth. 8vo. 1*s*. 6*d*. " A small number on a superfine paper." Frontispiece. B.M.
" May 18, 1715. Susannah Centlivre then received of Mr. Curll twenty guineas in full for the copy of my play called The Wonder; a Woman keeps a Secret." From a manuscript formerly in the possession of a Mr. Upcott, and printed in the *Gentleman's Magazine*. Mrs. Centlivre received the same sums for *The Cruel Gift* and *The Artifice*.

? June. [MANLEY (DELIA DE LA RIVIERE).] *The Adventures of Rivella;* or the History of the Author of the Atalantis. Deliver'd in a Conversation to the Young Chevalier D'Aumont . . . by Sir Charles Lovemore. Done into English from the French. " London : Printed in the Year M.DCC.XIV." 8vo. 2*s*. in Sheep, 2*s*. 6*d*. in Calf's Leather. Frontispiece. B.M.
Preface dated June 3rd, 1714.
See text.

June 4. [CENTLIVRE (SUSANNA).] *The Gamester.* A Comedy. The Third Edition. Knapton, Gosling, Bettesworth. " In an Elzevir Letter." 1*s*. B.M.

June 12. SEWELL (GEORGE). *Schism, Destructive of the Government,* both in Church and State. The Second Edition. 8vo. 6*d*. B.M.
The first edition luckily escaped me.

June 22. SHAKESPEARE (WILLIAM). *Sauny the Scot ;* or the Taming of the Shrew. Altered [by J. Lacy]. Bettesworth, Richardson. 12mo. 1*s.* (P.B.)
Bragge had published a previous edition in 1708.

June 26. *The Case of Impotency Debated,* in the late Famous Tryal at Paris, between the Marquis de Gesvres . . . and . . . his Lady. Done from the Paris Edition [by John Ozell]. 2 vols. 12mo. B.M.
The first of the best-sellers.

? June. *Memoirs of the Lives of King Edward IV. and Jane Shore.* Extracted from the best Historians. 4to. 6*d.* B.M.

? June. *The Life and Death of Jane Shore.* "Printed for J. Roberts, 1714." 4to. 6*d.* B.M.
A list of books lately published includes some of Curll's, and there are vague references to this pamphlet in some of the newspaper announcements.

July 10. BOILEAU DESPREAUX (NICHOLAS DE). *The Lutrin.* "The Third Edition, Corrected and Revis'd by the last Paris Edition." Burleigh. 12mo. 1*s.* 6*d.* Cuts. B.M.
"In justice to the Memory of Mr. [Samuel] Cobb, late Schoolmaster of *Christ-Hospital,* Mr. Ozell thinks himself oblig'd to own, That that ingenious Friend of his wrote many of the brightest Lines in the preceding Piece ; part whereof was likewise done by Mr. Johnson : the rest, perhaps the dullest part, as well as the greatest, was done by himself the said Ozell." Announcement on the last page. It was quite unlike Ozell to talk in this way. I think he must have been a little unwell at the time.

July 10. SEWELL (GEORGE). *Remarks upon a Pamphlet intitul'd A Vindication of the Earl of Nottingham.* 6*d.* (P.B.)

July 15. *Original Poems and Translations.* 12mo. 6*d.* B.M.
Contributors include Eusden, Thomas Hill, Broome and Dr. King.

July 20. ROWE (NICHOLAS). *Poems on Several Occasions.* The Third [Elzevir] Edition. Sm. 8vo. 6*d.* Frontispiece. B.M.

July 22. *An Account of the Life and Writings of John Locke.* Fo. 1*s.* (P.B.)

July 22. LOCKE (JOHN). *The Remains.* Fo. 1*s.* B.M.
Which sounds more impressive than it is.

July 22. [SEWELL (GEORGE).] *More News from Salisbury.* 8vo. 6*d.* B.M.

July 27. BOILEAU DESPREAUX (NICHOLAS DE). *The Art of Poetry.* "The Second Edition, Revis'd." (Sanger, Burleigh.) 1*s.* (P.B.)

July 31. AYLIFFE (JOHN). *The ancient and present State of the*

University of Oxford. 2 vols. 8vo. 12*s.* Some copies on large paper. B.M.

For which the author was summoned before the University Court " in two several Actions of Injury and Damage." Another proof of the unwisdom of annoying Vice-Chancellors. Ayliffe's chief complaint seems to have been that he was arrested in his own College Hall just as he was sitting down to dinner ; but that kind of thing *is* annoying.

Aug. 5. *The State of the Nation.* " Printed for J. Roberts." 8vo. 6*d.* B.M.

Repeatedly advertised by Curll, who must have been first in the field with a pamphlet concerning the Queen's Death. She had only been dead three days then, but her death even to-day is the subject of comment.

Aug. 14. JONES (SAMUEL, of Whitley). *Poetical Miscellanies on Several Occasions.* Bettesworth and local booksellers. 8vo. 1*s.* B.M.

At the end a list of " Books lately printed for A. Bettesworth . . . and E. Curll " includes two not elsewhere mentioned in connection with Curll. These are : *Matrimony unmask'd : Or, The Comforts and Discomforts of Marriage Display'd ; in several diverting poetical Dialogues. 1*s.*
WARD (JOHN, of Chester). *The Young Mathematician's Guide.* 6*s.*

Aug. 19. BARKER (JANE). *Exilius ; or the Banish'd Roman.* A new Romance. (Roberts.) 3*s.* (P.B.)

Aug. 21. JOSEPHUS (FLAVIUS). *The Jewish History* . . . The Second Edition. (P.B.)

Aug. 21. (dated 1715). TASSONI (ALESSANDRO). *The Rape of the Bucket.* The Second Edition. 1*s.* 6*d.* (Cat.)

Aug. 28. SEWELL (GEORGE). *Complete Collection of all . . . Tracts,* Written in Defence of the Church and Constitution. 4*s.* (P.B.)

Aug. 28 (dated 1715). YOUNG (EDWARD). *The Force of Religion.* The Second Edition. 8vo. 1*s.* and 1*s.* 6*d.* on large paper. Cuts. B.M.

Aug. 31. *The State of the Nation.* The Second Edition. (P.B.)

Sept. 2. *An Account of the Life and Writings of John Locke.* The Third Edition. (Clark.) Fo. 1*s.* (P.B.)

A second edition is not apparently mentioned.

Sept. 2. MONTFAUCON DE VILLARS (NICHOLAS DE). *The Count of Gabalis.* The Second Edition. (P.B.)

Sept. 2. *The Elzevir Miscellany.* Being a new Collection of

Original Poems. "In a neat Pocket Volume."
(Roberts.) 2s. 6d. (P.B.)

Sept. 19. *Miscellanies on several Curious Subjects*, Now first Publish'd
from their Respective Originals. 250 copies. 8vo. 3s.
Vignette portrait of Anthony à Wood. B.M.

Oct. 26 LE CLERC (JEAN). *Observations upon Mr. Addison's*
(dated *Travels through Italy.* Done from the French by Mr.
1715). [Lewis] Theobald. 8vo. 1s. B.M.

Oct. 30. *The Tunbridge and Bath Miscellany for the Year* 1714. 6d.
(P.B.)

Nov. 2. *Second and Last Part of the Case of Impotency* as Debated in
England. 2s. 6d., but subsequently enlarged, and sold
at 5s. (P.B.)
This includes the Essex case, already printed separately, the Castlehaven case, and the divorce of the Duke
of Norfolk.

Nov. 20. PITCAIRN[E] (ARCHIBALD). *The Works.* (" His Method
of Curing Smal-pox.") [Edited by George Sewell.]
(Pemberton, Taylor.) 5s. (P.B.)

Nov. 27 SMALRIDGE (GEORGE). *A Poem on the Death of our most*
(dated *Gracious Sovereign Queen Anne ;* and the Accession of . . .
1715). King George. Latin and English (the translator
admitting that he could not help himself, presumably on
account of the superb merits of the Latin lines).

? Dec. ASHMOLE (ELIAS). *The History of the Most Noble Order*
of the Garter. A new edition, "The Whole illustrated
with proper Sculptures." Bell, Taylor, Baker, Collins.
8vo. 7s. 6d. and 12s. on a superfine paper. Portrait
of George, Prince of Wales. B.M.
Curll's name is not on the title-page, but it is one of the
twenty volumes of what he called *Anglicana Illustrata.*
Lives and Characters of the most illustrious Persons who dyed
in 1712. 6s.
First advertised in *The Life . . . of Lady Jane Gray*,
and probably issued early in the year. Subsequently
advertised as in two volumes with those who had
" dyed " in 1711.
BOILEAU DESPREAUX (NICHOLAS DE). *The Works.* 3 vols.
8vo. 15s. B.M.
SEWELL (GEORGE). *Remarks upon a Pamphlet* Entitul'd,
Observations upon the State of the Nation in January
1712–13. The Third Edition. 8vo. 6d. B.M.
[GILDON (CHARLES)]. *A New Rehearsal, or Bays the*
Younger, containing an Examen of the Ambitious Step-
mother, &c. [by Rowe]. . . . Also a word upon Mr.
Pope's Rape of the Lock. " Printed for J. Roberts."
12mo. 1s. B.M.

Curll does not advertise this book until 1728, and perhaps it should not be included here. It is mentioned, however, in Pope's *Full and True Account of a Horrid and Barbarous Revenge . . . on . . . Mr. Edmund Curll* (1716), where Curll is made to say: "I protest I have no animosity to Mr. Rowe, having printed part of Callipædia, and an incorrect edition of his poems without his leave in quarto. Mr. Gildon's Rehearsal, or Bays the Younger, did more harm to me than to Mr. Rowe; though, upon the faith of an honest man, I paid him double for abusing both him and Mr. Pope." This pamphlet, of course, is satirical throughout, but Pope seems to have been furnished with fairly correct information about Curll's unavowed publications, and Curll himself mentions the book in his *Key* to the Dunciad. And it was seldom that he mentioned a rival's publication, unless to call it the silliest and falsest pyratical nonsense that had ever been sent to a printer.

State-Tracts. 8vo. 4s. B.M.

Various tracts, separately paged; some possibly excerpts from *The Secret History of Europe*.

HENLEY (JOHN). *Esther Queen of Persia.* An Historical Poem in Four Books. Pemberton, Bettesworth. 8vo. 1s. 6d. and 2s. Frontispiece. B.M.

The author was not yet notorious for his "Oratory."

SEWELL (GEORGE). *Poem on the King's Accession.* 6d.

Apparently not advertised until September, 1716, when it appears in Burleigh's list (all Curll publications) at the end of Chute's *Beauty and Virtue*.

It may be pointed out that *Poems and Translations, by Several Hands*. To which is added, The Hospital of Fools, by William Walsh (of which publication John Oldmixon was the editor), was published this year by Pemberton. Walsh's contribution, at any rate, was afterwards constantly being included in Curll's collections.

For the Year 1714, *a Catalogue of Books, Sold by Edmund Curll*, at his Shop in Tunbridge Wells; and at the Dial and Bible.

This is a list of his stock, not of his publications.

1715

Jan. WARREN (ROBERT). *Practical Discourses upon the most Fundamental Principles of Religion.* . . . Being the Second Part of The Christian's Devout Companion. (P.B.)

The two sold together for 6s.

Jan. 15.   SMALRIDGE (GEORGE). *Miscellanies*. 8vo. 2*s*. B.M.
Having become my Lord Bishop of Bristol, Smalridge is considered important enough to have three pieces already printed by Curll bound together with a general title-page.

Jan. 22.   A so-called Second Edition of *The Antiquities of* . . . *Westminster* is announced in the *Post Boy* " to the Death of Queen Anne." The price remains the same, but there may have been a further or revised supplement.

Feb. 8.   COCKER (EDWARD). *English Dictionary*. " The Second Edition, very much Enlarg'd and Alter'd : By John Hawkins." Norris, Bettesworth, Brown. 1*s*. 6*d*. and 2*s*. B.M.
Curll's name is not on the title-page, but the book is found in his advertisements.

Feb. 9.   DOGGET (THOMAS). *Hob ; or the Country Wake*. A Farce. Bettesworth. 12mo. 6*d*. B.M.

Feb. 26.   NELSON (ROBERT). *Companion for the Festivals and Fasts of the Church of England*. With some account of Mr. Nelson's Life and Writings. By William Kirke. Bettesworth. 12mo. 3*s*. Frontispiece. B.M.

Mar. 1.   *The German Atalantis*. Written by a Lady. " Printed and sold by most of the booksellers—viz. E. Curll . . . W. Hinchcliffe . . . J. Roberts . . . A. Bettesworth." (P.B.) 1*s*. 6*d*. and 2*s*.

Mar. 7.   The first pamphlet called *Homerides ;* or a Letter to Mr. Pope, Occasion'd by his intended Translation of Homer, By Sir Iliad Doggrel—i.e. Thomas Burnet, is often mentioned in connection with Curll. It was " sold by J. Roberts," but there is no evidence to show that Curll had a share in it. The same is true of George Sewell's *True Account of the Life and Writings of Thomas Burnett, Esq*, printed for A. Dodd, and issued four days later.

Mar. 26.   NOY (WILLIAM). *A Treatise of the Rights of the Crown* . . . written in 1634. Now first publish'd from the Original Manuscript. Lintott. 12mo. 2*s*. B.M. (? L.P.)
Preface by the publisher, unsigned.

Apr. 9.   *A True Copy of the Bishop of Salisbury's Last Will and Testament* . . . with an account of his Life and Times and his Character. (Pemberton, Roberts.) 6*d*. (P.B.)

Apr. 12.   PITTIS (WILLIAM). *Some Memoirs of the Life of John Radcliffe, M.D.* . . . also a true copy of his Last Will and Testament. 8vo. 2*s* in sheep, 2*s*. 6*d*. in calf. B.M.

Apr. 26.   *The Life of* . . . *Lady Jane Gray*. " On a superfine paper." 1*s*. 2 Cuts. (P.B.)
Presumably a re-issue.

Apr. 28. *Some Account of the Life and Writings of . . . Thomas Sprat*, late Lord Bishop of Rochester. With a True Copy of his Last Will and Testament. 8vo. 6*d.* B.M.

The Will, as usual, has a separate title-page : " London : Printed in the Year MDCCXV," ready to be bound up with anything else handy.

Advertised at the end is Robert Nelson's *An Address to Persons of Quality and Estate*, but it is not, I fancy, announced elsewhere as Curll's.

? May. PITTIS (WILLIAM). *Some Memoirs . . . of John Radcliffe.* . . . The Second Edition. 8vo. 2*s.*

Sheets of the first edition bound up with a supplement, which could be bought separately for 6*d.*

" Those Gentlemen who have any Memoirs to communicate, are desir'd to send them by Wednesday next, otherwise they cannot be inserted. N.B. The Packet out of Buckinghamshire is come to hand . . . for which Thanks are hereby return'd, and 6 Books, so soon as finished, shall be carefully sent, according to Direction, by E. CURLL." (*Post Boy*, 7th May.)

Showing Curll's methods of business.

" Whereas, since the Death of the late Dr. John Radcliffe, there have been two Books publish'd, the one with the Title of Dr. Radcliffe's Life and Letters, by E. Curll. . . . We the Executors . . . do think ourselves obliged to let the World know that both these Books were publish'd without our Consent, or Leave had from us, and without the Knowledge of any of the Doctor's Relations ; and we conceive they are highly injurious to the Memory of the Doctor, as well as a gross Imposition on the Publick : The former of them [Curll's] consisting of little else but a Number of false groundless Stories, and fictitious Letters. . . .

" Wm. Bromley   G. Beaumont
" Tho. Bacon   Anth. Kech."

But I would be willing to wager a small sum that " fictitious " is the wrong word. Curll was no forger. This, however, shows the results of his methods of business.

May 7. *A Proper Memorial for the* 29*th of May*. . . . Being an Account of Charles II's Escape after the Battle of Worcester. (Bettesworth, King, Hinchcliffe.) 1*s.* (P.B.)

May 24. *Memoirs of the Life of . . . Thomas, Late Marquis of Wharton.* With his Character by Sir Richard Steel[e]. " Printed for J. Roberts." 8vo. 1*s.* 6*d.* B.M.

?   *A True Copy of the Laſt Will and Teſtament of . . . Thomas, late Marquis of Wharton.* " Printed for J. Roberts . . . 1715." 8vo. 6*d.* B.M.

    Generally found with the *Memoirs.*

June 4.   *The Case of Impotency Debated. . . . The Second Edition.* 2 vols. 12mo. 5*s.* B.M.

    So popular was the book that the type was actually reset.

June 7.   SEWELL (GEORGE). *An Essay Towards a true Account of the . . . late Bishop of Salisbury.* 8vo. 3*s.* B.M.

    By this time he really ought to have found out something about the old gentleman.

June 23.   KNIPE (CHARLES). *A City Ramble ; Or, the Humours of the Compter.* A Comedy. Pemberton. 12mo. 1*s.* Frontispiece. B.M.

    Included in the liſt of " Books Printed for E. Curll and J. Pemberton " is *The Hiſtory of the moſt Serene Houses of Brunswick-Lunenbergh.* 6*s.* (Quite conceivably the title is altogether different.)

? June.   STAUGHTON ( ). *Secret Hiſtory of the Late Miniſtry . . . to the Death of the Queen.* (Baker.) 6*s.*

    I cannot identify this author. Could he have been Staunton ?

July 9.   SALIGNAC DE LA MOTHE FENELON (FRANCOIS). *The Adventures of Telemachus.* Translated by John Ozell. (Pemberton, Taylor.) 6*s.* (E.P.)

    On the appearance of which Churchill, moſt respectable of publishers, deprecates Ozell's misplaced zeal in the matter, and sells his version by Isaac Littlebury at 3*s.* This leads to an explanation on Ozell's part. England's foremoſt translator (*vide* the whole Bench of Bishops) complains of the egregious and numerous blunders of the earlier version, " not a fifth part of which," he maintains, " was done by Mr. Littlebury."

    But who cares ?

July 9.   NELSON (ROBERT). *Miscellaneous Works.* (Strahan, Bettesworth.) (*Eve. Post.*)

    Not, apparently, of much value to contemporary eyes. The executors complain that the book has been " issued without their approbation, is a wretched performance, with some actual falsehoods." (*Poſt Boy,* Sept. 13th.)

July 12.   [OLDMIXON (JOHN).] *The Secret Hiſtory of Europe.* Part IV. and Laſt. Pemberton. 8vo. 4*s.* B.M.

?   [OLDMIXON (JOHN).] *The Secret Hiſtory of Europe.* Part III. The Second Edition. Pemberton. 8vo. 4*s.* B.M.

July 12.   It is possible that " the Whole Works of the Celebrated

Monsieur Voiture " advertised in the *Post Boy* of this date is a new edition.

July 14.   ROWE (NICHOLAS). *The Tory's Downfall*, an Excellent new Ditty. 2*d.* (*Eve. Post.*)

July 19.   [NORTH (HON. ROGER).] *The Gentleman's Accomptant*. The Second Edition. 12mo. 3*s.*

The four pages of " Books Printed for Edmund Curll " include a series of seventeen " Classicks, &c. lately printed at Oxford and Cambridge."

July 19.   [BURNET (THOMAS).] *A Second Tale of a Tub*, or the History of Robert Powel, the Puppet Man. " Printed for J. Roberts." 8vo. 3*s.* 6*d.* B.M.

The B.M. copy contains an injudicious preface to Lord Halifax, which was cancelled, as well as the preface to Lord Oxford.

July 23.   BILTON (Capt.). *Journal of a late unfortunate Voyage, from Lisbon to Virginia.* (Bettesworth.) 6*d.* (P.B.)

July 28.   *Cases of Divorce for Several Reasons.* 12mo. 2*s.* 6*d.* Frontispiece (portrait of Beau Feilding). B.M. Contains the delectable cases of Feilding, Duchess of Cleaveland, John Dormer, and Sir George Downing. WARD (THOMAS). *England's Reformation.* A Poem. "Printed for J. Baker." 2 vols. 12mo. 5*s.* B.M.

Advertised in Curll's lists. Frequently reprinted.

July 28.   [OLDMIXON (JOHN).] *The Secret History of Europe.* [Part One.] The Third Edition. 8vo. 4*s.* (P.B.)

July 30.   [NORTH (HON. ROGER).] *A Discourse of Fish.* . . . The Second Edition. 12mo. 1*s.* 6*d.* B.M.

Aug. 2.   GAUGER (NICHOLAS). *Fires Improv'd.* Being a New Method Of Building Chimneys, So as to prevent their smoaking. Made English and improved by J[ohn] T[heophilus] Desaguiliers. Senex. 12mo. 3*s.* Nine folding plates. B.M.

" The whole being suited to the capacity of the meanest workman."

Even I understand it.

Aug. 6.   GREGORY (Dr.). *Elements of Catoptricks and Dioptricks, Improv'd.* Introduction by W. Browne. (Pemberton, Taylor.) 8vo. 5*s.* "With plates by Mr. Senex." (P.B.)

Ought one to know what these fearsome things are ?

Aug. 6.   ADDISON (JOSEPH). *The Knowledge of Medals.* The Second Edition. (Caldecott, Hooke.) 2*s.* 6*d.* (P.B.)

I have not found the date of the first edition, nor am I quite clear as to what the book contains.

Aug. 25.   SEWELL (GEORGE). *An Epistle to Joseph Addison.* . . . Occasion'd by the Death of . . . the Earl of Halifax. (Pemberton, Roberts.) (P.B.)

Aug. 27. SYMSON (WILLIAM). *A New Voyage to the West Indies.* "Printed by H. Meere." Bettesworth. 8vo. 3*s.* 6*d.* Map and plates. B.M.

Sept. 1. P. (D.). *Brief Reflections on Sir Richard Steele's Large Dedication to the Pope,* and his Preface to a Book Intituled, An Account of the Roman-Catholick Religion throughout the World. 8vo. 6*d.* B.M.

Sept. 1. HENLEY (JOHN). *Esther Queen of Persia.* The Second Edition. (Bettesworth, Pemberton.) 1*s.* 6*d.* (P.B.)

Sept. 3. LILLY (WILLIAM). *History of his Life and Times.* "Printed for J. Roberts." 8vo. 1*s.* 6*d.* and 2*s.* B.M.

Sept. 15. GALE (SAMUEL). *The History and Antiquities of the Cathedral Church of Winchester.* . . . Begun by . . . Henry, Earl of Clarendon. 8vo. 10*s.* and 12*s.* (on a superfine Genoa paper). 18 copper-plates. B.M.

Sept. 15. MONTAGU (CHARLES, EARL OF HALIFAX). *The Works and Life.* . . . Pemberton, Hooke. 8vo. 5*s.* Portrait. B.M.

Oct. 22. *The Bath Toasts for the Year* 1715. A Poem. To which are added, exact Descriptions of the Bath and Tunbridge Wells. 6*d.* (P.B.)

Nov. 1. NIXON (ROBERT). *Cheshire Prophecy.* The Third Edition. (Roberts.) 12mo. 4*d.* (P.B.)
This is the first edition in which Curll seems to have had an interest. He continued to reprint for thirty years.

Nov. 12. [BULLOCK (CHARLES).] *A Woman's Revenge; or, The Match in Newgate.* A Comedy. (Pemberton, Mears, Brown.) 12mo. 1*s.* Frontispiece. (P.B.)

Nov. 26. SALIGNAC DE LA MOTHE FENELON (FRANCOIS). *Conversations on the Plurality of Worlds.* Translated by W. Gardiner. (Bettesworth.) 2*s.* 6*d.* (P.B.)

Nov. 26. YOUNG (EDWARD). *A Poem on the Last Day.* The Third Edition, Corrected. Bettesworth, Pemberton. 8vo. 1*s.* Cuts. B.M.
A second edition (not Curll's) had been published at Oxford in 1713.

Dec. 3. PHILIPS (JOHN, the Dramatist). *The Earl of Mar marr'd;* With the Humours of Jockey, the Highlander. A Tragi-Comical Farce. 8vo. 6*d.* B.M.
Not acted; and I don't wonder.

Dec. 6 (dated 1716). *The Last Wills and Testaments of J. Partridge Student in Physick and Astrology, and Dr. Burnett, Master of the Charterhouse.* 8vo. 6*d.* B.M.
Separately paged, and also issued separately in later years.

Dec 17. PHILIPS (JOHN, the Dramatist). *The Earl of Mar marr'd.* The Second Edition. (P.B.)

Dec. 17. *The Lives and Characters of the most Illustrious Persons who died in the Years* 1713, 1714, *and* 1715. (Pemberton.) 2 vols. 11*s*. (P.B.)

Dec. 31. NIXON (ROBERT). *Cheshire Prophecy.* "The Fifth Edition, to which is added, Lilly's Remarkable Prophecy." (Pemberton, Roberts.) 12mo. 4*d*. (E.P.). Probably dated 1716. Fourth edition not advertised.

? Dec. *Wit at a Pinch; or The Lucky Prodigal.* A Comedy. Pemberton, Brown, Mears. 12mo. 1*s*. Frontispiece. B.M.

Dated 1715.

SEWELL (GEORGE). *The Life and Character of Mr. John Philips.* The Second Edition. 12mo. 1*s*. B.M.

A copy in the B.M. has in front of the title-page another : " Poems by Mr. Philips . . . to which is Prefix'd his Life. London. Printed in the Year MDCCXV," and the volume contains various pieces, separately paged, some bearing Clements's imprint.

[PHILIPS (JOHN).] *Ode ad Henricum S. John. Armig.* Editio Tertia.

Part of the *Works*, but, in spite of its pagination ([37]–[43]), is found separately, or with the translation by Newcombe.

ROWE (NICHOLAS). *The Poetical Works.* 8vo. 5*s*. B.M.

The title is euphemistic, the volume containing only those few things of Rowe's which Curll had already printed, with a new title-page.

GERHARD (JOHN). *The Christian's Support.* . . . Being the Divine Meditations. " The Second Edition, with Additions." Englished by Thomas Rowell. 8vo. Frontispiece. B.M.

A Character of . . . *Gilbert, Lord Bishop of Sarum :* with a True Copy of his Last Will and Testament. The Third Edition. 8vo. 6*d*. B.M.

Mostly Will.

[BOULTON (ROBERT).] *A Compleat History of Magick, Sorcery, and Witchcraft.* Vol. I. 12mo. Frontispiece. (Cat.)

Vol. II. issued in 1716.

Tory Pills to Purge Whig Melancholy. A Collection of Poems, Songs, &c. Written in Defence of Church and State. The Second Edition. " Printed for A. Moore." 12mo. 1*s*. 6*d*. B.M.

I have not seen the first edition. Advertised in Curll's lists.

OLDMIXON (JOHN). *The Life and Posthumous Works of*

Arthur Maynwaring. " Printed for A. Bell . . . W. Taylor . . . J. Baker." 8vo. B.M.

Mentioned in Pope's *Full and True Account* as one of Curll's publications, but not apparently advertised by him.

PRIDEAUX (HUMPHREY). *Directions to Church-Wardens.* The Third Edition. 1*s.* 6*d.*

Advertised in the Radcliffe *Memoirs.*

The Case of the Ld. John Drummond, In Relation to a Rape. " Printed for J. Roberts." 12mo. 6*d.* B.M.

Advertised in a 1741 list.

[BURNET (THOMAS)]. *A Second Tale of a Tub.* . . . The Second Edition. 8vo. Frontispiece. (Cat.)

[MANLEY (DELIA DE LA RIVIERE).] *The Adventures of Rivella.* . . . The Second Edition. 8vo. Frontispiece. (Cat.)

[HOLDSWORTH (EDWARD).] *The Mouse-Trap.* A Poem. Done from the Original Latin in Milton's Stile. Gosling, 1715. 8vo. (Cat.)

In this year *The Cases of Impotency and Divorce* were issued in four volume sets.

1716

Jan. 5. *The Case of the Earl of Mar and his Adherents fairly stated.* 6*d.* (E.P.)

Jan. 7. *A Memorial for the 30th January.* (Bettesworth.) 1*s.* (P.B.)

Jan. 16. *Memoirs of the Life and Times of . . . Thomas Tenison.* With his Will. " Printed for J. Roberts." 8vo. 2*s.* Portrait. B.M.

No date. Not to be confused with *The Last Will,* &c., issued by Wyat.

The same. The Third Edition. B.M.

Jan. 17. FREEMAN (PHILANAX), *pseud. The Mock Patriots;* or Highwaymen no Tories. 8vo. 6*d.* B.M.

Advertised in this book as printed for Curll, but not mentioned in the newspapers, are the two following books :

ANDREWS (CHARLES). *A Full and Authentick Narrative of the intended Horrid Conspiracy and Invasion.* The Second Edition. 6*d.*

The Real Antichrist : An Essay fully proving, That the Views of the Laity proceed from the Corruptions of the Clergy. 1*s.*

Jan. 21. STEELE (SIR RICHARD). *Account of the new Invention— Improv'd Fires.* " Given Gratis." (P.B.)

Jan. 21.   HOUGH (NATHANIEL). *The Spirit of Popery Set forth*, in a View of the Reformation. A Sermon. 8vo. 4*d.* B.M.

? Jan.   [WEST (RICHARD).] *A Discourse concerning Treasons*, and Bills of Attainder. " Printed for J. Roberts . . . 1716." 8vo. 1*s.* 6*d.* B.M.
Repeatedly advertised in Curll's lists.

Feb. 4.   ADAMS (SAMUEL). *Obedience due to the Higher Powers*. A Sermon. 8vo. 4*d.* B.M.

Feb. 4.   WISE (THOMAS). *The Pastoral Duty open'd*. A Visitation Sermon . . . at Canterbury. 6*d.* (E.P.)
You didn't know that Curll had produced all these godly things ?

Feb. 11.   *The Last Will and Testament . . . of . . . George Hickes*. 8vo. 6*d.* B.M.

Feb. 11.   HICKES (GEORGE). *A Caveat against Fanaticks under all Denominations*. 1*s.* (P.B.)

Mar. 7.   BLACKMORE (SIR RICHARD). *Essays upon Several Subjects*. Pemberton. 8vo. B.M.
The second volume, issued in 1717, was not printed for Curll. Obviously the City knight did not view with approval his Curllean colleagues. It was for this volume that Pope attacked him in the *Full and True Account*.

Mar. 17.   PRIOR (MATTHEW). *A Second Collection of Poems on Several Occasions*. " Printed for J. Roberts." 8vo. 1*s.* B.M.

Mar. 17.   [? ADDISON (JOSEPH).] *The Reasons which induced His Majesty to create Sir Thomas Parker . . . a Peer. . . .* 4to. 3*d.* (P.B.)

Mar. 24.   PHILIPS (JOHN, the Dramatist). *The Pretender's Flight, or, a Mock Coronation*. (A Sequel to The Earl of Mar marr'd.) 8vo. 6*d.* B.M.
Not intended for presentation—which was possibly lucky for John.

Mar. 26.   [POPE (ALEXANDER) and GAY (JOHN).] *Court Poems*. " Printed for J. Roberts." 8vo. 6*d.* (P.M.)
The date is misprinted 1706.
For the nice little row that followed, consult the text.

Mar. 27.   WALDRON (GEORGE). *A Persuasive Oration to the People of Great Britain*. " Printed for the Author." Sold by Harrison, Boulter, Graves. 8vo. 1*s.* B.M.
Curll's name not given on the title-page.

? Mar. 29. [POPE (ALEXANDER).] *A Full and True Account* of a Horrid and Barbarous Revenge by Poison on the Body of Mr. Edmund Curll, Bookseller. . . . " Publish'd by an Eye-Witness." Roberts, Morphew, Baker, Popping. sm. Fo. 3*d.* B.M.

This, of course, is not, strictly speaking, Curll's publication, but I dare say you could have bought as many copies as you wanted in his shop.

There are some lines on the title-page, by the way, which may be Pope's. Here they are :

" So when Curll's Stomach the strong Drench o'ercame,
(Infus'd in Vengeance of insulted Fame)
Th' Avenger sees, with a delighted Eye,
His long Jaws open, and his colour fly ;
And while his Guts the keen Emeticks urge,
Smiles on his Vomit, and enjoys the Purge."

Apr. 5.   H. (W.). *The Fate of Traytors.* A Poem upon the Rebellion. 8vo. 6d. B.M.

Apr. 10.   *An Account of the Tryal of the Earl of Winton.* " Printed for S. Popping." 2d. (*Flying Post.*)
For which Curll was taken into custody.

May 1.   POPE (ALEXANDER). *To the Ingenious Mr. Moore, Author of the Celebrated Worm Powder.* Fo. 2d. B.M.
Usually called " Mr. Pope's Worms."
Issued also as a single sheet " Adapted by Mr. William Turner to Ye Tune of Chivy Chace," but I cannot say whether Curll had anything to do with it.

May 5.   The same. The Second Edition. (P.M.)

May 5.   [BOULTON (RICHARD)]. *A Compleat History of Magick.* . . . Vol. II. (P.B.)

May 8.   PHILIPS (JOHN, the Dramatist). *The Earl of Mar marr'd.* The Third Edition. 8vo. 6d. B.M.

May 19.   *State Poems by the Most Eminent Hands.* " Printed for J. Roberts." 8vo. 6d. B.M.
Includes *The Worms, Verses upon the Sickness and Recovery of* . . . *R. Walpole, The Three Patriots,* and an *Epilogue for The Drummer.*

May 22.   DES CHAMPS ( ). *Cato of Utica.* A Tragedy. Translated from the French . . . by John Ozell. (E.P.)
The book had been announced in April, but publication was postponed owing to Ozell's presence being required at the rehearsals of his version. Curll also warned the public against " a pretended translation on the market." This was published on 12th May by Morphew, who retorted thus : " This [*i.e.,* his own blank verse translation] is done by a Club of Gentlemen of the two Universities ; that Mr. Curll might not impose a Cato upon the Publick, managed by himself and his Hirelings, which, our ingenious Author says, in the said Curll's last Will and Testament [*i.e.,* Pope's

Full and True Account], is damnably translated. But these Gentlemen humbly submit their Performance to the Censor of the Criticks in both Languages, notwithstanding the un-mannerly Quack-Advertisement of the aforesaid Curll, and his assuming Author J. Ozell."

And this to Ozell, Britain's foremost translator (*vide* the whole bench of bishops) !

May 26.   *Moore' Worms for the learned Mr. Curll, Bookseller.* (Sold by the Booksellers of London and Westminster.) (P.B.)

May 29.   [DUCKETT (GEORGE).] *Homerides ; or Homer's First Book Moderniz'd.* By Sir Iliad Doggrel. " Printed for R. Burleigh."

There is no direct evidence that Curll had a share in it, but nearly all his books were being advertised at this time in Burleigh's lists.

May 31.   [OLDMIXON (JOHN).] *The Catholick Poet ; or Protestant Barnaby's Sorrowful Lamentation.* An Excellent New Ballad. Morphew, Roberts. Fo. 3*d.* (Cat.)

May 31.   [DENNIS (JOHN).] *A True Character of Mr. Pope, and his Writings.* " Printed for S. Popping." 8vo. 3*d.* B.M.

Curll's advertisement (F.P.) runs : " Sold at the News shops, and by all the Booksellers in England, Dominion of Wales, and Town of Berwick upon Tweed."

Pope thought that Mrs. Centlivre and Gildon had a hand in the ballad, but Curll gives it all to Oldmixon.

May 31.   W[ORLIDGE] (J[OHN]). *A Compleat System of Husbandry and Gardening.* Pickard, Bettesworth. 8vo. 6*s.* B.M.

June 14.   DES CHAMPS (   ). *Cato of Utica.* The Second Edition. 1*s.* (P.M.)

June 14.   PRIDEAUX (HUMPHREY). *The True Nature of Imposture Fully Display'd in the Life of Mahomet.* The Sixth Edition, Corrected. Hooke, Caldecot. 12mo. 2*s.* 6*d.* B.M.

June 16.   POMFRET (JOHN). *Poems on Several Occasions.* The Fourth Edition. (Taylor.) 12mo. 2*s.* (P.M.)

Before   POPE (ALEXANDER). *Version of the First Psalm.* " Printed
June 20.   for R. Burleigh." 2*d.*

First advertisement seen is dated July 9th (E.P.), but Pope's letter to Swift of June 20th mentions the publication.

June 20.   COCKBURN (WILLIAM). *The Art of Midwifery, Improv'd.* Made English. (Pemberton, Taylor.) 6*s.* 38 cuts. (P.M.)

June 28.   GAY (JOSEPH) *pseud.* i.e. FRANCIS CHUTE. *The Petticoat.* An Heroi-Comical Poem. " Printed for R. Burleigh." 8vo. 1*s.* B.M.

" July 4, 1716. F. Chute received of Messrs. Curll

and Hooke full satisfaction for the sole right and title of the copy of a poem called The Petticoat." (Upcott MSS.)   Subsequently called *The Hoop Petticoat*.

Hitherto generally ascribed to J. D. Breval.

June 30.   BUTLER (SARAH). *Irish Tales*. (Hooke.)   1*s*. and 1*s*. 6*d*. (P.M.)

? June.   [POPE (ALEXANDER).]   *A Further Account of the most Deplorable Condition of Mr. Edmund Curl, Bookseller*, Since his being Poison'd on the 28th of March.   To be publish'd Weekly.   " Printed, and Sold by all the Pub-lishers, Mercuries, and Hawkers, within the Bills of Mortality."   (Cat.)

July 9.   GAY (JOSEPH), *pseud.* i.e. FRANCIS CHUTE.   *The Petticoat*. " The Second Edition, Corrected."   " Printed for R. Burleigh."   8vo.   B.M.

July 21.   *The Loyal Mourner for the best of Princes*.   Being a Collec-tion of Poems sacred to the Memory of Queen Anne. By various Hands. (Morphew.)   8vo.   1*s*. 6*d*.

" Re-publish'd " this day (P.B.).   Advertisements in 1719 add " Publish'd by Mr. Oldisworth."

I am not certain in which year the book first ap-peared.

July 26.   BARBER (JOHN).   *The Character of the Reverend and Learned Dr. Robert South*.   The Oration Spoken at his Funeral.   (In Latin and English.)   Burleigh.   8vo.   6*d*. B.M.   Frontispiece.

For which Curll was thrashed by the Westminster boys.   The frontispiece is the only really intimate por-trait of Curll that we have.

Sept. 15.   MONTAGU (CHARLES, EARL OF MONTAGU).   *The Poetical Works*.   The Second Edition.   Pemberton.   8vo.   5*s*. Portrait.   B.M.

" Prefix'd by the Character of His Lordship by Mr. Addison," with Memoirs.

Sept. 15   [POPE (ALEXANDER).]   *Court Poems*.   Part II.   " Printed
(dated   for J. Roberts."   12mo.   (E.P.)
1717).   Contains *The Dream, The Hyde Park Ramble, The Worms* and the *First Psalm*.

Sept. 15.   CHUTE (FRANCIS).   *Beauty and Virtue*.   A Poem Sacred to the Memory of Anne, late Countess of Sutherland. " Printed for R. Burleigh."   8vo.   6*d*.   B.M.

Sept. 15.   *The Case of Mr. [William] Paul and Mr. Hall*, with True Copies of their Papers, deliver'd at the Place of Execu-tion.   6*d*.   (E.P.)

In Burleigh's list.   A doubtful entry.

Sept. 25.   AGRICOLA (GEORG ANDREAS).   *The Artificial Gardiner*. Translated from the Dutch.   12mo.   6*d*.   B.M.

Advertises the following two books as " Sold by E. Curll " : BRADLEY (RICHARD) *Historia Plantarum Succulentarium*. The History of Succulent Plants. " Printed for the Author." 4to. B.M. PHILIPS (J. T.). *Dissertatio Historico Philosophica de Atheismo*. 8vo. 5s.

Also announces as in the press " Printed for E. Curll " :

HUET (PIERRE DAVID). *The History of the Commerce and Navigation of the Ancients*. Made English. " Printed for B. Lintot . . . and W. Mears . . . 1717." 8vo. 5s. B.M.

Oct. 6.   PITTIS (WILLIAM). *Dr. Radcliffe's Life and Letters*. The Third Edition. 12mo. 1s. 6d. B.M.

Oct. 9.   WILLIS (BROWN). *Survey of the Cathedral Church of St. David's*. " Printed for R. Gosling." 5s. (P.B.)

Oct. 25.   *The Life of Dr. Robert South*, with a true Copy of his . . . Last Will and Testament. With 3 Sermons. 5s. Frontispiece. (E.P.)

Oct. 27. (dated 1717).   OVIDIUS NASO. *Metamorphoses*. A New Translation by the most Eminent Hands, viz. Mr. Sewell, Mr. Philips, Mr. Hughes, Mr. Pope, Mr. Gay, &c. (Bettesworth, Taylor, Brown). 2 vols. 12mo. 16 plates. 6s. (E.P.)

Brought out in opposition to Garth's publication.

Nov. 16 (dated 1717).   PURNEY ( ). *Pastorals* : After the simple Manner of Theocritus. " Printed for . . . Brown . . . Burleigh." 8vo. 1s. B.M.

Nov. 17.   GAUGER (NICHOLAS). *Fires Improv'd*. With an Appendix. 3s. (P.B.)

Nov. 24.   *The English Theatre*. Being a Collection of Plays. 2 vols. 12mo. 7s. Cuts. (E.P.)

Separate plays with a new title-page. Almost certain to be dated 1717.

Nov. 29.   " This day is Republish'd on a Superfine Paper, The Whole Works of Robert Nelson. . . With a Character by Dr. Marshall." (Bettesworth.) 6s. and 7s. (E.P.)

Presumably a re-issue of the *Miscellaneous Works*.

Dec. 4 (dated 1717).   [OLDMIXON (JOHN).] *Court Tales ;* or, A History of the Amours of the Present Nobility ; with a Compleat Key. " Printed for J. Roberts." 8vo. 5s. Frontispiece. B.M.

Dec. 8 (dated 1717).   [? HUTCHINSON (F.).] *The Life of . . . Dr. John Tillotson*, late Archbishop of Canterbury. Taylor, Osborn. 8vo. 3s. 6d. Portrait. B.M.

Apparently also issued in folio at 3s. Alleged to have been " compiled from the Minutes of the Rev. Mr.

Young, Dean of Salisbury, by F. H., M.A." Some people would bet against this.

Dec. 13 (dated 1717). MANLEY (DELIA DE LA RIVIERE). *Memoirs of the Life of.* . . . To which is added a Compleat Key. The Third Edition. 8vo. 1s. 6d., 2s. and 2s. 6d. (E.P.)

Dec. 15 (dated 1717). ORLEANS (F.). *A Complete History of the Family of Stuarts.* Made English. (Baker.) 8vo. 5s. (Cat.)

Dec. 26 (dated 1717). PURNEY ( ). *Pastorals.* The Second Edition. (E.P.)

WESLEY (SAMUEL). *Neck or Nothing :* A Consolatory Letter from Mr. D–nt–n to Mr. C–rll upon his being Tost in a Blanket. " Sold by Charles King, 1716." 8vo. B.M. *The English Theatre for* 1716. 8vo. 4s. 6d.
   Plays bound up with a general title-page. Advertised in Curll's lists. Possibly dated 1717.

? year. DENNIS (JOHN). *Priestcraft Distinguish'd from Christianity.* The Second Edition. 1s.
   Advertised in the same author's *Remarks upon* . . . *Homer* (1717).

1717

Jan. 5. CENTLIVRE (SUSANNA). *The Cruel Gift.* A Tragedy. Bettesworth. 12mo. 1s. Frontispiece. B.M.

Feb. 26. DENNIS (JOHN). *Remarks upon Mr. Pope's Translation of Homer.* 8vo. 1s. 6d. B.M.

Mar. 7. B[REVAL] (J[OHN] D[URANT].) *The Art of Dress.* " Printed for R. Burleigh." 8vo. 1s. B.M.
   Contains also *Apple-Pye,* by William King. The Preface is signed J. D. B.
   "Feb. 13, 1716/17. John Durant Breval was paid by Mr. Curll four guineas for a poem called The Art of Dress." (Upcott MSS.)

Mar. 7. [BLACKMORE (SIR RICHARD).] *The Kit-Cats.* ? Another edition. 8vo. 1s. or 1s. 6d. on a Royal Paper. (Burleigh.) (P.B.)

Mar. 14. ERDESWICKE (SAMPSON). *A Survey of Staffordshire.* [Edited by Richard Rawlinson.] 8vo. 250 copies at 10s. B.M.

? CONGREVE (DR. THOMAS, of Wolverhampton). *A Scheme, or, Proposal For making a Navigable Communication Between the Rivers of Trent and Severn,* in the County of Stafford. 8vo. Folding maps. B.M.
   Dedication dated 6 Feb. 16/17. Issued with Mears's 1723 edition of the Erdeswicke book, and apparently printed for the subscribers of the first edition.

Mar. 14. *The Hiftory and Antiquities of the Cathedral Church of Rochefter.* 8vo. 5*s.* and 6*s.* "on the beft paper." B.M.
Mears bought the remaining sheets, and re-issued the book with a new title-page in 1723.

Apr. 16. HOWARD (HENRY, EARL OF SURREY). *Songes and Sonettes.* 8vo. "Reprinted from the 1567 edition, by E. Curll." 1*s.* and 2*s.* L.P. (Cat.)

Apr. 18. RAPIN (PAUL DE). *Dissertation sur les Whigs & les Torys.* Or an Hiftorical Dissertation of Whig and Tory. Made English by Mr. [John] Ozell. 8vo. 1*s.* B.M.

May 11. *The Life and Death of Lucius,* the 1ft Chriftian King of Britain. 6*d.* (P.B.)
A play on this subject by Mrs. Manley had juft been produced at Drury Lane. Curll's advertisement reads as though she had been the author of the pamphlet as well, although a closer examination will show that it is ambiguously worded. Of course she wasn't.

May 17. *A True Copy of the Laft Will and Teftament of . . . Daniel Williams, D.D.* "Printed for R. Burleigh." 8vo. 1*s.* B.M.

? *The Inscriptions upon the Tombs, Grave-Stones, &c in the Dissenters Burial place near Bunhill-Fields.* 8vo. 1*s.* 6*d.* B.M.
Advertised in the preceding book. Firft advertisement seen Feb. 25th, 1718. (P.B.)

May 23. *A True Copy of the Laft Will and Teftament of . . . Gilbert, Lord Bishop of Sarum. . . .* To which is added, The Inscription on the Monument erected to his Memory. The Fourth Edition. 8vo. 6*d.* B.M.

? *The Laft Will and Teftament of . . . Robert Nelson.*
Not apparently advertised before May 23rd, 1717, but almoft certainly of earlier date.

May 23. *The Loyalift's Memorial for the 29th of May.* "Re-publish'd." (Bettesworth.) 1*s.* (P.B.)
" Re-publish'd " may be anything you like to think.

June 6. PHILIPS (JOHN, the Dramatift). *The Inquisition.* A Farce. The Second Edition. (Warner.) 6*d.* (P.B.)
No mention of a firft edition seen.

June 6. WRIGHT (THOMAS). *The Female Virtuosoes, or Witty Ladies.* A Comedy. 8vo. 1*s.* (P.B.)
I am not sure of the date of this firft (Curll) edition. I am not even certain that the title is correct. Breval seems to have had something to do with it. The second edition of 1721 has an elaborately ironical title-page (q.v.).

June 6. DORIACK CHANCEL (A.). *A new Journey over Europe.* The Second Edition. (Harding, Taylor, Baker.) (D.C.

? June.   [AMHURST (NICHOLAS).] *An Epiſtle to the Chevalier ;* and a Congratulatory Poem to Mr. Secretary Addison. 1*s.* (P.B.)

? June.   POPE (ALEXANDER). *Miscellany in Two Parts.* (Burleigh only.) 12mo. 6*d.* (P.B.)

Part I. contains the *Court Poems*, with *The Worms* and the *Firſt Psalm.* Part II. contains *The Hyde Park Ramble, The Parson's Daughter, The Court Ballad, Court Epigrams,* and *The Weſtminſter Ballad* by " Mr. Joseph Gay."

Of these nearly all were also published separately. The *Court Ballad* appeared this year, sm. Fo. 2*d.* " Printed for A. Smith." And also " The Second Edition, Correᴄted." B.M. As did also

WYVILL (CHRISTOPHER). *The Parson's Daughter.* A Tale. " For the use of pretty Girls with small Fortunes." 8vo. 6*d.* But whether the copy in the B.M. " Printed for J. Harris near St. James's Bagnio, 1717," and including the *Còurt Epigrams* and the *Court Ballad,* was Curll's or a piracy, I do not know. Smith's edition of the *Ballad* advertised Pope's *Miscellany,* the second edition.

?   The same. The Second Edition. " Printed for R. Burleigh." 12mo. 6*d.* B.M.

P.S. I am inclined to think that when in after years Curll was advertising *The Parson's Daughter* he really meant the *Miscellany.* It was an old dodge of his to take one item from a colleᴄtion and announce it as though it ſtood by itself—a new and original piece.

June 23.   B[REVAL] (J[OHN] D[URANT].) *The Art of Dress.* The Second Edition. (P.B.)

July 23.   NEWCOMBE (THOMAS). *An Ode sacred to the Memory of . . . the Countess of Berkeley.* 8vo. 1*s.* (P.B.)

With a letter from Edward Young, printed on the back of the title-page, advising Curll to print the poem, though Young afterwards announced that he had done so without authority. (Cat.) Which seems odd.

July 23.   *The British Court ; or Poetical Characters of the Royal Family.* By a Person of Quality. 6*d.* (P.B.)

July 23.   PLACE (CONYERS). *The Thoughts of an Honeſt Whig.* 6*d.* 8vo. B.M.

Concerns the Bangorian controversy, and advertises *A Complete Collection* of all the Papers which have pass'd between the Bishop of Bangor, Dr. Snape, the Bishop of Carlisle, and Dr. Kennet. 6*d.*

?   PLACE (CONYERS). *An Impartial Account of the Tories,* from His Majeſty's happy Accession to the Present Time. 6*d.*

Advertised in *The Thoughts of an Honest Whig*, but not mentioned in the newspapers until November.

?   [? COLLINS (ANTHONY).]   *Howel and Hoadly ;* or the Church of England crucify'd between two ——   6*d.* (P.B.)

Aug. 10.   A View of the Duke of Marlborough's Battles, painted by Mr. Languerec, in his Grace's Palace at St. James's. (P.B.)
? engraving.

Aug. 10.   HOWARD (HENRY, EARL OF SURREY) and WYAT (SIR THOMAS).   *Poems.*   2*s.* 6*d.* or 5*s.* on large paper.   (P.B.)
Candidly I am not clear about the several 1717 editions that appeared. The one most usually seen bears the names of Mears and Brown on the title-page, but there were at least two others. George Sewell edited one of them.

Aug. 13.   [BREVAL (JOHN DURANT).]   *Mac-Dermot ;* Or, the Irish Fortune-Hunter.   A Poem.   8vo.   1*s.*   B.M.

Nov. 2.   " Re-publish'd this day " *The Whole Works of Robert Nelson.* ? second edition. Also *The Last Day* by Edward Young. "A new edition on a fine paper." 3 cuts. (Bettesworth).   1*s.*   (P.B.)
But I do not know whether they really were new.

Nov. 5.   " This Day re-publish'd " :
Fenelon's *Plurality of Worlds.*   2*s.* 6*d.*   ? second edition.
Symson's *New Voyage to the East Indies.*   3*s.* 6*d.*   ? second edition (but see under 1720).
Hanover Tales.   1*s.* 6*d.* and 2*s.*
Callipædia.   4*s.* and 7*s.* 6*d.* L.P.

Nov. 19.   G—— (   ). *The Apparition.* A Poem. Address'd to the Earl of Clarendon. (Baker.)   1*s.*   (P.B.)

Dec. 19. (dated 1718).   *Petri Abaelardi, Abbatis Ruyensis et Heloissæ, Abbatissæ Paracletensis Epistolæ.* . . . Richardi Rawlinson. Taylor. 8vo.   6*s.*   B.M.
Memoirs of the Life of that learned Antiquary, Elias Ashmole, Esq. ; Drawn up by himself by way of Diary. 8vo. " Printed for J. Roberts, 1717." (Cat.)
"Publish'd by Charles Burman, Esq." In Curll's lists.
[BURNET (THOMAS).]   *A Second Tale of a Tub.* The Third Edition. Roberts only. 8vo. (Cat.)
[SOLORZANO] (ALONZO DE CASTILLO). *The Spanish Pole-Cat ; or, the Adventures of Seniora Rufina.* Begun to be translated by Sir Roger L'Estrange. And Finished by Mr. Ozell. Taylor. 8vo.   4*s.*   B.M.
SOUTH (ROBERT). *Posthumous Works.* 8vo.   5*s.*   Portrait.   B.M.

Edited by Edmund Curll. A notice dated July 26th, 1716, bids the public take no notice of any attacks on the proposed printing of this work, on the ground that it is unauthorized. "Concerning these particulars," it concludes, "any Person who has Authority to enquire, may receive full Satisfaction of Mr. *Curll*, and of which, his [South's] Executors are desir'd to inform themselves before they consent to the Inserting of any more Scandalous Advertisements against a Work, of the Contents of which, they are wholly Ignorant." But they knew their Curll.

GAY (JOSEPH), *pseud.* i.e. J. D. BREVAL. *The Confederates.* A Farce. "Printed for R. Burleigh." 8vo. 1*s.* Figures on title-page. B.M.

Not advertised by Curll, but almost certainly his.

HELIODORUS. *The Adventures of Theagenes and Clariclea.* Translated from the Greek. Taylor, Gosling, Hooke, Brown, Osborn. 2 vols. 12mo. 5*s.* B.M.

Dedication signed C. G., i.e. Charles Gildon.

At the end is a list of "Books lately Printed for E. Curll, W. Taylor, J. Hooke, and Jon. Browne." Of these the first two pages are Curll's.

EARBERY (MATTHIAS). *The Pretended Reformers.* Made English from the French Original. [Part I. only.] "Printed for A. Smith." 2*s.* B.M.

Frequently advertised in Curll's lists.

The English Theatre for 1717. 8vo. 3*s.* 6*d.*

Plays bound up with a general title-page.

JACOB (GILES). *The Rape of the Smock;* An Heroi-Comical Poem. "Printed for R. Burleigh." 1717. Frontispiece. 8vo. (Cat.)

Not apparently advertised by Curll, though the second edition of 1727 bears his son's name on the title-page.

A Complete Key to Three Hours after Marriage. "Printed, and Sold by E. Berrington, 1717." 6*d.*

Curll seems to have had some share in this pamphlet, which he advertises in one of his lists, and which is included in his *Miscellanies upon Several Subjects,* 1719.

1718

Jan. 6. GAY (JOSEPH) *pseud.* i.e. J. D. BREVAL. *A Compleat Key to the Non-Juror.* 8vo. 6*d.* B.M.

Also attributed to Pope ; why I don't know.

Jan. 8. The same. The Second Edition. 8vo. 6*d.* B.M.

Jan. 8. *Letters, Poems, and Tales :* Amorous, Satyrical, and Gallant. Which passed between Several Persons of

Distinction. (Includes the Decree for concluding the Treaty between Dr. Swift and Mrs. Long.) 8vo. 2s. (P.B.)

This was the book which led Lady Elizabeth Germain to ask Swift to commit her letters " instantly to the flames ; for you, being stigmatized with the name of a wit, Mr. Curll will rake to the dung-hill for your correspondence, and, as to my part, I am satisfied with having been honoured in print by our amorous, satirical and gallant letters." (May 27th, 1735.)

Jan. 30.   ADDISON (JOSEPH). *The Resurrection. 6d.* 8vo. Frontispiece. (P.B.)

The Latin text with a translation [by Nicholas Amhurst].

The first of Curll's very delightfully produced translations of the *Poemata.*

Feb. 6.   [? ANCILLON (CHARLES).] *Eunuchism Display'd.* Describing all the different Sorts of Eunuchs. Written by a Person of Honour. 12mo. 3s.

" Occasion'd by a young Lady's falling in Love with *Nicolini,* who sung in the Opera at the *Hay-Market,* and to whom she had like to have been Married." The *tragic* things that happen in our midst !

A twelve-page catalogue of " Books Printed " is found at the end. About Charles Ancillon I can find nothing, or, rather, I have found nothing, because I have not worried myself. Robert Samber was the translator if the book was originally written in French. Otherwise he was its author.

Feb. 15.   GAY (JOSEPH), *pseud.* i.e. J. D. BREVAL. *A Compleat Key to the Non-Juror.* The Third Edition. 8vo. 6d. B.M.

At the end is advertised :

CONGREVE (WILLIAM). *The Way of the World.* But I do not think Curll had a special edition of his own.

Feb. 15.   *A Clue to the Comedy of the Non-Juror. . . .* In a Letter to N. Rowe, Esq. 8vo. B.M.

Feb. 18.   *The Verses which were presented on Sunday last to the Prince . . .* occasion'd by the Death of the young Prince [George William]. 8vo. 4d. (P.B.)

Feb. 18.   *The Lady's Miscellany.* 8vo. 5s. (P.B.)

A made-up volume, containing *The Art of Dress, The Fan, The Hoop Petticoat, The Rape of the Smock, Hyde Park Ramble, Court Poems,* and *The Worms.* Subsequently a different series was issued under the same title. (Quite a new departure for Curll to have two different books issued under the same title !)

The Fan was not Gay's poem, but a few lines by Atterbury.

Feb. 25. [DEFOE (DANIEL).] *Memoirs of the Life of . . . Daniel Williams*, D.D. 8vo. 2*s.* and 2*s.* 6*d.* B.M.
Includes the *Will*, separately paged.

Feb. 26. ADDISON (JOSEPH). *Dissertatio de Insignioribus Romanorum Poetis.* 1*s.* L.P. copies 2*s.* (P.B.)
Apparently only the Latin text.

Feb. 26. SALIGNAC DE LA MOTHE FENELON (FRANCOIS). *The Christian Pilgrimage.* Made English by Mrs. Jane Barker. Rivington. 12mo. 1*s.* 6*d.* sheep, 2*s.* calf. Frontispiece. B.M.

Mar. 11. ADDISON (JOSEPH). *The Resurrection.* The Third Edition. (P.B.)

Mar. 26. *The Plot Discover'd, or a Clue to the Comedy of the Non-Juror.* The Second Edition. 8vo. B.M.

Mar. 22. *Onanism Display'd.* Made English from the Paris Original [almost certainly by Robert Samber]. 2*s.* 6*d.* (P.B.)

Apr. 10. [GILDON (CHARLES).] *Memoirs of the Life of William Wycherley, Esq.* With a Character of his Writings, by Lord Lansdowne. 8vo. 1*s.* B.M.
The title-page is so worded that at a first glance Lord Lansdowne appears to have written the whole of the book. A fierce attack on Pope is included, which led to the well-known couplet about wishing the man a dinner.

Apr. 10. SALIGNAC DE LA MOTHE FENELON (FRANCOIS). *Reflections upon Learning.* Made English by Mr. Ozell. To which is added, An Essay Concerning Humour in Comedy, by Mr. Congreve. 8vo. 2*s.* (P.B.)

Apr. 22. [AMHURST (NICHOLAS).] *Protestant Popery; or the Convocation.* A Poem. 8vo. 1*s.* 6*d.* Portrait of Hoadly. B.M.
" Whereas a Poem, entituled, The Convocation, or *Protestant* Popery, has been falsely imputed to me as the Author thereof : I do hereby most solemnly declare, that I never writ so much as one Line of the said Poem ; that I have not read three Pages of it ; and that (I hope every one who knows me, will believe) I could not be guilty of such Scurrility and Nonsense ; I do this the rather, because many very trifling and silly Things have been charged to my Account, which I had not the least Concern in, not having for these two Years put my Papers to the Press, unless with the Name of
" G. SEWELL. May 12, 1718." (P.B.)
Needless to say, Sewell had quarrelled with Curll about two years before this date.

? May. ADDISON (JOSEPH). *Two Poems*, viz. On the Deluge, Paradise, the Burning of the World . . . An Ode to

Dr. Burnet. II. In Praise of Physick and Poetry. An Ode to Dr. Hannes. 8vo. B.M.

"Letter to Mr. Curll from Univ. Coll. Oxon. April 13, 1718.

"Mr. Curll,

"Your Design of obliging the Public with a correct Edition of all Mr. Addison's *Latin* Poems, and Translations of them, meets here with a general Approbation.

"According to my Promise I have sent you the two Odes : You promis'd to conceal my Name, which I insist on. I will be answerable to the World for the Justness of the Translation. . . . Next Week you shall have (what I can't help calling Mr. Addison's Masterpiece) his Poem on the Peace of Reswick. . . ."

A modest fellow.

May 1. MOLLOY (CHARLES). *The Coquet ; or, the English Chevalier.* A Comedy. Francklin. 8vo. 1s. 6d. or 2s. with gilt leaves. B.M.

"April 23, 1718. Charles Molloy received of Mr. Curll five guineas, and a note of hand for the like sum, conditionally payable upon the sale of 900 of a play called The Coquet, Acted at Lincoln's Inn Fields' Theatre, April 19, and two following nights." (Upcott MSS.)

May 8. FARQUHAR (GEORGE). *The Stage Coach.* To which is prefix'd some Account of his Writings. (Francklin.) 12mo. 1s. Frontispiece. (P.B.)

May 29. [AMHURST (NICHOLAS).] *A Congratulatory Epistle from His Holiness the Pope,* to the Reverend Mr. Snape. 8vo. 6d. and 1s. B.M.

May. [AMHURST (NICHOLAS).] *An Epistle to the Chevalier.* The Second Edition.

Advertised in the *Congratulatory Epistle,* and again in the P.B. of Dec. 30th, where it is sold at 6d. and 1s.

May 31. [CURLL (EDMUND).] *Curlicism Display'd ;* or an Appeal to the Church ; being just Observations upon some Books publish'd by Mr. Curll. "Printed for the Author." 12mo. 6d. B.L.O.

June 10. *The Lover's Week ;* or the six Days Adventures of Philander and Amaryllis. Written by a young Lady. (Francklin.) 1s. (P.B.)

July 8. PACK (RICHARDSON). *Miscellanies in Verse and Prose.* 3s. (P.B.)

July 15. ADDISON (JOSEPH). *Poems on Several Occasions.* 5s. (P.B.)

Presumably the same as the 1719 edition (q.v.), with an earlier title-page, but possibly identical. Curll did not mind post-dating his books, though six months is rather a long look ahead.

Nov. 4 (dated 1719). CORNELIUS NEPOS. *The Life of T[itus] P[omponius] Atticus.* With Remarks. [Translated] By Richardson Pack. 8vo. 3*s.* and 4*s.* B.M.

Nov. 13. SALIGNAC DE LA MOTHE FENELON (FRANCOIS). *The Adventures of Telemachus.* Translated by Mr. Ozell. The Second Edition. (Pemberton.) 8vo. 6*s.* (P.B.)

Nov. 15 (dated 1719). SEYMOUR (RICHARD). *The Court Gamester.* sm. 8vo. 1*s.* 6*d.* and 2*s.* (P.B.)

Nov. 25. *The Female Deserters ;* or, the Amours of some Ladies of Quality. A Novel. Written by a Young Lady. (Graves, Francklin, Lewis, Harrison, Roberts.) 1*s.* 6*d.* (P.B.)

Nov. 25. *The Lover's Week.* The Second Edition. (P.B.)

Dec. 4. *The Fair of St. Germain's.* Translated by John Ozell. The Second Edition. (Chetwood, Roberts.) (D.C.)
This is the only advertisement seen. The play was at this time being acted in French at the Theatre in Lincoln's Inn Fields.

Dec. 4 (dated 1719). JACOB (GILES). *The Poetical Register,* or the Lives and Characters of the English Dramatick Poets. Vol. I. 8vo. 6*s.* or 12*s.* on royal paper. Frontispiece with five vignettes, and several portraits. (P.B.)
Curll had now removed to " Next the Temple Coffee-House."

Dec. 11. BUTLER (SARAH). *Milesian Tales,* or Instructive Novels for the Proper Conduct of Life. (Roberts.) 1*s.* 6*d.* and 2*s.* (P.B.)

Dec. 16. OVIDIUS NASO. *The Nooning.* A Poem. Translated . . . by Richardson Pack. 4*d.* (P.B.)

Dec. 20 (dated 1719). GAY (JOSEPH), *pseud.,* i.e. J. D. BREVAL. *Ovid in Masquerade ;* being a Burlesque upon the XIII Book of his Metamorphoses. 8vo. 1*s.* B.M.

Dec. 30. *The English Theatre for the Year* 1718 : consisting of all the New Comedies Acted at Both Houses. (Francklin.) (P.B.)
A copy advertised recently for sale contained *The Non-Juror,* fourth edition, published by Lintott ; *The Plot Discover'd,* or a Clue to . . . the Non-Juror, second edition ; *The Artful Wife, The Coquet,* and *Love in a Veil,* the last of which is dated 1719 (see below).
With its predecessors this is advertised as " The English Theatre in 3 vols, with cuts. 13*s.* Any may be had separately."

[BREVAL (JOHN DURANT).] *Calpe or Gibraltar.* Burleigh only. 8vo. 6*d*.
Advertised in Curll's lists.

MEIBOMIUS (JOHN HENRY). *A Treatise of the Use of Flogging in Venereal Affairs.* . . . Made English . . . by a Physician [i.e., George Sewell]. To which is added a Treatise of Hermaphrodites [by Giles Jacob]. 3*s*.
One of the two books which gave the Judges of the King's Bench so much trouble. " Translated," Curll tells us, " by George Sewell, M.D. in the Year 1718, on Occasion of the untimely Death of Mr. *Peter Motteaux* (who lost his Life in a Brothel through an Act of *unnatural Lewdness*) no Objection was made to it in Eight Years *Time ;* nor was it published with the least immoral Intent." *(Curliad.)* So there !

Love's Invention, or the Recreation in Vogue. An excellent new Ballad upon the Masquerade. (Francklin.) 8vo.
The same. The Second Edition.
On the half-title is printed " Mr. Pope's Worms." (Cat.)

TAVERNER (WILLIAM). *The Artful Wife.* A Comedy. " Printed for and sold by J. Roberts . . . 1718." 8vo. 1*s*. B.M.

PRIDEAUX (HUMPHREY). *The True Nature of Imposture.* . . . The Seventh Edition. Hooke, Mears, Clay. 8vo. B.M.

EVELYN (CHARLES). *The Lady's Recreation ;* or, the Art of Gardening further improv'd. To which are added, Some curious Observations concerning Variegated Greens, by John Lawrence. The Second Edition. Roberts. 8vo. 2*s*. Frontispiece. B.M.
The first edition, issued in the previous year, has a slightly different title-page, which does not bear Curll's name, and was not advertised by him. It is really a third part of Evelyn's *The Art of Gardening Improv'd*, issued by another publisher.

[JACOB (GILES).] *Lex Mercatoria : or, the Merchant's Companion.* " In the Savoy : Printed by Eliz. Nutt, and R. Gosling (Assignees of Edw. Sayer, Esq. ; for E. Curll . . . and W. Taylor . . . MDCCXVIII." 8vo. 5*s*. B.M.
The 1729 edition is reset and revised, and Curll had nothing to do with it.
" In 1718 was published an edition of the Poems of . . . Rochester and . . . Roscommon . . . which does not bear Curll's name on the title-page [though] he had clearly an interest in it, for a note, p. viii., vol. ii., refers

to Mr. Pomfret's Poems printed by E. Curll." W. H. Thoms, *Curll Papers*.

Included in a 1718 list of Curll's books (and not seen) are :

The History and present State of France . . . by a Gentleman return'd from his Travels. 2 vols. 6s.

BLACKALL (OFFSPRING). *Sermons on Several Occasions.* 2 vols. 8s.

The Elzevir Miscellany. The Second Edition.

Also four volumes of Antiquities :

AUBREY (JOHN). *Introduction towards a Natural History of Wiltshire.* With other Curious Miscellanies. 3s.

The History and Antiquities of the City and Cathedral Church of Hereford. 7s. and 10s.

ABINGDON (   ). *Survey of the Cathedral Church of Worcester . . . Litchfield and Chichester.*

AUBREY (JOHN). *The Natural History and Antiquities of Surrey.* 4 vols. £4 6s. the Large, £2 3s. the Small Paper.

1719

? Dec. 1718.   SAVAGE (RICHARD). *Love in a Veil.* A Comedy. Francklin, Chetwood. 8vo. 1s. 6d. B.M.

? Jan.   EVELYN (CHARLES). *The Lady's Recreation.* . . . The Third Edition. Roberts. 8vo. 2s. Frontispiece. B.M.

Jan. 24.   *Onanism Display'd.* The Second Edition. 1s. 6d. (P.B.)

Jan. 27.   ASHMOLE (ELIAS). The *Antiquities of Berkshire.* . . . 3 vols. Sm. paper £1 15s., L.P. £3 10s. (P.B.)

"N.B. The Price of this valuable Work will be raised at Lady-Day next, there being but a few Copies left unsubscrib'd for. E. Curll."

Jan. 29.   [? BRERETON (   ).] *The Criticks* : or, The Taste of the Times expos'd as to Operas, Plays, Masquerades, and Fashions. Volume I. (? all published.) " Printed for W. Chetwood." 12mo. 2s. 6d. B.M.

Advertised in one of the 1740 lists. Chetwood had been Curll's apprentice.

Jan. 29.   SEWELL (GEORGE). *Poems on Several Occasions.* With a Preface by the Author concerning the present Edition. Pemberton. 8vo. 1s. 6d. B.M.

" Where may be had, The Tragedy of Sir Walter Raleigh." The title-page bears these words. Pemberton's name is alone on the title-page of the play, which is nowhere else advertised by Curll.

Jan. 31.   *Musarum Lachrymæ :* or Poems To the Memory of Nicholas Rowe, Esq. ; By Several Hands. To which are prefix'd : Some Memoirs of his Life and Writings. By Mr. [Stephen] Hales. 12mo. 1s. 6d. B.M.

Jan. 31.   Another edition of Rowe's Poems is advertised in one volume at 4s. (P.B.)

Feb. 4.   BUDGELL (EUSTACE). *A Letter to the Lord xxxx.* The Fourth Edition. With a Postscript. 8vo. 6d. (P.B.) Previous editions (1718) lack the postscript, bear Roberts's name only on the title-page, and were not advertised by Curll.

Feb. 28.   The same. The Fifth Edition. 8vo. 6d. B.M.
       South Sea oratory.

Feb. 28.   *A Letter from a West Country Freeholder to the Right Honourable Mr. Secretary Web——r.* Occasion'd by Mr. Budgell's Letter to Lord xxxx. (P.B.)

Feb. 28.   GAY (JOSEPH), *pseud.* i.e. J. D. BREVAL. *The Church Scuffle ;* or, News from S. Andrews. A Ballad. The Second Edition.
       No mention seen of a first edition. Reprinted more than once in the various Miscellanies.

Feb. 28.   [POPE (ALEXANDER).] *News from Court.* An excellent new Ballad. The Second Edition. (P.B.)
       ? 1st edition issued in Dec., 1718, by Chetwood. A copy with this date is known " Printed for S. Huddleston," which may be Curll's.

Feb. 28.   PACK (RICHARDSON). *The Miscellanies in Prose and Verse.* The Second Edition. 8vo. 3s. 6d. B.M.

Feb. 28.   [PRIOR (MATTHEW)] or [HARCOURT (HON. SIMON).] *The Female Phæton.* Warner. sm. Fo. 2d. B.M.
       This is advertised in the P.B. as The Third Edition. The B.M. copy has a printed note : " N.B. The Copy before publish'd, has not one Stanza printed right." I am not clear as to the actual date of the first edition, and better critics than myself are not clear as to who was the author. The verses are addressed to " Prior's Kitty," the Lady Catherine Hyde who afterwards became Gay's Duchess of Queensbury. They are certainly Prior-ish, but in several places Curll says definitely that " Mr. Harcourt " was the author. I put " Simon " as his first name, because there was a Simon Harcourt at the time ; but there was also a James (who died young). Somebody will some day prove conclusively that Prior was the author, and somebody will prove as conclusively that he wasn't. Perhaps they already have.
       Prior's *Horace and Venus,* by the way, " a Song never before published " is advertised with the above, but without a price, which leads me to suppose that it may have been sold with the Verses.

Mar. 14.   *The Tryal of Sir Edward Moseley, Bart.,* indicted . . . for committing a Rape upon the Body of Mrs. Anne

Swinnerton. To which are added the Depositions against Mr. Clark [in the matter of] the Widow Coleman. "Printed by E. G. for W. L. 1647. Reprinted by E. Curll, 1719." 12mo. 6d. B.M.

See text for details of this unhappy affair. Advertised pleasantly as " The Backsliding Teacher."

?   HICKES (GEORGE). *A Caveat against all Fanaticks.* . . . The Third Edition.

Advertised in the above.

Mar. 20.   ADDISON (JOSEPH). *Poems on Several Occasions.* With a Dissertation upon the Roman Poets. 8vo. Portrait. (P.B.)

Apr. 2.   SALIGNAC DE LA MOTHE FENELON (FRANCOIS). *Private Thoughts upon Religion,* in Several Letters. " Printed for the Author. MDCCXIX." 12mo. 3s. 6d. B.M.

Preface signed J. Delacoste.

Spring.   Certain early numbers of *The Moderator* are sold by Curll, whose name, however, soon drops out of the advertisements.

?   *The Court Miscellany in Prose and Verse.* [No. I.] 8vo. (Cat.) " To be continued occasionally."

Apr. 14.   *The Court Miscellany,* No. II. 8vo. 6d. (P.B.)

Contains Henley's poem *Of Laughing,* Newcombe's *Verses on the Lady Catherine Wyndham,* the *Fable of Amillius, and the Statue of Venus, News from the Masquerade,* and *Verses to Lord Berkeley.*

Apr. 14.   NIXON (ROBERT). *Cheshire Prophecy at Large.* With his Life [by John Oldmixon]. The Sixth Edition. Roberts only. 8vo. 6d. B.M.

Apr. 21.   [? AMHURST (NICHOLAS).] *The Protestant Session.* A Poem. By a Member of the Constitutional Club at Oxford. 8vo. 6d. or 1s. L.P. B.M.

D.N.B. thinks that Amhurst was the author. Let him have it.

Apr. 21.   [AMHURST (NICHOLAS).] *Political Poems.* 8vo. 2s. 6d. (P.B.) A made-up volume of such of Amhurst's pieces as Curll had printed.

Apr. 30.   BULL (GEORGE, late Lord Bishop of St. David's). *A Vindication of the Church of England.* 8vo. 4s. B.M.

May 7.   ? WREN (SIR CHRISTOPHER). *The History and Antiquities of the Cathedral Church of Salisbury, and the Abbey Church of Bath.* 8vo. 15s. or 30s. L.P.

May 28.   AMELOT DE LA HOUSSAYE (ABRAHAM NICHOLAS). *The History of the Spaniards Conspiracy against the Republic of Venice.* Made English. (Hartin, Graves, Popping.) 1s. 6d. (P.B.)

May 28.   ADDISON (JOSEPH). *Poems on Several Occasions.* " The Second Edition, Corrected." 5s. (P.B.) 8vo.

July 2.   BARKER (JANE).   *The Entertaining Novels.* . . . With
Verses to her by Mr. Sewell. (Bettesworth.) 5*s*. (P.B.)

July 2.   ADDISON (JOSEPH).   *Maxims, Observations, and Reflections,
Moral, Political and Divine.* " Methodiz'd and connected
by Mr. [Charles] Beckingham." (P.B.) With a Copy of
the Will. 8vo. 1*s*. 6*d*. Portrait.

Aug. 6.   MOMOPHILUS CARTHUSIENSIS (? RICHARD MEAD).   *A
Serious Conference between Scaramouch and Harlequin,* Concerning Three and One. Roberts only. 8vo. 6*d*. B.M.

A satire against Dr. Woodward. Advertised as " The
Triumvirate : or, the Battle of the Physicians. As it is
now acted in the Cities of London and Westminster."

Aug. 6.   [? JACOB (GILES)].   *Memoirs of the Life of . . . Joseph
Addison.* . . . With a particular Account of his Writings.
8vo. 1*s*. B.M.

Dedication (to the Countess of Warwick) signed G.J.
" Memoirs " is not perhaps quite the right word.

Aug. 6.   [? SWIFT (JONATHAN)].   *Ars Pun-ica sive Flos Linguarum ;
The Art of Punning.* . . . By the Labour and Industry of
Tom Pun-Sibi. " Printed for J. Roberts." 8vo. 1*s*.
(Cat.)

Sept.   The same. The Second Edition. " Printed at Dublin
in the Year 1719. Reprinted at London for J. Roberts."
8vo. 1*s*. B.M.

Sept. 16.   The same. The Third Edition. (D.C.)

Nov. 6   LOGGIN (ROBERT).   *The Present Management of the
(dated   Customs.* " Printed for the Author, and sold by J.
1720).   Roberts, J. Brotherton, E. Curll and J. Fox." 8vo. 1*s*.
B.M.

John Rotherham is part-author.

It is worth while noticing that when exception was
taken to this book, Curll was the only bookseller called
on to apologise, which he did on Feb. 17th, 1720 (D.C.) :

" Whereas I E. Curll, of London, Bookseller have
thro' Inadvertency been concern'd in publishing an
Advertisement in the Daily Courant of Friday the 6th
of November last, notifying that on that Day was publish'd a Pamphlet, entitled The Present Management of
the Customs, &c. Printed for (and at the Expence of)
Robert Loggin the Author, (then my Lodger,) unjustly
reflecting upon the Hon. His Majesty's Commissioners
of the Customs : Now I do hereby declare, that I am
seriously concern'd for having been any Way Instru-
mental in publishing the said false scandalous and
malicious Libel, and I do hereby ask Pardon of the Commissioners for the Offence they have taken thereat ; I
do also acknowledge the Favours I have receiv'd from

them, and shall always be more proud of retracting an Error than persisting in one.

E. Curll."

" Inadvertency " is good. But do you think he gave notice to Mr. Loggin ?

Nov. 10 (dated 1720).
ALEXANDER (WILLIAM, EARL OF STERLINE). *Doomsday, Or, the Last Judgment*. (Boreham, Rivington, Brotherton, Jauncy.) 1s. Preface by A. Johnstoun, i.e. Edmund Curll.

Nov. 21 (dated 1720).
BECKINGHAM (CHARLES). *The Tragedy of King Henry the Fourth, of France*. Jauncy, Bettesworth, Brotherton. 8vo. 1s. 6d. Portrait. B.M.

" Nov. 13, 1719. Charles Beckingham received of Mr. Curll, for the sole right and title to the copy of a play by me written, intitled The Tragedy of King Henry the Fourth of France ; and also of my translation of Rapin's Christus Patiens, fifty guineas." (Upcott MSS.)

Dec. 10 (dated 1720).
The same. The Second Edition. (D.C.)

Dec. 10 (dated 1720).
LEIGH (JOHN). *Kensington Gardens ; or, The Pretenders*. A Comedy. Jauncy, Bettesworth, Brotherton. 8vo. 1s. 6d. B.M.

" Nov. 28, 1719. John Leigh received of Mr. Curll, for a copy of a play called Kensington Gardens, or the Pretenders, forty-five guineas." (Upcott MSS.)

POPE (ALEXANDER). *Court Poems in Two Parts Compleat*. To which are added 1. Venus upon Prudery. 2. An Epitaph upon John Hewitt and Mary Drew, who were killed by Lightning. . . . " Printed for R. Burleigh, 1719." 1s. (Cat.)

With two inner title-pages. . . . Pope's Miscellany I. & II.

The Cases of Impotency Debated. . . . The Third Edition. 5 vols. 12mo. 12s. 6d.

Not all the volumes are third editions.

CENTLIVRE (SUSANNA). *The Wonder : A Woman keeps a Secret*. The Second Edition. Bettesworth. 12mo. 1s. Frontispiece. B.M.

GAY (JOSEPH), *pseud*. i.e. J. D. BREVAL. *Miscellanies upon Several Subjects ;* Occasionally Written. 8vo. B.M.

Various pieces bound up.

[GILDON (CHARLES)]. *The Life and Strange, Surprizing Adventures of Mr. D—— De F——, of London, Hosier*. . . . The Second Edition. 1719. (Cat.)

Curll advertises this book at the end of 1721.

The Famous Tryal of the Reverend and Learned Mr. James Grame [for heresy]. 8vo. 2s. 6d. B.M.

An edition of this book is advertised in a 1740 list at 3s., and the tract is included in Curll's *Bibliotheca Recondita,* 1739.

1720

Jan. 2.   SEYMOUR (RICHARD). *The Court Gamester.* The Second Edition, Corrected. Sm. 8vo. 1s. 6d. and 2s. B.M.

Jan. 7.   HAMMOND (ANTHONY). *The Character of His Royal Highness Prince Frederick, Duke of Gloucester.* (Chetwood, Taylor, Boreham, King, Jauncy, Crownfield, Clements.) 6d. (P.B.)

Jan. 12.   LEIGH (JOHN). *Kensington Gardens.* . . . The Second Edition. (P.B.)

Jan. 12.   [LEIGH (JOHN).] *Hob's Wedding.* A New Farce. Jauncy. 12mo. 6d. B.M.

     A sequel to *Hob, or the Country Wake.*

Jan. 18.   COBDEN (EDWARD). *A Poem on the Death of* . . . *Joseph Addison.* Bettesworth, Brotherton, Graves. 8vo. 6d. B.M.

Jan. 18.   ASGILL (JOHN). *Several Assertions proved,* in order to create another Species of Money than Gold and Silver. . . . With a Postscript. The Second Edition. (Roberts.) 1s. (D.P.)

     First edition issued in 1696.

Jan. 18.   ASGILL (JOHN). *A Brief Answer to* . . . *the Question Between the Printed and Painted Calicoes.* The Second Edition. "Printed for J. Roberts." With an Appendix on the Spinster. 8vo. 6d. B.M.

     The first edition, also printed for Roberts, is dated 1719, issued at 3d., and without the Appendix. Curll only advertises the second.

     Asgill was an earnest political gentleman, and, like Curll, got into trouble.

Feb. 5.   DENNIS (JOHN) and GILDON (CHARLES). *A new Project for the Regeneration of the Stage.* (Boreham, Chetwood, Graves.) (D.P.)

     "Occasion'd by the silencing of the Drury Lane Players." Hence, too, Pope in the *Dunciad,* Book III., in ironical reply to Dennis's statement that he had never written in concert with Gildon :

       " Ah Dennis ! Gildon ah ! what ill-starr'd rage
       Divides a friendship long confirm'd by age ?
       Blockheads with reason wicked wits abhor ;
       But fool with fool is bar'brous civil war.
       Embrace, embrace, my sons ! be foes no more ! "

Feb. 6. ASGILL (JOHN). *An Essay on a Registry for Titles of Lands.* (Roberts, Jauncy.) 6*d*. (P.B.)

Feb. 8. DENNIS (JOHN) and GILDON (CHARLES). *A new Project.* . . . The Second Edition. (D.P.)

Feb. 12. SWIFT (JONATHAN). *The Right of Precedence Between Physicians and Civilians Enquir'd into.* "Dublin : Printed : And Reprinted at London for J. Roberts." 8vo. 6*d*. B.M.

The same, with a letter dated Feb. 3, 1720, from Dublin Castle, on verso of title-page, saying that the piece is Swift's.

Feb. 13. The same. The Second Edition. "Printed at Dublin in the Year 1720 ; and Reprinted at London for J. Roberts." 8vo. 6*d*. B.M.

Feb. 20. PACK (RICHARDSON). *Religion and Philosophy.* A Tale. With 5 other Poems. 8vo. 6*d*. B.M.

Feb. 20. [PACK (RICHARDSON).] *Select Translations from Catullus, Tibullus, and Ovid.* With an Essay on the Roman Elegiac Poets. 1*s*. (P.B.)

I am a little uncertain about this entry.

Feb. 23. *A Catalogue* of Poems, Plays and Novels, Printed for, and Sold by E. Curll next the Temple Coffee-House in Fleet-Street. Gratis.

This includes, besides those I have already mentioned, the following four books :

Heideigger's Masquerade ; Or, the Bell. A Satire. 6*d*.
The Sick Lady's Cure : Or, a City Intrigue. A Poem. 6*d*.
The Olympic Odes of Pindar. In English Meetre. 6*d*.
Ignoramus Comœdia ; Authore T. Ruggle. Cantab. 1*s*. 6*d*. (of which there were many editions).

? SEWELL (GEORGE). *The Life and Character of Mr. John Philips.* The Third Edition. 12mo. 1*s*. B.M.

Feb. 26. *Three Poems*, viz. I. Reason : a Satire . . . by the Reverend Mr. [John] Pomfret. . . . Written in . . . 1700, II. The Female Phæton, by Mr. Harcourt, III. The Judgment of Venus, by the same. 8vo. 6*d*. B.M.

Here, you see, the authorship of the *Female Phæton* is given to Harcourt and not Prior.

Mar. 17. PHILIPS (JOHN). *The Whole Works* . . . with . . . Life by . . . Sewell. "Printed for J. Tonson and T. Jauncy." 8vo. Portrait. B.M.

No mention of Curll on the general title, but included is *Poems on Several Occasions.* The Third Edition. "Printed for J. Tonson, E. Curll, and T. Jauncy. M.DCC.XX." 2*s*. 6*d*. *Cyder* is included, separately paged.

Feb. 22. ADDISON (JOSEPH). *Scating :* a Poem. Latin text with translation [by Thomas Newcombe], and Pope's verses to Lady Mary Wortley Montagu. 8vo. 6*d.* B.M.
Preface signed T. N. The Pope verses were separately advertised as " The Second Eve."

Apr. 7. ADDISON (JOSEPH). *Maxims, Observations, and Reflexions.* Part II. (Bickerton.) 1*s.* 6*d.* (P.B.)
Charles Beckingham, editor.

Apr. 19. SALIGNAC DE LA MOTHE FENELON (FRANCOIS). *The Adventures of Telemachus.* . . . " The Third Edition. To which is added that celebrated Piece, The Adventures of Ariſtonous, written in imitation of Telemachus." (Taylor, Pemberton.) 6*s.* (P.B.)

April. [DEFOE (DANIEL).] *The Hiſtory of the Life and Adventures of Mr. Duncan Campbell.* Mears, Jauncy, Meadows, Bettesworth, Lewis, Graves. 8vo. 5*s.* Portrait and 3 plates. B.M.

June 12. HAMMOND (ANTHONY), *Ed. A New Miscellany of Original Poems, Translations and Imitations.* By the moſt eminent Hands. . . . With some Familiar Letters by the late Earl of Rocheſter. Jauncy. 8vo. (Cat.)
Mentioned in one of Curll's liſts.

July 12. ROWE (NICHOLAS). *The Poetical Works.* The Second Edition. Tonson, Jauncy, Bell, Bettesworth, Pemberton, Hooke, Rivington, Cruttenden, Cox, Battely, Clay, Symon. 12mo. 3*s.* B.M.
Advertised by Jauncy in the P.B. of this date, but not by Curll, though his name appears on the title-page with the others. Many of Curll's books appear at this time in Jauncy's liſts.

July 12. RAPIN (RENÉ). *Chriſtus Patiens : or, the Sufferings of Chriſt.* An Heroic Poem, in Two Books. Made English by Charles Beckingham. Rivington, Brotherton. 8vo. 1*s.* 6*d.* Frontispiece. B.M.
Advertised by Jauncy on this date. (P.B.)

July 16. RAMSAY (ALLEN). *Content :* A Poem. 8vo. B.M.
" Having been honour'd by a Noble Peer in Scotland with a Present of the complete Works of this Author, I have for some time been preparing them for the Press, with such Notes as are requisite for explaining the Beauties of the Scots Dialeƈt, &c. This excellent Poem is firſt publish'd as a Specimen of the Whole. The Titles of the reſt being as follows : viz. I. Tartana : Or, the Plaid. II. The Morning Interview : An Heroi-Comical Poem. III. Chriſt's Kirk on the Green. In Three Cantos. IV. Scots Songs. V. The Scribblers lash'd. VI. Elegies on several Occasions. VII. Edinburgh's

Address to the Country. VIII. Familiar Epistles. At the Desire of several Persons of Quality, a small Number will be done on a superfine Royal Paper.

"Pater-Noster-Row, July 9, 1720. E. Curll." (P.B.)

I am not sure whether Curll issued any or all of the others. On the other hand Jauncy was advertising Ramsay's *Wealth* in the following week, and Pemberton subsequently published *Patie and Roger : a Pastoral*. It may be that the Beauties of the Scots Dialect were too much for London.

July 16.   JACOB (GILES). *The Poetical Register.* . . . Vol. II. 8vo. 6*s*. Cuts.

The cuts might be had separate at 6*d*. each or 6*s*. the set on a royal paper.

July 21.   [RAWLINSON (RICHARD).] *The English Topographer*, or an Historical Account . . . of all the Pieces that have been Written relating to the Antiquities. By an Impartial Hand. "Printed for T. Jauncy." 8vo. 10*s*. 25 copies on a superfine paper at £1 1*s*. B.M.

Ten copper-plates advertised but not issued.

Aug. 4.   [DEFOE (DANIEL).] *The* : . . *History* . . . *of* . . . *Duncan Campbell*. The Second Edition. With Additions. 8vo. 5*s*. Portrait and plates.

The additions and the plates could both be had separately.

Sept. 13.   EARBERY (MATTHIAS). *The Pretended Reformers ;* or a True History of the German Reformation . . . [Part II.]. Jauncy only. 8vo. 2*s*. B.M.

Sept. 13.   SWIFT (JONATHAN). *A Second Collection of Miscellanies.* 4*s*. (P.B.)

Contains *The Art of Punning, The Right of Precedence, The Defence of English Commodities, The Swearer's Bank, Elegy*, and *Letters to* . . . *Mrs. Long.*

Sept. 29.   BUDGELL (EUSTACE). *Letter to Lord xxxx.* The Fifth Edition. (P.B.)

Sept. 29.   BUDGELL (EUSTACE). *The Speech* made . . . at the last General Court of the South Sea Company in Merchant Taylors Hall on Tuesday 20th inst. The Third Edition. 3*d*. (P.B.)

Previous editions not apparently advertised.

Entered at Stationers' Hall.

"N.B. The above-mentioned Speech having been procured contrary to Act of Parliament, the Offenders are now under a Prosecution for the same." Curll's own advertisement, showing that he made the best of a bad job. I can find nothing of the prosecution. Roberts afterwards published another of Budgell's speeches, and

Boreham a pamphlet to prove that he hadn't made the one that Curll printed. But he was always making speeches, though there was some excuse on this occasion, when he is supposed to have lost £20,000.

Oct. 31. STANHOPE (HENRY) ? *pseud.* of Edward Bond. *An Epistle to his Royal Highness the Prince of Wales ;* Occasion'd by the State of the Nation. 8vo. 6*d.* B.M.

A satirical piece which enjoyed unusual success. It contains the well-known lines :

" Here, those, that on his Menials joy'd to wait,
    With *South-Sea* Squibs, besiege a Duke's Estate ;
    For *Cypher-Scrolls* his Rent Rolls they command,
    He gets their *Paper*, and they get his *Land*."

Whether Stanhope was Bond or not I do not know for certain, though I think he was, from something that Curll says in the *Curliad.*

Nov. 2. The same. The Second Edition. (P.B.)

" N.B. If any Person shall presume to Pyrate this Poem, they shall be prosecuted as the Act of Parliament directs, by H. Stanhope."

Nov. 3. ADDISON (JOSEPH). *Dissertation on the Roman Poets.* [Latin text.] The Third Edition. With an Essay (in Latin and English) on his Writings by R. Young. 12mo. 1*s.* 6*d.* B.M.

Nov. 4. STANHOPE (HENRY) ? *pseud. An Epistle to . . . the Prince of Wales.* The Third Edition. 8vo. 6*d.* B.M.

Nov. 5. A Key to Mr. Stanhope's Epistle. . . . (D.P.)

Which, however, may not have been issued separately.

Nov. 11. ARUNDELL (" of St. Martin's "). *The Directors.* A Poem in Defence of the South Sea Company. Address'd to Mr. Stanhope. With Verses by John Cowper [advertised as *Bagpipes no Musick*]. 8vo. 6*d.* (D.P.)

Contains a couplet applicable to other ages than his own :

" If Great Men Tradesmen turn with one Accord,
    Why mayn't each Tradesman strive to be a Lord ? "

Also a letter to Curll :

" If, 'midst the most Refin'd, you'll not refuse,
    T'accept the Labours of a Rural Muse,
    Thy Name to Distant Villages shall spread,
    Still shall thy Name be with the Muses read ;
    And on thy Grave-Stone let it graven be,
    Thou wert a Friend to *Poets*, They to Thee."

Which shows that some poets can be good business men.

Nov. 15. The same. The Second Edition. 8vo. 6d. B.M.

Nov. 15. STANHOPE (HENRY) ? *pseud.* *An Epistle.* . . . The Fourth Edition. 8vo. 6d. (P.B.)

Nov. 15. [WYVILL (CHRISTOPHER).] *The Parson's Daughter.* A Tale. For the Use of pretty Girls with Small Fortunes. 8vo. 6d. (P.B.)

A copy in the B.M. is " Printed for J. Harris near St. James's Bagnio, 1717." (q.v.)

Nov. 26. STANHOPE (HENRY) ? *pseud.* *The Governor.* A Poem on the present Posture of Affairs at Home and the Proceedings of some Foreign Courts. 6d. (P.B.)

Nov. 30. The same. The Second Edition. (D.P.)

Dec. 3. [OLDMIXON (JOHN).] *Court Tales.* " The Second Edition, with a complete Key." 12mo. 5s. (P.B)

Dec. 29. FOXTON (THOMAS). *Jesina.* Or, Delusive Gold. A Pastoral. Lamenting the Misfortunes of a Young Lady of Quality, ruined by the South Sea. 6d. (P.B.)

Who Foxton was I have not a notion, but he was a prolific gentleman.

Dec. 29. HASTINGS ( ). *The Czar.* A Poem. 6d. (P.B.)

Autumn. NORDEN (JOHN). *Speculi Britanniæ.* Pars Altera : or, a Delineation of Northamptonshire. " Printed in the Year M.DCC.XX." 8vo. 2s. 6d. 25 copies at 5s. L.P. B.M.

SYMSON (WILLIAM). *A New Voyage to the East Indies.* The Second Edition. Bettesworth. 12mo. 3s. 6d. Cuts. B.M.

The same as the 1715 edition, with a new title-page. See also under 1717.

HALES (JOHN). *A Discourse of the Several Dignities, and Coruptions of Man's Nature, since the Fall.* 8vo. 3s. B.M.

" With a complete Index by the late Rev. Mr. Lawrence Howel."

GAY (JOSEPH), *pseud.* i.e. FRANCIS CHUTE. *The Hoop Petticoat.* The Third Edition. 8vo. (Cat.)

Title slightly altered.

In this year a pamphlet was advertised to appear in April called *The Popeish Controversy Compleat.* This, if it exists, is not the same as the collection of squibs on the *Dunciad.* It was announced to contain amongst other items the *True and Full Account* and Mr. Curll's Conversion to Judaism.

HOLDSWORTH (EDWARD). *Muscipula ; or the Mouse-Trap.* In Latin and English. Translated by Samuel Cobb. The Second Edition. 8vo. (Cat.)

CLARKE (WILLIAM). *Party Revenge :* or, [a] Narrative of his Case and Sufferings. . . . With an Account of the

Prosecution and Indictment of E. CURL, Bookseller at the Old Bailey for printing a scandalous Libel. . . . " Printed and Sold by A. Woodcock. . . . 1720. 8vo. 6d. B.M.

1721

Jan. 12. FOXTON (THOMAS). *The Character of a Fine Gentleman.* . . . To which is added, Five Pieces . . . all by Mr. Addison. 8vo. 1s. 6d. Vignette on title-page. B.M.

Foxton signs preface in full, but Addison's is the only name on the title-page, which is so arranged as to suggest at a first glance that the whole book had been Addison's work.

Jan. 14. WRIGHT (THOMAS). *No Fools like Wits ; or the Female Virtuosoes.* A Comedy . . . or, The Refusal ; or, The Ladies Philosophy. The Second Edition. 8vo. B.M.

An ironical title relating to a theatrical quarrel of the day. Curll has a long preface, attacking Cibber on the grounds of his plagiarisms from Molière and almost everybody else.

> " Impartial *Cibber* now does freely own,
> ' *There's no Imposing Wit upon the Town ;*
> His *Title*, not his Play, we set to Sale :
> If *Patch-work* pleases, *Molière's* Sense can't fail."

From this preface it appears that *The Female Virtuosoes* had first been acted in 1693, and was revived this year, under the title of *No Fools like Wits*, but with alterations by the " Reviver " by no means to the bookseller's liking. In fact to him Mr. Cibber's production is about as bad as it can be.

> " There's no Imagination that can strike it,
> 'Tis so *like* Nothing, that there's Nothing *like* it."

Jan. 19. *The Ladies Miscellany.* The Second Edition. (P.B.)

Jan. 24. HEARNE (Mrs.). *Honour the Victory, and Love the Prize.* Illustrated in Ten Diverting Novels. 2s. 6d. " sowed up," 3s. bound. (P.B.)

Jan. 24. *A Detection of the whole Management of the South Sea Company.* In a Letter to John Ward of Hackney, Esq. (Roberts, Meadows, Griffiths.) 6d. (P.B.)

Jan. 28. *Memoirs of the Life of Dr. South.* The Second Edition. 8vo. 5s. Portrait. B.M.

With the inscription on his monument, written by Dr. Freind.

Jan. 28. SOUTH (ROBERT). *Opera Posthuma.* 3s. 6d. (P.B.)

Possibly a new edition, as the price has been altered.

Jan. 31. [PLACE (CONYERS).] *Priestianity ; or a View of the Dis-*

parity between the Apostles and the Modern Inferior Clergy.
"A New Impression." (Meadows, Graves, Griffith.)
1*s.* (P.B.)

The first edition was "Printed for A Moore. . . .
MDCCXX." and not advertised as Curll's.

There is an interesting, but (to me) wholly un-
intelligible postscript to the advertisement of this book.
"—— The Author of the SPY is desired to read and
censure this Piece, otherwise his Master Signor *Curillo*
will turn him off."

Jan. 31. *Ten New Poems :* viz. I. The Pleasures of Co-t-on, or the
Nightly Sports of Venus, translated from Bonefonius.
II. An Ode in Praise of Melancholy. III. The Fox-
hunter. IV. The Sick Wife Cur'd, a Tale. V. The Tea-
pot. VI. The Disappointment. VII. The Midsummer
Wish. VIII. Abelard to Eloisa, by Mr. Beckingham.
IX. The Fair Vestal. By Mr. Addison. X. The Power
of Musick . . . by Mr. Parnell. (Graves, Griffith.) 1*s.*
(P.B.)

It might seem odd to find Archdeacon Parnell in this
gallery, but he was conveniently dead.

Feb. 2. HALES (JOHN). *The Golden Remains.* . . . 5*s.* (P.B.)

Feb. 2. AUBREY (JOHN). *Miscellanies upon the Following Subjects :*
Day-Fatality, Local-Fatality, Ostenta, Omens, Dreams,
Apparitions, Magick, Oracles, &c. The Second
Edition. With some Account of his Life. (Bettes-
worth.) 8vo. Frontispiece. Some copies on large
paper. (P.B.)

Feb. 6. THEOCRITUS. *The Idylliums.* With Rapin's Discourse
upon Pastorals. Made English by Mr. Creech. . . . The
Third Edition. 8vo. 3*s.* 6*d.* Portrait of Creech. B.M.

Feb. 6. GAY (JOSEPH), *pseud.* i.e. J. D. BREVAL. *Ovid in Masquerade.* . . . The Second Edition. 1*s.* (D.P.)

Advertised as "The Force of Eloquence Illustrated,
in Two Witty Orations . . . merrily translated into
Burlesque Verse."

Feb. 14. LILLY (WILLIAM). *The History of the Life and Times of.*
. . . The Second Edition. 3*s.* (P.B.)

Feb. 17. "This Day is re-publish'd " [BOULTON (ROBERT)]. *A
Compleat History of Magick.* . . . (Pemberton.) 5*s.* (D.P.)
? a new edition.

Feb. 26. GERHARD (JOHN). *The Christian's Support.* . . . Being
the Divine Meditations. . . . The Third Edition. 3*s.*
(P.B.)

Mar. 2. [NORTH (HON. ROGER).] *The Gentleman's Accomptant.*
The Third Edition. 12 mo. 3*s.* B.M.

Mar. 4. The Works of Voiture " re-publish'd " this day (P.B.) but I doubt whether it is a new edition.

Mar. 6. *Ten New Poems.* The Second Edition. (D.P.)
Advertised as " The Pleasures of Coition."

Mar. 13. *South-Sea-Pills to purge Court Melancholy.* Being a Collection of Poems, Satires, &c. . . . occasion'd by the ruinous State of the Nation. 8vo. 1s. 6d. (D.P.)
Contributions by Stanhope, Arundell, Cowper, and Foxton, and probably a made-up volume.

Mar. 13. " A very curious Print of the Rev. Dr. Swift, Engrav'd from the Original Painting by Mr. Vertue." 6d. (D.P.)

Mar. 27. BONEFONIUS. *Pancharis, Queen of Love;* or Woman Unveil'd. Being the Basia . . . containing the whole Art of Kissing, and original Poems [by Parnell, Foxton, Beckingham and J. Philips]. 8vo. 1s. Frontispiece. B.M.
Parnell's *Original Poems upon Several Occasions* is advertised separately (D.P.), but must belong to this collection.

Apr. 21. BONEFONIUS. *Cupid's Bee-Hive, or the Sting of Love.* Translated by several Hands. With some Original Poems. . . . Now first publish'd from the Original by Mr. [John] Addison. 8vo. 1s. 6d. (D.P.)
John, you notice.

Apr. 28. *Hanover Tales;* or, the Secret History of Count Fradonia and the Unfortunate Barilia. Done from the French by a Lady. The Second Edition. Bettesworth. 12mo. 1s. 6d. and 2s. B.M.

Apr. 29. DART (JOHN). *Westminster Abbey.* A Poem. (Batley, Chetwood, Griffith, Graves, King, Meadows.) 1s. (P.B.)

May 10. A " Second Edition " of the *Callipædia* is announced at 1s. 6d. (D.P.)

May 15. *Three New Poems.* Viz : I. Family Duty, or the Monk and the Merchant's Wife. Being the Shipman's Tale from Chaucer, moderniz'd. II. The Curious Wife ; A Tale, devised in the Manner of Chaucer, by Mr. Fenton, now moderniz'd. III. Buckingham House, with the Duke's Character of Queen Anne. 1s. (D.P.)
One of the pamphlets to which the authorities took exception, and defended by Curll in his *Humble Petition.*

May 19. *Proposals for printing by Subscription the Memoirs of Henry Pulleine, Esq.* (late Governor of Bermuda). Gratis. (D.P.)
Which apparently came to nothing.

July 1. PHILALETHES. *Ars Punica, Pars Altera;* or Truth Vindicated from the Misrepresentations of the Dean of

Worcester [Hare]. " Printed for A. Moore, and Sold by him (under the Rose) near St. Paul's." 8vo. 6d. B.M.

Philalethes might be anybody.

Aug. 22. GEDDE (JOHN). *The English Apiary : or the Compleat Bee-Master*. Mears, Corbet. 12mo. 2s. B.M.

Preface signed Cha. Nourse, who thanks the booksellers for sending him the manuscript (to edit).

Oct. 30 (dated 1722). EARBURY (MATTHIAS). *A Modest Vindication of the Clergy of the Church of England*. " Printed for J. Roberts . . . 1722." 8vo. B.M.

Early Nov. (Dated 1722.) C[RULL] (J[OHN].) *The History and Antiquities of Westminster Abbey*. The Third Edition. Bell, Darby, Bettesworth, Gosling, Pemberton, Fayram, Hooke, Rivington, Clay, Batley, Symon. 2 vols. 8vo. 8s. or 15s. L.P. B.M.

Early Nov. (Dated 1722.) ORLEANS (F. J.). *History of the Revolutions in England under the Stuarts*. Made English. The Second Edition. (Gosling, Pemberton.) 5s. (D.P.)

Nov. 4. POMFRET (JOHN). *A Pindarick Ode upon the last Day*. 6d. (D.P.)

Nov. 9. BONEFONIUS. *The Love Poems*. The Second Edition. With cuts. 3s. 6d. (P.B.)

Apparently a made-up volume. I am not sure about the general title.

Nov. 10. PRIOR (MATTHEW). *A Supplement to . . . Poems*. 1s. 6d. (D.P.)

" Consisting of such Pieces as were (for Private Reasons) omitted in the Collection of his Works in his Life Time ; and of others, now first published from the Original Manuscripts in the Custody of his Friends. To which is added, Threnus, or Stanzas upon his Death. By a Fellow Collegian."

Dec. 12 (dated 1722). *Some Memoirs of the Life and Publick Employments of Matthew Prior, Esq.* . . . With his Will. 8vo. B.M.

The manuscript was sent, we are told, to Giles Jacob, who wrote part of the Memoirs. The will is separately paged.

Dec. 12. *The Court of Honour ;* or the Laws . . . establish'd for the Suppression of Duels in France. . . . With Observations . . . by Sir Richard Steele. 1s. 6d. (P.B.)

Dec. 12. SHEFFIELD (JOHN, DUKE OF BUCKINGHAMSHIRE). *The Works*. " Published, By his Grace, in his Life Time." 8vo. 3s. 6d. Vignette on title. B.M.

Edited by John Henley, who announced that " the verses were delivered to Mr. Gildon, in 1721, corrected by the author." Curll was afterwards in trouble over a projected issue of the complete works.

Dec. 13 (dated 1722). SWIFT (JONATHAN). *Miscellanies*. The Fourth Edition. "London : Printed in the Year MDCCXXII." 12mo. 2*s*. 6*d*. B.M.

This contains *The Benefit of Farting*, with a mock title-page, *The Wonderful Wonder of Wonders*, *The Art of Punning* (4th ed. 1719), *The Right of Precedence* (4th ed., 1720), *Advice to a Young Poet* (4th ed., 1720), *The Swearer's Bank* (4th ed., 1720), *A Defence of English Commodities* (1720), *An Imitation of Horace*, *Letters*, *Poems*, *Tales*, &c. (2nd ed., "First Printed in the Year 1718"). Pagination, however, runs on.

Dec. 16. BROWN (MOSES). *The Richmond Beauties*. A Poem. To which are added 3 others. 6*d*. (P.B.)

Probably dated 1722, but possibly another book altogether. Mr. Brown's contribution, I mean, may be so modest that in a hurried glance at some other pamphlet I may have missed him altogether.

Dec. 19 (dated 1722). BELLARMINE (ROBERTO, Cardinal). *The Joys of the Blessed*. A Poetical Discourse . . . Translated . . . by Thomas Foxton. To which is prefix'd An Essay upon the State of Departed Souls. By Mr. Addison. 8vo. 3*s*. B.M.

DE LA MOTTE (A.). *One Hundred Court Fables*, written for the Instruction of Princes. . . . Made English from the Paris Edition by Mr. [Robert] Samber. 12mo. 4*s*. (Cat.)

An edition of Amhurst's *Poems on Several Occasions*, at 5*s*., is advertised as being sold in the autumn by Curll. I presume this must be Francklin's edition of 1720.

DENNIS (JOHN). *Original Letters, Familiar, Moral and Critical*. 2 vols. "Printed for W. Mears, 1721." (Cat.)

This occurs in one of Curll's lists.

A Catalogue of new Books publish'd this Autumn. Gratis.

1722

? HOBBES (THOMAS). *A True Ecclesiastical History from Moses to the Time of Martin Luther, in Verse*. Translated from the Latin Original. 8vo. 3*s*. 6*d*. B.M.

The Latin text was offered at 2*s*. Advertised on July 14th, 1721 (D.P.), and probably issued in the autumn of that year.

? BUCHANAN (GEORGE). *History of Scotland*. The Second Edition, Revised and Corrected by Mr. Bond. Bettenham, printer. Bettesworth, Taylor, Bickerton, Batley, Mears, Rivington, Lacy. 2 vols. 8vo. Plates. B.M.

Advertised as " now in the Press and speedily will be publish'd " on 24th Sept., 1720. (P.B.)

Jan. 10.   " There is now preparing for the Press (by several Hands) a Translation of Pliny's Epistles. With his panegyrick upon the Emperor Trajan. To which will be prefix'd, The Life of Pliny.

☞ If any Gentlemen have, for their private Amusement, translated any of these Epistles, and will be pleased to communicate them to the Editor (directed to Mr. Curll's over against Catherine-Street in the Strand) the Favour will be gratefully acknowledged." (D.P.)

It cheerfully remained in the press for some time. The editor turns out to be John Henley. Ultimately the book was published by Mears 2nd July, 1724.

? Jan.   [STAUNTON (WILLIAM).] A *Packet of Letters ;* which lately passed between . . . and the Rev. Dr. Waterland. 4*s.*

? Jan.   [STAUNTON (WILLIAM).] *Reason and Revelation stated.* . . . By the same Hand that wrote the Packet of Letters to Dr. Waterland. 8vo. 1*s.* B.M.

Feb. 3.   *The Gentleman's Miscellany.* 2 vols. 8vo. Cuts. 10*s.* (P.B.)

Feb. 13.   [? SWIFT (JONATHAN).] *The Wonderful Wonder of Wonders.* The Fifth Edition. " Printed from the Original Copy from Dublin, and Sold by A. Moore." 8vo. 4*d.* B.M.

Feb. 17.   SHAKESPEARE (WILLIAM). *The Tragedy of K. Richard II.* Alter'd . . . by Mr. Theobald. 1*s.* 6*d.* (P.B.)

I cannot trace this edition, unless it be the 1720 edition printed for Strahan, Mears, Meighan, Barker and Morphew.

Feb. 20.   OSBORN[E] (FRANCIS). *The Miscellaneous Works.* . . . The Eleventh Edition. Bell, Darby, Bettesworth, Taylor, Pemberton, Fayram, Mears, Hooke, Rivington, Clay, Batley, Symon. 2 vols. 12mo. 6*s.* B.M. " Printed by T. Wood," vol. II.

Feb. 20.   [? SWIFT (JONATHAN).] *The Wonderful Wonder of Wonders,* or The Hole History of the Life and Actions of Mr. Breech. The Sixth Edition. 8vo. 4*d.* B.M.

Feb. 24.   DYCHE (THOMAS). *A Practical Grammar of the English Tongue.* In Two Parts. 1*s.* and 1*s.* 6*d.* (P.B.)

Specially, and no doubt wisely, recommended to the Fair Sex.

Feb. 27.   BROADBENT (HUMPHREY). *The Domestick Coffee-Man ;* showing the true Way of preparing and making of

Chocolate, Coffee, and Tea. Bickerton. 8vo. 6*d*. B.M.

Mar. 15.   LE CLERC (JEAN). *A Critical Examination of the Reverend Mr. Dean Prideaux's Connection of the Old and New Testaments.* . . . Made English. " Printed for J. Roberts." 8vo. 1*s*. B.M.

May 5.   " To prevent any Imposition upon the Publick, this is to give Notice that speedily will be publish'd, a new Edition of The Compleat Works of Mr. John Locke, in 3 Volumes in Folio . . . to which is added, a Supplement containing some Pieces which were omitted in the former Edition. Also a Life. Printed for A. Churchill, E. Curll, T. Woodward, R. Francklin." (D.P.)

" Whereas there was an Advertisement [as above]. . . . This is to give Notice, that Mr. Churchill is in no way concerned in the said Supplement or Account of Mr. Locke's Life, but that a new Edition of Mr. Locke's Works is reprinting in the same Manner as the former Edition was, printed for A. Churchill and S. Manship, and sold by W. Taylor." 10th May. (D.P.)

A little piece of Curllean bluff. His own *Remains* would go very nicely with the new edition, and in this way might seem to belong to it.

May 24.   RICE (THOMAS). *The Resurrection of the Same-Body, and the Immortality of the Soul, Asserted.* In a (very Remarkable) Sermon. 4*d*. (P.B.)

July 3.   SALIGNAC DE LA MOTHE FENELON (FRANCOIS). *A Treatise on the Usefulness of Eloquence.* . . . Translated by John Ozell. To which is added, An Essay upon Humour, by Mr. Congreve. (Payne.) 12mo. 2*s*. 6*d*. (P.B.)

A pleasant little dispute followed the appearance of a rival edition by Walthoe, who in the P.B. of 5th July said : " N.B. This Translation is illustrated and adorn'd with more than a HUNDRED QUOTATIONS from *Tully*, *Quintilian*, *Longinus*, and others of the finest Writers, both Ancient and Modern, that are not in the French Edition, nor in the ABRIDGEMENT thereof publish'd on Tuesday last by E. CURLL, under the disguis'd title of *A Treatise upon the Usefulness of Eloquence*, &c., which Quotations, tho' printed in a small Character, have increased the Bulk of this Edition considerably, and will be reckoned by all good Judges as valuable as any part of the Book."

Curll of course accepted the challenge, and in advertising his Ozell version two days later, pointed out that it was very fortunately " not loaded with Notes, to enhance the Price ; the Repetition of the Dialogue is likewise avoided, and only *such Rules retained* as are useful to the *English Pleader* and *Preacher*."

Aug. 23. " In the Press and speedily will be publish'd " *Occult Philosophy* or an Historical Treatise of the Diving Rod. From the French of de Vallamont. (Payne, Brotherton, Graves.

No further advertisements seen.

Oct. 11. SADLER (JOHN). *The Lady's Physician.* Being a Treatise of all Uterine Diseases. (Johnston, Goddard.) 1*s.* 6*d.* (P.B.)

Oct. 16. " This Day, New Editions of the Last Wills and Testaments of the following : " Tenison, Gilbert Burnet, Wharton, Halifax, Hickes, Thomas Burnet, Partridge, Nelson, Radcliffe, Prior, and South. To be had, either collected into volumes, or single. (P.B.)

Oct. 27. CENTLIVRE (SUSANNA). *The Artifice.* A Comedy. " Printed for T. Payne." 8vo. 1*s.* 6*d.* B.M.

Reprinted in 1735 (12mo.) for Mears, and in the following year for Feales. At this time Payne was in close partnership with Curll.

BONEFONIUS. *Pancharis, or the Queen of Love.* The Second Edition. H. Curll. (Cat.)

SEYMOUR (RICHARD). *The Court Gamester.* The Third Edition, Corrected. 12mo. 1*s.* 6*d.* and 2*s.* B.M.

1723

Jan. 8. " Speedily will be publish'd " *The Memorable Lovers,* or the Amours of the Countess de Vergi and the Chevalier de Vaudray. From the French by Mr. [Joseph] Morgan. (P.B.)

Jan. 17. SIMON (RICHARD). *De Statu Mortuorum : an Historico-Theological Dissertation concerning the Dead.* Made English by Mr. [Joseph] Morgan. 8vo. 1*s.* B.M.

Jan. 17. JACOB (GILES). *The Poetical Register.* 2 vols. 8vo. Plates.

A re-issue, without Curll's name. Advertised by Bettesworth, Baker and Taylor.

This was a time when Curll was meditating retirement.

Apr. 6. *Cytheria : or, New Poems upon Love and Intrigue.* With Mr. Pope's Character of Addison. [Edited by Jeremiah Markland.] Payne. 8vo. 1*s.* 6*d.* B.M.

Long supposed to be the first appearance of Pope's poem in print, but as a matter of fact it had previously appeared in the *St. James's Journal.*

Apr. 13. AMHURST (NICHOLAS). *The Satirical Works.* 8vo. 5*s.*
(E.P.)
Includes only the pieces (to be " had single ") which
Curll had printed.

? April. *Cases of Divorce for Several Reasons.* The Second Edition.
12mo. B.M.
With slight additions.

May 18. OINOPHILUS (BONIFACE), *pseud.*, i.e. A. H. DE SALLENGRE.
Ebrietatis Encomium ; or the Praise of Drunkenness. 12mo.
2*s.* 6*d.* Frontispiece. B.M.
" Written by a Person of Honour (who is a Free-
Mason). Author of Eunuchism Display'd." (E.P.)
" Feb. 20, 1723. Robert Samber was paid by Mr.
Curll four guineas for the sole right and title to the copy
of a book by me written, intituled The Praise of Drunken-
ness, with a reserved right of twelve copies bound."
(Upcott MSS.)

June 8. ATTERBURY (FRANCIS). *Maxims, Reflections, and Observations, Divine, Moral, and Political.* " Printed in the
Year M.DCC.XXIII." 8vo. 1*s.* 6*d.* B.M.

June 13. BARKER (JANE). *A Patch-Work Screen for the Ladies.*
. . . In a Collection of new Instructive Novels. Payne.
12mo. 2*s.* 6*d.* B.M.

June 29. FOXTON (THOMAS). *Serino ; or the Character of a Fine
Gentleman.* With 5 Poems by Mr. Addison. The Second
Edition. 8vo. 1*s.* B.M.

Aug. 8. [STACKHOUSE (THOMAS).] *Memoirs of . . . Dr. Francis
Atterbury.* " Printed in the Year, M.DCC.XXIII."
8vo. 2*s.* Portrait. B.M. Preface signed Philalethes.
" Sept. 16, 1723. Thomas Stackhouse received of Mr.
Curll ten guineas for writing The Life of Bishop Atter-
bury." (Upcott MSS.)

Aug. 29. [HAUKSBEE (FRANCIS).] *The Patch.* An Heroi-Comical
Poem. With *The Wild Wedding.* (Nutt, Dodd, Griffith.)
1*s.* (E.P.)

Nov. 28. DEVENTER (HENDRIK VAN). *New Improvements in the Art
of Midwifery.* [A Supplement.] 2*s.* and 2*s.* 6*d.* (P.B.)
STAUNTON (WILLIAM). *A Review of Mr. Whiston's
XXIII Propositions* Concerning the Primitive Faith of
Christians about the Trinity and the Incarnation. 8vo.
2*s.* 6*d.* B.M.
STAUNTON (WILLIAM). *A Discourse of Repentance and
Faith.* 8vo. 6*d.* B.M.
PRIDEAUX (HUMPHREY). *The True Nature of Imposture
Fully Display'd in the Life of Mahomet.* The Eighth
Edition, Corrected. Hooke, Mears, Clay. 8vo. B.M.

? 1723.   STAUNTON (WILLIAM). *Thoughts of a Christian upon the Godhead.* 8vo.

RABADAN (MAHOMET). *Mahometism Fully Explain'd* . . . written in Spanish and Arabic in the Year MDCIII. Translated by Mr. [Joseph] Morgan. " Printed for W. Mears." 8vo. 5s. B.M.

This is Vol. I. Vol. II., issued in 1725.

WOODWARD (JOHN). *Remarks upon the Ancient and Present State of London,* Occasion'd by some Roman Urns . . . Lately discover'd. The Third Edition. Bettesworth, Taylor, Gosling, Clarke. 8vo. B.M.

Curll's name does not appear on the title-page, but the tract is advertised in some of the later catalogues, and it is also included in *Bibliotheca Recondita,* 1739.

1724

Jan. 15.   A Catalogue of very curious Books . . . to be sold by Auction . . . at the Chapter Coffee-House in Pater-Noster-Row. Gratis.

Feb. 1.   BALDASSARE (COUNT CASTIGLIONE). *The Courtier.* [Translated by Robert Samber.] (Bettesworth, Batley, Clarke.) 6s. (E.P.)

Feb. 8.   DACIER (Mme.). *Remarks upon Mr. Pope's Translation of Homer.* " Translated by Mr. Parnell." 6d. (P.B.)

Mar. 7.   STAUNTON (WILLIAM). *Five Theological Tracts.* 8vo. 6s. (P.B.)

Mar. 26.   WALKER (CHARLES). *Authentick Memoirs of the Life* . . . *of Sally Salisbury.* The Second Edition. (Warner.) 8vo. 2s. Portrait. (P.B.)

The first edition " Printed in the Year M.DCC.XX.III." was not advertised by Curll.

Apr. 2.   Various Lives (Hamilton, Mohun, Leeds, Godolphin, &c.) are issued together. 6s. (P.B.)

?   STAUNTON (WILLIAM). *A Familiar Discourse,* shewing that the Gospel is a Comment upon the Law of Nature. 8vo. 1s. B.M.

?   STAUNTON (WILLIAM). *An Epistolary Conference with the Reverend Dr. Waterland.* The Second Edition. 8vo. B.M.

Apr. 17.   STAUNTON (WILLIAM). *Six Tracts* [called] The Second Edition. 7s. 6d. (D.J.)

The preceding piece has been added to the others.

?   STAUNTON (WILLIAM). *A Letter to the Reverend Mr. Samuel Croxall.* 8vo. B.M.

Apr. 20.   POMFRET (JOHN). *Poems.* The Sixth Edition. (D.J.)

July 11.   LE CLERC (JEAN). *Critical Examination* . . . upon Dean Prideaux's Connection. . . . Part II. (E.P.)

The two parts sold at 1s. 6d.

July 11.   STAUNTON (WILLIAM). *Seven Tracts.* 8vo. 8s. (E.P.)
The last of him, and about time too.

Oct. 10   MANLEY (DELIA DE LA RIVIERE). *History of her own Life*
(dated   *and Times.* The Fourth Edition. Pemberton. 8vo.
1725).   1s. 6d. and 2s. 6d. Frontispiece. B.M.
       With a preface by Curll.

Oct. 15.   " In the Press " Le Clerc's *Remarks on Bishop Burnet's*
History of His Own Times, translated by Mr. Morgan.
(P.B.)

Oct. 15.   *Venus in the Cloister ; or the Nun in her Smock.* [From the
French by Robert Samber.] 2s. and 2s. 6d. Frontis-
piece.
       No booksellers' names on the advertisement. See
text.

Nov. 10.   [? KENNET (BASIL).] *Armour, or the never failing Engine.*
A Poem. 6d. (E.P.)
       Reprinted in *The Potent Ally,* (1741).
       Just the kind of poem that you might expect from a
Bishop's son.
[JACOB (GILES).] *Memoirs of . . . Joseph Addison. . . .*
The Second Edition. 8vo. 6d. B.M.

1725

? Jan.   MAGNUS (ALBERTUS). *De Secretis Mulierum ; or, the*
Mysteries of Human Generation Fully Revealed. . . . Faithfully rendered into English, with Explanatory Notes
and Approved by the late John Quincy, M.D. 12mo.
2s. B.M.

? Jan.   CURLL (EDMUND). *The Humble Representation of . . .*
Concerning Five Books, complained of to the Secretary
of State. 8vo.
       The five books being *The Treatise of Flogging, Venus in*
the Cloister, Ebrietatis Encomium, Three New Poems, and
De Secretis Mulierum.

Feb. 2.   ADDISON (JOSEPH). *Miscellanies in Prose and Verse.* 8vo.
10s. (P.B.) 12mo. 3s. Portrait. B.M.
       Contains Preface, *Poems on Several Occasions* (2nd ed.
1724), *Serino* (2nd ed. 1723), *Dissertation on the Roman*
Poets (3rd ed., 1721), *Content* (by Allan Ramsay), *Art of*
Dress (2nd ed.) and three of Amhurst's satirical pieces.

Feb. 4.   *Venus in the Cloister. . . .* The Second Edition. (E.P.)
? May.   MANLEY (DELIA DE LA RIVIERE). *A Stage-Coach*
Journey to Exeter. . . . To which is added The Force of
Love . . . by [Richardson] Pack. " Printed for J.
Roberts." 1s. (E.P.)
       A doubtful entry.

June 24.   The same. The Second Edition. B.M.
Curll's books are advertised, anonymously, at the end
of the book.
He was then in prison.

June 24.   PACK (RICHARDSON). *A New Collection of Miscellanies in
Prose and Verse.* 8vo.   3s. and 5s.   L.P.   B.M.

Sept. 2.   PLANTE-AMOUR, *pseud.,* i.e. F. BRUYS.   *The Adventures of
Pomponius,* a Roman Knight ; or the History of Our
Times.   Made English from the Rome Edition of the
French Original by Spring Macky.   12mo.   2s. 6d.
B.M.
[Part I. only.]

Sept. 4.   ALBERTUS (MAGNUS).   *De Secretis Mulierum.* . . . The
Second Edition.   To which is added, *The Lady's Physician* . . . by John Sadler.   4s.   (F.P.)

Sept. 7.   " Now in the Press " *Practical Discourses* . . . by
Richard Duke.   Curll says that he intends to include
Memoirs of Duke's Life, and asks for information.
(F.P.)   I cannot find that the project ever came to any-
thing.

Sept. 28.   QUEULLETTE (THOMAS SIMON).   *Chinese Tales ;* or the
Wonderful Adventures of the Mandarin Fum Hoam.
Done from the French . . . by Thomas Stackhouse.
Also a Compleat Key.   (Edlin.)   2 vols.   12mo.   4s.
Cuts.   (W. E. P.)
" N.B.   Beware of a spurious and very defective trans-
lation of this Work, obtruded upon the Publick, by a
nameless and scandalous Scribbler." (Henry Curll's
1728 list.)
" N.B.   In Justice to the Publick, we hereby declare,
that we have compared the two Versions of the Chinese
Tales . . . and do find, that the Anonymous Transla-
tion lately obtruded upon the World by Meadows and
Brotherton . . . both for Justness and Beauty of Expression, is no way comparable to Mr. Stackhouse's.   Witness our Hands.
                M. HALPENN, Great Pulteney-street
                JOHN MORGAN, of Highgate
                WILLIAM COOKE, Middle Temple
                CHA. AYRES, Lincolns-Inn-Fields."
We are not impressed.

Oct. 6.   " In the Press " Thomas Stackhouse's new translation
of Charles Drelincourt's *Consolations against the Fear of
Death.* (P.B.)

Oct. 12   BARKER (JANE).   *The Lining of the Patch-Work Screen.*
(dated   " Printed for A. Bettesworth." 12mo.   2s. 6a.   B.M.
1726).

Nov. 11.
(dated
1726).
PLANTE-AMOUR, *pseud.*, i.e. F. BRUYS. *The Adventures of Pomponius.* . . . Translated by Spring Macky. Part II. 12mo. 2*s.* and 2*s.* 6*d.* B.M.

Nov. 11.
R. (W.) *The Mandate of the Archbishop of Paris.* Occasion'd by the Miracles wrought there, May 31. With Remarks. 1*s.* (P.B.)

Dec. 16
(dated
1726).
The Gentleman 'Pothecary. A True Story. Done out of the French by Sir Roger L'Estrange, Knt., in the Year 1678. The Second Edition. 12mo. 1*s.* Frontispiece. B.M.

One of the impounded books.

" March 3, 1724/5. Ann Brome received then of Mr. Edmund Curll one guinea in full satisfaction for all my right, property, and interest to and in the following copy, viz. The Gentleman Apothecary ; being a late and true Story, turned out of French, with several Letters, 8vo, which said copy was the property of my late husband, Mr. Charles Brome, deceased." (Upcott MSS.)

Dec. 23
(dated
1726).
The Case of Seduction. Translated from the French by Mr. Rogers. Being the . . . Proceedings . . . against the . . . Abbé des Rues. 12mo. 2*s.* 6*d.* B.M.

Subsequently advertised when any other clergyman got into similar trouble. When a certain Father Girard went rather too far, Curll printed, and probably composed, the following couplet :

" Father Girard, by far, is by Des Rues out-done,
One Hundred Virgins, He seduc'd ; Girard but one."

Dec. 23.
The Stamford Toasts ; or, Panegyrical Characters of the Fair Ones. . . . With some other Poetical Amusements. By Mr. Pope, not the Undertaker." (P.B.)

Probably dated 1726, with Henry Curll's name.

ROUSE (LEWIS). *Tunbridge Wells ; or, a Directory for the Drinking of Those Waters.* Made English from the Latin Original. " Printed for J. Roberts." 8vo. 1*s.* 6*d.* B.M.

Contains, separately paged, *A Physico-Mechanical Dissertation Concerning Water.*

RABADAN (MAHOMET). *Mahometism Explain'd.* Vol. II. " Printed for the Author MDCCXXV." 8vo. 6*s.* B.M.

Copies of John Philips's *Works,* with Sewell's Life, may be found with the general title-page dated 1725. (Cat.)

1726

Feb. 8.
[NORTH (HON. ROGER).] *The Gentleman Farmer ;* or Certain Observations made . . . upon the Husbandry

of Flanders. . . . By a Person of Honour in the County
of Norfolk. 2s. 6d. (W. E. P.)
"Who wrote the Gentleman Accomptant." Curll's
announcement.

Apr. 9. MARVELL (ANDREW). *The Works.* 2 vols. 12mo. 5s.
Portrait and plates. "Printed for H. Curll." (P.B.)
"April, 1726. Thomas Cooke was paid by Mr. Curll
£5 for writing Mr. Marvell's Life, procuring some of
his Letters, and publishing his Works." (Upcott MSS.)

Apr. 26. PACK (RICHARDSON). *All the Works* . . . [in one
volume]. 3s. or 6s. L.P. (W.E.P.)

June 9. KER (JOHN, of Kersland). *The Memoirs.* Containing
His secret Transactions and Negotiations in Scotland,
England, the Courts of Vienna, Hanover, and other
Foreign Parts. . . . Published by Himself. "Printed in
the Year M.DCC.XXVI." 8vo. 3s. 6d. B.M.
[Part I. only.]
Contains Henry Curll's list of books before Phila-
lethes's (i.e. Curll's) "Letter Sent on Reading the
Following Memoirs."

July 14. POPE (ALEXANDER), &c. *Miscellanea.* 2 vols. 12mo.
5s. (P.B.)
"Vol. I. contains I. Familiar Letters written to Henry
Cromwell, Esq., by Mr. Pope. II. Occasional Poems by
Mr. Pope, Mr. Cromwell, Dean Swift, &c. Letters from
Mr. Dryden, to a Lady, in the Year 1699. Vol. II. con-
tains I. An Essay on Giving Fortunes with Women on
Marriage. II. The Praise of Women, done out of the
French by Mr. Macky. III. An Essay on Gibing. IV.
Swifteana ; or Poems by Dean Swift, and several of his
Friends. V. Laus Ululæ. The Praise of Owls."
Swifteana also published separately.
"N.B. There is also in the Press, Whartoniana ; or
Poems by his Grace the Duke of Wharton and several
other Persons of Eminence. The Original Manuscripts
of all the above Miscellanea I am ready to produce to
any Gentleman who desires to see them : Also a correct
Copy of *Cadenus* and *Vanessa,* &c. HENRY CURLL."
(P.B.)
The Pope letters had been purchased from Mrs.
Thomas, Cromwell's erstwhile mistress.

July 14. SWIFT (JONATHAN). *Cadenus and Vanessa.* A Poem.
6d. (P.B.)
The advertisement states that this poem "the only
true copy" is furnished with a Key. That "printed and
sold by J. Roberts" has no key, but may be the one
referred to. Various editions were issued within a very

few weeks, and of course every publisher printed his version from " the only true copy."

Aug. 20
(dated
1727).
FOXTON (THOMAS). *The Tower.* A Poem. " Printed in the year 1727." 12mo. 1*s.* B.M.
Included in Whartoniana, vol. I.

Aug. 23
(dated
1727).
MOYLE (WALTER). *The Whole Works.* . . . That were Published by Himself. To which is prefixed Some Account of his Life and Writings [by Anthony Hammond]. With a Preface, signed E. C[urll]. Knapton, Bettesworth, Pemberton, Batley. 8vo. 5*s.* B.M.

Aug. 23
(dated
1727).
[CURLL (EDMUND).] *An Apology for the Writings of Walter Moyle, Esq.* " Printed in the Year M.DCC.XXVII." 8vo. 6*d.* B.M.
With various letters of Curll's.
At the end Henry Curll advertises " Mr. Moyle's Works in 3 Volumes, price 15*s.*"

Aug. 23.
[CURLL (EDMUND).] *The Prisoner's Advocate ;* or Caveat against under Sheriffs and their Officers ; Jayl Keepers and their Agents. " Printed for W. Osborn." 8vo. 1*s.* B.L.O.
Introduction signed " Philalethes."

Aug. 25.
A New Miscellany of Original Poems. Published by Anthony Hammond. 8vo. 5*s.* (E.P.)

Sept. 15.
PARKER (SAMUEL). *History of his Own Times,* beginning at the Year 1660. Faithfully Translated. With proper Remarks throughout . . . by Edmund Curll from the Latin Original. [Book one, only.] 8vo. 1*s.* 6*d.* (W.E.P.)

Sept. 20.
KER (JOHN, of Kersland). *The Memoirs.* . . . Part II. " Printed in the Year M.DCC.XXVI."
For which Curll stood in the pillory.

Sept. 24
(dated
1727).
Whartoniana, or Miscellanies in Verse and Prose, by the Wharton Family, &c. " Printed in the Year 1727." 2 vols. 12mo. 5*s.* Frontispiece and Portrait.
Preface by Curll, who also prints three of his own short poems. One of these is printed in the text. The others are :

" *On the Duke of* Wharton *renouncing the* Protestant Religion.

A *Whig* He was bred, but at length is turn'd *Papist,*
Pray God send the next Remove be not an *Atheist.*"

" *On the revived* Controversy *of the* Thundering Legion.

Since Whiston and Woolston their Shafts have let fly,
To *Catechise* Truth, and *Confirm* an old Lye ;

> Would make Thunder, Hail, Lightning, for Miracles pass,
> And who'er disbelieved—is accounted an Ass,
> The Church Cant let's reverse then, and own the true Foyle,
> Of Religion, is Reason, and found in a Moyle."

Oct. 6. The *Poems* of Nicholas Rowe are now sold with the *Callipædia* in one volume at 6s. (W.E.P.)

Oct. 6. POPE (ALEXANDER). *Court Poems.* 12mo. (E.P.) Contents differ from the 1716 edition. (Cat.)

Oct. 29. *A Guide to the Oratory, Being a full Account of the new Sect of the Henleyarians.* (Osborn, Brotherton, Jackson, Blandford.) (E.P.)

? Nov. KER (JOHN, of Kersland). *The Memoirs.* . . . Part III and Last. 8vo. B.M.
Contains, separately paged, Mr. Consul [William] Ker's *Remarks upon Holland, Germany &c.*

Nov. 1. PARKER (SAMUEL). *History of his Own Times.* Faithfully translated. With proper Remarks . . . by Edmund Curll. Book II. 1s. 6d. (W.E.P.)

Nov. 1. LE CLERC (JEAN). *Two Tracts.* I. Remarks upon Mr. Addison's Travels through Italy. II. A Supplement to Sir William Temple's Observations on the Netherlands. Both translated . . . by Mr. Theobald. 1s. (W.E.P.)

Nov. 1. HOLDSWORTH (EDWARD). *Muscipula* . . . with the Translation. "A new Edition." 1s. (W.E.P.)
Possibly dated 1727.

Nov. 1 (dated 1727). JACOB (GILES). *The Rape of the Smock.* The Second Edition. H. Curll. 8vo. 1s. Frontispiece. B.M.

Nov. 24. COROLINI, *pseud.* A Key, being observations and explanatory Notes, upon the Travels of Lemuel Gulliver. In a Letter to Dean Swift. Translated from the Italian Original. "Printed in the Year MDCCXXVI." 8vo. Parts I. to III. (All with same imprint.)
Title-page to Part II. : *The Brobdingnagians. Being a Key.* . . . In a Second Letter to Dean Swift.
Part III. *The Flying Island, &c.* . . . In a Third Letter to Dean Swift.
All separately paged.
It was a neat project, which skilfully advertised a number of recent Curllean publications, regretting that they were not to be found in the libraries of the various Royal palaces which Gulliver visited.
The advertisement was so worded as to make it seem

that Motte, the publisher of *Gulliver's Travels*, had also published this Key.

Dec. 20. COROLINI, *pseud. The Kingdom of Horses. Being a Key.* . . . In a Fourth Letter to Dean Swift. Same imprint. 8vo. 6*d*. B.M.

Dec. The four parts issued together with a general title-page and a page or two of verses : *Lemuel Gulliver's Travels into Several Remote Nations of the World. Compendiously methodiz'd.* " Printed in the Year MDCCXXVI." 8vo. 2*s*. 6*d*. Frontispiece. B.M.

Dec. 24. PITCAIRN[E] (ARCHIBALD). *The Whole Works.* The Second Edition. 5*s*. (E.P.)

Dec. 24. ROSE (Dr.). *Treatise of the Small Pox, whether Natural or Inoculated.* 1*s*. 6*d*. (E.P.)
A Catalogue of Books Printed for H. Curll over against Catherine Street in the Strand, 8vo, 16 pp., n.d., must, I think, have been issued either in the autumn of 1726 or the spring of 1727.

1727

? ATTERBURY (FRANCIS). *Oratio* V.R. . . . S.T.P. Hab. Oxon, die Admiss. ad Decanatam. Aed. Christi, 1711. Impensis H. Curll, 1727.
Note in Parker's *History of his own Times.*

Jan. 5. *Atterburyana.* Being Miscellanies. With I. a Collection of Original Letters, &c. II. The Virgin Seducer. III. The Batchelor-Keeper. By Philaretus [i.e. John Clarke]. " Printed in the Year MDCCXXVII." 12mo. 2*s*. 6*d*. B.M.
Dedication signed E. Curll, who explains why he makes use of Atterbury's name in a collection which contains so little of the ex-Bishop's.
" Oct. 1726. John Clarke received of Mr. Curll two payments of one guinea each in part of the copy-money of two novels, The Virgin Seducer. 2. The Batchelor's Keeper ; agreed to be printed in duodecimo at half-a-guinea per sheet, according to a specimen of The Essay on Gibing." (Upcott MSS.)

Jan. SEVIGNE (MARIE DE). *Court Secrets :* or the Lady's Chronicle Historical and Gallant . . . Extracted from the Letters . . . suppressed at Paris. " Printed in the Year 1727." 12mo.
Included in *Atterburyana*, where it is separately paged, but possibly not issued by itself, although several advertisements make particular reference to it, in order to counteract J. Peele's announcement of a rival edition.

Feb. 25. MAHOMET (LEWIS MAXIMILIAN). *Some Memoirs of the Life of.* . . . 8vo. 6*d.* B.M.
> Contains Pope's Epitaph to the Memory of Mr. Secretary Craggs.

Mar. 21. *A Dissertation concerning the Rights of the East India Company.* 2*s.* 6*d.* (W.E.P.)
> " To be had of H. Curl. Brought from Holland."

Mar. 21. " Now in the Press : *Memoirs of the Life of the late Lord Bolingbroke.*" (W.E.P.)
> But were they ?
> No.

Apr. 1. *The Altar of Love.* A Poetical Miscellany. 8vo. 6*s.* Frontispiece. (E.P.)

Apr. 11. STANHOPE (JAMES, EARL OF). *Queries Sent to the Abbot Vertot, relating to the Constitution of the Roman Senate.* 6*d.* (W.E.P.)

Apr. 11. SWIFT (JONATHAN). *The Swearer's Bank.* The Third Edition. 6*d.* (W.E.P.)
> A " third edition " had appeared in Dublin in 1721.

Apr. 13. STACKHOUSE (THOMAS). *Memoirs of the Life . . . of Dr. Francis Atterbury.* . . . The Second Edition. " Printed in the Year MDCCXXVII. 8vo. 2*s.* 6*d.* B.M.
> Identical with the first, but new title-page now giving Stackhouse's name.

Apr. 13. H. Curll appears as the first of several booksellers, selling three books by William Willymott, Vice Provost of King's Coll. Camb.
> 1. *The Lord Bacon's Essays.* 2 vols. 8vo. 10*s.* (A copy in the B.M. is dated 1720).
> 2. *A Collection of Devotions for the Altar.* 2 vols. 10*s.*
> 3. *Thomas à Kempis.* Translated. 8vo. 6*s.* (B.M. copy dated 1722.)

May 11. [SOLORZANO] (ALONZO DE CASTILLO). *Spanish Amusements :* or the Adventures of . . . Rufina call'd, The Pole-Cat of Seville. . . The Second Edition. 8vo. 4*s.* B.M.
> At the end is printed " Books lately printed for E. Curll . . . and W. Taylor."

June 3. JESUP (EDWARD) and BOND (WILLIAM). *The Lives of Mons. Pascal and Picus, Prince of Mirandola.* 3*s.* (S.J.E.P.)
> A rival edition on the market.

June 8. *The Altar of Love.* The Second Edition. 8vo. (S.J.E.P.)
> Contents probably differ from the first. Both are made-up volumes.

July 1. KER (JOHN, of Kersland). *The Memoirs.* 3rd Part. The Second Edition. 6*s.* (E.P.)

July 18. PATTISON (WILLIAM). *An Epistle to His Majesty on his*

Accession to the Throne. 8vo. 1*s.* Portrait of the Prince of Wales. (E.P.)

July 20. *The Northern Heroine ;* Being Authentick Memoirs of the late Czarina, Empress of Russia. With Verses thereon, by Aaron Hill, Esq. 8vo. 6*d.* B.M.

July 27. BURNET (THOMAS, of the Charterhouse). *Of the State of the Dead.* . . . Translated . . . by Matthias Earbery. [Part I.] 2*s.* 6*d.* 8vo. B.M.

Aug. 9. *Whartoniana.* " A New Impression." 2 vols. 5*s.* 12mo. (E.P.)

    Surely the first known use of the word " impression " in this sense ?

Sept. 9. PATTISON (WILLIAM). *The Poetical Works.* 8vo. 6*s.* B.M. [Vol. I. only.]

    Includes Memoirs of the Author's Life.

    " N. B. This Gentleman fell a Victim to the Small Pox, on the 10th Instant (in the 21st Year of his Age) the Day on which he was to have been introduc'd to their Majesties. He was one of the greatest poetick Geniuses of his Time, as his Volume of Miscellanies will sufficiently manifest. . . .H. Curll."

    Henry may have been unduly optimistic, though I believe that the critics have found many agreeable lines in the unfortunate young man's work.

Sept. 21. *A Compleat Key to Gulliver's Travels.* A New Impression. (E.P.)

    This must be the Corolini production.

Sept. 26. BURNET (THOMAS, of the Charterhouse). *Of the State of the Dead.* . . . Translated by Matthias Earbery. Part II. 8vo. 6*s.* (both parts). (S.J.E.P.)

Oct. 3. *The Velvet Coffee-Woman ;* or the Life, Gallantries, and Amours of the late Famous Mrs. Anne Rochford. " Westminster : Printed for Simon Green. . . ." 8vo. 1*s.* B.M.

    The Altar of Love is advertised on p. 46.

Oct. 21. The same. The Second Edition. (S.J.E.P.)

Oct. 24 *The Lives and Last Wills and Testaments of the Following*
(dated *Eminent Persons :* (Gil. Burnet, Thos. Burnet, Hickes,
1728). Dan. Williams, Addison, Prior, and Mr. Mahomet.) 5*s.* 8vo. B.M.

    " With several other valuable tracts " to make up the required thickness. Later the volume is advertised at 6*s.*, when no doubt further valuable tracts were added.

Nov. 7. RICHARDS ( ). *Hoglandia ; or Hogland.* Being a description of Hampshire. 1*s.* (S.J.E.P.)

    I rather fancy that there had been an edition of this poem a number of years before.

Nov. 11. POPE (ALEXANDER). *Familiar Letters.* A new edition. 5*s.* (S.J.E.P.)

Dec. 16 (dated 1728). PATTISON (WILLIAM). *Cupid's Metamorphosis;* or Love in all Shapes. Being the Second and Last Volume of the Poetical Works. " Printed in the Year M.DCC.XXVIII." 8vo. 6*s.* Portrait. B.M.

Letter to Florio at York, signed E.C.

BRITANNUS. *An Answer to Mr. Mist's Journal of January,* No. 93. In a Letter to the Author of it. " For N. Blandford . . . 1727."

For some reason this has been ascribed to Curll, as author, I mean, but on what grounds I do not know.

The Totness Address Transversed by Captain Gulliver.

In one of Curll's lists.

The Gentleman Fisher : or, The Whole Art of Fishing. The Second Edition. 12mo. Frontispiece. (Cat.)

1728

Dec. 30, 1727. " Shortly will be publish'd " *A Faithful Account of the Life and Writings of Dr. William Sherlock.* Master of the Temple. 1*s.* (S.J.E.P.)

Jan. 13. DAVIES (SIR JOHN). *The Soul.* A Poem. 2*s.* 6*d.* (S.J.E.P.)

Jan. 13. CORNWALLIS ( ). *The Jealous Husband; or Virtue in Distress.* A Venetian Story. 1*s.* (S.J.E.P.)

Jan. 13. *A Catalogue of Books Printed for H. Curll* is advertised again, but I think it is the one I have already mentioned, 1726/7.

Jan. 23. *Proposals for a Subscription to Memoirs of the Life of Edmund Curll,* Bookseller and Citizen of London. . . . Written by Himself. Gratis. (E.P.)

But the idiots refused to subscribe. I would give much to see a copy of the *Proposals,* but doubt whether many will have survived.

Feb. 27. SEYMOUR (RICHARD). *The Court Gamester.* The Fourth Edition, Improved. 12mo. 2*s.* B.M.

Mar. 28. HOWARD (HENRY, EARL OF SURREY) and WYAT (SIR THOMAS). *The Praise of Geraldine* . . . being the Celebrated Love Poems of Hy. Howard . . . also the Poetical Recreations of Sir Thos. Wyate. " Printed for Henry Curll." 8vo. (Cat.)

Almost certain to be the old sheets with a new title-page.

Apr. 11. BURNET (THOMAS, of the Charterhouse). *Of the State of Those that are to Rise.* Translated from the Latin Original . . . By Mr. Earbery. The Last Part. " Printed int Year M.DCC.XX.VIII." 8vo. B.M.

The three parts are usually found in two volumes.

Apr. 27.   ADDISON (JOSEPH). *The Chriſtian Poet.* A Miscellany of Divine Poems . . . with Memoirs. 8vo. 4*s.* Frontispiece. B.M.

May 18.   [POPE (ALEXANDER).] *The Dunciad.* " Dublin printed, London Reprinted, for A. Dodd." 12mo. 6*d.* B.M. *The Progress of Dulness* is advertised on verso of p. 51.

I shall not here go into the vexed queſtions of the various " ſtates " and " varieties," and I do not know on what date the so-called " Curll's pirated edition " appeared. (Lefferts No. 2.) But as it may really have been Curll's, I suppose I ought to mention that the Owl frontispiece is without legend and the lettering of the scroll in the bird's beak runs upward. Also l. 76 reads " Gold Chains " inſtead of " Glad Chains." On the assumption, however, that Curll may have had something to do with the Dodd issues, I shall mention them as they occur in the advertisements I have seen.

May.   [CURLL (EDMUND).] *A Compleat Key to the Dunciad.* " Printed for A. Dodd." 8vo. 6*d.* B.M.
Not yet advertised by Curll, but containing two pages of his advertisements at the end.
Where, also, is advertised :
The Knight of the Kirk : or the Eccleſiaſtical Adventures of Sir John Presbyter. A Burlesque Epic-Poem. The Third Edition. (Not seen.)

May.   [BULLOCK (CHARLES).] *Woman's Revenge ; or a Match in Newgate.* A Comedy . . . to which is added a Compleat Key to the Beggar's Opera. By Peter Padwell of Paddington [*pseud.*]. " Printed for J. Roberts." 8vo. 1*s.* 6*d.* Frontispiece.
A rival edition on the market (without the Key).

?   The same. The Second Edition. B.M.

May 25.   [POPE (ALEXANDER).] *The Dunciad.* The Second Edition. " Dublin printed ; London, reprinted for A. Dodd." 12mo. 6*d.* Owl frontispiece. B.M.

June 1.   *A Popp upon Pope.* (A. Moore only). 1*d.* (S.J.E.P.) Included in *The Popiad,* etc.

June 4.   [CURLL (EDMUND).] *A Compleat Key to the Dunciad.* With a Charaƈter of Mr. Pope's Profane Writings. By Sir Richard Blackmore. The Second Edition. 6*d.*
With emendations and additions, and a notice announcing that Mrs. Dodd has been forbidden to sell any more copies of the Key.

June 8.   [POPE (ALEXANDER).] *The Dunciad.* The Third Edition. (E.P.)

June 11.   [STANHOPE (HENRY).], *pseud.* ? William Bond. *The*

    Progress of Dulness. "Printed in the Year M.DCC.XXVIII." 8vo. 1s. B.M.

June 20. [DEFOE (DANIEL).] *The Supernatural Philosopher ;* or the Mysteries of Magick in all its Branches, clearly Unfolded . . . in the History of . . . Duncan Campbell. . . . The Second Edition. 8vo. 5s. B.M.

    Contains Stanhope's Verses to Campbell, i.e. *The Progress of Dulness,* separately paged, but with the exception of the altered title-page, the book is the old *History of the Life and Adventures.*

June 25. [STANHOPE (HENRY)], *pseud.,* ? William Bond. *The Progress of Dulness.* "New Edition." (S.J.E.P.)

July 2. [CURLL (EDMUND).] *A Compleat Key to the Dunciad.* . . . The Third Edition. 8vo. 6d. B.M.

July 2. [CURLL (EDMUND).] *The Popiad.* "Printed in the Year M.DCC.XXVIII." 12mo. 1s. B.M.

July 4. BURNET (THOMAS, of the Charterhouse). *Of the State of the Dead.* . . . Translated. . . . The Second Edition. 2 vols. 8vo. 10s. 6d. B.M.

July 18. [CURLL (EDMUND).] *The Popiad.* "New Edition." (E.P.)

July 23. SALIGNAC DE LA MOTHE FENELON (FRANCOIS). *Conversations on the Plurality of Worlds.* The Second Edition. 2s. 6d. (S.J.E.P.)

July. D'ANVERS (CALEB), *pseud.,* i.e. NICHOLAS AMHURST. *The Twickenham Hotch-Potch.* . . . Being a Sequel to the Beggar's Opera. "Printed for J. Roberts." 1s. 8vo. B.M.

Aug. 8. *The Female Dunciad.* "Printed for T. Read . . . and Sold by the Booksellers of London and Westminster." 8vo. 1s. B.M.

    Contains letters and poems by Pope, an Eliza Haywood novel, *Female Worthies* by the Bishop of Peterborough, "The Whole being a continuation of The Twickenham Hotch-Potch."

Aug. 29. *The History of That most Eminent Statesman, Sir John Perrott* . . . Lord Lieutenant of Ireland. 8vo. 6s. B.M.

    Edited by Richard Rawlinson.

Sept. 3. BURNET (THOMAS, of the Charterhouse). *Archæologiæ Philosophicæ ;* or the Ancient Doctrine concerning the Originall of Things. . . . Translated by Thomas Foxton. 8vo. 3s. B.M.

    "Risen from the Grave of a Chancery-Injunction, and publish'd. . . . Some of my timorous Brethren, thro' the ridiculous Threats of Mr. Wilkinson [Burnet's literary executor], late of Lincoln's Inn, having let a

Translation of Dr. Burnet's Archæologia, &c. lye suppress'd near 7 Years, it now happens that the said Wilkinson's Death, proves to be Dr. Burnet's Resurrection. Therefore the Publick, and Mr. Wilkinson's Successors, may be hereby assured I shall go through with a Translation of all Dr. Burnet's Works, and that, his own Commentary upon his Theory of the Earth will be publish'd in a Month's time. E. CURLL." (S.J.E.P.)

Sept. 5.   [CURLL (EDMUND) and THOMAS (ELIZABETH).] *Codrus : or, The Dunciad Dissected.* . . . To which is added, *Farmer Pope and his Son.* A Tale by Mr. [Ambrose] Philips. 8vo. 6d. B.M.
Of Pope it says :

> " At laſt, he felt 'twas native Spite,
> That any but himself should write."

Sept. 17.   [POPE (ALEXANDER).] *The Art of Sinking in Poetry.* (Chapman, Turner, Brotherton.) 1s. (S.J.E.P.)
Sept. 21.   Shakespeare's *Poems* are " republish'd " at 6s. (S.J.E.P.)
Sept. 28.   MOSS (ROBERT). *Divine Poems.* The Second Edition. (S.J.E.P.)
Oct. 15   BURNET (THOMAS, of the Charterhouse). *Theory of the*
(dated   *Visible World.* By way of Commentary on his own
1729).   Theory of the Earth. Being the Second Part of his Archæologiæ Philosophicæ. Translated by Thomas Foxton. 8vo. 3s. B.L.O.
Nov. 14   CASTIGLIONE (COUNT BALTHAZAR). *The Courtier : Or,*
(dated   *The Complete Gentleman and Gentlewoman.* Translated
1729).   from the Italian . . . by Robert Samber. 8vo. 6s. B.M.
Old sheets with a new title-page.
Dec. 3.   FOWKE (MARTHA) and BOND (WILLIAM). *The Epiſtles of Clio and Strephon.* The Third Edition. 1s. (S.J.E.P.)
I cannot positively identify this edition. An 8vo edition in 1720 had been printed for Hooke, Gyles and Boreham. A " Second Edition," in 12mo was issued by J. Hooke in 1729 (and this may be the one advertised above), and a third edition, with a new title-page, *The Platonic Lovers,* came out in 1732, printed for Wilford and Chandler, but containing at the end Hooke's old liſt of books, which, incidentally, included many of Curll's. Which sounds a great deal of fuss about very little, but I am told that Martha Fowke was a very remarkable woman. I am quite willing to believe that William Bond was a very remarkable man, particularly if he was also Henry Stanhope.

Dec. 17 (dated 1729).

BURNET (THOMAS, of the Charterhouse). *Appendix to the Ninth Chapter of the State of the Dead.* Translated by Thomas Foxton. 8vo. 2s. 6d. B.M.

Includes a letter to Foxton, dated 28th Nov., 1728, and signed Philalethes, i.e. Curll, who says that he has been looking up the Will of the detested Francis Wilkinson—a rich man at the time of his death, but by no means religious.

SAINT EVREMOND (CHARLES DE MARGUETEL DE SAINT-DENIS). *The Works.* . . . Made English. . . . To which are added The Memoirs of the Dutchess of Mazarin. The Second Edition, corrected and enlarged. Knapton, Darby, Bettesworth, Round, Gosling, Fayram, Harris, Pemberton, Osborn (J.), Longman, Hooke, Rivington, Clay, Batley, Osborn (T.). 3 vols. 8vo. B.M. *Petri Abælardi Abbatis Ruyensis et Heloïssæ.* . . . "Oxonii: E. Theatro Sheldoniano. M.DCC.XXVIII." 5s.

A reprint of Rawlinson's edition. (H. Curll's Cat.)

ADDISON (JOSEPH). *The Resurrection.* The Sixth Edition.

? year. Title-page not seen. Bound in with B.M. copy of Burnet's *State of the Dead.*

PHILIPS (JOHN). *Poems on Several Occasions.* The Fourth Edition. "Printed and Sold by Thomas Astley. . . . 1728." 12mo. 2s. 6d. Frontispiece. B.M.

Contains the *Ode ad Henricum Saint John*, with Newcombe's translation, *The Splendid Shilling*, with separate title-page " To which is added Blenheim . . . London, Printed for E. Curll, 1728," and *Cyder*, the third edition (Tonson, 1727).

SEWELL (GEORGE). *Posthumous Works.* "Printed for Henry Curll in Clement's Inn, M.DCC.XXVIII." 8vo. B.M.

Contains The Tragedy of Richard I., an *Essay on the Usefulness of Snails in Medicine*, two *Moral Essays*, and the *Poems on Several Occasions* (separately paged). Edited by Gregory Sewell.

PARKER (SAMUEL). *History of his Own Times.* In Four Books. "Printed for H. Curll in the Strand, M.DCC.XXVIII." 8vo. B.M.

The complete book, edited by Curll.

A Complete Collection of all the Verses, Essays, Letters and Advertisements, which have been occasioned by the publication of three volumes of Miscellanies, by Pope and Company . . . "Printed for A. Moore, 1728." 8vo. Frontispiece. B.M.

I am doubtful about this. Curll often advertised such collections, but whether he really had an interest in this particular one I do not know. He would appreciate the frontispiece, however, and I have reproduced it.

[? WESLEY (SAMUEL).] *Hereditary Rights Exemplified ;* or a Letter of Condolance from Mr. Ed——d C——l to his Son H——y, Upon His Late Discipline at Westminster. " Printed for A. Moor." 8vo. 6d. B.M.

1729

? ROUSE (LEWIS). *Memoirs of the Life of Dr. John Freind.* " In the Press " August, 1728. Advertised " Just Publish'd " 6th Feb., 1731.

Jan. 4. KER (JOHN, of Kersland). *Memoirs.* 3 vols. 12s. (S.J.E.P.)
" Just Re-printed in Holland, Ireland, &c."

Feb. 25. *Memoirs of the Life and Writings of Richardson Pack.* 2 vols. 7s. 6d. (S.J.E.P.)
" Contains all his Works," and I should imagine very little else.

Feb. 27. POPE (ALEXANDER). *Miscellanea.* . . . " A new edition." 2 vols. 12mo. 5s.

Apr. 3. SEYMOUR (RICHARD). *The Knowledge of Play.* . . To which is added, The Gaming Lady of Quality, a Tale by Dean Swift and Mr. Pope. 1s. 6d. B.M.

Apr. 10. POPE (ALEXANDER). *The Dunciad* (variorum). " A. Dob." " A correct and neat edition." 2s.
The printer offers to give separately and for nothing the corrections made by Pope in the several editions of the poem. He says that Dodd's quarto edition is " pretentious." Who " he " was I don't know. It may have been Curll, but it may have been anybody else you like to think.

Spring. [CURLL (EDMUND).] *The Curliad.* A Hypercritic upon the Dunciad Variorum. With a farther Key to the New Characters. " Printed for the Author." 12mo. 1s. B.M.
Most valuable to me.

May 27. *The Last Will and Testament of* . . . *William Congreve.* With Characters of his Writings, &c. 8vo. 1s. B.M.

? CONGREVE (WILLIAM). *A Letter . . . to . . . the Lord Viscount Cobham.* " Printed for A. Dodd . . . and E. Nutt. . . . 1729." 8vo. 3d. (Cat.)
Mentioned in one of Curll's lists, and printed in the preceding pamphlet.

May 27. GRAY (SUSANNA). *The Lady's Preservative ;* in the three

Characteristics of Beauty, the Hair, Complexion and Teeth. 6d. (S.J.E.P.)

July 22. *The Pope-ish Controversy Compleat.* 12mo. 4s. (S.J.E.P.)

The five attacks on Pope printed by Curll gathered together, with, I fancy, a general title-page. (Not seen.)

? JAMES, DUKE OF YORK (KING JAMES II.) *Memoirs of the English Affairs, chiefly Naval,* from the Year 1660 to 1673. " Printed in the Year M.DCC.XX.IX." 8vo. Frontispiece. 5s. B.M.

Advertised in the 1735 cat.

Aug. 12 WILSON (CHARLES), *pseud.,* i.e. JOHN OLDMIXON.
(dated *Memoirs of the Life of Mr. Congreve.* 8vo. 5s. Portrait.
1730). B.M.

Two parts, separately paged. Contains Congreve's short novel *Incognita.*

Prints a letter from Congreve to Curll at the time that Jacob was compiling his *Register.*

" Surrey-street, July 7, 1719.

" Sir,

" I much approve the Usefulness of your Work ; any Morning, about Eleven, I shall be very ready to give you the Account of my own poor Trifles & self, or any thing else that has fallen within the compass of my Knowledge, relating to any of my Poetical Friends.

" I am, Sir,

" your Humble Servant,

" William Congreve."

Nov. 6. Three new translations from the French are announced, of which I have been unable to trace two :
The Life of Mahmoud, Sultan of Gazna.
The Jesuits Art of Love.

? year. WYNDHAM (Mr., of Norfolk) *History of the Great St. Athanasius.* Mentioned in a note in Curll's *Life of Wilks* as having been a small pamphlet printed by him.

1730

Jan. 1. " To prevent the Propagation of further Daily Journal Falsehoods " Curll announces that the executors of Mr. A. Boyer have sold nothing to that newspaper, and that on 12th Feb., and every month, there will appear *A New Political State of Great Britain,* Collated and Compiled by Mr. Morgan. Printed for T. Payne, B. Creake, and E. Curll."

The advertisements of the first two numbers bear Curll's name, after which, however, he drops out. (S.J.E.P.)

Jan. 13. WILSON (CHARLES), *pseud.*, i.e. JOHN OLDMIXON. *Memoirs of the Life . . . of Mr. Congreve.* The Second Edition. 8vo. 5*s.* Portrait. (S.J.E.P.)

Feb. 21. *A Collection of Miscellanies, in Prose and Verse.* A New Edition. 5 vols. 12*s.* 6*d.*

Which is vague, but I can't help it.

Nov. 10. PLANTE (AMOUR), *pseud.*, i.e. J. BRUYS. *The Art of Knowing Women ; or The Female Sex Dissected.* Written in French . . . and translated by Spring Macky. " Printed in the Year M,DCC,XXX." 8vo. 4*s.* B.M. PARKER (SAMUEL). *History of his Own Times . . .* " Printed in the Year 1730." 8vo. 6*s.*

I fancy this is Curll's version with a new title-page, but am not quite certain.

The Last Will and Teſtament of . . . Mr. Congreve. The Second Edition. 8vo. B.M.

1731

Feb. 6. BURNET (GILBERT). *Two Diſſertations.* 8vo. 2*s.* 6*d.* (S.J.E.P.). Containing A Defence of Polygamy, and the Lawfulness of Divorce, with a Life of Steele.

Feb. 26. EGERTON (WILLIAM), *pseud.*, i.e. E. CURLL. *Faithful Memoirs of the Life of . . . Mrs. Anne Oldfield.* (Brotherton, Payne, Edlin, Jackson only.) 3*s.* and 3*s.* 6*d.* (S.J.E.P.)

Mar. 9. " Shortly " *The Benefit of Piſſing ;* or the whole Art of exercising that Engine of Nature in Both Sexes. 6*d.*

I have not seen this presumably physiological thesis.

May 15. *The Altar of Love.* The Third Edition. 8vo. 6*s.* Cuts. (S.J.E.P.)

This differs in its contents from earlier editions, and quite possibly copies differ from each other.

May 29. *A Letter to his Grace the Archbishop of Canterbury,* concerning Mr. Henley's Oratory. (Brotherton, Gilliver, Jackson, Dodd.) 3*d.* (S.J.E.P.)

Aug. 12. BURNET (GILBERT). *Two Diſſertations. . . .* The Third Edition. (P.B.)

Sept. 2. RAPIN (PAUL DE). *Diſſertation sur les Whigs & les Tories. . . .* Translated by John Ozell. The Fourth Edition. 1*s.* 6*d.* (S.J.E.P.)

Sept. 2. ZENOPHON. *The Banquet,* translated by James Welwood, is advertised again at 1*s.* 6*d.*, and may have a new title-page.

Sept. 16 (dated 1732). OLDMIXON (JOHN). *Court Tales.* " The Second Edition." 2*s.* 6*d.* (Cat.)

In 1720 a " Second Edition " had been issued, but in a different format.

Sept. 28.   *The Life of Sir Robert Walpole.* [Part I.] 8vo. 1s. B.M.

Oct. 5.   The same. The Second Edition. (S.J.E.P.)

Nov. 18.   The same. The Third Edition. (S.J.E.P.)

Dec. 21.   NICHOLSON (Dr.). *A Conference Between the Soul and the Body, concerning the Present and Future State.* The Third Edition. 3s. and 3s. 6d. (S.J.E.P.)

        A second edition had been issued in 1705 by Richard Smith. Probably dated 1732.

Dec.   A Catalogue of " Books printed only for E. Curll, at Congreve's Head, in Burleigh Street in the Strand." 8vo, n.d. [1731].

        This includes three books which I have not found in the newspaper advertisements. These are :

A Companion for Lent ; or, Meditations on the Passion, Death, Resurrection & Ascension of Christ. With Suitable Prayers. 2s. (I admit, however, that this would suit several of the books already mentioned.)

CENTLIVRE (SUSANNA). *The Goatham Election.*

Memoirs of the Lives and Families of Thirty Persons of Distinction. 2 vols. 8vo. 12s.

        This may be *The Memoirs of the Earls of Nottingham, Portmore, Lord Trevor, Bp. Sprat, &c.,* mentioned as " just publish'd " on Feb. 6th, 1731 (S.J.E.P.), or, rather, it may have engulfed it, as that book is sold at 2s. 6d.

Pylades and Corinna : or, Memoirs of the Lives, Amours and Writings of Richard Gwinnett Esq. . . . and Mrs. Elizabeth Thomas Jun. . . . To which is prefix'd, The Life of Corinna. Written by Herself. " Printed in the Year M.DCC.XXXI." 8vo. 5s. Frontispiece. B.M.

        Preface by Philalethes (? Curll).

        Almost every note refers to a book which has been published by Curll. He lost no chances.

        Vol. II. issued in 1732.

1732

Jan. 28.   Curll seems to have been interested in the first two numbers of *Milton Restor'd, and Bentley Dethron'd.* 6d. (G.S.J.)

Mar. 11.   BOWMAN (WILLIAM). *Poems.* The Second Edition, Corrected. 8vo. 1s. 6d. B.M.

        The preface is dated 1727, which may be the date of the first edition.

Mar. 14.   CRAWFURD (JOHN). *The Cases of Impotency and Virginity fully discuss'd.* 8vo. 2s. 6d. B.M.

Contains the case of the Hon. Catherine Weld, and, in a separately paged Appendix, " The Invalidity of an un-consummated Marriage."

Here somebody had got in first, and Curll appealed to the public " not to be impos'd on by a sham, anonymous Pamphlet." And, really by this time, you would have thought that he had secured a monopoly in such things. The anonymous compiler, however, retorted by announcing that his version appeared " By Authority," though whose authority he did not state. Regrettably he was thus able to issue a third edition within a very short while.

Mar. 25. The same. The Second Edition. 8vo. B.M.

Apr. 27. PLANTE-AMOUR, *pseud.*, i.e. J. BRUYS. *The Art of Knowing Women.* . . . The Second Edition. Payne. 2s. 6d. Frontispiece. B.M.

May 13. MUSGRAVE (WILLIAM). *Genuine Memoirs of the Life and Character of . . . Sir Robert Walpole.* 8vo. 3s. B.M.

Preface signed Philalethes. Contains The Life of Walpole [Part I.] and, separately paged, *Memoirs of the Family of Walpole.*

" Note, Whereas the *First Part* (being only the Introduction to this Work) was sold for 1s. those who have purchased the *same* may have the *Second Part* separate, to perfect their Books. Price 2s." (S.J.E.P.)

? GWINNETT (RICHARD). *The Country 'Squire, or a Christmas Gambol.* A Comedy. 8vo. (Cat.)

? *The Honourable Lovers :* or, the Second and Last Volume of Pylades and Corinna. . . . " Printed in the Year M.DCC.XXXII." 8vo. 5s. B.M. Frontispiece.

Preface, unsigned, dated New Year's Day, 1732.

Contains the preceding comedy, with separate half-title.

Oct. 9 (dated 1733). MACKY (JOHN). *Memoirs of the Secret Services of.* . . . With two Letters from his son, Spring Macky. " Printed in the Year M.DCC.XXXIII." 8vo. 5s. B.M.

? The same. The Second Edition. B.M.

The old sheets, with an altered title-page.

Dec. 7 (dated 1733). [CURLL (EDMUND).] *The Life of that Eminent Comedian, Robert Wilks, Esq.* 8vo. 1s. Vignette of title. 1s. 6d. B.M.

With testimonials from the family. See text.

Dec. 7 (dated 1733). CURLL (EDMUND). *Ed.* *Some Private Passages of the Life of Sir Thomas Pengelly, late Lord Chief Baron.* . . . Written by a Lady, his intimate Friend. 8vo. 1s. 6d. B.M.

Dedication signed Philalethes.

Advertised first October 7th, 1731 (S.J.E.P.), but apparently not ready for two years.

TAVERNER (WILLIAM). *The Maid the Mistress*. The Second Edition. " Printed and sold by F. Feales . . . 1732." 12mo. 1s. B.M.

Contains a page of Curll's " Single Plays " before the Prologue, Some Account of the Author and his Writings, and at the end a long list of Poetry lately Printed, all Curll's. No newspaper advertisements seen.

KING (WILLIAM). *The Life and Posthumous Works in Verse and Prose*. 8vo. 5s.

Advertised in the 1735 catalogue.

An edition in the B.M. is thus titled : *Remains of the Late Learned and Ingenious Dr. William King* . . . containing Miscellaneous Pieces in Verse and Prose. . . . ' Printed for W. Mears . . . MDCCXXXII.' 8vo. This is probably the one meant.

Two translations from the French of " Count Passerau," belonging to this year, are advertised in a 1740 list. These are :

A Parallel between Muhamed & Sosem [i.e. Moses]. 8vo. " Sold by J. Harbert." 8vo. 1s. B.M.

The History of the Abdication of Victor Amadeus II, Late King of Sardinia. " Printed and Sold by J. Harbert." 8vo. 1s.

But another edition of this book, " Printed and Sold by A. Dodd . . . E. Nutt . . . E. Cook . . . and by the Booksellers and Pamphlet-Sellers of London and Westminster, MDCCXXXII " has a more Curll-like sound about it.

The Clarendon Family Vindicated. " Printed for E. Curll, 1732." Mentioned in *Mr. Pope's Literary Correspondence* (note in Vol. III.). Included in the 1733 edition of Oldmixon's *Secret History of Europe*, but apparently issued separately as well.

A Miscellany of Taste. " Printed and sold by G. Lawton . . . T. Osborne . . . and J. Hughes . . . 1732." 8vo. 1s. Frontispiece. B.M.

I suspect Curll. There are detailed and sarcastic notes in the Curllean manner, a Key, and Congreve's Epistle to Lord Cobham ; also much that appears in *The Female Dunciad*.

Who, too, is G. Lawton ? A real bookseller, or Mr. Lawton Gilliver transposed for the occasion ?

1733

Feb. 1. [CURLL (EDMUND).] *The Life of Mr. Gay.* 8vo. 1*s.* 6*d.* Vignette on title. B.M.

Curll signs dedication to Gay's two sisters. The book, announced " by approbation," might just as well have been called " A Selection from Mr. Gay's Works " for all the Memoirs it contains, but the vignette is excellent.

Feb. 3. [GRAINGER (LYDIA).] *Modern Amours ;* or the Secret History of the Adventures of some Persons of the First Rank. With a Key. " Printed in the Year M.DCC.XXX.III." 12mo. 1*s.* 6*d.* B.M.

Apparently Part I. only.

Feb. 24. ? SWIFT (JONATHAN). *A Panegyrical Poem on the Hornbook.* With a Surprising Satire upon a very Surprising Lord. 6*d.* (Joliffe, Brindley, Isted.) 6*d.* (D.J.)

Feb. 28. [CURLL (EDMUND).] *The Life of Gay.* The Second Edition. 1*s.* 6*d.* (D.J.)

Mar. 22. BUCHANAN (GEORGE). *History of Scotland.* The Third Edition. 2 vols. 12*s.* (D.J.)

Apr. 30. *A True Copy of the Last Will and Testament of the late Honourable Robert Price, Esq.* 1*s.* (D.J.)

June 6. *Love without Artifice ; or, the Disappointed Peer.* A History of the Amour of Elizabeth Fitz-Maurice, alias Leeson, and the Lord William Fitz-Maurice. 8vo. 1*s.* B.M.

June 8. D. J. announces *The Pleasures and Mysteries of the Marriage Bed modestly unveil'd.* An Instructive Poem for young Brides. Translated by Nick. Rowe. This suggests that it might be *Callipædia,* but for the fact that " the two first books " are " now offer'd, the two last at the end of the month." Nutt and Dodd are mentioned with Curll, and the price is 1*s.* 6*d.*

July 24. Henry Curll announces *An Historical Account of the Lives and Writings of the most Eminent English Poets* in one volume at 6*s.* The 12 cuts at 6*d.* each or 3*s.* the set.

He calls it " The Second Edition," and says that it is " Compleat." So I suppose that it is another edition of Jacob's *Register* printed in a smaller type, but I have not seen a copy.

Aug. 2. [OLDMIXON (JOHN).] *The Secret History of Europe.* A New Edition. (H. Curll and Joliffe.) The whole in 1 vol. 5*s.* " To which is subjoined The Clarendon Family Vindicated." (D.J.)

Aug. 6. *A Particular of Two Estates and Two Manors* (within Six Miles of Coventry in Warwickshire) to be Let on Old

Rents at £350 per Annum. "Printed and delivered Gratis by Mr. Curll." (D.J.)

Aug. 29. *A True Copy of the Last Will and Testament of Matthew Tindall, LL.D.* 6d. (D.J.)

Sept. 3. The same. "A new Edition." 6d. (D.J.)

Sept. 17. [CURLL (EDMUND).] *Memoirs of the Life and Writings of Matthew Tindall, LL.D.* With a History of the Controversies Wherein he was Engaged. With his Will. 8vo. 2s. B.M.

Curll signs preface: "Those who have bought the Doctor's Will may have his Life separate. Pr. 1s. 6d."

See text for all the fuss and the rumpus that the old gentleman caused by his peculiar Will, or, rather, by the Will that was written out for him.

Oct. 19. TINDAL (MATTHEW). *An Essay concerning the Law of Nations and the Rights of Sovereigns.* The Third Edition. 1s. 6d. (D.J.)

Advertised with this were two other essays of Tindal's:

I. *An Essay on the Inconsistency of Absolute Submission to Princes*, and

II. *A Pastoral to H.H. the Prince of Orange.*

Also *A Letter to Mr. Curll . . . from the Rev. Nicholas Tindall.*

"All sold by Mrs. Nutt . . . H. Curll . . . and all Booksellers." I am not sure, however, whether they were issued separately.

Oct. 22. TINDAL (MATTHEW). *Answer to the Bishop of London's Pastoral Letter.* 1s. (D.J.)

In a letter, written a little while before, Curll had said that the works of Tindal had become very scarce, and that he proposed to reprint them ; so perhaps they really are all separate.

Nov. 21. PRIOR (MATTHEW). *Poems on Several Occasions. Volume the Third, and Last.* The Third Edition, to which is Prefix'd The Life of Mr. Prior, by Samuel Humphreys. Adorned with [a new Sett of] Cuts. "Printed and Sold by S. Birt . . . W. Feales." 12mo. 2s. 6d. B.M.

Nov. 21. GRAINGER (LYDIA). *Modern Amours. . . .* "A New Edition." 1s. 6d. and 2s. (D.J.)

BURNET (THOMAS, of the Charterhouse). *De Futura Judæorum Restauratione.* A Treatise of the Future Restauration of the Jews. Made English. . . . By Thomas Foxton. 8vo. 2s. 6d. (Cat.)

GAY (JOSEPH), *pseud.* (?). *The Lure of Venus : Or, a Harlot's Progress.* A Heroi-Comical Poem, in Six Cantos. . . . Founded on Mr. Hogarth's Six Prints, and illustrated with them. (? Wilford only). 1733. 8vo. 1s. 6d. B.M. (Lacks title-page.) Preface dated Nov. 30, 1732.

Announces as in the press and " Printed and Sold by J. Wilford " a new edition of Mr. Joseph Gay's cele- brated Poem The Hoop Petticoat, though this does not make Chute the author of the new poem.

Advertised in Curll's 1735 Catalogue.

In a 1740 list is advertised *The Life and Trial of Mr. Woolston* for writing against Christ's Miracles. 8vo. 6d. This is probably *The Life of Mr. Woolston, With an Impartial Account of his Writings*. " Printed for J. Roberts . . . 1733."

1734

? *Loyal Honourable and True Memoirs of . . . the late Duchess of Ormonde. . . .* Now first publish'd by a Lady to whom Mrs. Manley gave them in the Year 1722. With her Grace's Last Will and Testament. 8vo.

Advertised as in the press, Nov. 21, 1733. Vignette on title. Included in *Mr. Pope's Literary Correspond- ence*, Vol. III.

Jan. 1. CENTLIVRE (SUSANNA). *The Wonder : A Woman Keeps a Secret*. A Comedy. The Second Edition. Bettes- worth, Feales. 12mo. 1s. Frontispiece. B.M.

The third edition, 1736, bears only Feales's name.

Jan. 8. In the press a re-setting of SALIGNAC DE LA MOTHE FENELON (FRANCOIS). *The Adventures of Telemachus. . . .* Translated by John Ozell. The Third Edition. 2 vols. [Vol. I. dated 1735, Vol. II. 1734.] " Printed for W. Innys & R. Manby . . . S. Birt . . . W. Feales." 8vo. B.M.

Apparently Ozell was endeavouring to negotiate with other firms, for Curll, after mentioning that Pemberton and Innys were associated with him in the new venture, printed the following (D.J.) : " To Mr. Ozell——Sir, *We shall not suffer you to sell our Property to others, as we hear you are about to do.*"

Jan. 8. In the press, a new edition of *The Life of the Right Hon. John, Lord Somers*. (D.J.) The first edition had been printed in 1716 for J. Roberts, but not advertised as Curll's.

Jan. 8. SEYMOUR (RICHARD). *The Compleat Gamester*. The Fifth Edition. Wilford. 12mo. 2s. 6d. B.M.
" In the Press " on this day.

Jan. 23. [CURLL (EDMUND).] *The Life of the late Honourable*

Robert Price, Esq. " Printed by the Appointment of the Family, 1734." 8vo. 3*s.* and 3*s.* 6*d.* Vignette on title. B.M.

With separately paged Will, and an Appendix of " Letters to his Mother."

Jan. 23. CENTLIVRE (SUSANNA). *The Cruel Gift.* A Tragedy. The Second Edition. Bettesworth, Feales. 12mo. 1*s.* Frontispiece. B.M.

The third edition, 1736, contains only Feales's name.

" In the Press " this day.

Jan. 23. In the press " a new edition of the Poetical Works of Lord Halifax." (D.J.)

Mar. 14. " Speedily will be publish'd *An Appendix to the Second Volume of Bishop Burnet's History of his own Time.* Fo. 5*s.*" (D.J.)

" N.B. Any Gentleman, of Worth and Honour, shall be inform'd of the Particulars contain'd in this Appendix, if they please call at Mr. Curll's Printing-Office, in Rose Street, Covent Garden."

June 7. [QUEULLETTE (THOMAS SIMON).] *Peruvian Tales.* From the French by Samuel Humphreys. (Jackson.) 3*s.* (D.J.)

? The same, but enlarged to two volumes. 6*s.* (1735 cat.) Subsequently enlarged to four.

July 12. FLEURY (CLAUDE, Abbé). *A New Ecclesiastical History.* Translated from the French by George Jeffreys. (Jackson, Jolliffe, Payne, Clarke.) 4*s.* (D.J.)

JOHNSTOUN (JAMES). *A Juridical Dissertation concerning the Scripture Doctrine of Marriage Contracts.* " Printed for the Author, 1734." 8vo. 1*s.*

Advertised in Curll's 1735 Catalogue.

Love and Artifice. . . . Being the Case of Elizabeth Fitz-Maurice. The Second Edition. 8vo. 1*s.* B.M.

[GORDON (THOMAS).] *The Tryal of William Whiston, Clerk.* In Defaming and Denying the Holy Trinity, before the Lord Chief Justice Reason. " Printed in the Year MDCCXXXIV."

Advertised in Curll's later catalogues, though his interest in the squib may only have followed on its initial success. The second and third editions are definitely his.

ROMAN (EDWARD, bricklayer). *The Gentleman's and Builder's Director.* The Second Edition. " Printed for H. Curll, in Burghley Street. . . . 1734." 8vo. 6*d.* B.M.

Preface dated 1705.

1735

Mar. 15. GREGORY (Dr.). *Elements of Catoptrics and Dioptrics.* Translated from the Latin Original . . . by William Brown. The Second Edition. To which is added, an Appendix by J. T. Desaguiliers. 8vo. 5s. B.M.

> I am glad that these strange things survived so long.

May 12. POPE (ALEXANDER). *Letters* of . . . and Several Eminent Persons, From the Year 1705 to 1711. Vol. I. and II. "Printed and Sold by the Booksellers of London and Westminster." 8vo. 5s. B.M.

> The sheets sent to Curll by P. T. At least two varieties. See text, where, however, I have not gone into bibliographical details, having been forestalled long ago.

? May 22. POPE (ALEXANDER). *Literary Correspondence for Thirty Years.* Vol. I. "Printed for E. Curll." 8vo. Plates. B.M.

> The first of Curll's printing.

June 26. *The Poet finished in Prose.* Being a Dialogue concerning Mr. Pope and his Writings. (Dodd, Nutt, Jolliffe.) (G.E.P.)

June 28. POPE (ALEXANDER). *Literary Correspondence.* "Printed with a new Letter, adorn'd with Cuts, improved by an Index and compleat Key, with a true Narrative of the Publishing of these Letters. Price 2s. 6d. in 12ves, and 5s. in 8°. The Third Edition."

? July 7. POPE (ALEXANDER). *Literary Correspondence.* Vol. II. 8vo. Portrait. B.M.

? July 14. The same. Volume the Third.

> I am not sure of this date, though the authorities give it. I would put it later myself.

Nov. 1 (dated 1736). [CURLL (EDMUND).] *The Rarities of Richmond.* Being Exact Descriptions of the Royal Hermitage, and Merlin's Cave. [Part I.] 8vo. 1s. Folding plate. B.M.

> Preface signed E.C.
> For the succeeding parts in 8vo., see next year.

? Nov. 1. CURLL (EDMUND). *Ed. Impartial Memorials of the Life and Writings of Thomas Hearne* . . . with his Last Will and Testament. By Several Hands. "Printed in the Year MDCCXXXVI." 8vo. 5s. B.M.

> Introduction, with letters to Curll, signed Philalethes.

Dec. 1. *A Catalogue of Books Printed for E. Curll at Pope's Head,* in Rose Street, Covent Garden. 8vo. 16pp. With vignette of Pope on p. 1.

> See illustration.

CRAWFURD (JOHN). *Arches-Court Law . . . Containing*

Three Remarkable Cases. "Printed in the year MDCCXXXV."

This is a volume made up of the 1732 edition of *The Cases of Impotency and Virginity* (Weld), *A Sequel to the Case of the Honourable Mrs. Weld,* " printed for W. Mears, MDCCXXXIV.," and *Love and Artifice* (Leeson) 1734.

NEPOS (CORNELIUS). *The Lives of Titus Pomponius Atticus, Miltiades and Cimon.* Translated by Richardson Pack. To which is added L'Abbe Bellegarde's *Treatise on Fashions, with an Essay on Entertainments.* 8vo. 3*s.* 6*d.* Frontispiece. B.M.

The *Treatise* is separately paged, and was issued by itself.

The 1735 catalogue advertises also :

WYVILL (CHRISTOPHER). *The Parson's Daughter.* 1*s.* ? new ed.

An Ode Sacred to the Memory of Dr. Francis Atterbury. With his Picture. Written by a very near Relation.

1736

From now onwards the advertisements become irregular, or I have not seen the right papers, and the dates are often very uncertain. But Curll was becoming tired, and only seems to have issued new books by fits and starts, though he advertised the old ones (sometimes under difficult aliases) often enough.

[CURLL (EDMUND).] *The Rarities of Richmond.* . . . Parts II. to V. 8vo. 1*s.* each. Plates. B.M.

Part II. " Printed in the Year 1736," but pagination is not separate. Bound in with it are a letter from Curll to Mr. [Stephen] Duck and the *Cheshire Prophet*, both separately paged.

Parts III. to V. have title-pages of their own, but pagination continues. The complete volume should have frontispiece and 3 folding plates.

The same. 12mo. Five parts. 6*d.* each. Plates. B.L.O.

Merlin ; or The British Inchanter. And King Arthur, The British Worthy. A Dramatic Opera. 8vo. 1*s.* B.M.

This contains *The Royal Chase, or Merlin's Hermitage and Cave.*

Feb. CORDONNIER de-Saint-Hyacinthe (H.) *Histoire du Prince Titi, A.R. : The History of Prince Titi,* a Royal Allegory. Translated by a Lady [Eliza Stanley]. Books I., II., & III. 12mo. 3*s.* 3 plates. B.M.

A rival translation, the work of James Ralph, was

issued almost simultaneously by Mrs. Dodd, who complained bitterly of Curll's attack on it as an incomplete work.   It was a satire on the British Royal Family, and had two sequels (q.v.)

Before
May.
POPE (ALEXANDER). *Seven Select Pieces.*

Includes *Essay on Criticism, Ode to Music, Windsor Forest, Eloisa and Abelard, Temple of Fame, Messiah,* and the *Elegy on an unfortunate Young Lady.* Cuts. 4s. (L.E.P.)

In the same advertisement is announced *The Honour of Parnassus :* Being a curious Draught of Mr. Pope's House, with Verses. 2s. 6d. Also " Four Prints of Mr. Pope " 6d. each.

May 1.
POPE (ALEXANDER). *Literary Correspondence.* Volume the Fourth. 8vo. 5s. (L.E.P.) Portraits.

But no more than a miscellany.

I give Curll's own poetical contribution :

" Court Poems to this Work are join'd,
    That all the World may see ;
Pope's Falshoods manifested here,
    Hinc illæ Lacrymæ."

The same advertisement announces that the first three volumes have been re-issued in 12mo. at 7s. 6d. the set.

May 4.
CORDONNIER de Sainte-Hyacinthe (H.). *Ismenia and the Prince, or the Royal Marriage.* " Done from the Italian " [by Eliza Stanley]. A Sequel to Prince Titi. 12mo. 1s. (or bound in with *Titi,* 3s. 6d.)

" N.B. The Publick are now fully convinc'd of the Imposition of a counterfeit and very defective Edition of this Book [i.e. *Prince Titi*], stuff'd with many Impertinences not in the Original, and the Author's Meaning throughout grosly perverted. This Sequel will not be sold to any (but the Purchasers of the above Translation) under 1s. 6d. Eliza Stanley." (L.E.P.)

May 4.
POPE (ALEXANDER). *Essay on Man.* 8vo. 1s. (L.E.P.)

" This Edition was sold, ready printed (as his Letters were) to Mr. Curll, in Rose-street, Covent Garden."

Quite so, but not necessarily by Mr. Pope.

May 11.
FONTAINE (JEAN DE LA). *Tales and Novels in Verse.* [Translated by Prior, Congreve, &c. Published by S. Humphreys.] 8vo. 5s. (L.E.P.)

May 13.
BARKER (JANE). *The Entertaining Novels. . . .* The Third Edition. Bettesworth, Hitch. 2 vols. 12mo. 5s. Portraits. B.M.

On the same day are advertised (L.E.P.) a list of nine other pocket volumes of novels, some of which may bear this date. These are : *Spanish Amusements, Court Tales,*

Modern Amours, Court Poems, The Gentleman 'Pothecary
with *The Case of Seduction, The Virgin Seducer* with *The
Batchelor Keeper*, and *Letters, Fables, &c.* (probably from
Whartoniana or the other *Miscellanies*).

May 20.   *The Law of Liberty and Property ; or a New Year's Gift
for Mr. Pope.* Wherein those between Men and Women
are particularly recited, relating to double Marriages,
Stealing Heiresses, Rapes, Sodomy, &c., by Giles Jacob,
Gent. *2s.* (L.E.P.)

     I cannot identify this queer-sounding volume at all.

? May.   WALSH (WILLIAM). *The Works of* . . . in Prose and
Verse. 12mo. *4s.* B.M.

     With Pope's Character of the poet.

May 22.   *The Life of the late Right Honourable George, Lord Carpenter.*
With his . . . Last Will and Testament. 8vo. *1s. 6d.*
B.M.

     Vignette on title, and frontispiece. B.M.

May 22.   VOLTAIRE (FRANCOIS MARIE AROUET DE). *Alzira, or the
Americans.* A Tragedy. Done from the French . . .
by Mr. Goston [?]. 8vo. *1s. 6d.* (L.E.P.)

     An edition of this year in the B.M. was printed for
J. Osborn, and translated by Aaron Hill.

May 25.   FRACASTORO (GIROLAMO). *Syphilis ; Sive Morbus Gallicus.*
A Poem on the Rise, Progress, and various Stages of the
Venereal Disease. 8vo. *2s. 6d.* (A small number on a
superfine paper at *4s.*)

     Many times reprinted by the various booksellers.

May 25.   This day Curll also advertises : I. *Pædotrophiæ ; sive de
Puerorum Educatione.* A Poem on the Art of Nursing
and Education of Children. By Samarthanus. (This,
I suppose, is either Rowe's translation of the *Callipædia*,
or Morphew's edition of 1710.) II. *Titi Petronii
Arbitrii Satiricon.* Edidit A. Tooke. *2s. 6d.* Which
may, or may not, be a new edition.

June 1.   BLAND (JAMES). *The Charms of Women ; or, A Mirror for
the Ladies.* 8vo. *4s.* B.M.

     This is made up of sheets of the 1723 edition (issued
as *An Essay in the Praise of Women*) printed for the
author and sold by several booksellers (not Curll).

June 5.   BROWNE (SIR THOMAS). *Religio Medici ;* or the Christian
Religion as professed by a Physician. . . . The Tenth
Edition. 8vo. *1s. 6d.* Portrait and plates. B.M.

     There was some annoyance expressed at the time that
a distinguished writer like Sir Thomas should be added
to the number of Curll's " victims," but—

     " N.B. Beware of a paltry, pyratical Edition of this
Book, impos'd upon the Publick at *2s. 6d.* full of gross
Blunders in almost every Page, and loaded with silly

Notes, wholly useless, the learned Author having sufficiently illustrated his own Meaning." (L.E.P. Curll's advt.) And—

" All the Manuscripts left by Sir Thomas Browne, were put into Mr. Curll's Hands, 1712, by Owen Brigstocke, Esq; (his Grandson by Marriage) as will be testified by Sir Hans Sloane and Dr. Rawlinson : So that it is hop'd the Publick will not be impos'd on by any Pretence whatever, Mr. Curll acting by Direction of the Family, Sir Thomas Browne's own Daughter (Mrs. Lyttelton) being now living. . . . John Harvey." (L.E.P.)

Curiously enough, his own edition was also attacked for being printed " with a gouty letter." Usually his letters were singularly good for the times.

June 8. MORABIN ( ). *An Enquiry into the Life and Writings of Cicero*, including the History of his Banishment. 8vo. 5s. B.M.

In his first announcements Curll merely announced that it " is said to have been written in Allusion to (or by way of Parallel of) the Case of Dr. Atterbury," but later in the year, he took advantage of the imprisonment of and great interest in the " Rev." George Kelly to announce that gentleman as the translator. There may, therefore, be two different title-pages. In any case, the book is made up wholly of Bowyer's 1725 edition, a fact which the G.S.J. was delighted to point out.

June 8. VOITURE (VINCENT). *The Works*. The Third Edition. Bettesworth, Pemberton. 2 vols. 8vo. 7s. Portrait. B.M.

Curll prints a notice from Ozell " to the Booksellers," and a letter of his own to him, saying that the new edition has been put into his hands, and that J. Webster is the editor.

June 17. *The Pleadings at Large before the House of Lords*, 1723, by Sir Constantine Phipps & Mr. Sergeant Wynne, upon the Trial . . . of Dr. Atterbury . . . 8vo. 2s. 6d. (L.E.P.)

July 6. POPE (ALEXANDER). *An Essay on Human Life*. 6d. (L.E.P.)

July 6. POPE (ALEXANDER). *Literary Correspondence*. Volume the Fourth. The Second Edition.

An advertisement says that the Fifth Volume will not appear until after the " Guinea Subscription Volume " of the First Volume is ready. I cannot believe that he kept his word.

July 10. *Post-Office Intelligence : or, Universal Gallantry*. Being a

Collection of Love Letters. With Rational Remarks upon Mr. Pope's Letters. 8vo. 3s. Frontispiece. B.M.

July 22. DENNIS (JOHN), &c. *A Collection of the Several Critiques which have been written upon Mr. Pope's Works.* . . . 2 vols. 10s. "Any Piece single at 1s." (L.E.P.)

Nine in number, "all printed for, and only sold by, E. Curll." These include *The New Rehearsal.*

July 26. *The Pleadings . . . of Sir Constantine Phipps . . . upon the Trial . . . of Dr. Atterbury.* The Second Edition. 2s. 6d. (L.E.P.)

Aug. 17. POPE (ALEXANDER). *Literary Correspondence.* The Third Edition. 4 vols. 20s. (L.E.P.)

Aug. 17. The same. The Second Edition. 4 vols. 12mo. (L.E.P.)

Aug. 28. BROWNE (SIR THOMAS). *Hydriotaphia : or, Urn Burial* [also] *The Garden of Cyrus.* The Fourth Edition. 8vo. 1s. 6d. Frontispiece. B.M.

Advertisement states that this is the second of twelve proposed numbers of a collected edition. The third, the *Vulgar Errors,* is announced as in the press.

"Beware of Pyratical Counterfeits, who dare not proceed any further."

But did Curll?

Sept. 14. *London's Wonder ; Or, The Chaste Old Batchellor,* Being, A Faithful Account of the Family, Life, and Legacies of Mr. Samuel Wright . . . Gent. With his Will. 8vo. 1s. B.M.

For some reason Mr. Wright's death seems to have excited the town.

Oct. 5 (dated 1737). ROWE (ELIZABETH). *Philomela : or, Poems by Mrs. Elizabeth Singer* [*now Rowe*]. The Second Edition. 8vo. 3s. Frontispiece. B.M.

Contains a letter from Curll to Pope about the authoress, also one from her to Curll, assuring him that "no Body will dispute his Right" to republish her writings, if he cares to do so.

Oct. 12. BURNET (THOMAS, of the Charterhouse). *Doctrina Antiqua de Rerum Originibus ;* or, an Enquiry into the Doctrine of the Philosophers of all Nations, Concerning the Original of the World. Translated by Mr. [Richard] Mead and Mr. [Thomas] Foxton. 8vo. 5s. B.M.

Dec. 7. CORDONNIER de-Sainte-Hyacinthe (H.). *Pausanias and Aurora :* Being the Conclusion of Prince Titi's History. 12mo. 3s. (L.E.P.)

New editions of the two previous volumes are also announced.

PITTIS (WILLIAM). *Dr. Radcliffe's Life and Letters.* The Fourth Edition. Bettesworth, Pemberton. 8vo. B.M.

JACOB (GILES). *The Rape of the Smock.* . . . The Third Edition. With other Miscellanies [separately paged]. 8vo. 1*s.* Vignette of Pope on title. B.M.

" Tassoni sings the *Bucket*, Pope the *Lock*, My daring Muse prefers the *Rape of Smock.*"

[BROWNE, ISAAC HAWKINS.] *Of Smoking. Four Poems in Praise of Tobacco.* An Imitation of the Style of Four Modern Poets [Pope, Ambrose Philips, Young, and Thomson]. 8vo. B.M.

Memoirs of the Life, Travels and Transactions, of the Reverend Mr. George Kelly. 8vo. 1*s.* B.M.

With a separately-paged Appendix containing Kelly's speech at his trial.

Attacked, at great length, in the G.S.J.

" In 1736 he [Curll] brought out an edition of Pope's Sober Advice, with this notice upon the title-page : ' Printed for T. Boreman, at the Cock on Ludgate Hill, 1735, who having taken the liberty to print some poems which are my property, I here return him the same compliment in part, as I always will, whoever attacks me, by way of *Lex Talionis*, i.e. the juſt law of retribution.' " Note in Appendix I., Elwin & Courthope's *Pope*, Vol. X.

1737

RAPIN (RENÉ). *Chriſtus Patiens.* . . . An Heroic Poem. From the Latin by Mr. [Charles] Beckingham. The Second Edition. 8vo. Frontispiece. (Cat.)

[CURLL (EDMUND).] *The Honour of the Seals;* or, Memoirs of the Noble Family of Talbot. 8vo. 1*s.* B.M.

" Printed for E. Curll " [*sic*].

Usually attributed to a Dr. Johnſton, or Johnſtoun, but really by Curll.

POPE (ALEXANDER). *Literary Correſpondence.* The Fifth Volume. 8vo. B.M.

B.M. copy has two title-pages. The firſt is " *New Letters of Mr. Alexander Pope.* . . . Printed Anno Reformationis, 1737."

See text.

1738

STUART (ALEXANDER). *New Discoveries and Improvements in the moſt considerable Branches of Anatomy and Surgery.* " Printed for the Author, M.DCC.XXX.VIII." 8vo. 1*s.* B.M.

Advertised in Beckett's *Chirurgical Tracts,* 1740.
Slightly quackish.

CROUSAZ (PIERRE DE). *A Commentary upon Mr. Pope's Four Ethic Epistles,* intituled, An Essay on Man . . . Translated from the French Original . . . with Remarks. 12mo. B.M.

A translation of Crousaz's *Examination of Mr. Pope's Essay on Man,* Printed for A. Dodd, 1737, and " The Third Edition of the *Literary Correspondence,* 5 vols., 8vo with 13 cuts," are advertised in this book.

MUSGRAVE (WILLIAM). *A Brief and True History of Sir Robert Walpole, and his Family.* . . . 8vo. 2s. B.M.

The sheets of *Memoirs of the Family of Walpole* with a new title-page.

HOLDSWORTH (EDWARD). The Mouse-Trap. (Cat.)

But this may not be Curll's.

1739

[GORDON (THOMAS).] *The Trial of Wm. Whiston.* . . . To which is subjoined, A New Catechism for The Fine Ladies. With a Specimen of a New Version of the Psalms, By Mr. Pope, &c. The Second Edition. " Printed by a Society for the Encouragement of Learning (proper to be bound up with *The Scheme for Amending the Ten Commandments*) sold by Mr. *Minors* . . . to be had at all the Pamphlet Shops . . . 1739." 8vo. 1s. 6d. B.M.

Advertised in a 1741 list.

CHAMBERS (JOHN). *Ed. Bibliotheca Recondita :* Or, a Collection of curious private Pieces ; Some of which Great Endeavours have been used To Conceal from Public View. 2 vols. 8vo. 12s.

Old tracts, and not very curious.

GERHARD (JOHN). *The Christian's Support* . . . being the Divine Meditations. Englished by Thomas Rowell. The Third Edition. Bettesworth, Hitch, Longman, Wood. 8vo. 3s. B.M.

The School for Venus ; or The Lady's Miscellany. Being, A Collection of Original Poems and Novels relating to Love and Gallantry. The Second Edition. 8vo. 6s. Frontispiece. B.M.

Includes *The Art of Dress,* 3rd ed., *The Patch,* 2nd ed., *The Hoop Petticoat,* 4th ed., and *Post-Office Intelligence.*

Nov. 3
(dated
1740).

PRIOR (MATTHEW). *The History of His Own Time compiled from the Original Manuscript.* . . . By Mr. Adrian Drift. " Printed for the Editor." 8vo. 6s. B.M.

The first volume of the *Miscellaneous Works* in 2 vols., issued in 1740.

NIXON (ROBERT). *Cheshire Prophecy at Large.* With his Life. . . . "A New Edition." 6*d.*

Advertised in Swift's *Prophecy of St. Patrick,* as belonging to this year, and, as a matter of fact, hardly a year did pass without at least one new edition.

1740

? Mar.   BECKETT (WILLIAM). *Practical Surgery Illustrated and Improved.* Corbett, Rivington, Birt, Ware, Longman, Hitch, Wood, Strahan, Clark. 8vo. 4*s.* B.M.

?   *Bibliotheca Beckettiana,* Or, the Small but Curious Library of Books collected by William Beckett, Surgeon . . . sold . . . by E. Curll. 8vo. Gratis.

Advertised in the preceding volume, together with a Life of Beckett (? printed).

Apr. 5.   FULLER (FRANCIS). *Medicina Gymnastica :* or, a Treatise concerning the Power of Exercise. The Second Edition. (Rivington, Longman, Hitch, Wood, Birt, Ware, Clements.) 8vo. 4*s.* (C.)

Previous edition in 1718.

Aug. 2.   BECKETT (WILLIAM). *A Collection of Chirurgical Tracts.* Rivington, Birt, Ware, Longman, Hitch, Wood, Clark, Hodges. 8vo. 4*s.* B.M.

Aug. 30.   *The History of the Life and Death of David.* Translated from the French. "Printed for the Editor, and sold only by E. Curll and G. Hawkins in Tunbridge Wells." (C.)

Aug. 30.   PRIOR (MATTHEW). *The Miscellaneous Works.* Vol. II. 8vo. Frontispiece. (Cat.)

Aug. 30.   [GORDON (THOMAS).] *The Tryal of William Whiston.* . . . The Third Edition. "Printed by a Society for the Encouragement of Learning. Sold by J. Cooper in Fleet Street." 1*s.* 6*d.* 8vo. B.M.

J. Cooper, not the well-known T.

The following books are advertised in this book :

A New Collection of Poems, Translations, and Imitations. Published by Anthony Hammond. The Second Edition.

WALSH (WILLIAM). *Æsculapius ; or the Hospital of Fools.* The Third Edition. (Also included in various collections.)

JOHNSON (EDWARD). *A Primitive Discourse upon Prayer.* 8vo. 1*s.*

JOHNSON (EDWARD). *A Plain Account of the Trinity* . . . wherein it is . . . proved, that the Belief of this

Doctrine . . . is a Human Invention, and not to be found in the Scriptures. 2s. Also
One Thousand Seven Hundred Thirty Nine. A Rhapsody. The first edition of this last-mentioned pamphlet was " Printed for J. Cooper in Fleet-Street, MDCCXL. . . . Where may be had all Mr. Pope's Works." 8vo. 6d. B.M. This looks Curllean.

Nov. 1. STRETSER (THOMAS). *A New Description of Merryland.* " Bath : Printed and Sold by the Booksellers there." 8vo. 1s. 6d. (C.)

I fancy Leake's name is mentioned on the title-page.

This peculiar production had an enormous sale, and went to six or seven editions. The Bath imprint was a bluff. Incidentally, its success led Curll to issue a whole series of imitations, all more or less pornographic. It also led him to print an attack on the original piece, no doubt to stimulate the waning interest in it. Ultimately all the Merryland tracts were issued together.

Nov. 15. The same. The Third Edition. (C.)
Dec. 6. The same. " The Fourth Genuine Edition." 8vo. 1s. 6d. Frontispiece. (C.)

I presume there were imitations, not put forth by him.

OGLE (LUKE). *The Natural History of Both Sexes, or a Modest Defence of Public Stews.* With an Account of the Present State of Whoring in these Kingdoms. The Fourth Edition. " London : Printed in the Year M.DCC.XL." 8vo. 2s. 6d. B.M.

Dedication " To the Societies for the Reformation of Manners," signed Philo-Porney.

Earlier editions not seen.

Advertised in a 1741 list.

PRIOR (MATTHEW). *The History of his own Time.* . . . The Second Edition. 8vo. 6s. B.M.

? SWIFT (JONATHAN). *True, Genuine and Authentic Copy of that most Strange, Wonderful, and Surprising Prophecy, Written by Saint Patrick.* . . . The Second Edition. " Dublin printed by W. Faulkner. Reprinted at London . . . 1740." 8vo. 6d. B.M.

The Tryal of Colley Cibber, Comedian, &c. For Writing a Book intituled An Apology for his Life. . . . Together with an Indictment exhibited against Alexander Pope . . . for not exerting his Talents at this Juncture. " Printed for the Author," and sold by Lewis, Dodsley, Jackson, Jolliffe, Brindley. 8vo. 1s. B.M.

Preface signed T. Johnson.

PENNYMAN (MARGARET, LADY). *Miscellanies in Prose and*

Verse. With some other curious Pieces. 12mo. 3*s*.
Portrait. B.M.

An anonymous preface, probably by Curll, who calls
the authoress the Hon. Lady Margaret Pennyman, but
he was not very good on titles : cf. the Lady Price in
The Budgell Will affair.

The following three books are advertised in a list at
the end, amongst others already mentioned :

*A Surprising Account of the Apparition of a Young
Woman*, who appear'd to the Reverend Mr. Ruddle of
Launceston. 8vo. 6*d*.

*Coffee : A Satire on Ecclesiastical Courts and Church
Authority*. 8vo. 1*s*.

BOND (WILLIAM). *Congreve and Cobham*. A Poem to the
Memory of the Former.

? Dec.
(dated
1741).
The Potent Ally ; or Succours from Merryland. To which
is added, The Present State of Bettyland. By Charles
Cotton. 8vo. 1*s*. 6*d*.

[STRETSER (THOMAS).] *A New Description of Merryland*
The Fifth Edition. (Cat.)

1741

Jan. 3.
The Potent Ally. . . . The Second Edition. " Paris,
Printed by Direction of the Author, and sold by the
Booksellers of London and Westminster." 8vo. 1*s*. 6*d*.
B.M.

At the end, separately paged, is *Arbor Vitæ*, a most
Curlicilian satire in prose.

I like the Paris imprint.

Jan. 17.
YOUNG (EDWARD). *The Poetical Works*. Tonson,
Walthoe, Hitch, Gilliver, Browne, Jackson, Corbett,
Lintot, Pemberton. 2 vols. 8vo. 9*s*. Cuts. B.M.

Dedicated to Lord Carpenter by Curll, who prints a
letter from Young to himself.

Very respectable company after the Merrylanders.

Feb. 28.
The Confederacy : or, Boarding School Rapes, being the
Tryal At Large . . . between Abraham Magny, a Jew,
John Crab and Others . . . for seducing . . . Mrs.
Mary King. 8vo. 2*s*. 6*d*. B.M.

But we soon return to more familiar waters.

Mar. 28.
Satan turns Moralist ; or, the Devil's Will and Testament.
A Satire. 1*s*. (C.)

Mar. 28.
GRAINGER (LYDIA). *New Court Tales*. 2*s*. 6*d*. (C.)
Apparently a new edition.

Mar. 28.
NIXON (ROBERT). *Cheshire Prophecy at Large*. With the
Life. A new edition. 6*d*. (C.)

Apr. 11.
CHAUCER (GEOFFREY). *The Canterbury Tales, rendered*

into Modern Verse . . . by . . . Dryden, Pope, &c. Published by George Ogle. (Dodsley, Jackson, Jolliffe, Chapell, Brackiston, Isted.) 3 vols. 8vo. 15*s.*

A rival edition, but also published by Ogle, was issued in 2 vols. by Tonson. There had been a previous edition of this in 1737.

May 16. *Spanish Amusements* : Being a curious Collection of Fifteen Novels. Translated . . . by Mr. Ozell. 2 vols. 7*s.* (C.)

This cannot be all Alonzo de Castillo's work.

May 30. SWIFT (JONATHAN). *Literary Correspondence, for Twenty-Four Years.* 8vo. 5*s.* B.M.

Edited by Curll, who reprints from Faulkner's edition with an extra letter and notes. See text.

June 13. BETTERTON (THOMAS) [in reality William Oldys]. *The History of the English Stage from the Restauration to the Present Time.* 8vo. Portrait and vignettes in text.

Dedication signed by Curll.

This should contain an abbreviated *Memoirs of Mrs. Anne Oldfield.* " Printed in the Year, M,DCC,XLI " with vignette on the title.

June 20. KING (WILLIAM). *The Oxford Shepherds.* A Pastoral Satire. . . . Done from the Latin Original. 1*s.* (C.)

June 20. [STRETSER (THOMAS).] *A New Description of Merryland.* The Sixth Edition. (C.)

A Sixth Volume of Pope's *Literary Correspondence* is announced, but this is the volume of Swift's letters.

Aug. 22. [CURLL (EDMUND).] *Ed.* *An Impartial History of the Life, Character, Amours, Travels, and Transactions of Mr. John Barber, City-Printer, and Lord Mayor of London.* Written by several Hands. 8vo. 2*s.* 6*d.* B.M.

Preface signed Philalethes, i.e. Curll, who contributes a concise if not too accurate description of the book :

" His private and his publick Life are shown,
    Void of all Virtues ; ev'ry Vice his own."

Attacks a previous whitewashing Life. Prints letter signed Amicus, which " Mr. [Norton] De Foe himself delivered to Mr. Curll, who has the Original to produce." Apparently Amicus had promised to reveal new and most savoury details, but Curll would not have them.

Sept. 5. *An Account of the Progress of an Epidemical Madness.* In a Letter to the President and Fellows of the College of Physicians. 1*s.* (C.)

Oct. 10. [STRETSER (THOMAS).] *A New Description of Merryland.* The Seventh Edition. 8vo. 1*s.* 6*d.*

With (apparently) *The Potent Ally.*

Nov. 7.   [A. (P.).] *Consummation : or, the Rape of Adonis.* 8vo. 1*s.* (C.)

Nov. 7.   [STRETSER (THOMAS).] *Merryland Display'd,* or Plagiarism, Ignorance, and Impudence Detected. 1*s.* 6*d.* 8vo. (C.)

    This appears to be the most forthright attack on the *New Description,* but is not. Curll makes up an amusing yarn about its acceptance by the publisher, who had " turned down " the *Description,* and allows himself to be insulted as usual. See also p. 314.

The Altar of Love. 2 vols. 8vo. 12*s.* Cuts. (C.)
    Contents not seen.

Merryland Display'd. The Second Edition. " Bath : Printed for the Author, and sold by J. Leake ; and the Booksellers of London and Westminster." 8vo. 1*s.* 6*d.* B.M.

A Catalogue of Books Printed for E. Curll. . . . 8vo.
    This includes *Twenty Years Literary Correspondence between John Locke,* &c. . . . and his Life and Writings by Le Clerc. The Third Edition. 4*s.* This may be the two Locke tracts issued by Curll put together.

1742

Feb. 13. *The Merryland Miscellany.* 8vo. 5*s.* (C.)
    Contains ten pieces, including the *Poetical History of Pandora's Box, Armour, Consummation, Resurrection* and *ΚΥΝΔΥΜΟΓΕΝΙΑ.*

Dec. 8. *A Short Description of the Roads which lead to that delightful Country call'd Merryland.* 8vo. 1*s.* 6*d.* (D.A.)

MORABIN ( ). *L'Exile de Ciceron : or, The History of Cicero's Banishment.* . . . Translated from the French . . . by the Reverend Mr. George Kelly. The Second Edition. 8vo. 5*s.* B.M.

    The old sheets of Bowyer's 1725 edition, with Bowyer's advertisements at the end.

1743

OINOPHILUS (BONIFACE), *pseud.,* i.e. A. H. DE SALLENGRE. *Ebrietatis Encomium : or, the Praise of Drunkenness.* The Second Edition. [Translated by Robert Samber.] 12mo. 2*s.* 6*d.* Frontispiece. B.M.
    The old sheets with a new title-page.

PRIOR (MATTHEW). *Solomon de Mundi Vanitate, Liber Secundus, cui Titulus inscribitur Voluptas, Poema . . . Latine Traductum. Cantabrigiæ. . . .* Tonson, Vaillant, Dodsley, Crownfield, Thurbourn, Fletcher, Pote. 4to. 5*s.*

No mention of Curll, but the book is mentioned in one of his lists.

D'AUBEUF (AUBERT DE VERTOT). *The History of the Revolution in Sweden*, Occasion'd by the Changes of Religion, and Alterations of Government, in that Kingdom. . . . Done into English by J. Mitchel, M.D. The Seventh Edition. Wood, Knapton, Longman, Brindley, Hitch, Corbett, Caldwell, Wellington, New. 8vo.

1744

Jan. 2. NIXON (ROBERT). *Cheshire Prophecy at Large*. With his Life by John Oldmixon. Corbett. The Thirteenth Edition. 8vo. 6*d*. Frontispiece. (D.A.)

PHILIPS (JOHN). *Poems attempted in the Style of Milton.* With his Life by Dr. Sewell. 12mo. Portrait. (Cat.)

1745

Jan. 8. AYRE (WILLIAM), *pseud.*, i.e. E. CURLL. *Memoirs of the Life and Writings of Alexander Pope.* 2 vols. Sm. 8vo. 7*s*. B.M.
Curll's " masterpiece."

Jan. 30. H. (J.). ? John Henley, or John Hill. *Remarks on 'Squire Ayre's Memoirs of the Life and Writings of Mr. Pope.* In a Letter to Mr. Edmund Curl, Bookseller. . . . Cooper only. 8vo.

Apr. 4. MUSGRAVE (WILLIAM). *The Life of the Late Right Honourable Robert Earl of Oxford* . . . including a Brief History of his Whole Family. The Second Edition. 8vo. 2*s*. B.M.
Old sheets, with a new title-page and " Postcript."

Apr. 25. QUEULLETTE (THOMAS SIMON). *Peruvian Tales.* The Second Edition. 4 vols. 12mo. 13*s*. (S.J.E.P.)

May 23. *Presbyterian Persecution exemplified* in the famous Trial of the late Reverend and Learned Mr. James Graham. 8vo. 3*s*. 6*d*. (S.J.E.P.)
? A new edition.

May 23. *A Collection of seven most surprising Trials before the Parliament of Paris for Rapes.* Translated from the French. 3*s*. (S.J.E.P.)
The title may be *Seven Trials at Paris.*

June 25. *The Merryland Miscellany.* 2 vols. 8vo. 10*s*. (S.J.E.P.)
There are now twelve pieces. These are : 1. *A New Voyage to Merryland.* 2. *The Potent Ally.* 3. *Merryland Display'd.* 4. *The Present State of Bettyland.* 5. *Arbor Vitæ.* 6. *A Short Description of the Roads leading to these Countries.* 7. *The Pleasures of Coition.* 8. *Consummation.* 9. *Armour of the Gods, or Vulcans Prerogative.* 10. *Primi-*

tive Rakes. 11. *Adam's Errors ; or the Road Mistaken.*
12. *The Secret Natural History of Both Sexes.* The one or
two of these which have not been mentioned may
probably be found separate.

? Spring. NIXON (ROBERT). *Cheshire Prophecy at Large.* Printed
from the Lady Cowper's Original, in the Reign of Queen
Anne. . . . Also his Life. By John Oldmixon. The
fifteenth Edition. Corbett. 8vo. 6d. Frontispiece.
B.M.

July 2. *Delirium Poeticum : Or, the History of Poetical Lunacy ;*
Being Critical and Rational Remarks on some of the
most Considerable Pieces of Poetry which have been
published within these ten Years past, chiefly Satire ;
by Dr. Young, Mr. Pope, the Laureat, Messrs. Fielding,
Ralph, and other less considerable Authors. 5s.
(S.J.E.P.)

July 18. *Iberian Tales and Novels.* Translated from the Spanish
Originals. " Printed in the Year M,DCC,XLV."
12mo. 4s. B.M.
" By the Lady Donna Isabella."

Sept. 12. POPE (ALEXANDER). *Miscellaneous Poems.* Approved and
prepared for the Press by the late Mr. Pope. Containing.
1. An Essay on Painting. 2. Orpheus and Eurydice.
3. A Contius to Cydippe. 4. Several Translations from
Virgil, Statius, &c. 5. Divine Poems on select Subjects.
6. Soliloquy to his Soul from Chaucer. 8vo. 4s.
(S.J.E.P.)

Oct. 29. BONEFONIUS. *The Love Poems* . . . with *The Pleasures of
Coition.* 2s. 6d. (S.J.E.P.)

Nov. 19. NIXON (ROBERT). *Cheshire Prophecy at Large.* . . . The
Seventeenth Edition. (Corbett.) 8vo. 6d. Frontispiece. (S.J.E.P.)

1746

Jan. 25. GWINNETT (RICHARD) and THOMAS (ELIZABETH). *Pylades and Corinna.* The Second Edition. 2 vols. 8vo.
10s. (L.E.P.)

Feb. 6. ? SWIFT (JONATHAN). *The Art of Punning.* The Fifth
Edition. 3s. (L.E.P.)

Apr. 8. Curll advertises his old *Impotency* volumes, suitably
disguised, but I do not think they are new editions.

Aug. 20. *Achates to Varus.* An Epistle Describing some late
Wonderful Appearances That ensued from a Touch of
Ithuriel's Spear. Together with a large Preface, In the
Style and Manner of some distinguished Authors. 8vo.
1s. 6d. B.M.
Entered at Stationers' Hall.

ADDENDA

1718

ADDISON (JOSEPH). *A Dissertation Upon the most Celebrated Roman Poets*. Made English by Christopher Hayes, Esq. " Printed for E. Curll in Fleet-street, MDCCXVIII."

This was included in the 1719 edition of *Poems on Several Occasions*, but was separately paged. It contains both Latin and English texts, and is obviously the book advertised under the Latin title in the *Post-Boy* of February 26th.

1730

A Young Student's Library, or A Catalogue of Books belonging to the late Mr. Lusher, of Pembroke College, Oxon., consisting of 500 articles in Greek, Latin, Italian, Spanish, French and English. 8vo. n.d. (but issued by Curll from his Literatory). (Cat.)

1740

A New Description of Merryland.

" Nov. 10, 1740, Thomas Stretser received of Mr. Curll full satisfaction for the sole right and title to the copy of a book entitled A New Description of Merryland."

No sum mentioned. In like manner on " Oct. 17, 1741, was transferred the copy of a book entitled Merryland Display'd." (Upcott MSS.). So Stretser was the author of both books.

INDEX [1]

A

A., T., 70, 71
Abbot, George, Archbishop of Canterbury, 81, 91
Abchurch Lane, 59
Account of the Tryal of the Earl of Winton, 65 *et seq.*
Achilles, 132, 133
Achilles Dissected, 141 *n.*
Addison, John, 25
Addison, Joseph, 9, 127, 129 *n.* ; his *Campaign*, 9 ; his *Cato*, 9 ; his *Pœmata*, 86
Æneas, 133
Amey, William, 118 *n.*
Amhurst, Nicholas, 48, 77 ; his *Twickenham Hotch-Potch*, 131
Amory, Thomas, 37, 43, 47, 48
Amsterdam, 66
Ananias, 182
Angel and Bible, The, 15
Anne, Queen, 7, 10, 13, 26, 100, 105, 121 ; her Royal Warrant to Ker, 112, 113, 121
Applebee's Original Weekly Journal, 114 *n.*, 119
Arbuthnot, John, 10, 40, 139, 148, 182, 187
Arlington Street, 113
Art of Politicks, The, 98
Art of Sinking in Poetry, The, 128 *n.*
Atalantis, The New, 44, 95
Atherton, John, Bishop of Clogher, 33
Atterbury, Francis, Bishop of Rochester, 70, 142, 179, 183
Auctions, 18
Author to Let, An, 43, 44
" Ayre, William," 194 *et seq.*

B

Bacon, Sir Francis, 157
Baily's Dictionary, 79 *n.*
Baker, J., 22, 31, 54 *n.*

Banstead, 39
Barber, John, Alderman, 45, 46, 191, 192
Barber, John, of Westminster School, 70, 71
Battle of the Books, The, 35
Bavius, Mr., 142 *et seq.*, 152 *n.*
Beckett, William, 33 *n.*
Bedford, Duke of, 37
Bedlam, 14
Bee, The, 149, 151
Beeding, 115
Beggar's Opera, The, 78, 124
Black Rod, 67, 93, 165, 166, 168
Blackmore, Sir Richard, 10, 22, 57, 59, 63 ; his *Essays*, 60
Bladen, Martin, 15 ; his *Cæsar*, 15, 21 ; his *Solon*, 15
Bloomsbury, 157
Blount, Teresa, 70, 131
Boddington, bookseller, 76
Bodleian Library, 123 *n.*
Bohour, Father, 43
Bond, William, 133
Booth the actor, 145 *n.*
Bosvile, Alexander, 33
Bow Street, 140, 146
Bracegirdle, Mrs., 139
Bramston, James, 98
Breval, John Durant, 48, 77, 78, 86, 133 ; his *Confederates*, 64
Bridge, Daniel, 67
Brindley, James, 186
British Journal, The, 128 *n.*
British Museum, 37 *n.*
Bromley, Mr., 156
Broome, William, 134
Brown, Tom, 18
Brunswick, Duke of, 187
Buckingham Court, 61
Buckinghamshire, Duke of. See Sheffield, John.
Buckley, Mr., 95
Budgell, Eustace, 87, 149 *et seq.*
Bull Tavern, The, 111
Buncle, John, 37, 43, 47, 48

[1] *The Index refers only to Part I.*

Date Due

Demco 38-297